The Theologies of the Law in Martin Luther and John Wesley

The Asbury Theological Seminary Series in Pietist/Wesleyan Studies

Kiyeong Chang

EMETH PRESS
www.emethpress.com

*The Theologies of the Law in
Martin Luther and John Wesley*

Copyright © 2014 Kiyeong Chang
Printed in the United States of America on acid-free paper

All rights reserved. No part of this book may be reproduced, or stored in a retrieval system or transmitted in any form or by any means, electronic, mechanical, photocopying, recording, scanning or otherwise, except as permitted by the 1976 United States Copyright Act, or with the prior written permission of Emeth Press. Requests for permission should be addressed to: Emeth Press, P. O. Box 23961, Lexington, KY 40523-3961. http://www.emethpress.com.

Library of Congress Cataloging-in-Publication Data

Chang, Kiyeong.
  The theologies of the law in Martin Luther and John Wesley / Kiyeong Chang.
      pages cm. -- (Asbury Theological Seminary series in Pietist/Wesleyan studies)
  ISBN 978-1-60947-074-6 (alk. paper)
  1. Luther, Martin, 1483-1546. 2. Wesley, John, 1703-1791. 3. Christianity and law--History of doctrines. 4. Law and gospel--History of doctrines. I. Title.
  BR333.5.L3C43 2014
  241'.2--dc23
                              2013048210

The Asbury Theological Seminary Series in Christian Revitalization Studies

This volume is published in collaboration with the Center for the Study of World Christian Revitalization Movements, a cooperative initiative of Asbury Theological Seminary faculty. Building on the work of the previous Wesleyan/Holiness Studies Center at the Seminary, the Center provides a focus for research in the Wesleyan Holiness and other related Christian renewal movements, including Pietism and Pentecostal movements, which have had a world impact. The research seeks to develop analytical models of these movements, including their biblical and theological assessment. Using an interdisciplinary approach, the Center bridges relevant discourses in several areas in order to gain insights for effective Christian mission globally. It recognizes the need for conducting research that combines insights from the history of evangelical renewal and revival movements with anthropological and religious studies literature on revitalization movements. It also networks with similar or related research and study centers around the world, in addition to sponsoring its own research projects.

An important theological issue in understanding movements of Christian revitalization is to explore how new life in Christ through the Holy Spirit interfaces with the theology of law. Kiyeong Chang's careful research on the theology of law in Martin Luther and John Wesley offers much insight in this discussion, particularly from the standpoint of its exposition of Wesley's evangelical synergism of holiness and grace. This twofold axial theme is examined in light of Luther's foundational treatment of law as the dialectical counterpart to his primary focus on salvation sola gratia. This study is deeply grounded in primary sources from both theologians, providing a solid research base for the conclusions that are drawn. In giving focus to this theme, this study appears as an entry in the Pietist and Wesleyan Studies sub series of The Asbury Theological Seminary Studies in Christian Revitalization Studies.

J. Steven O'Malley
General Editor
The Asbury Theological Seminary Studies in Christian
Revitatliztion Movements

Contents

Abbreviations / vii

Preface / xv

Acknowledgements / xvii

Introduction / 1

Chapter 1: The Concept of the Law / 11

Chapter 2: God the Father and the Law / 53

Chapter 3: Christ the Son and the Law / 83

Chapter 4: The Holy Spirit and the Law / 119

Chapter 5: Faith and Works in Soteriology / 153

Chapter 6: Humanity and the Law / 191

Chapter 7: The Law in Practice / 225

Conclusion / 257

Bibliography / 265

Index / 279

Abbreviations

Books

Agape	Anders Nygren, *Agape and Eros*, tr. Philip S. Watson (London: S.P.C.K., 1953)
'Anthropology'	Young Taek Kim, 'John Wesley's Anthropology: Restoration of the Imago Dei as a Framework for Wesley's Theology', (Ph.D. thesis, Drew University, 2006)
Beyond	Carter Lindberg, *Beyond Charity: Reformation Initiatives for the Poor* (Minneapolis: Fortress Press, 1993)
BC	*The Book of Concord: The Confessions of the Evan gelical Lutheran Church*, ed. and tr. T. G. Tappert (Philadephia: Fortress, 1959)
BE	Bicentennial Edition of The Works of John Wesley, General Editors, Frank Baker, Richard Heitzenrater, Oxford: Clarendon Press, Nashville: Abingdon Press, 1975-
Christ	Ian D. Kingston Siggins, *Martin Luther's Doctrine of Christ* (New Haven and London: Yale University Press, 1970)
Deschner, Christology	John Deschner, *Wesley's Christology: An Interpretation* (Grand Rapids: Francis Asbury Press, 1988)
Lienhard, Christology	Marc Lienhard, *Luther: Witness to Jesus Christ: Stages and Themes of the Reformer's Christology*, tr. by Edwin H. Robertson (Minneapolis: Augsburg Publishing House, 1982)
Cross	Gerhard O. Forde, *On Being a Theologian of the Cross: Reflections on Luther's Heidelberg Disputation, 1518* (Grand Rapids: Wm. B. Eerdmans, 1997)
ENNT	Explanatory Notes on the New Testament
ENOT	Explanatory Notes on the Old Testament
'God'	Yang Jung, 'The Doctrine of God in the Theology of John Wesley', (Ph.D. thesis, University of Aberdeen, 2003)
Heritage	Albert C. Outler, *The Wesleyan Theological Heritage*, eds. Thomas C. Oden & Leicester R.

	Longden (Grand Rapids: Zondervan Publishing House, 1991)
Journals	*The Journal of the Rev. John Wesley, A.M.*, ed. Nehemiah Curnock, 8 vols, London: Robert Cullery.
Justice	Irv A. Brendlinger, *Social Justice Through the Eyes of Wesley: John Wesley's Theological Challenge to Slavery* (Ontario: Joshua Press, 2006)
Collins, 'Law'	Kenneth J. Collins, 'John Wesley's Theology of Law', (Ph.D. thesis, Drew University, 1984)
Elert, Law	Werner Elert, *Law and Gospel*, tr. Edward H. Schroeder (Philadelphia: Fortress Press, 1967)
Let	Philip Watson, *Let God Be God: An Interpretation of the Theology of Martin Luther* (Philadelphia: Fortress, 1947)
Letters	*The Letters of the Rev. John Wesley, A.M.*, ed. John Telford, 8 vols, London: Epworth Press, 1931.
LEX	Johannes Heckel, *LEX CHARITATIS: A Juristic Disquisition on Law in the Theology of Martin Luther*, tr. and ed. by Gottfried G. Krodel, Henning F. Falkenstein, and Jack A. Hiller (Grand Rapids: Wm. B. Eerdmans, 2010)
Luther	Gerhard Ebeling, *Luther: An Introduction to his Thought* (Philadelphia: Fortress Press, 1970)
LW	Martin Luther, Luther's Works, ed. J. Pelikan et al. (St Louis: Concordia and Philadelphia: Fortress, 1955-86)
Moral	D. Stephen Long, *John Wesley's Moral Theology: A Quest for God and Goodness* (Nashville: Kingswood Books and Abingdon Press, 2005)
Mount	Tore Meistad, *Martin Luther and John Wesley on the Sermon on the Mount* (Lanham, Md.: Scarecrow Press, 1999)
NPNF	Schaff, Philip. ed. *A Select Library of the Nicene and Post-Nicene Fathers of the Christian Church.* 14 vols. Buffalo: The Christian literature Co., 1886.

Old	Heinrich Bornkamm, *Luther and the Old Testament*, trs. Eric W. & Ruth C. Gritsch, ed. Victor I. Gruhn (Philadelphia: Fortress Press, 1969)
'Perceptible'	Joseph W. Cunningham, 'Perceptible Inspiration: A Model for John Wesley's Pneumatology', (Ph.D. thesis, The University of Manchester [Nazarene Theological College], 2010)
Plain Account	John Wesley, *A Plain Account of Christian Perfection* (Massachusetts: Hendrickson Publishers, 2007)
Present	Tuomo Mannermaa, *Christ Present In Faith: Luther's View of Justification*, ed. Kirsi. Stjerna (Minneapolis: Fortress Press, 2005)
Preached	Gerhard O. Forde, *The Preached God: Proclamation in Word and Sacrament*, eds. Mark C. Mattes & Steven D. Paulson (Grand Rapids: Wm. B. Eerdmans, 2007)
Radical	Gerhard O. Forde, *A More Radical Gospel: Essays on Eschatology, Authority. Atonement and Ecumenism*, eds. Mark C. Mattes & Steven D. Paulson (Grand Rapids: Wm. B. Eerdmans, 2004)
Reason	Brian. A. Gerrish, *Grace and Reason: A Study in the Theology of Luther* (Oxford: Clarendon, 1962)
Responsible	Randy Maddox, *Responsible Grace: John Wesley's Practical Theology* (Nashville: Kingswood Books, 1994)
Sanctification	Harald Lindström, *Wesley and Sanctification: A Study in the Doctrine of Salvation* (Nashville: Abingdon Press)
Social	Manfred Marquardt, *John Wesley's Social Ethics: Praxis and Principles*, trs. John E. Steely & W. Stephen Gunter (Nashville: Abingdon Press, 1992)
Spirit	Lycurgus Starkey, *The Work of the Holy Spirit: A Study in Wesleyan Theology* (Nashville: Abingdon Press, 1962)

Spiritus	Regin Prenter, *Spiritus Creator*, tr. John M. Jensen (Philadelphia: Muhlenberg Press, 1953)
ST	Thomas Aquinas, *SummaTheologica*, tr. Fathers of the English Dominical Province. 5 vols. (New York: Benziger Brothers, 1948)
Sufficient	Herbert Boyd McGonigle, *Sufficient Saving Grace: John Wesley's Evangelical Arminianism* (Carlisle: Paternoster, 2001)
Lohse, Theology	Bernhard Lohse, *Martin Luther's Theology: Its Historical and Systematic Development*, tr. and ed. Roy A. Harrisville (Deinburgh: T&T Clark,1999)
Collins, Theology	Kenneth J. Collins, *The Theology of John Wesley: Holy Love and the Shape of Grace* (Nashville: Abingdon Press, 2007)
Althaus, Theology	Paul Althaus, *The Theology of Martin Luther*, tr. Robert C. Schultz (Philadelphia: Fortress press, 1966)
WAD.	Martin Luther's Werke. Kritische Gesamtausgabe. Weimar, 1883-.
Where	Gerhard O. Forde, *Where God Meets Man: Luther's Down-To-Earth Approach to the Gospel* (Minneapolis: Augsburg Publishing House, 1972)
WW	*The Works of John Wesley*, ed. Thomas A. Jackson, 14 volumes.

Journals

CJ	Concordia Journal
CTQ	Concordia Theological Quarterly
LQ	Lutheran Quarterly
MH	Methodist History
WTJ	Wesleyan Theological Journal

Articles and Chapters

'Cross'	Robert Kolb, 'Luther on the Theology of the Cross', *LQ* 16:4 (Winter 2002)
'God'	Dale A. Johnson, 'Luther's Understanding of God', *LQ* 16:1 (Feb. 1964)

'Holiness'	John W. Kleinig, 'Luther on the Reception in God's Holiness', *Pro Ecclesia* 17:1 (Winter 2008)
'Image'	Nathan Jastram, 'Man as Male and Female: Created in the Image of God', *CTQ* 68:1 (Jan. 2004)
'Natural Law'	Gifford Grobien, 'A Lutheran Understanding of Natural Law in the Three Estates', *CTQ* 73 (2009)
'Pietist'	Frederick Dreyer, 'John Wesley: ein englischer Pietist', *MH* 15 (2001-02)
'Unknown'	Brian A. Gerrish, 'To the Unknown God', in *The Old Protestantism and the New* (Chicago: The University of Chicago Press, 1982)

Abbreviations of Wesley's Sermons (in the Order of the BE)

Salvation	Salvation by Faith
Almost	Almost Christian
Awake	'Awake, Thou That Sleepest'
Scriptural	Scriptural Christianity
Justification	Justification by Faith
Righteousness	The Righteousness of Faith
Way (1)	The Way to the Kingdom
Fruits	The First fruits of the Spirit
Witness (1)	The Witness of the Spirit, I
Witness (2)	The Witness of the Spirit, II
Witness (3)	The Witness of Our Own Spirit
Sin	On Sin in Believers
Repentance	The Repentance of Believers
Assize	The Great Assize
Means	The Means of Grace
Circumcision	The Circumcision of the Heart
Marks	The Marks of the New Birth
Privilege	The Great Privilege of Those That Are Born of God
Lord	The Lord Our Righteousness
Mount (1)	Upon Our Lord's Sermon on the Mount, I
Mount (2)	Upon Our Lord's Sermon on the Mount, II
Mount (3)	Upon Our Lord's Sermon on the Mount, III
Mount (4)	Upon Our Lord's Sermon on the Mount, IV

Mount (5)	Upon Our Lord's Sermon on the Mount, V
Mount (6)	Upon Our Lord's Sermon on the Mount, VI
Mount (7)	Upon Our Lord's Sermon on the Mount, VII
Mount (8)	Upon Our Lord's Sermon on the Mount, VIII
Mount (9)	Upon Our Lord's Sermon on the Mount, IX
Mount (10)	Upon Our Lord's Sermon on the Mount, X
Mount (11)	Upon Our Lord's Sermon on the Mount, XI
Mount (12)	Upon Our Lord's Sermon on the Mount, XII
Mount (13)	Upon Our Lord's Sermon on the Mount, XIII
Law	The Original, Nature, Properties, and Use of the Law
Established (1)	The Law Established through Faith, I
Established (2)	The Law Established through Faith, II
Enthusiasm	The Nature of Enthusiasm
Bigotry	A Caution against Bigotry
Catholic	Catholic Spirit
Perfection (1)	Christian Perfection
Wandering	Wandering Thoughts
Satan's	Satan's Devices
Way (2)	The Scripture Way of Salvation
Original	Original Sin
New (1)	The New Birth
Wilderness	The Wilderness State
Heaviness	Heaviness through Manifold Temptations
Denial	Self-Denial
Speaking	The Cure of Evil-Speaking
Money	The Use of Money
Steward	The Good Steward
Manners	The Reformation of Manners
Whitefield	On the Death of George Whitefield
Eternity	On Eternity
Trinity	On the Trinity
Approbation	God's Approbation of His Works
Fall	On the Fall of Man
Predestination	On Predestination
Love (1)	God's Love to Fallen man
Deliverance	The General Deliverance
Iniquity	The Mystery of Iniquity
Coming	The End of Christ's Coming
Spread	The General Spread of the Gospel
New (2)	The New Creation

Reproving	The Duty of Reproving Our Neighbour
Signs	The Signs of Times
Providence	On Divine Providence
Counsels	The Wisdom of God's Counsels
Knowledge	The Imperfection of Human Knowledge
Reason	The Case of Reason Impartially Considered
Good	Of Good Angels
Evil	Of Evil Angels
Hell	Of Hell
Church	Of the Church
Schism	On Schism
Perfection (2)	On Perfection
Worship	Spiritual Worship
Idolatry	Spiritual Idolatry
Dissipation	On Dissipation
World	On Friendship with the World
Temptation	On Temptation
Patience	On Patience
Question	The Important Question
Working	On Working Out Our Own Salvation
Backsliders	A Call to Backsliders
Riches (1)	The Danger of Riches
Dress	On Dress
Excellent	The More Excellent Way
Israelite	An Israelite Indeed
Charity	On Charity
Zeal	On Zeal
Time	On Redeeming the Time
Family	On Family Religion
Children	On the Education of Children
Parents	On Obedience to Parents
Pastors	On Obedience to Pastors
Sick	On Visiting the Sick
Reward	The Reward of Righteousness
Pleasing	On Pleasing All Men
Communion	The Duty of Constant Communion
Former	Of Former Times
Man (1)	What Is Man? (Psalm 8:3-4)
Attending	On Attending the Church Service
Conscience	On Conscience
Faith (1)	On Faith (Heb 11:6)

Vineyard	On God's Vineyard
Riches (2)	On Riches
Free	Free Grace
National	National Sins and Miseries
America	The Late Work of God in North America
Lazarus	The Rich Man and Lazarus
Man (2)	What is Man?
Discoveries	On the Discoveries of Faith
Omnipresence	On the Omnipresence of God
Walking	Walking by Sight and Walking by Faith
Unity	The Unity of the Divine Being
Inefficacy	Causes of the Inefficacy of Christianity
Dream	Human Life a Dream
Eye	On a Single Eye
Folly	On Worldly Folly
Garment	On the Wedding Garment
Deceitfulness	The Deceitfulness of the Human Heart
Treasure	Heavenly Treasure in Earthen Vessels
Without	On Living without God
Riches (3)	The Danger of Increasing Riches
Faith (2)	On Faith
Mourning	On Mourning for the Dead
Image	The Image of God
Winning	The Wisdom of Winning Souls
Diversions	Public Diversions Denounced
Love (2)	The Love of God
Needful	The One Thing Needful
Love (3)	On Love
Leave	In What Sense We Are to Leave the World
Understanding	The Promise of Understanding
Flesh	On Knowing Christ after the Flesh
Adoption	The Spirit of Bondage and of Adoption

Preface

This book is a comparative study of the theologies of the law in Martin Luther and John Wesley. Though Luther's view of the law has been investigated by many Luther scholars, and Wesley's view by a few Wesley scholars, no one has yet attempted to compare and contrast both theologians' views of the law as a book-length project. This book contributes to scholarship, firstly, by investigating their theologies of the law in relation to subjects of systematic theology, namely, their views of God, Christology, Pneumatology, soteriology, anthropology, and Christian ethics. On the basis of a reliable examination of both theologians' views of the law, this book also analyses the similarities and differences between them. For both theologians, the law was not just one subject among many, but an essential element that penetrated every topic they dealt with. This book makes clear the different motives and the characteristics of their theologies of the law in all of the subjects discussed in this book. Doing this, this book not only deals with long debated questions, such as whether Luther taught justification by imputed righteousness or by *theosis*, and whether he taught the so-called third use of the law, but also examines subjects which have not been fully explored, such as Wesley's views of the three offices of Christ with regard to the law, and of the role of the Holy Spirit in revealing and enabling fulfilment of the law.

To provide a contextual analysis, their theologies of the law have been considered in their respective historical and religious situations. In Luther's view, his reformation was an attempt to correct a human-centred religion of the Catholic Church characterized by intellectualism and moralism, which he believed was caused by misapplication and distortion of the law as meritorious cause. Employing Philip Watson's theocentric motif, and Brian Gerrish's emphasis on justification by faith and two kingdoms as a framework for interpreting Luther's theology, this book demonstrates that Luther represented all aspects of God's all-sufficiency, His absolute freedom, imputation of Christ's righteousness, spiritual trials and comfort by the Holy Spirit, justification and sanctification by faith, human beings as earthly creatures, Christians as saints and sinners, two uses of the law in God's two kingdoms, as countermeasures against a human-centred religion of the Catholic Church.

In his own historical context, what Wesley aimed to correct was not only the Catholic Church's legalism, but also the Protestant Church's antinomianism which he thought Luther's negative representation of the law caused owing to his over-reaction against the Catholic doctrine of meritorious salvation. On the foundation of Luther's teaching of *sola gratia*, Wesley endeavoured to bring Luther's negative view of the law back to a balanced theology of the law. Employing Kenneth Collins' analysis of the two-fold axial theme in Wesley's theology – holiness (holy love) and grace (free and co-operant) – as a framework for understanding Wesley's theology of the law, this book shows that in all subjects of God's works, the three offices of Christ, the witness and empowerment of the Holy Spirit, the relationship between faith and love, human beings as the image of God, and sanctification as renewal of person and cosmos, Wesley's evangelical synergism makes room for the role of the law on the foundation of God's grace.

Acknowledgements

This book is a revision of my Ph.D. thesis. During my Ph.D. study I experienced spiritual trials ('*Anfechtung*') like Luther, though the reason for mine was different from his. In *Anfechtung* I have also experienced the comforts of God Who supports the poor in need, gives wisdom to the foolish, and strengthens the feeble. He came to me wearing various masks, as follows.

Firstly, my parents and parents in law have shown me a sacrificial love like Christ's love for me and my family. In their weakness and poverty, they supported my study with prayer, with all money they have, and with an endless love.

Secondly, my teachers have been wonderful to me. I would like to express my gratitude to Dr. Young Tae Han who taught me Wesley's theology as well as scholarly devotion based upon a deep piety. I thank Dr. Kenneth Collins for accepting me as his M.A. and Ph.D. student (as co-supervisor), and for having been a very supportive supervisor. The first Wesleyan Studies Summer Seminar at Asbury Theological Seminary to which he invited me was greatly helpful for my study.

I appreciate Dr. Herbert McGonigle for his encouragement, support, and patience. Especially, I cannot thank Dr. Geordan Hammond enough for being an excellent supervisor. Without his kind help and Christ-like friendship, I could not have written my thesis and this book. He helped my study by providing supervision, proofreading, and advice and guidance. I hope to be a wonderful helper like him for my future students. I also want to extend my thanks to the faculty and staff of Nazarene Theological College for all their kind and generous support during my study there.

Thirdly, I thank all who have supported me and my family spiritually or financially until now. Without their support, I could have not continued my study.

Finally, because of my happy life with my lovely daughters Sungkyeol and Yeokyeol, and my wonderful spouse Eunyoung, I was able to overcome all stress and adverse circumstances. I will not forget all their sacrifices, hardships and the loneliness they suffered in order to support my study.

I praise God Who has enabled me to do all I have done until now. As Wesley taught, because He first gives all things to me, I believe I *can* and *should* live for His glory and for the benefit of others, sharing what I have learned about the theologies of Martin Luther and John Wesley.

Introduction

'Come, let us go up to the mountain of the Lord' (Isa 2:3).

The purpose of this study is twofold: firstly, to understand the theologies of the law in Martin Luther and John Wesley in their respective theological systems. For both theologians, as Timothy Wengert maintains, the subject of the law 'can never be reduced to one topic among many in an orderly theological system', but 'every topic in Christian theology is penetrated by law and gospel'.[1] Tore Meistad states, the understanding of the law forms, or is well harmonized with, 'the image of God, Christology, anthropology, soteriology, the relations between gospel and law, and ethics'.[2] In this book, both theologians' views of the law will be investigated in relation to the other subjects of systematic theology, namely, their views of God, Christology, Pneumatology, soteriology, anthropology, and Christian ethics.

The second purpose of this study is, on the basis of a reliable achievement of the first goal, to compare and contrast the two theologians' theologies of the law. In almost all works of Luther scholars the subject of the law has been dealt with seriously.[3] Among Wesley scholars, Kenneth J. Collins in his doctoral dissertation of 1984 investigates Wesley's theology of the law mainly in relation to the Wes-

---

[1] Timothy Wengert, 'Fear and Love in the Ten Commandments', *CJ* 21.1 (1995), 15.
[2] Meistad, *Mount*, 26.
[3] Among others, see Althaus, *Theology*; Heckel, *LEX*; Thomas M. McDonough, *The Law and the Gospel in Luther: A Study of Martin Luther's Confessional Writings* (London: Oxford University Press, 1963).

leyan order of salvation.⁴ However, there are few works that deal with both theologians' theologies in general, and their theologies of the law in particular. The work of Franz Hildebrandt, *From Luther to Wesley* (1948), seeing Wesley's Methodism as a branch of Lutheran Pietism, seeks to find unified confessions of faith in both theologians according to major subjects of systematic theology. However, it focuses on their similarities rather than on differences.⁵ A more recent work of Tore Meistad, *Martin Luther and John Wesley on the Sermon on the Mount* (1999) compares and contrasts the overall theologies and ethics of Luther and Wesley. But, Meistad limits his discussion within the boundary of the two theologians' views of Christ's Sermon on the Mount, though for this study, most importantly, he deals with the subject of the law.⁶

The significance of this book is two-fold. Firstly, this book investigates the theologies of the law in Luther and Wesley respectively in their systematic theology, which, with the exception of the works mentioned above, has not yet been done. Secondly, this book is the first attempt to compare and contrast both theologians' theologies of the law in a thorough way according to major subjects of systematic theology.

In 1530 Luther wrote that as one of the most difficult subjects, 'many have wrestled with it [the law] in different ways, but no one has ever solved it'.⁷ It is not an exaggeration to say that Luther's reformation was a reformation of the theology of the law within the religious and historical situations of his time. Wesley, however, wrote in 1750 that there were few subjects within the whole of Christianity which had been so little understood as the law,⁸ or that the law has been 'little considered or understood'.⁹ He did not think that Luther taught the law properly. On the contrary, he regarded his own view of the law as a correction of Luther's view. Therefore, it is

---

⁴ Collins, 'Law'; There are a few other works dealing with Wesley's view of the law, such as Charles Randall Wilson, 'The Correlation of Love and Law in the Theology of John Wesley', (Ph.D. thesis, Vanderbilt University, 1959), John Horton Tyson's 'Interdependence of Law and Grace in John Wesley's Teaching and Preaching', (Ph.D. thesis, University of Edinburgh, 1991), and Chang Hoon Park's 'The Theology of John Wesley as "Checks to Antinomianism"', (Ph.D. dissertation, Drew University, 2002).
⁵ Franz Hildebrandt, *From Luther To Wesley* (London: Lutterworth Press, 1951).
⁶ Meistad, *Mount*.
⁷ Luther to Philip Melanchthon: 4 Aug. 1530, Appendix II: WA.B 5:529.1. Quoted by Heckel, *LEX*, 19;
⁸ S. Law, Intro. 1.
⁹ S. Established (2), I. 3.

expected that Luther's and Wesley's theologies of law have considerable differences as well as similarities.

Their different views of the law were partly fruits of their own times and religious situations. According to Luther, as Christians we are living where Satan, the world, sin, the flesh, and death assail us. We are not safe 'for even one moment' from 'spiritual adultery'; from 'fear of death ... of any other danger'; from anxiety; and, above all, from fear of God's wrath.[10] While Luther's spiritual journey was a pursuit for a safe place from all fears, what he saw on Mount Sinai was the 'lightning, thunder, rain, and earthquake' of the law which frightened sinners by revealing their sins.[11] Through his 'Tower Experience', which gave him a new understanding of the gospel,[12] he realized that rest from a guilty conscience can be found 'on Calvary, where Christ offered Himself for the sins of the world'.[13] Having a new insight into the gospel, Luther realized that his fear was caused not only by 'considerable confusion within the late medieval church concerning the doctrine of justification',[14] but also by what he believed was the deliberate inducement of the Catholic Church which aimed at ruling over her adherents, which Roland H. Bainton describes:

> Hell was stoked ... in order to instil enough fear to drive them to the sacraments of the Church. If they were petrified with terror, purgatory was introduced by way of mitigation as an intermediate place where those not bad enough for hell nor good enough for heaven might make further expiation. If this alleviation inspired complacency, the temperature was advanced on purgatory, and then the pressure was again relaxed through indulgences.[15]

In the Catholic Church, Luther saw that the burden of the law of Moses was already 'truly heavy', nevertheless, 'tyranny of church law' was so much heavier that 'the whole world would not be able to carry them'.[16] From the beginning of the Reformation, Luther regarded the law as 'a main topic in his theological work'. Johannes Heckel points out that the 'concepts of medieval doctrine of law were

---

[10] LW 16:30; LW 1:60-65.
[11] LW 15:348-349.
[12] LW 34:336-337; see LW 12:313; LW 22:145-146.
[13] LW 1:310.
[14] Alister E. McGrath, *Luther's Theology of the Cross: Martin Luther's Theological Breakthrough* (Oxford: Basil Blackwell, 1985), 7-12.
[15] Roland H. Bainton, *Here I Stand: A Life of Martin Luther* (Tring: Lion Publishing plc, 1987), 28.
[16] LW 14:337.

second nature to all clergy ... the scholarly ABC of every clergyman. Luther could not have avoided coming to terms with the traditional idea of law – to the contrary, he was pushed into doing so'.[17] Luther took seriously his view that the law was abused 'by those who want to excuse Christians from it [the law] altogether', imagining that 'Christian liberty is carnal license to do whatever they please'. However, in the Catholic Church, the law was abused differently 'by all the self-righteous and the hypocrites, who imagine that men are justified by the law', as well as 'by those who, when they feel its terrors, do not understand that these are to last only until Christ'. Luther saw that whereas in the latter 'the abuse is a cause for despair', in the former the abuse is 'a cause for pride and presumption'.[18]

To correct the Catholic Church's abuse of the law in doctrines and practices, Luther consciously launched his concentrated attack on doctrines. George Wolfgang Forell notes that 'for Luther, if only the word remained pure, there was always the hope that the life would also be straightened out through the power of this word. But if the word was missing there was also no hope for a changed life'.[19] Luther said:

> Doctrine and life must be distinguished. Life is bad among us, as it is among the papists, but we don't fight about life and condemn the papists on that account. Wycliffe and Huss didn't know this and attacked [the papacy] for its life. I don't scold myself into becoming good, but I fight over the word and whether our adversaries teach it in its purity. That doctrine should be attacked – this has never before happened. This is my calling.[20]

Luther's method of correcting the Catholic Church's error was to distinguish the law clearly from the gospel.[21] By the distinction, Luther believed not only that the purity of the gospel 'can be kept sound',[22] but also that a dilemma between Christian freedom and laxity[23] can be solved. Luther's distinction was not to abolish the law with the gospel, but to teach that 'the law can be satisfied' by the

---

[17] Heckel, *LEX*, 18-19.
[18] LW 26:344-345.
[19] George Wolfgang Forell, 'Justification and Eschatology in Luther's Thought', *Church History* 38:2 (1969), 164-174.
[20] LW 54:110.
[21] Gerhard Ebeling, *Luther: An Introduction to his Thought* (Philadelphia: Fortress Press, 1970), 111.
[22] LW 26:313.
[23] LW 27:75. 'If we teach faith, carnal people will neglect works; but if we urge works, faith and the comfort of consciences will be lost'.

gospel, not by human works.[24] For him, only the pure gospel gives a diligent life and freedom from all fear. Therefore, when we feel God's wrath through any misfortune in life or through any fear in conscience, Luther taught, we should constantly visit the mountain of the gospel 'to hear the word of God constantly, to proclaim the death of Christ constantly, and to ponder constantly'.[25] In his *Lectures on Galatians* (1535) Luther urged his followers first to 'persevere in the doctrine of faith', and on the basis of this, to 'be devoted to one another through love'. He said that 'this is the perfect doctrine ... the shortest and the longest kind of theology – the shortest so far as words and sentences are concerned; but in practice and in fact it is wider, longer, deeper, and higher than the whole world'.[26]

Hildebrandt points out that in spite of differences in their theologies, Wesley was 'the great mediator between Luther and our generation' of Methodists, who handed down Luther's doctrine of justification by faith.[27] According to Albert C. Outler, before Wesley, 'there was no consensus as to "the doctrine of the Church of England" on justification, and never had been'.[28] Consistently, Hildebrandt points out that 'English Church history' was very 'closely touched by Luther ... in John and Charles Wesley'.[29] John B. Cobb, Jr. sees Wesley as 'the last of the great Reformers', who organized their followers into religious movements; shared similar worldviews based on Scripture and Christian tradition, being unchallenged by scientific discoveries; and endeavoured to find answers to questions about 'the relation of faith and works, regeneration and justification, assurance and sanctification, law and gospel' with common concern for salvation.[30]

Wesley was 'a man of tradition',[31] especially the tradition of the Church of England.[32] This means not only that the problems with which Wesley struggled were much different from those of Luther, but also that his solutions did not come out of a vacuum. Against an antinomian tendency within Protestantism both in England and in

---

[24] LW 12:19-20.
[25] LW 16:30; Johnson, 'God', 59-60.
[26] LW 27:59.
[27] Hildebrandt, *From Luther To Wesley*, 14-25.
[28] Outler, *Heritage*, 66.
[29] Hildebrandt, *From Luther To Wesley*, 15.
[30] John B. Cobb, Jr., *Grace and Responsibility: A Wesleyan Theology for Today* (Nashville: Abingdon Press, 1995), 21-23.
[31] Outler, *Heritage*, 109.
[32] Long, *Moral*, 171-172; Frank Baker, *John Wesley and the Church of England* (London: Epworth Press, 1970), 7-25.

the whole Protestant world of the eighteenth century, John Fletcher analyzed, 'We stand now as much in need of a reformation from antinomianism, as our ancestors did of a reformation from Popery'.[33] Wesley would agree with this. He saw that most Christians had been 'as far from it [holiness] as hell is from heaven'.[34] The Church came to have as her members numerous baptized sinners.[35] There had been innumerable vices among Christian kingdoms, in Christian Churches, Christian cities, and Christian families.[36] Wesley described numberless phases of depravity in Church history as 'the general, the almost universal contagion'.[37]

Wesley believed that such low ebb of spirituality was partly caused by the tendency among the Protestants that hesitated to vindicate the importance of obedience to God's law or of doing good works in fear of being considered legalistic. Denying that good works are 'splendid sins' or 'hindrances of our salvation' with which people establish their own righteousness, he traced such distortion to solafidianism as a result of Luther's over-reaction to the Catholic doctrine of meritorious salvation. He stressed that if good works spring from love, they become 'the highest of all Christian graces' as well as 'sacrifices wherewith God is well pleased'.[38]

According to Fletcher's analysis, the Methodist movement can be regarded as a new reformation that brought Luther's negative representation of the law back into a balanced theology of the law.[39] Wesley, thinking that Protestantism lacked the doctrine of sanctification, whereas the Roman Catholicism lacked a proper teaching of justification by faith, endeavoured to preserve both doctrines of justification and sanctification by restoring the Scriptural teaching of the law.[40] Whereas Wesley's view of justification owed much to Luther through the Moravians, his positive representation of the role the law for sanctification can be traced mainly to his Anglican background, in

---

[33] Benson, *The Life of the Rev. John W. de la Flechere*, 160. Quoted by Laurence W. Wood, *The Meaning of Pentecost in Early Methodism* (Lanham: Scarecrow Press, 2002), 102.

[34] S. Spread, 7; see S. Inefficacy, 6; S. Attending, 17-18; S. Established (2), I. 5; S. Denial, I. 1.

[35] S. Marks, IV. 3.

[36] S. Mount (2), III. 18; S. Garment, 13-14.

[37] S. Iniquity, 36.

[38] S. Reward, I. 1-6.

[39] See Fletcher, *Works* 1:431-47, 438-442. Quoted by Wood, *The Meaning of Pentecost in Early Methodism*, 102.

[40] S. Reward, I. 1-6.

which various Christian traditions, such as Christian primitivism,[41] especially of the Eastern Fathers,[42] Roman Catholicism,[43] Arminianism,[44] Puritanism,[45] German Pietism and the holy living tradition[46] stood together in a coherent way to emphasize some portion of human responsibility for salvation and for a holy and devoted life after salvation. They helped Wesley consider the role of the law positively. Thus, as Collins contends, Wesley had not only Protestant but also 'catholic' understanding of grace embracing a divine and human co-operation.[47]

Ernest F. Kevan's *The Grace of Law* (1964) outlines the Puritan understanding of the law in a way that Wesley scholars can easily see that the Puritan theology of the law has impressive similarities to Wesley's theology of the law.[48] The space and the scope of this book does not allow a detailed analysis of similarities and differences between the Methodist and the Puritan theologies of the law, which would require extensive scholarly work. However, it is certainly worthwhile to mention that for Wesley's view of the law, the Puritan tradition probably became one of his major sources. In this sense, Wesley was indebted to Calvin's positive teaching of the law for the Christian life, mediated and strengthened by the Puritans.

Interacting with various Christian traditions Wesley encountered what he believed were problematic doctrines and practices such as legalism, solafideism and stillness. For the purpose of establishing the law, on the one hand, Wesley not only corrected doctrinal errors in those arguments, but also inspected even prevalent doctrines, conceptions, or expressions in Protestantism, such as the imputed righteousness of Christ, bondage of will, or predestination, for antinomian tendencies in order to caution against them. On the other hand, synthesizing useful insights and practices from Christian tradi-

---

[41] Geordan Hammond, 'Restoring Primitive Christianity: John Wesley and Georgia, 1735-1737', (Ph.D. thesis, The University of Manchester, 2008).
[42] Outler, *Heritage*, 98-110.
[43] Long, *Moral*, 171-207.
[44] McGonigle, *Sufficient*, 73-105.
[45] Robert C. Monk, *John Wesley and His Puritan Heritage: A Study of the Christian Life* (London: Epworth Press, 1966), 137-243.
[46] Kenneth J. Collins, *John Wesley: A Theological Journey* (Nashville: Abingdon Press, 2003), 29-53.
[47] Collins, *Theology*, 289.
[48] Ernest F. Kevan, *The Grace of Law: A Study in Puritan Theology* (London: The Carey Kingsgate Press Limited, 1964).

tions into the Scriptural teaching of the law, Wesley exerted himself to teach Christian duties according to the law.

Wesley believed that to lay equal stress on both justification and sanctification, and to synthesize them into one Christian theology was his theological enterprise and the great mission of the Methodists entrusted by God.[49] Wesley not only pointed to Luther's insight on the law's role of revealing the depravity of humanity against irrelevant confidence in the moral ability of humanity,[50] but also went farther than Calvin's teaching of the third use of the law for believers,[51] contending that with God's grace, obeying the law becomes possible and obligatory for believers, combating both Luther's and Calvin's negative presentation about the possibility of achieving the law.[52]

Viewed from different historical and theological settings in which Luther and Wesley developed their theologies of the law, the most challenging aspect in comparing and contrasting the two theologians' views of the law is not that they never met each other, but that even when they used the same terms and expressions, there existed fundamental differences in their concepts, intentions, or their opponents' errors which they endeavoured to correct. Also, as leaders of new movements, Luther and Wesley were not genuinely systematists like Calvin, but 'occasional' writers who addressed specific circumstances. Moreover, some of their early points of view underwent transition with the gradual maturation of their theological thought. Sometimes their teachings, especially Luther's, lacked an inner harmony, containing conflicting views or expressions, which often became their opponents' points of attack.[53]

To appraise their theologies of the law properly, the different historical and theological settings in which Luther and Wesley lived should be kept in mind. Accordingly, this study will focus more on the two theologians' implications and intentions than on their express terms or expressions. As examples, Luther's negative description of the law did not necessarily mean that he recklessly disregarded good works, as Wesley misunderstood him to have taught.

---

[49] S. Vineyard, I. 5-8; S. Garment, 18.
[50] S. Righteousness, II. 1-5.
[51] By the third use, Calvin referred to the use of the law for Christian holy life after salvation. John Calvin, *Institutes of the Christian Religion*, tr. J. T. McNeil (Louisville: Westminster Press, 1960), II. 7. 12-13.
[52] See S. Working; *Institutes* II. 7. 5.
[53] Gerrish, *Reason*, 7-8, 57-58; Outler, *Heritage*, 39-54; McGonigle, *Sufficient*, 217-239.

Similarly, Wesley's contention of human cooperation in salvation through obedience to the law did not exclude divine grace as the source of human response. Wesley's positive presentation of the law cannot be identified with legalism, which might be a Lutheran criticism of Wesley's theology.

In Luther's theology, Brian A. Gerrish notes, though there is an astonishing variety of ideas, the entire structure is determined by the doctrines of the two kingdoms and of the forgiveness of sins.[54] Philip Watson points out, theocentricity also works as a prime motif in Luther's theology against Catholicism in which Luther thought human beings occupied the centre of the religious stage.[55] In his *Lectures on Galatians* (1535) Luther characterized his own theology as the one which gives all glory to God.[56] Watson asserts that the watchword, *soli Deo gloria*, is no less applicable to Luther than Calvin.[57] In this book, theocentricity and the two doctrines of justification by faith and the two kingdoms of God will be used as a framework for investigating Luther's theology of the law.

In Wesley's theology, Collins observes, holiness (holy love) and grace (free & co-operant) make a two-fold axial theme. Collins contends, in Wesley's concept of holy love, which expresses the essence of his thought on divine nature and on the earnest Christian life, holiness that entails separation and purity from sin, is held together with love which involves engagement and communion. Also, in Wesley's concept of grace, a Catholic emphasis on co-operant grace is in conjunction with the Protestant emphasis on *sola gratia*; grace as 'undeserved favour' of God is in conjunction with grace as the 'transforming, assisting, and renewing' power of the Holy Spirit. For Wesley, while holy love, showing that God's grace is not 'amorphous' but 'normed grace', makes room for the law to be a norm of Christian life, free and co-operative grace shows how this norm can be realized in our lives.[58] Collins' analysis of the two-fold axial theme and the related conjunctions in Wesley's theology, which sheds light on the nature and the importance of the law in Wesley's thought, will be used as a framework for examining Wesley's theology of the law.

It is not an easy task to invite to a discussion table two theologians between whom there exists a time gap of two centuries and dif-

---

[54] Gerrish, *Reason*, 8-9.
[55] Watson, *Let*, 37-38.
[56] LW 26:66.
[57] Watson, *Let*, 14.
[58] Collins, *Theology*, 5-15, 20-22.

ferences in regions, cultures, languages, histories, and Christian traditions. The critical appraisal of their different views of the law will be based on a proper understanding of their overall theologies. In cases when their mature theological thoughts differed from their early ones, priority will normally be given to their mature views, taking into account transition or development.

This book consists of seven chapters, in which Martin Luther's and John Wesley's views of the law will be dealt with in relation to subjects of systematic theology: firstly, in their respective theologies, followed by comparing and contrasting them. The first chapter will investigate the concepts of the law in Luther and Wesley. The second chapter will deal with the law in relation to God the Father. The third chapter will be allotted to both theologians' views of the law with regard to Christology, and the fourth chapter, in relation to Pneumatology. The relationship between faith and works in soteriology will be examined in the fifth chapter. The sixth chapter will compare and contrast both theologians' views of humanity in connection with their theologies of the law. The last chapter will examine their views of the law's uses for the Church (means of grace) and for the world (Christian personal and social ethics). In conclusion, the findings of this book will be summarized and appraised.

> *'Come, let us go up to the mountain*
> *of the Lord' (Isa 2:3).*

Chapter 1

The Concept of the Law

A. Martin Luther

I. The Definition, Sources, History, and Types of the Law

i. Definition

How Luther defined the law is shown in his distinction between the law and the gospel. The law 'commands and requires us to do certain things ... what we are to do or to avoid', whereas the gospel reveals what 'God has done for you'.[1] The law includes examples of 'how these laws are kept or broken',[2] words concerning consequences of obeying or disobeying God, such as 'benefits, dangers, advantages, and disadvantages',[3] and 'all statements of Scripture that uncover the sin of humans and accuse them'.[4] As faithful expositors of Luther's theology, the writers of *The Book of Concord* defined that 'the law is a divine doctrine which teaches what is right and God-pleasing and which condemns everything that is sinful and contrary to God's will. Therefore everything which condemns sin is and belongs to the proclamation of the law'.[5]

Marcus Wriedt notes that for Luther, the law or the gospel cannot be confined within the Scriptural texts.[6] Timothy Wengert points out that for Luther the law and the gospel are not mere descriptions of what kinds of words God speaks between commands and promises, but whatever 'proclaim[s] God in action, putting to death the old

---

[1] LW 35:162, 236-237.
[2] LW 35:236.
[3] *BC*, 345.
[4] Donald K. McKim ed., *The Cambridge Companion to Martin Luther* (Cambridge: Cambridge University Press, 2003), 106.
[5] *BC*, 478.
[6] McKim ed., *The Cambridge Companion to Martin Luther*, 106.

creature with its false belief in itself ... and bring to life the new creature through faith'.[7] Paul Althaus notes that the law may exist in various forms that are not 'expressly imperative, accusatory, or judgmental',[8] as Luther maintained that the gospel *paradoxically* condemns human sins,[9] illustrating the wrath of God most dreadfully on Christ's cross.[10]

Sometimes Luther used the law interchangeably not only with 'the word of God' from the viewpoint of its source,[11] but also with good works from the viewpoint of its objects.[12] Into the defining elements of the law, Regin Prenter includes 'the motion' of human heart: Whatever eliminates 'all pride and all egotism' from the heart and moves it 'toward Christ' is the gospel; whatever detaches the human heart from Christ, such as pride and self-righteousness, is the law.[13] George W. Forell states that for Luther, 'actions, faculties ... standards [of good and evil]' of human beings cannot be allotted to either the law or the gospel 'in a static sense'. Even if they are once classified into either of the law or the gospel, it is not necessarily 'forever', but is 'dynamic', that is, according to whether they help or hinder the human relationship with God.[14] The gospel can easily degenerate to the law, Gerhard O. Forde contends, if believers ascribe their salvation or good works, not to God but to themselves.[15] By teaching that baptism does not work in a 'once-for-all' way, but must be daily renewed in the heart, Luther warned that 'yesterday's faith easily tends to slip into' the law, if our dependence on God's grace and denial of the self are not daily renewed.[16]

Luther argued that 'in the broadest possible sense ... whatever is not grace is law'.[17] Whatever brings accusation in the sight of God is the law,[18] whether it is God's providence, Christ's cross, the Spirit's revelation, or our attitudes. Luther said, 'from the beginning to the

---

[7] Wengert, 'Fear and Love in the Ten Commandments', 15; see George Wolfgang Forell, *Faith Active in Love: An Investigation of the Principles Underlying Luther's Social Ethics* (Minneapolis: Augsburg Publishing House, 1954), 60-61, n. 28.
[8] Althaus, *Theology*, 261.
[9] LW 26:13.
[10] LW 47:113.
[11] Siggins, *Christ*, 71-72.
[12] LW 26:333.
[13] Prenter, *Spiritus*, 110-111.
[14] Forell, *Faith Active in Love*, 54-55.
[15] Forde, *Cross*, 24-25.
[16] Forde, *Where*, 38-40; Forde, *Cross*, 108-109.
[17] LW 26:42.
[18] LW 26:122-123.

end no one can excuse himself [for] the Spirit never stops speaking this law in the hearts of all men'.[19] The law, as Forde states, 'is sure to sound anew in countless subtle ways': through accusation; in the form of the third use of the law;[20] even through 'the demand that today I recapture yesterday's faith'.[21]

ii. Sources

Luther acknowledged the efficacy of the Old Testament as 'a book of laws'.[22] In 'the books of Moses' the law was declared 'to perfection'.[23] 'The prophets and the histories' are 'nothing else than what Moses is ... the knowledge of the law'.[24]

Luther found the law in the New Testament as well, especially in Christ's Sermon on the Mount.[25] The Lord's Prayer and the other prayers reveal human sins in the form of confession and repentance.[26] Christ is the source of the law by His teaching of the law, by being an example for Christians, and in His death on the cross.[27] 'The apostolic directives' contain abundant implications regarding the law.[28]

From the viewpoint of the gospel, the relationship of the Old and the New Testaments can be regarded respectively as the promise and the fulfilment of the gospel.[29] From the viewpoint of the law, however, the New Testament depends on the Old Testament, since the law was declared there as perfectly as 'not even Christ Himself can improve upon the law'.[30]

Insisting that '[Christ] interprets the law perfectly and spiritually', whereas the spiritual meaning of the law 'was hidden in the Deca-

---

[19] LW 27:355.
[20] The third use refers to the law as 'a definite rule according to which they [the regenerate] should pattern and regulate their entire life', as explained in the *Formula of Concord*, Article VI in *BC*, 479.
[21] Forde, *Where*, 40; Forde, *Cross*, 108-109.
[22] LW 35:236.
[23] LW 35:238, 246.
[24] LW 35:246-247.
[25] See Meistad, *Mount*.
[26] Althaus, *Theology*, 261; WA 391, 351.
[27] Forde, *Cross*, 1-18; Osward Bayer, *Martin Luther's Theology: A Contemporary Interpretation*, tr. Thomas H. Trapp (Grand Rapids: Wm. B. Eerdmans, 2008), 63-64; Meistad, *Mount*, 24; Lienhard, *Christology*, 142; Althaus, *Theology*, 261-266.
[28] Althaus, *Theology*, 271.
[29] LW 35:236-237.
[30] LW 21:69; Althaus, *Theology*, 261.

logue',[31] Johannes Heckel erroneously insists that Luther ascribed the full exposition of the law not to Moses but to Christ exclusively.[32] Heckel's error results from his identification between the declaration of the law and believers' capacity to understand it. For Luther, this capability is given only through faith.[33] Thus, those who have faith recognize the full depth of spirituality in the law of Moses as well as in the law of Christ. Christ by His teaching did not deepen or add more contents to Moses' teaching of the law. He only confirmed and interpreted the already declared perfect law of Moses.[34]

iii. The Law in History

a. The Law before the Fall

Luther distinguished between the laws given in creation and given after the fall. Adam was created as 'a partaker of divinity and immortality' as the image of God,[35] and he loved God and His creatures in his original righteousness.[36] Adam kept the natural law without compulsion in his 'pure and sinless' nature; being already 'as he should be', he was already doing what he should do.[37]

Denying the argument that since the law is given for sinners (1 Tim. 1:9), what was given innocent Adam was not the law but a mere exhortation, Luther contended that 1 Tim. 1:9 mentions the law given after the fall, which should not be confused with the law before the fall; 'the law given to the unrighteous is not the same law that was given to righteous Adam'.[38] David S. Yeago characterizes the law before the fall; on the foundation of humans' righteous relationship with God in their spiritual wholeness of the heart and works, it was given to the righteous and deified human beings as a form of worship of God: 'The commandment [not to eat of the tree of knowledge] is not given to Adam so that he might *become* a lover of God by keeping it; Adam already *is* a lover of God ... The commandment is given, rather, in order to allow Adam's love for God to take form in an historically concrete way of life ... the concrete social practice of wor-

---

[31] Heckel, *LEX*, 87.
[32] WA 39.I:452.12. Cited from Heckel, *LEX*, 358.
[33] Heckel, *LEX*, 89.
[34] LW 21:69; Althaus, *Theology*, 261.
[35] LW 1:115, 62-63, 65.
[36] LW 1:113.
[37] LW 24:255; LW 34:187.
[38] LW 1:109.

ship'.[39] Yeago represents the righteous relationship between God and human beings in terms of 'thorough integration' between God's grace and human response in which the law is 'neither correlative with sin nor antithetical to grace'.[40] Luther explained, God's command not to eat from the tree for distinguishing of good and evil was given to Adam in order to give him 'a definite way to express his worship' of God.[41]

However, such condition before the fall became 'something unknown', thus, something that 'can be inferred' now, because the innocent state of humanity is no longer available for anyone after the fall.[42] The harmony from the creation between human righteousness and the demand of the law was broken.[43] The role of the law as the expression of innocent worship of God was permanently 'lost through sin in Paradise'.[44]

b. The Natural Law

Since 'after sin Adam is not the person he was before sin in the state of innocence', there should be a 'distinction between the law given before sin and that given after sin'.[45] The law after the fall reflects the condition of human sin.[46] According to a chronological order, Luther distinguished the law after the fall into three: the 'natural law, the written law, and the law of the gospel'.[47]

The natural law becomes 'the key for understanding the essence of divine law'.[48] Though the natural law has lost the role of teaching innocent worship of God as in creation, it, remaining 'a practical first principle in the sphere of morality',[49] becomes 'the fundamental lo-

---

[39] David S. Yeago, 'Martin Luther on Grace, Law, and Moral Life', in *The Thomist* 62 (1998) no. 2, 163-191.
[40] Ibid.
[41] LW 1:94.
[42] LW 1:63, 113.
[43] WA 31:1:478, 454. 'God was compelled to renew these laws [the natural law] through Moses ... in order to present to us what we were before the fall of Adam and what someday we are to be in Christ'. Quoted by Martin Luther, *What Luther Says: An Anthology*, ed. Ewald M. Plass, 3 vols. (St. Louis: Concordia, 1959), 2:748. (hereafter *Anthology*).
[44] LW 1:65.
[45] LW 1:109.
[46] LW 26:309.
[47] LW 27:354.
[48] Heckel, *LEX*, 45.
[49] LW 54:293.

cus of the law for the human person'.⁵⁰ Because it is written on the human heart by God,⁵¹ it could have been 'already operative independent of God's Sinaitic legislation' in the forms of God's juridical actions and verdicts and of works of human conscience.⁵² Since the natural law remains effective, being continuously revitalized in the human heart, God's law or judgmental activities either on or after Sinai can be understood and accepted; 'it is certain that the law might be preached to us for a hundred years in vain, if it were not written on our heart so that when we are admonished we instantly say: Yes, that is so'.⁵³ The natural law is 'inborn and present in creation, not given; found at hand, not handed down ... alive, not contained in letters';⁵⁴ it exists as God's 'ceaselessly active, living word' in all human hearts.⁵⁵

The demands of the natural law are two in general: 'the duty of worshiping God' and 'the love of neighbour'.⁵⁶ In relation to God, it, reminding human beings of what they owe to their Creator, accuses those who do not ascribe their life, blessings, and glory to their Creator.⁵⁷ In relation to neighbours, the natural law demands the Golden Rule (Matt. 7:12; Luke 6:31) and to 'love your neighbour as yourself' (Rom 13:9).⁵⁸

c. The Law of Moses (or Written Law)

The law of Moses was given because the natural law become so 'weak and obscured' by the devil to the point that sinners care neither for God nor for others in their sins.⁵⁹ God gave this further law to make sinners 'find and feel the law in itself [in their heart]' again by re-impressing His law on sinners' hearts on which the natural law was inscribed, in order that the law works properly in their hearts

---

[50] Grobien, 'Natural Law', 212; LW 40:97-98.
[51] LW 47:110; LW 35:164-168; LW 54:293.
[52] Elert, *Law*, 10-11; *BC*, 365-368; LW 13:364-365; Althaus, *Theology*, 145.
[53] W.A. 56.447.10ff. Quoted by Watson, *Let*, 99; LW 40:96; LW 26:399-400.
[54] LW 25:182.
[55] Heckel, *LEX*, 45.
[56] Bornkamm, *Old*, 124-125.
[57] LW 1:15; LW 40-96-97; LW 13:364-365; *BC*, 365-368; see Althaus, *Theology*, 145.
[58] LW 40:96-97; LW 45:128; Luther taught that Lev 19:18, Rom 13:8-10, 1 Cor 13, and Matt 7:12 are the same commandments. See LW 27:348-358; WA 17II, 102:15. Quoted by Bornkamm, *Old*, 125.
[59] WA 31:1:478, 454. Quoted by Plass ed., *What Luther Says*, 2:748; WA 39.1.361.19ff. Quoted by Watson, *Let*, 99; LW 40:96-98.

with God's assistance and illumination.⁶⁰ The basis from which the law of Moses revitalizes the natural law is the unity of the contents of the law. In terms of the contents of the law, both the Mosaic law and the law of the gospel 'differ not so much' from the natural law; the other two laws are none other than the restatement of the natural law.⁶¹ Luther asserted that 'they all come together and are summed up in one', that is, love:⁶²

> This written law, 'You shall love your neighbour as yourself', says exactly what the natural law says, namely, 'Whatever you wish that men would do to you [this, of course, is to love oneself], do so to them [as is clear, this certainly means to love others as oneself]'. But what else does the entire gospel teach? Therefore there is one law which runs through all ages, is known to all men, is written in the hearts of all people, and leaves no one from beginning to end with an excuse.⁶³

Heckel explains, since the natural law was 'repeated' in the Decalogue, 'in terms of their content, the Ten Commandments are natural law; in terms of their form they are ... the divine positive law'.⁶⁴ The Mosaic law as positive law differs from the natural law. Firstly, whereas the natural law exists as a principle, positive law takes into account the recipients' situation, culture, time, and spiritual state. As an example, if the principle natural law, 'do good and not evil', is applied to the case of theft, positive law, subdividing kinds and levels of the crime, works in a complicated way with so many articles and clauses to decide suitable punishment.⁶⁵ According to their respective natures, whereas positive law works very complicatedly with so many articles and clauses of duties, the natural law deals with the principle that 'lays its hand on the head, on the source, on the root' of all positive law.⁶⁶ Grobien states:

> It is actually the character of natural law to be general so that it applies in all situation and times through its practical articulations in positive law. The natural law is supposed to be general and universal ... so that it can be applied in all places and under all circumstances. Thus, natural law may

---

⁶⁰ LW 40:97; Grobien, 'Natural Law', 214.
⁶¹ LW 40:98; LW 47:89; Althaus, *Theology*, 253.
⁶² LW 27:354; WA 31:1:478, 454. Quoted by Plass ed., *Anthology*, 2:748.
⁶³ LW 27:355.
⁶⁴ Heckel, *LEX*, 45.
⁶⁵ Grobien, 'Natural Law', 216; LW 54:293; LW 27:349-352.
⁶⁶ LW 27:349-352. The context mainly deals with love as the demand of the law. However, Luther's teaching of the natural law is consistent with this explanation.

always need the positive law to expand and apply it, but, on the other hand, the natural law serves as the principle for all positive law.[67]

Secondly, whereas 'the basis of natural law is God', 'the basis of positive law is civil authority'.[68] To generalize this statement, not only civil authorities but also all human beings are responsible for proper interpretation and execution of the natural law in their own life.[69] Since human beings have finitude in judging everything accurately, not strictness but tolerance and exceptions are necessary for anybody to avoid injustice toward other people.[70]

d. The Law of Christ (or the Law of the Gospel)

Luther consistently contended that Christ is not superior to Moses in His teaching of the law. Moses' teaching of the law was so perfect and spiritual that there is no need for a new Prophet of the law:[71]

> The Law has been transmitted most perfectly and amply by Moses, so that nothing further can be added. For what could be added to the Decalogue...? What loftier thing can be taught than to believe, trust, love, and fear God with one's whole heart, not to tempt God, etc.? Furthermore, what rules can be more just and holy than those which Moses ordains concerning the external worship of God, government, and love for one's neighbour? ... Moses interprets himself in this book so well that there is no need of another; nor can another add one jot or tittle to make him clearer or more perfect. Since, therefore, there cannot be another word beyond the perfect teaching of the Law unless it were the Word of grace, it follows that this Prophet will not be a teacher of the Law but a minister of grace.[72]

The essence of the law of Christ is love, like the other laws.[73] Christ added nothing to the law of Moses as well as to the natural law: 'the law of Christ is the law of love. After redeeming and regenerating us and constituting us as His church, Christ did not give us any new law except the law of mutual love'.[74]

If there is no difference in the contents of the law, what characterizes the law of Christ? Luther stressed that, unlike the law of Moses that threatened sinners harshly 'with horrible punishments', Christ

---

[67] Grobien, 'Natural Law', 216.
[68] LW 54:293.
[69] Grobien, 'Natural Law', 216; LW 13:160-164.
[70] LW 46:99-103.
[71] LW 27:113.
[72] LW 9:176-177; LW 35:246
[73] LW 27:391.
[74] LW 27:113.

delivered it 'in a loving and friendly way',[75] even though the law of Christ reflects the truth that there are faults and sins in every human being and in every station of human society.[76] The law of Christ deals with human sins in order to 'kill the remnants of the old man in the flesh'.[77] Nevertheless, Christ is not under the authority of Moses, the supreme teacher of the law, who delivered the law with threats and punishments. As a teacher of the gospel He terminated and replaced Moses. It does not mean that Christ does not teach the law, teaching only the gospel, but that He establishes His law on the entirely different foundation of the gospel. While Christ teaches 'something far greater and better' than what Moses taught, the basis of Christ's superior teaching is Who He is; the Saviour and the Preacher of the gospel. His teaching of the law presupposes what He does for sinners, that is, the gospel.[78]

Denying Ernst Troeltsch's correct observation that whereas Luther regarded the Sermon on the Mount as the Christian standard for individual ethics, he considered some other sort of natural law such as the Decalogue the standard for social ethics, George W. Forell does not distinguish between the law of Christ and the law of Moses, basing all ethics of Luther, either individual or social, on God's forgiveness of sin.[79] However, Tore Meistad properly points out that there are 'two different sets' of the law for Christians. One is a 'universal' law 'for the entire humanity' based on human reason. This law, in forms of 'the natural law, human reason, and the secular law', serves as moral standard for every human being and society. Another one pertains exclusively to Christians 'by the most rigid kind of distinction'[80] for their 'Christian way of life';[81] 'this sermon [Christ's Sermon on the Mount] is intended only for those who are Christians'.[82]

The law of Christ has 'justification by faith alone' as its 'soteriological basis'.[83] As the Lord of the gospel Who Himself has gone through the punishments of the law for sinners, Christ gives His law

---

[75] LW 35:120-121.
[76] LW 27:114; LW 27:391-392.
[77] LW 9:179; LW 40:97; cf. *BC*, 567.
[78] LW 26:293.
[79] Forell, *Active*, 63; Ernst Troeltsch, *The Social Teaching of the Christian Church* II, tr. Olive Wyon (London: George Allen & Unwin LTD, 1931), 507-508.
[80] LW 10:403-404.
[81] LW 21:45.
[82] LW 21:25.
[83] Meistad, *Mount*, 19.

to believers from whom all threats and punishments of the law have been removed permanently.[84] 'Christ is speaking to Christians, who are above every law and do more than the laws ordain',[85] and for whom 'the law, which is intended only for the humiliation of the ungodly through the recognition of their sin and weakness, is already abolished'.[86] Believers do not obey the law of Christ 'from necessity or contrary to their own will' because of the threat of the law. Their spirit 'hastens' to do what Christ commands 'of its own accord' or 'spontaneously', since they have the source from which they receive 'the power to fulfil the law', that is, the incomparable love of Christ that produces their responsive love.[87] To 'think of what I [Christ] have done for you' compels believers to keep His law with a grateful love.[88]

The law of Christ is totally different from the law of Moses or the natural law in terms of the sources from which the doers of the law receive the power to fulfil it. As the source, the law of Christ points to God's grace, Christ's sacrificial love, and the Spirit's revealing and empowering presence at God's side, and faith, love, and spiritual renewal in the believer, whereas the other laws depend on sinners' limited and contaminated resources in fulfilling the same will of God.[89] The law of Christ is the law in appearance, but, more exactly, it denotes the state that the law is already fulfilled; gratitude, praise, and returning love toward the love of God through faith in the gospel.[90] Luther identified the law of Christ with 'the law of peace', 'the law of grace', 'the law of life', 'the law of faith', 'the law of love', 'the new law', or, in his most clear expression, with 'the gospel' itself, whereas he identified the law of Moses with 'the law of works', 'the law of the flesh', 'the law of sin', 'the law of wrath', or 'the law of death'.[91] Because of the freeing but motivating, not forcing, character of the gospel, the law of Christ, though it is the law, changes into 'a benefit just like any other work of Christ'.[92]

---

[84] LW 9:179; LW 27:114.
[85] LW 9:144; LW 11:527.
[86] LW 9:179; LW 27:114. 'The law of Christ for Christians'.
[87] LW 9:179.
[88] LW 24:101-102; BC, 147.
[89] LW 21:69.
[90] LW 11:285-288; LW 10:152-154.
[91] LW 10:403; LW 25:67, 187; LW 27:114, 234-235; LW 35:120-121.
[92] LW 35:120-121.

iv. Types of the Law

In his *Preface to the Old Testament* (1545), Luther distinguished the law of Moses into three: the civil or the political, the ceremonial, and the moral:

> The laws are of three kinds. Some speak only of temporal things, as do our imperial laws... because of the wicked, that they may not do worse things ...[93]

> Since this life ... cannot be without external forms of worship, God ... included them in his commandment ... Room, place, time, person, work, and form are all more than adequately determined and prescribed, so that the people cannot complain and need not follow simply the example of alien worship.[94]

> Over and above these two are the laws about faith and love ... faith and love are always to be mistresses of the law and to have all laws in their power. For since all laws aim at faith and love, none of them can be valid ... if it conflicts with faith or love.[95]

a. The Moral Law

The moral law commands faith and love. Though it was given to the Jews, it has a binding force for all Christians since it is consistent with the natural law.[96] Luther said, 'The natural laws were never so orderly and well written as by Moses',[97] thus, 'the Mosaic law [the moral law] and the natural law are one'.[98] In this sense, 'the Decalogue is not of Moses. Nor did God give them first to him. On the contrary, the Decalogue belongs to the whole world. It was written and engraved in the minds of all human beings from the beginning of the world'.[99]

b. The Civil Law

Luther found the first instance of the civil law in the Scripture from the post-deluge covenant God established with Noah's family, in which God ordered death penalty toward murderers.[100] In that if there had been no fall, no murder, or no sin, such penalty would not

---

[93] LW 35:240.
[94] LW 35:239-240.
[95] LW 35:240.
[96] Bornkamm, *Old*, 124-126.
[97] LW 35:165-170; LW 40:95-98; Grobien, 'Natural Law', 213-214.
[98] LW 40:96-98.
[99] WA 31:1:478, 454. Quoted by Plass ed., *What Luther Says*, 2:748.
[100] LW 2:139; LW 45:86. Luther thought God's prohibition not to kill Cain in Gen. 4:15 as a sort of civil law, but he gave more importance to the command after deluge, in that no death penalty was commanded in the case of Cain.

have been needed, the civil law is required as consequence of the human fall.[101] Because the devil 'reigns in the whole world and drives men to all sorts of' sins, God has ordained civic ordinances 'to bind the hands of the Devil'. The wicked, being afraid of executioner's sword, refrain from sinning, such as murdering, committing adultery, and stealing, just as a rope keeps a furious beast from attacking people.[102] Negatively, civil law restrains human sins through force and punishment. Positively, it keeps people's life peaceful and preserves God's created orders in all realms of earthly life such as family, the church, and the state.

For Luther, the civil law of Moses was only for the Israelites and does not apply to Christians; 'I dismiss the commandments given to the people of Israel. They neither urge nor compel me'.[103] However, representing Moses as an excellent expositor of the natural law in the realm of the civil law, he quickly added, 'if I were emperor, I would take from Moses a model for [my] statutes … there are … extraordinarily fine rules in Moses … the emperor could here take an example for setting up a good government'.[104] Luther thought that good examples of the civil law in the Mosaic law are applicable to contemporary positive laws, 'not because Moses gave commandments', but they correspond with the principles of the natural law that 'have been implanted in me by nature'.[105]

c. The Ceremonial Law

All the three types of the Mosaic law – the civil, the moral, or the ceremonial – reveal the state of human sin. Especially the ceremonial law was devised by God as a method for training the Israelites in becoming conscious of sin in a radical way:

> The true intention of Moses is through the law to reveal sin and put to shame all presumption as to human ability … he not only gives laws like the Ten Commandments that speak of natural and true sins, but he also makes sins of things that are in their nature not sins. Moses thus forces and presses sins upon them in heaps. For unbelief and evil desire are in their nature sins, and worthy of death. But to eat leavened bread at the Passover and to eat an unclean animal or make a mark on the body, and all those things that the Levitical priesthood deals with as sin—these are not in their nature sinful

---

[101] LW 1:104.
[102] LW 26:308
[103] LW 35:164-168.
[104] LW 35:166-167.
[105] LW 2:340.

and evil. Rather they became sins only because they are forbidden by the law.[106]

Because the purpose of revealing sin is to point out Christ as Saviour, the ceremonial law finished its role when Christ died as the 'only one propitiatory sacrifice'. After Christ's cross, the old ceremonies that accumulated human sins were replaced by the 'Eucharistic Sacrifice' in the New Testament, through which believers 'give thanks or show their gratitude for the forgiveness of sins'.[107] Luther found a more universal value than mere racial preferences of the Jews in the ceremonial law of Moses, whose ceremonies, he believed, can help Christian faith if used properly.[108] Being 'external forms of worship',[109] ceremonies remain in the New Testament in reformed ways.[110]

When 'the law' is used as an antithesis to grace or the gospel, they do not just mean 'the ceremonial law', but 'the entire law', 'whether it be the civil law, the ceremonial law, or the Decalogue [the moral law]'.[111] If sin is understood as violations of the ceremonial law, the 'remission of sin' is limited to offenses of it as well; 'It follows... that Christ achieved nothing by His death except that He redeemed the Jews alone from the ceremonial law'. Against this Luther asserted that Christ saves from 'the sin and death of the whole world'; from violations not only of the ceremonial law but also of the 'moral law ... its total power and force'.[112] In Luther's soteriology, the most important law is the moral law; 'Paul speaks of the law simply and in a total sense, but especially about the moral law'.[113]

II. Nature, Effect, and Uses of the Law

i. The Nature of the Law

Luther contended that 'the law is holy and good; in view of its authorship God's commandment cannot be evil and wrong'.[114] He also emphasized that the law is spiritual. Sinners who have lost spirituali-

---

[106] LW 35:242-243.
[107] *BC*, 252-253.
[108] LW 40:96-98; LW 35:169-173; LW 35:239-240; LW 44:35.
[109] LW 35:240.
[110] LW 40:96-98; LW 35:169-173, 239-240; LW 44:35; Heckel, *LEX*, 85.
[111] LW 26:122.
[112] LW 34:114-120.
[113] LW 34:114.
[114] LW 22:140.

ty by departing from God, understand the law in terms of morality and external behaviours. However, since God is Spirit Who 'judges according to what is in the depths of the heart',[115] concrete practices and external behaviours are not sufficient in obeying God without having love and pleasure in His law: 'since it is spiritual, no one can satisfy it, unless all that you do is done from the bottom of your heart'.[116] In order that sinners love God and His law, it is necessary that 'faith alone makes a person righteous'.[117] Luther subordinated morality to spirituality; external works to inner righteousness; and good works to faith.

In addition to holiness and spirituality, Luther taught the strictness of God's law. Heckel properly states, the law 'gives just one choice to man: everything or nothing! ... Because of its strictness, divine law is for natural man a law which he is unable to obey ... even man's smallest and most secret notions of disobeying God's law are punished ... with the most severe punishment ... death'.[118] Luther contended, the law was never intended as a means of justification, either before or after justification.[119] Because the law requires the impossible thing of spiritual wholeness from sinners, the only way for sinners to fulfil it is 'to have another person ... who can keep it', that is, Christ, the only fulfiller of the law. When sinners have Christ in faith they become the doers of the law through Him and in Him.[120]

ii. The Effect of the Law

If 'the law is holy, righteous, and good', the consequence should be that 'the works of the law are holy, righteous, and good' as well. 'Nevertheless', Luther said, 'a man is not justified in the sight of God through them'.[121] Why cannot the holy law be a way of justifying sinners? Luther answered, 'after sin Adam is not the person he was before sin'.[122] Whereas the law remains the same law, what has changed is humanity to whom the law is applied. What is problematic is not the law but sinners who have lost their original righteous-

---

[115] LW 35:365-380; Yeago, 'Martin Luther on Grace, Law, and Moral Life', 163-191.
[116] LW 35:366-368.
[117] LW 35:368-369.
[118] Heckel, *LEX*, 17.
[119] LW 26:123-124.
[120] LW 25:326.
[121] LW 26:123.
[122] LW 1:109.

ness with which they could fulfil the law before the fall.[123] The requirement of the law is 'in contrast with' the human state that cannot fulfil the law.[124] Because of this, the law came to have the function of revealing and accusing human sins.[125] What has changed in the law after the fall is not the contents of the law, but its role toward human beings who have become sinners. Like a stick is used when a child is bad, the law came to accuse sinners.[126]

For Luther, the roles of 'showing up of sin' and 'demanding of good' in the law cannot be separated from each other; as much as the law shows people the way to life, it reveals how much they are far from it.[127] The law reveals corruption of human nature, gives the feeling that '[God] hates you', and sentences human beings to the judgment of God.[128] The law produces in sinners a troubled heart and an evil conscience.[129] Thereof, wishing that 'there were no God',[130] sinners reject God.[131] Having all these effects of the law in mind, Luther asserted that the law makes sin grow and be multiplied through sinners' hatred of the law.[132]

iii. Two Uses of the Law

The law relates to sin in both the civil and the theological uses. While the civil use is for preserving social orders of families, the churches, and secular governments for earthly life, this work is done by punishing sinners through the swords of civil authorities.

The theological use deals with human sins in front of God. After human beings have lost their original righteousness, 'the true function and the chief and proper use of the law is to reveal to man his sin, blindness, misery, wickedness, ignorance, hate and contempt of God, death, hell, judgment, and the well-deserved wrath of God'.[133] This theological use intensifies in believers the struggle and the conflict between the remaining sin and the flesh on the one hand, and the Spirit and faith on the other hand; the more godly believers be-

---

[123] Yeago, 'Martin Luther on Grace, Law, and Moral Life', 163-191.
[124] LW 25:342.
[125] LW 1:109; LW 26:123.
[126] LW 1:109.
[127] LW 35:237.
[128] LW 32:223-224; LW 26:309; WA 40.II:351.5. Quoted by Heckel, *LEX*, 243.
[129] LW 31:231; LW 24:101.
[130] WA12:569.35. Quoted by Heckel, *LEX*, 18.
[131] WA 40.I:362.4. Quoted by Heckel, *LEX*, 246.
[132] LW 35:367; LW 26:309.
[133] LW 26:309.

come, the more conflict they experience.[134] What makes them obey the law is neither the demand of the law nor human performance, but 'our illumination by the Holy Spirit, our regeneration by the Word of God, and our faith in Christ'.[135]

III. The Law and the Gospel

i. The Dialectic between the Law and the Gospel

For Luther, through the accusing role, the law leads sinners to Christ. Sin, working in a hidden way, pervades in whatever sinners think good, natural, and moral;[136] 'while it is active, it is not felt ... because these [the ill effects which sin brings on] lie hidden, we proceed smugly to the deed itself'.[137] The presumption of sinners is so great that they regard themselves as righteous, if they do not commit murder, adultery, or theft, which causes in them pride, smugness, and contempt of grace. Against hidden works of sin, God employs the law as a means of showing sinners their damnation and misery.[138] As the tremendous spectacle on Mt Sinai symbolizes,[139] the law becomes a 'powerful hammer' to crush sinners' self-righteousness;[140] 'when later on sin is revealed through the law, then it weighs too heavily on man'.[141]

When sinners fall into despair by the law, the gospel declares: 'Behold that one who alone fulfils the law for you, whom God has made to be your righteousness, sanctification, wisdom, and redemption, for all those who believe in him'.[142] Insofar as believers are sinners, the law convicts them of their remaining sin and leads them to Christ. Like the sun replaces the moon, Christ replaces Moses, and the gospel replaces the law: 'righteousness replaces sin; reconciliation and grace replace wrath; life replaces death; and eternal salvation replaces damnation'.[143]

---

[134] LW 26:390-391; LW 27:70-75.
[135] LW 22:143-145.
[136] LW 32:225-226.
[137] LW 1:163
[138] LW 26:309-310.
[139] LW 26:64, 310.
[140] LW 26:310.
[141] LW 1:163.
[142] LW 31:231.
[143] LW 26:151.

For Luther, God's intention of employing the law is not accusation itself, but that by revealing human sins, the law helps His plan of salvation. The law aims at salvation through the negative role of accusation:

> When God begins to justify a man, he first of all condemns him; him whom he wishes to raise up, he destroys; him whom he wishes to heal, he smites; and the one to whom he wishes to give life, he kills ... sinners are turned to hell and their faces are filled with shame ... However, in this consternation is the beginning of salvation ... in short, God works a strange work in order that he may work his own work.[144]

The law serves the gospel by driving sinners to the gospel. Insofar as believers are sinners, they also need accusation of the law to convict them of their remaining sin and to lead them to the gospel of Christ. In this sense, regarding the law as a minister for the gospel,[145] Luther advised preachers to begin with the law and proceed to the gospel. Then, sinners become humbled by the law, and next consoled by the gospel, confessing the words in Psalm 30:5, 'Weeping may tarry for the night, but joy comes with the morning'.[146]

Lest Christians remove the law, Luther stressed, the gospel is of no use without the law: 'Where there is no law there is no sin. And if there is no sin, then Christ is nothing ... How can one know what sin is without the law and conscience? And how will we learn what Christ is, what He did for us, if we do not know what the law is that he fulfilled for us and what sin is, for which he made satisfaction?'.[147]

ii. Abolition of the Law

Believers are freed from the law in the sense that the law loses its right to condemn. Even if a believers' conscience feels the terrors of the law, it cannot be brought to despair. In this sense, the law has been abrogated for believers;[148] 'When Christ comes the law ceases, especially the Levitical law which ... makes sins of things that in their nature are not sins. The Ten Commandments also cease, not in the sense that they are no longer to be kept or fulfilled, but in the sense that the office of Moses ... no longer increases sin ... and sin is no longer the sting of death'.[149]

---

[144] LW 31:99.
[145] LW 26:314-315.
[146] LW 31:364.
[147] LW 47:110-113.
[148] LW 27:446-447.
[149] LW 35:244.

However, Luther limited the meaning of the abolition. Firstly, as dualistic beings who are simultaneously holy and sinful, believers are not entirely free from the accusation of the law.[150] In spite that God completely accepts them because His grace is complete, the gospel itself continually reminds them of what punishment they deserve.[151] It is still necessary for believers to confess their sinfulness in order that they purely praise God's grace. To forget their sinfulness produces ingratitude toward God and an injury to His grace.[152]

Secondly, Luther limited the abolition of the law to the matter of salvation in God's spiritual kingdom. Distinguishing between the proper areas and times either for the law or for the gospel, Luther contended that the law should be despised when the conscience is terrified, 'in a matter apart from conscience, when outward duties must be performed ... whether you are a preacher, a magistrate, a husband, a teacher, a pupil, etc., this is no time to listen to the Gospel. You must listen to the law and follow your vocation'.[153]

---

[150] LW 32:226-229.
[151] LW 47:113.
[152] LW 27:229-230.
[153] LW 26:117.

B. John Wesley

I. The Definition, Sources, History, and Types of the Law

i. Definition

Wesley defined the law as 'the immutable rule of right and wrong',[1] 'a complete model of all truth',[2] or God's words as enjoinment and forbiddance according to the rule or the model.[3] The law for Wesley could mean inclusively, as Collins defines, 'any commandment, rule, stricture or code which is considered as an expression of the will of God with respect to the conduct of His creatures'.[4]

Though the definition is simple, the law relates to an exceedingly broad range of objectives. As the word 'conversation'[5] comprises boundless aspects of life including 'every inward as well as outward circumstance ... every motion of our heart, of our tongue ... and bodily members... all our powers and faculties; to the manner of using every talent ... with respect either to God or man',[6] Wesley explained, 'the commandment of God is exceeding broad; as extending not only to all our actions, but to every word which goeth out of our lips, yea, every thought'.[7] The law deals with all of human heart and life.

Negatively speaking, the law is God's words which perform 'the convincing men of sin; the awakening those who are still asleep on the brink of hell',[8] threatening sinners with the judgments of God;[9] 'reproving their superstition, ignorance, and idolatry; and strongly moving them to repent, from the consideration of a future judgment, and of the resurrection from the dead' or preaching Christ to sinners 'by reasoning of righteousness, temperance, and judgment to

---

[1] S. Law, III. 8.
[2] S. Law, I. 2.
[3] Wesley, *Plain Account*, 18; S. Established (2), I. 2.
[4] Collins, 'Law', Intro. vii.
[5] By 'conversation', Wesley often meant 'manner of life' in today's general English. Cf. Howard Snyder, 'Translating Wesley's Writings into Late 20th Century General English', n.p. [Conferred 10 Oct. 2013]. http://wesley.nnu.edu/john-wesley/translating-wesleys-writings-into-late-20th-century-american-general-english
[6] S. Witness (3), 9.
[7] S. Mount (11), I. 2.
[8] S. Established (1), I. 3.
[9] S. Established (1), I. 6.

come'.¹⁰ Sin that the law exposes is as broad as the law in that any breach of the commandment is sin.¹¹

In cases of disputable things in which the human conscience cannot judge between good and evil easily,¹² or of neutral diversions which may take away time and money, the law warns against 'every mistake which tends to evil', irresponsibility, or extravagancy.¹³ As a high standard of Christian holiness, the law continually warns against even the subtleties of temptations and asks to gain early victory over each of them as it arises.¹⁴ Speaking of fasting, giving alms, and prayer, Wesley taught that not only express enjoinments but also the Scriptural teachings on 'directions how to' do something have the same authority as the law.¹⁵ In an exhaustive way, Wesley stressed that all God's words which 'relate to the power of godliness, and ... require us to "pass the time of our sojourning in fear", to "work out our salvation with fear and trembling", to "strive", or agonize, "to enter in at the strait gate"' are 'all the great and weighty branches of his [God's] law'.¹⁶ From this inclusive understanding of the law, Wesley derived 'numerous concrete rules for Christian living' from Scriptural texts, as Deschner enumerates:

> The Methodist must not swear, become drunk, hold slaves, smuggle, take unlawful interest. He must care for the hungry and sick, instruct and reprove all men, and use all the means of grace ... eat only what is needful and cheapest; do nothing merely to gratify curiosity; allow no superfluity or finery or fashionable elegance in furniture or apparel; regard only cleanliness, necessity, or at the most very moderate convenience; allow no idle talk. Use of curled hair, gold, and costly raiment is expressly forbidden to Christian women, and in this respect, 'no art of man can reconcile with the Christian profession the wilful violation of an express command'.¹⁷

---

¹⁰ S. Established (1), I. 8.
¹¹ Wesley defined sin as 'a voluntary transgression of a known law of God'. *Plain Account*, 55; S. Privilege, II. 2; S. Mount (11), I. 2. Wesley contended that sin is 'a thousand times broader' than the way of keeping the law, reasoning that 'there is only one way of keeping the commandment ... we do not properly keep it, unless both the thing done, the manner of doing it, and all the other circumstances, are right: But there are a thousand ways of breaking every commandment; so that this gate is wide indeed'.
¹² S. Reproving, I. 3.
¹³ S. Reproving, I. 2; S. Diversions, IV.
¹⁴ S. Privilege, III. 1.
¹⁵ S. Mount (7), II. 12.
¹⁶ S. Mount (5), III. 6.
¹⁷ Deschner, *Christology*, 94; S. Established (1), III. 4-6; ENNT I Tim 2:9 and I Pet 3:3.

However, very concrete requirements of the law cannot be reduced to collections of external rules. In 1738 Wesley classified Christian duties into three: using 'all the ordinances which He [God] hath appointed'; doing 'all the good works'; and bearing 'all holy and heavenly tempers'.[18] Later in 1781, he subdivided Christian duties into five categories: love, holy tempers, works of mercy, works of piety, and the Church.[19] Wesley always emphasized the comprehensive essence of the law: to have holy love after God's nature; to have the mind which was in Christ and imitate Him; to receive the Holy Spirit and produce the fruits of the Spirit; and, thus, to recover the lost image of God.

ii. Sources

Wesley found the law in the 'two tables of stone' which God inscribed.[20] It was not added to but 'only declared, explained, or enforced' by the prophets.[21] In the category of the law, Wesley included the examples of God's love which believers should follow.[22] Through the teaching of Christ, the same law was established 'in its fullness', especially in the Sermon on the Mount.[23] The law was expounded and instructed by His apostles,[24] to which Wesley attached the same authority as to the Decalogue or Christ's Sermon on the Mount.[25] In order to make the law profit Christians, Wesley emphasized, 'All that is written in the book of God' should be declared;[26] the law is as broad as God's words in its broadest sense.

iii. The Law in History

Wesley dealt with various concepts of covenants, dispensations, and types of the law, following the outline of the Westminster Confession. In Deschner's formulation:

1. Covenant of works (applying to Adam alone): moral law as norm, obedience as condition of fellowship with God.

---

[18] S. Salvation, III. 2; Deschner, *Christology*, 94; S. Mount (5), IV. 11; S. Vineyard, III. 1.
[19] S. Zeal, II. 5.
[20] S. Law, I. 5.
[21] S. Mount (5), I. 2; III. 2.
[22] S. Love (1), I. 5; WW 10:68-71.
[23] S. Mount (5), I. 3-4; see Kenneth Collins, *The Scripture Way of Salvation* (Nashville: Abingdon Press, 1997), 52.
[24] S. Established (2), I. 1-2; see Deschner, *Christology*, 93-94.
[25] S. Speaking, Intro. 1.
[26] S. Established (2), I. 5.

2. Covenant of grace: moral law as norm, faith as condition of fellowship with God.

     a. Mosaic dispensation: moral law as norm, faith in ceremonial mediation, leading to obedience of the letter, as condition of fellowship.

     b. Gospel dispensation: moral law as norm, faith in Christ-mediation – whose authenticity is attested by spiritual, lovin- obedience – as the condition of fellowship with God.[27]

a. Two Covenants

Wesley classified the law according to the covenants between God and human beings into two: the law under 'the covenant of works' – the Adamic law – and the law under 'the covenant of grace' after the fall of humanity – the natural law, the law of Moses, and the law of Christ. The former required 'all righteousness, inward and outward, negative and positive'; the obedience and the holiness should be perfect in degree and in continuation.[28] Being 'created free from any defect, either in his understanding or his affections', innocent Adam was able to fulfil the law. Since 'God could not but require the service he was able to pay', the law was 'proportioned to his [Adam's] original powers'.[29] Though Adam was capable of this law and could continue holy and happy life at Paradise forever, he disobeyed God and was sentenced to death.[30]

When it became impossible for sinners to seek life by works of the law, God instituted 'a new covenant of salvation' in order that human beings 'might not be lost'.[31] 'The covenant of grace' is the only covenant which God has established with every human being after the fall.[32] This new covenant reflects human condition after the fall, that is, the loss of the moral image and the mar of the natural and the political images of God in human beings.[33] Even the entirely sanctified believers who are recovered to the moral image of God cannot be

---

[27] Deschner, *Christology*, 112-114.
[28] S. Righteousness, Intro. 1, I. 1-5; *Plain Account*, 83-84; S. Justification, I. 2.
[29] *Plain Account*, 83-84; S. Image, I. 1-4; S. Justification, I. 2-3; S. Deliverance, I. 2; S. New (1), I. 1.
[30] S. Justification, I. 4-5; S. New (1), I. 2; S. Justification, I. 3; S. Fall, Intro. 1; S. New (1), I. 2; WW 9:402; ENOT Gen 2:7; 3:6-8.
[31] Rogers, 'The Concept of Prevenient Grace in the Theology of John Wesley', 113-127.
[32] S. Righteousness, Intro. 1.
[33] Works 9:381; S. Fall, II. 6; S. Image, I. 1; S. New (1), I. 1; Leo G. Cox, *John Wesley's Concept of Perfection* (Kansas City: Beacon Hill Press, 1968), 148-149.

freed from many kinds of infirmities by the mar of the other images of God.³⁴ In this state, no one can fulfil the demands of the law perfectly.³⁵

Because it became impossible for sinners to seek life by the works of the law, Wesley explained, Christ died and put an end to the covenant of works, which means that 'the obligation to observe [the Adamic law]... is vanished away'.³⁶ The Apostle Paul's declaration that 'Christ is the end of the law' means that Christ has put an end to the covenant of the law,³⁷ since human capacity is no longer capable of it.³⁸

The demand of the covenant of grace is only 'to believe'.³⁹ 'Everyone that believeth ... is justified, sanctified, and glorified', and, in this sense, the law under the covenant of grace is identified with 'the law of faith'.⁴⁰ Wesley harmonized the necessity of the law with faith as the sole requirement of the covenant of grace by investigating the character of faith; 'the whole law under which we now are [the law of faith], is fulfilled by love (Rom. 13:8, 10). Faith working or animated by love is all that God now requires of man'.⁴¹

Wesley diligently allied faith with love in various ways. Faith is given as a free gift by God who is 'the great ocean of love'.⁴² The essential content of faith is 'the love of God the Father, through the Son of His love'.⁴³ Faith in God's love gives believers a most powerful motive to love God and neighbour. If believers love God and neighbours, inwardly 'no wrong temper, none contrary to love, remains in the soul', and outwardly 'all the thoughts, words and actions, are governed by pure love'.⁴⁴ Asking 'What room is there for sin therein?'⁴⁵ Wesley asserted that love fulfils the law both by doing no evil and by doing good to all people:⁴⁶

---

³⁴ See Chapter 6 of this book; S. Perfection (1), I. 8; S. Perfection (2), I. 3-4; *Plain Account*, 21-22, 84; Leo G. Cox, *John Wesley's Concept of Perfection*, (Kansas City: Beacon Hill Press, 1964), 148-149.
³⁵ S. Righteousness, II. 5.
³⁶ *Plain Account*, 84; S. Righteousness, I. 1-3.
³⁷ S. Righteousness, I. 1-3.
³⁸ Letters 4:98.
³⁹ S. Righteousness, Intro. 3; I. 8.
⁴⁰ *Plain Account*, 84.
⁴¹ *Plain Account*, 85; S. Patience, 10; Letters 4:155.
⁴² S. Salvation, III. 3; S. Established (2), II. 3-6.
⁴³ S. Scriptural, I. 2
⁴⁴ Works, 11:394, 416.
⁴⁵ S. Way (2), III. 14.
⁴⁶ S. Established (2), III. 3.

Now is not this love 'the fulfilling of the law?' the sum of all Christian righteousness? ... it necessarily implies bowels of mercies, humbleness of mind ... gentleness, meekness, long-suffering ... And of all outward righteousness; for 'love worketh no evil to his neighbor' ... it is zealous of good works ... 'full of mercy and good fruits'.[47]

Calling this love as the 'evangelical law',[48] Wesley asserted that 'He [God] has substituted... love, in the room of angelic perfection',[49] or that the evangelical law took place of the Adamic law.[50]

Being consistent with the substitution of the law, Wesley defined sin as 'every voluntary breach of the law of love'.[51] Distinguishing between voluntary transgression of the law of love and involuntary mistakes, Wesley related sin only to the former;[52] 'Mistakes, and whatever infirmities necessarily flow from the corruptible state of the body, are no way contrary to love; nor therefore, in the Scripture sense, sin'.[53] Without voluntary transgression, 'there may be ten thousand wandering thoughts, and forgetful intervals, without any breach of love, though not without transgressing the Adamic law'.[54]

The law of faith or the law of love does not require as perfect obedience without any mistake or infirmities as the Adamic law did. Faith working through love is the requirement of the covenant of grace, adjusted and proportioned to human capacity after the fall.[55] With the assistance of the Spirit of God, this requirement can be fulfilled.[56]

b. The Law under the Covenant of Grace

The law under the covenant of grace can be classified into three: the law of nature, the law of Moses, and the law of Christ. 'The law of nature' indicates the law given to all human hearts 'in some measure'[57] objectively through prevenient grace,[58] or, in Deschner's

---

[47] S. Way (1), I. 9.
[48] S. Patience, 10.
[49] *Plain Account*, 85.
[50] S. Patience, 10.
[51] Works, 12:394.
[52] S. Perfection (2), II. 9.
[53] *Plain Account*, 55.
[54] Works, 12:394.
[55] Letters 4:155.
[56] S. Righteousness, I. 8.
[57] S. Law, I. 4.
[58] ENNT Rom 2:12-14; By the term, 'nature', Wesley meant that God inscribed the law objectively in all human heart *without any outward or written form*, not that the law is intrinsic in human nature without any work of God's grace; for the distinction

words, 'prevenient re-inscription of the law'.[59] While the basis of this law is that God has been 'reconciled to man' through the atoning work of 'the Son of His love', its goal is to 'bring those who faithfully receive it to saving grace'.[60] It is not salvation itself, but an initiator of it. The light of the law by prevenient grace is as bright as to make every person to be convicted of their having sinned against God 'without having any written law'.[61] However, since sinners suffocate prevenient grace, they can proceed to a deeper understanding of God's law only when a further grace of the Holy Spirit's revelation of the written law is added.[62]

The law of Moses was proclaimed to give 'a more perfect knowledge of His law'. Compared with the law of nature, the law of Moses gives a more 'accurate knowledge' of God's will than the law in a corrupted human heart.[63]

The law of Christ is 'as old as the creation' in terms of its contents.[64] However, it is distinguished from the law of Moses in terms of profundity of the teaching. Christ has established the law 'in its fullness', clarifying any obscurity in the law and declaring the 'full import of every part of it'.[65] The law of Christ is regarded as 'new' not because of new contents, but because of the new 'degree' of the demand of the law, that is, the new depth of love consistent with the love Christ has shown to us.[66]

c. Two Dispensations

The difference between the law of Moses and the law of Christ can be explained in terms of 'the wide difference ... between the Jewish and the Christian dispensation'.[67] From Christ's words at Matt. 11:11, Wesley extracted a syllogism. Firstly, before Christ's coming, 'among

---

between the objectivity of the law of nature in all human beings and the subjectivity of the law in believers' heart, see Collins, 'Law', 95; Deschner, *Christology*, 96.
[59] Deschner, *Christology*, 97.
[60] Tae Hyoung Kwon, *John Wesley's Doctrine of Prevenient Grace: Its Impact on Contemporary Missiological Dialogue* (Ph.D. Dissertation, Temple University, 1996), 26; S. Law, I. 4.
[61] S. Working, II. 1.
[62] S. Working, III. 4.
[63] S. Law, I. 5; ENNT Rom 2:14; 2:20; 3:9.
[64] S. Mount (5), I. 4; S. Law, III. 11.
[65] S. Mount (5), I. 3.
[66] ENNT John 13:34. 'A new commandment – Not new in itself; but new... as to the degree of it, as I have loved you'.
[67] S. Perfection (1), II. 8, 11, 13; Letters 7:252; ENNT 1 John 2:8; ENNT Heb 8:7-8.

all the children of men there had not been one greater than John the Baptist ... neither Abraham, David, nor any Jew was greater than John'. Secondly, 'he which is least ... in that kingdom which he [Christ] came to set up on earth ... is greater than he'. The conclusion is that the Christian dispensation exceeds the Jewish dispensation, though the latter had its own glory.[68] Commenting on Heb 8:7-8, Wesley enumerated the superiority of the Christian dispensation: 'It is new in many respects, though not as to the substance of it: 1. Being ratified by the death of Christ. 2. Freed from those burdensome rites and ceremonies. 3. Containing a more full and clear account of spiritual religion. 4. Attended with larger influences of the Spirit 5. Extended to all men. And, 6. Never to be abolished'.[69]

The superiority of the law under Christian dispensation is twofold: Christ's revelation of the spiritual meaning of the law and the Holy Spirit's empowerment for keeping the law. Under the Jewish dispensation the law was understood as the outward rules and believers were not yet given the sanctifying grace. Under the Christian dispensation, the law stands on 'a different foundation from what it did before', that is, serving God 'in newness of spirit';[70] whereas 'the glory of the whole Mosaic dispensation was chiefly visible and external', 'the glory of the Christian dispensation is of an invisible and spiritual nature'.[71] Furthermore, God 'by requiring engages to work in us'.[72] When believers do their best to keep the law, Christ together with the Spirit not only forgives believers of their trespasses against the law, but also, making them 'more than conquerors over sin',[73] 'empowers them to do what His law commands'.[74] Therefore, every Christian in the Christian dispensation, even a babe in Christ, may become 'so far perfect as not to commit sin'.[75] Under the Christian dispensation the law must not be understood as impossible to be obeyed.

---

[68] S. Perfection (1), II. 8.
[69] ENNT Heb 8:7-8.
[70] S. Law, Intro. 2-3.
[71] WW 11: 472; Scott J. Jones, *John Wesley's Conception and Use of Scripture* (Nashville: Kingwood Books, 1995), 105.
[72] S. Mount (9), 5.
[73] S. Perfection (1), II. 11.
[74] S. Law, IV. 4.
[75] S. Perfection (1), II. 20-21.

iv. Types of the Law

Following the Thirty-nine Articles and the Reformers, Wesley classified the law into three types: 'the political [or civil], moral, and ceremonial'.[76] He sometimes omitted the civil law.[77]

a. The Moral Law

Wesley expressed explicitly that when he used the term 'the law' without any explanation, it meant only the moral law.[78] As a guidance of proper relationships between God, human beings, and the other creatures, the moral law requires holy love in all relationships. Coming out from the nature of God that is not liable to change, and being written on the hearts of all human beings, the moral law will remain in force permanently upon all human beings.[79]

b. The Civil Law

He expressed his thought on the civil law in respect of the roles of political authorities.[80] In his sermon, 'The Great Assize' (1758), Wesley established their authority on divine foundation, representing them as 'ministers of God'. Their responsibility is to work for both spiritual and secular welfare, by punishing wrongdoers, supporting the public tranquillity, securing people's temporal blessings, and encouraging innocence and virtue.[81] In another sermon, 'The Reformation of Manners' (1763), Wesley admitted the peculiar roles of the civil law distinguished from the moral law. While spiritual ministers work for the changes of human hearts through God's word, magistrates work for outward soundness of human life through the civil law:

> The Word of God is the chief, ordinary means, whereby he changes both the hearts and lives of sinners; and he does this chiefly by the Ministers of the gospel. But it is likewise true, that the Magistrate is 'the minister of God'; and that he is designed of God 'to be a terror to evil-doers', by executing human laws upon them. If this does not change the heart, yet to prevent outward sin is one valuable point gained. There is so much the less dishonour done to God, less scandal brought on our holy religion; less curse and reproach upon

---

[76] *Plain Account*, 83.
[77] ENNT Acts 13:39; Deshner, *Christology*, 93.
[78] S. Law, II. 6.
[79] S. Mount (5), I. 1-2.
[80] See S. Assize, IV. 1-2; S. Manners, I-II; S. America, II; S. Vineyard, IV. 2-4.
[81] S. Assize, IV. 1-3.

our nation; less temptation laid in the way of others; yea, and less wrath heaped up by the sinners themselves against the day of wrath.[82]

The civil (or positive) law is based upon the moral (natural) law. The civil and the moral laws are complementary and cooperative. When the civil law shows its limitations in solving problems of human societies, the moral law can help efficiently: 'it concerns all that fear God, that love mankind, and that wish well to their king and country, to pursue this design [the reformation of manners] with the same vigour as if there were no such officers existing'.[83]

For Wesley, biblical teachings on political order, authority, and responsibility are not necessarily restricted to the civil law, in that the moral law has already ample implications for proper relationships between people[84] as well as between God and people.[85] This explains why Wesley did not deal with Luther's 'political use' in any formal way.

c. The Ceremonial Law

Wesley defined the ceremonial law as 'all the injunctions and ordinances' that God laid through Moses upon 'the children of Israel' concerning 'the old sacrifices and service of the temple'. The ceremonial law was designed to restrain disobedient and stiff-necked people temporarily. But, as 'a type of Christ' that 'pointed us to Him [Christ]' the ceremonial law was utterly abolished by Christ's coming.[86]

II. Nature, Effect, and Uses of the Law

i. The Nature of the Law

For Wesley, the nature of God is 'the fountain whence it [the law] flowed'.[87] As an expression of God's nature, the law is holy in its nature.[88] The law is good because God is good.[89] Like the law reflects the nature of God, it also contains all 'virtue … wisdom, and knowledge, and love' in it. When Wesley explained the law as 'holy,

---

[82] S. Manners, II. 8.
[83] S. Manners, II. 5.
[84] See S. Assize; S. Family; S. Children; S. Parents; S. Pastors; S. National.
[85] S. Law, I. 1.
[86] S. Mount (5), I. 1; ENNT Gal 3:19, I Tim 1:8.
[87] S. Law, III. 10.
[88] S. Law, III. 1-3.
[89] S. Law, III. 10.

just, and good' following Paul's teaching in Rom. 7:12, he always had in mind the nature of God.[90]

ii. The Effect of the Law

Since the law originates from God's nature, the substance or the nature of the law does not change by the fall of humanity. What has changed because of the fall is the effects of the law.[91] Before the fall, the law was the way of 'the pure, clean, unpolluted worship of God'.[92] Because of the fall, the law came to have the other effects which had never previously existed; by the law 'sin appears to be sin' or 'sin... becomes exceeding sinful' (Rom. 7:13). This means that because the law is good, pure, and holy in its nature, if it is applied to sin, it takes effect as a detector of sin.[93] Sin has already existed, not exposing itself, but the law makes it 'far more odious both to God and man'.[94]

If sin is uncovered by the law, it rages all the more; if sin is restrained, it bursts out with greater violence.[95] Though sin abuses the law in this way, the law itself cannot be defiled; 'the heart of man is desperately wicked. But the law of God is holy still'.[96] To avoid confusion, Wesley stressed that though the law relates to human sin, its nature must be understood from its origin of God's nature. When the law is explained as holy in the Pauline Epistles, Wesley contended, 'the Apostle does not ... speak of its effects, but ... of its nature'.[97] Wesley affirmed, 'It [the law] has no fellowship with sin of any kind ... As sin is, in its very nature, enmity to God, so His law is enmity to sin'.[98]

iii. Three Uses of the Law

In his sermon, 'The Original, Nature, Property and Use of the Law' (1750), Wesley represented the uses of the law as three:

> To slay the sinner is ... the first use of the law; to destroy the life and strength wherein he trusts, and convince him that he is dead ... unto God, void of all spiritual life, 'dead in trespasses and sins'. The second use of it is, to bring

---

[90] S. Law, III. 1-2.
[91] S. Law, III. 2.
[92] S. Law, III. 2.
[93] S. Law, III. 4.
[94] S. Law, III. 4.
[95] S. Law, III. 4.
[96] S. Law, III. 4.
[97] S. Law, III. 2.
[98] S. Law, III. 3; Intro. 3.

him unto life, unto Christ ... The third use of the law is, to keep us alive ... to keep us with him ... the more they [we] see of its height, and depth, and length, and breadth ... the more ... closer and closer let us cleave to His beloved embrace.[99]

These three uses of the law are not only consistent with Wesley's view of the progress in salvation of non-believers: prevenient (convincing) grace, justification, and sanctification, but pertain to the process of 'promoting sanctification in the believer'.[100]

III. The Law and the Gospel

i. The Correlation between the Law and the Gospel

Wesley related both the nature and the uses of the law to God's love. Love is 'the spring' of the first use that 'drives us by force', as well as the second use that leads to Christ.[101]

God's love is related to the law in another way in Wesley's concept of 'covered promise', which means that every command of God can be kept with the help of His grace.[102] Wesley said:

> The law ... requires us to love God, to love our neighbour, to be meek, humble, or holy. We feel ... that 'with man this is impossible:' But we see a promise of God, to give us that love, and to make us humble, meek, and holy: We lay hold of this gospel ... it is done unto us according to our faith; and 'the righteousness of the law is fulfilled in us', through faith which is in Christ Jesus ... every command in holy writ is only a covered promise. For by that solemn declaration, 'This is the covenant I will make ... I will put my laws in your minds, and write them in your hearts', God hath engaged to give whatsoever he commands ... to 'pray without ceasing?' To 'rejoice evermore?' 'To be holy as He is holy?' ... He will work in us this very thing. It shall be unto us according to his word.[103]

For instance, the love for God promised in Deut. 30:6 is ordered as a command in Matt. 22:37; the latter is 'no less a promise, though in the form of a command'.[104] Similarly, the promise in Jeremiah 31:33 is commanded in Philippians 2:5.[105] The imperative to produce the fruits of the Spirit (Gal. 5:22-23) is 'a promise ... provided we are

---

[99] S. Law, IV. 2-3.
[100] Collins, 'Law', 205.
[101] S. Law, IV. 2.
[102] S. Mount (5), II. 3; See Outler, *Heritage*, 153, n. 14. According to Outler, Wesley picked up the concept of the covered promise from Thomas Drayton, *The Proviso or Condition of the Promises* (1657), 1-2.
[103] S. Mount (5), II. 3.
[104] S. Perfection (2), II. 1.
[105] S. Perfection (2), II. 2.

led by the Spirit'.[106] To the list of covered promises Wesley added biblical verses such as 1 Thess. 5:23, Psa. 130:8, Heb. 7:25, Ezek. 36:25-27, Lk. 1:73-75, and 1 Pet. 1:15.[107]

Wesley explained the fulfilment of covered promises in terms of both God's will and His ability; 'Nothing can be wanting on God's part: As He has called us to holiness, He is undoubtedly willing, as well as able, to work this holiness in us'.[108] Since God's grace gives as well as promises, Wesley contended:

> There is no contrariety at all between the law and the gospel; that there is no need for the law to pass away, in order to the establishing of the gospel. Indeed neither of them supersedes the other, but they agree perfectly well together. Yea, the very same words, considered in different respects, are parts both of the law and of the gospel. If they are considered as commandments, they are parts of the law: if as promises, of the gospel. Thus, 'Thou shalt love the Lord thy God with all thy heart', when considered as a commandment, is a branch of the law; when regarded as a promise, is an essential part of the gospel; ... the gospel being no other than the commands of the law proposed by way of promises. Accordingly poverty of spirit, purity of heart, and whatever else is enjoined in the holy law of God, are no other, when viewed in a gospel light, than so many great and precious promises.[109]

Though Wesley taught that God makes sinners realize their sins by the law, he denied that after justification God still makes believers humble with the law they are not capable of fulfilling. Against the argumentation that believers inevitably commit sins, he said, 'Least of all can you with any colour of argument infer, that any man *must* commit sin at all. No: God forbid we should thus speak! No necessity of sinning was laid upon them. The grace of God was surely sufficient ... for us at this day'.[110] The law can be fulfilled by God's grace. God makes believers humble by not removing their infirmities in this life.[111]

ii. Abolition of the Law

Wesley taught that those who 'openly and explicitly judge the law, and speak evil of the law' are in 'the highest rank of the enemies of the gospel of Christ'.[112] In the first conversation of the *Minutes of*

---

[106] S. Perfection (2), II. 3.
[107] S. Perfection (2), II. 4-7.
[108] S. Perfection (2), II. 5.
[109] S. Mount (5), II. 2.
[110] S. Perfection (1), II. 14.
[111] S. Coming, III. 3; S. Treasure, II. 5.
[112] S. Mount (5), III. 7; WW 8:278.

Some Late Conversations Between the Rev. Mr. Wesleys and Others (25th June 1744), Wesley, defining the antinomianism as 'the doctrine which makes void the law through faith', summarized the pillars of the insistence of antinomians:

> (1) Christ abolished the moral law; (2) therefore Christians are not obliged to observe it; (3) one branch of Christian liberty is, liberty from obeying the commandments of God; (4) it is bondage to do a thing because it is commanded, or forbear it because it is forbidden; (5) a believers is not obliged to use the ordinances of God, or to do good works; (6) a preacher ought not to exhort to good works; not unbelievers, because it is hurtful; not believers, because it is needless.[113]

For Wesley, the error comes from the mistake that they apply the word 'abolition' to the whole law without proper distinction between the temporary and the everlasting aspects in the law. The law abolished by Christ is, first, the Adamic law under the covenant of works.[114] Secondly, the law abolished is the ceremonial law of the Mosaic law, because Christ brought 'a better righteousness' by cleansing 'the inmost soul' of believers 'through His blood';[115] 'all things by the law were *purged with blood* ... But the blood of Christ being shed, all bloody ordinances are now abolished'.[116]

Finally, the law abolished by Christ is the moral law in the sense that 'the fulfilling it, the keeping all the commandments' is not required as 'the condition of our justification':[117] 'we have done with the moral law, as a means of procuring our justification; for we are 'justified freely by His grace, through the redemption that is in Jesus'.[118] The correct meaning of abolition when it is applied to the moral law is that the moral law is necessary 'on a different foundation' from what it was before.[119] Applying the law to believers on the way to entire sanctification, as well as to non-believers in the process of salvation,[120] Wesley affirmed:

> We have not done with this [the moral] law. For it is still of unspeakable use, first, in convincing us of the sin that yet remains both in our hearts and lives, and thereby keeping us close to Christ, that His blood may cleanse us every moment; Secondly, in deriving strength from our Head into His living

---

[113] Works 8:278.
[114] S. Righteousness, I. 1-3.
[115] S. Mount (9), 21; S. Law, Intro. 2; ENOT Gen 17:10; ENNT Matt 27:62; Gal 2:15; Eph 2:15; Heb 8:8; Rev 7:7; WW 8:278.
[116] ENOT Gen. 17:10.
[117] S. Established (2), Intro. 2.
[118] S. Law, IV. 4.
[119] S. Law, Intro. 3.
[120] S. Law, IV. 2-3.

members, whereby He empowers them to do what His law commands; and, Thirdly, in confirming our hope of whatsoever it commands and we have not yet attained, of receiving grace upon grace, till we are in actual possession of the fullness of His promises.[121]

C. Observations and Analysis

I. Function (Accusation) vs. Contents (Accusation & Prescription)

What is the law? In defining and understanding the law, there exist fundamental agreements between Luther and Wesley. Both Luther and Wesley taught that the law has holy love as its nature. It is spiritual. Also it has the strictness that gives just one choice between perfect obedience and punishment, judging our conformity to God in all subtle aspects of our behaviour, words, and thoughts. The law has various forms: moral and spiritual senses in the human heart; explicit enjoinment or forbiddance in Scripture; examples of good or bad behaviour of others with their respective rewards or punishments; providential events that reveal God's warning or wrath; and the pivotal historical events of Christ's life, teaching, and death. The law is well represented in the Scripture either by Moses or by Christ.

However, at the same time, the two theologians' views of the law diverge at various points. Firstly, they diverged concerning the ways of relating the nature to the effect of the law. Werner Elert aptly states, for Luther, while the law is something like a fence and sin is transgression into forbidden territory over that fence, the law after the fall relates only to transgressors whose 'entire life's journey from beginning to end is on the wrong side of the fence'. Human beings after the fall were all sinners both before and after the law was re-declared on Sinai to expose their sins more explicitly.[122]

Luther's focus was laid on the impossibility of sinners fulfilling the law. To reveal how much human nature has depraved from the nature of holy love of God, is an inevitable consequence of applying the law to sinners.[123] After the fall, the law's relation to the righteous human – prescription without accusation – is possible either hypothetically or only as the hope of future blessing. Elert properly as-

---

[121] S. Law, IV. 4.
[122] Elert, *Law*, 10-11.
[123] Elert, *Law*, 11.

serts that the quintessence of Luther's teaching of the law after the fall is that '*Lex semper accusat* (the law always accuses)'.[124]

Wesley distinguished between the nature and the effect of the law, as Luther did. However, he moved the focus of the discussion of the law from the effect to the nature of the law to remove the negative appraisal that the law causes or multiplies sins, which he thought is the inevitable consequence of relating the law merely to its effect. For Wesley, the law's relation to depraved humanity cannot exhaust the use of the law. If there were no salvation, to relate the law only to accusation could have been justified. However, salvation in a broad context of creation, fall, and recreation makes accusation merely a part of more comprehensive works of the law. Denying that the accusation is the sole and the major use, Wesley taught that the law eventually aims to point out sanctification as the teleological end of salvation. Since the law retains the nature of God's holy love as its nature, it informs the original state of human righteousness. To conform to God's law becomes a way of renewing human nature according to God's nature. The law works for our salvation not only by negative accusation but also by positive prescription.

Secondly, Luther and Wesley diverged from each other concerning the law's relation to God. In Luther's teaching, God confronts sinners directly though various forms of the law. God's law is not merely commandments, examples, or events, but God Himself acting and speaking through them. It is not only what is spoken, but also what is done to sinners. Luther scholars have a general agreement in describing Luther's definition of the law as 'everything that makes us realize our sin and accuses and terrifies the conscience, regardless of whether one finds it in Christ or in Moses',[125] in God's creation or in historical events,[126] or in the voice of human conscience.[127] In all of those things, sinners confront a wrathful God, not dead letters.

In a diametrically opposite way to the works of the gospel 'for me', God of the law aims 'against me' every moment through everything around me and even through myself.[128] By extending the effect of the law to the whole area of human existence Luther emphasized that sinners have no way to avoid the law. Also, by relating the law to the very words and works of God Himself, which are enough to over-

---

[124] Elert, *Law*, 10-11; *BC*, 112, 125, 130, 135, 150,
[125] Althaus, *Theology*, 261.
[126] Gerrish, 'Unknown', 132-149.
[127] Bornkamm, *Old*, 128-129; Forde, *Where*, 13-16.
[128] Siggins, *Christ*, 110-113.

power human pride, egotism, and ingratitude, Luther could teach that the law really kills and humiliates sinners, in spite of their resistance to it or misusing it as a means of self-defence and self-righteousness. This grants the law a very 'existential' character in the sense that the law deals 'not with a [theological] system' but sinners' status before God the Judge, not metaphysically but as a real experience.[129]

This existential character of the law characterizes a sinners' relationship with God. The possibility of sinners' repentance depends solely on the power of God. Revealing the true meaning of the spiritual law through the Holy Spirit and, thus, confronting sinners with His wrath and punishment, God changes a distorted gospel, with which sinners presumptuously defend their self-complacency and avoid God's demands of repentance, into the law. Even when the natural law or the written law cannot play its role of giving sinners self-knowledge, being misunderstood, resisted, and distorted by human sin, God Who Himself is the existential law is always before and around sinners.

The existential character of the law determines Luther's view of the gospel as well. For Luther, believers cannot have faith in the 'once-for-all' manner; we 'cannot live today on yesterday's faith'. By interpreting whatever becomes an existential threat to us as the message of the divine law, sinners can renew their dependence on God. When the law inevitably arises anytime, anywhere, and by anything, 'the only way to deal with such problems is ... to go every day to the cross, and begin again ... Faith in the gospel has to be renewed each day. Each day we must hear anew that Christ is the end of the law and the gift of new life'.[130]

In contrast with Luther, Deschner states, Wesley's concept of the law has 'a semi-independent role' in relation to God, in the sense that 'once given' by God the Creator, the law 'acquires a kind of state of its own, over against the Giver'. Whereas God created His world and gave His law from His absolute freedom, after creation, God 'looks first of all not to His own free will, but to creation, and conforms His direct command to what is established there'. This means that the law is confirmed in the way that according to His prior declaration of the law, God makes the law objective – 'fixed, eternal, and immuta-

---

[129] Forell, *Faith Active in Love*, 47.
[130] Forde, *Where*, 40.

ble' – information of God's will as a means of 'a more abstract, stylized kind of holiness'.[131]

Wesley's discussion of the law was focused on law in Scripture. Deschner points out, 'Wesley has a strong tendency to derive his laws from Scriptures'.[132] Similarly to Luther, Wesley admitted that God can convict sinners either with or without the law. Also, Wesley would agree with Luther that the natural law is not in itself sufficient for leading sinners to repentance without further grace of God, since they suffocate prevenient grace. However, if the written law that provides sufficient information of God's will is employed as a means of convincing sinners by the Holy Spirit, it turns into very dreadful power of wrathful God enough to remove any hindrances to repentance from sinners. Wesley emphasized, 'the ordinary method of the Spirit of God' is the law of the Scripture. It teaches God's will most clearly.[133]

Thirdly, the fundamental difference in the views of Luther and Wesley can be described as the one between monergism and evangelical synergism, which will be dealt with in more details in Chapter 5. In Luther's monergistic view, the law's accusation against every human being functions as an essential theological pair with *sola gratia*. For him, not only the gospel, but also the real function of the law is attributed solely to God.

In contrast, for Wesley, God's sovereign re-inscription of the moral law through prevenient grace is God's direct work. It is not synergistic. Wesley also represented convincing grace as a direct work of God. However, in his evangelical synergism, to respond properly to prevenient grace or the law in the Scripture is necessary as a means with which sinners and believers are not only led to initial or evangelical repentance respectively, but also are prepared for further grace of justification or sanctification. In the evangelical synergism in which God's grace motivates and empowers, and human beings respond and cooperate with grace, the law works for our salvation by both accusation and prescription. There exists a synergism between God's direct work and human use of the already declared law.

---

[131] Deschner, *Christology*, 102-106.
[132] Deschner, *Christology*, 93-94.
[133] S. Law, IV. 1.

II. Two Uses and Two Kingdoms vs. Prevenient Grace and Three Uses

Luther taught that all three types of the law – the civil, the ceremonial, and the moral laws – compose a valid paradigm of Christian life and religion. The civil law demonstrates God's government in His earthly kingdom. The ceremonial law, though its meaning has changed, is an important element of the worship of God. The moral law becomes a spur for believers who are still sinners to constantly depend on God's grace. Wesley also knew all three types of the law. However, it seems that he discussed the civil affairs in relation to prevenient grace or the moral law. The ceremonial law, he explained, was 'utterly' abolished by Christ's coming.[134] Wesley's discussion of the law was focused mainly on the moral law.

Differently from Luther's two uses of the law – civil (*'usus politicus'*) and theological (*'usus theologicus'*) – Wesley taught three use of the law: 'to slay the sinner', 'to bring him ... unto Christ', and 'to keep us with Him'. Collins notes that among Wesley's three uses, there is no political use like Luther's, and all three uses are 'theological' ones. His first two uses of convincing sinners and of leading to Christ are equivalent to Luther's theological use. His third use is consistent with the third use of the law Melanchthon and Calvin taught, whereas Luther did not teach the third use.[135]

Luther's two uses and Wesley's three uses reflect different views of the fall and salvation. Luther thought that the righteousness with which we can fulfil the law is not given in this life except through the imputed righteousness of Christ. Until believers receive the future blessing of perfect righteousness, the two uses of the law together with three types of the law continue to deal with sins in people's civil lives and their spiritual life before God.

For Wesley, though the original righteousness is lost, the foundation of believers' recovering of inherent righteousness was laid by God Himself. Firstly, through the covenant of grace, believers' works done in faith are regarded as righteous by a gracious God.[136] Secondly, though the covenant of grace opens the possibility that works can be counted as righteous, the covenant is not the righteousness itself. What changes the possibility into reality is the empowerment of the

---

[134] S. Mount (5), I. 1.
[135] Collins, 'Law', 183.
[136] Wilson, 'The Correlation of Love and Law in the Theology of John Wesley', 100-101; WW 8:289.

Holy Spirit for believers to fulfil the law. On the foundation of both the covenant of grace and the Spirit's empowerment, Wesley maintained that the law not only accuses but restores believers to their inherent righteousness.

Luther's understanding of the law forms the framework of his theology, that is, justification by faith and the two kingdoms. Christian relationship with the secular kingdom is two-fold. On the one hand, believers and non-believers are alike in the secular kingdom, in that the natural law becomes their standard of personal ethics, and the civil law which originates from the natural law, becomes their public positive law. In the secular kingdom, everybody follows their own reason personally, or is governed by the civil law publicly.[137] In that interpretation of the natural law depends on human reason, Luther insisted that in the earthly kingdom, 'we could be our own teachers',[138] or that 'you are your own Bible, your own teacher, your own theologian, and your own preacher'.[139] Believers and non-believers alike have their own righteousness 'to be lived out' within their own life stations; 'this righteousness has nothing to do with Christ, but it works independently on the basis of inherent human capacities'.[140]

On the other hand, only true believers, who live according to the law of Christ, can love their neighbours in a special way, having a 'religious basis' for their neighbourly love.[141] Whereas non-believers find ethical implications from the natural law and the civil law, believers regard the requirements of both laws as the way of fulfilling their Christian vocation in God's secular kingdom.

For Wesley, three uses of the law, which are all theological uses, do not exhaust the works of the law. What is equivalent to Luther's civil law in Wesley's teaching is prevenient grace. Through a certain measure of capacity 'in distinguishing between the morally good and the morally evil', prevenient grace works for 'condemning morally reprehensible conduct toward their fellow human beings', like Luther's civil law does.[142] Similarly to Luther's view of the two kingdoms, Charles R. Wilson observes, Wesley distinguished between two realms of history God rules over; on the one hand, 'general uni-

---

[137] Meistad, *Mount*, 60-61, 147.
[138] LW 21:235.
[139] LW 21:236-237.
[140] Meistad, *Mount*, 110; LW 21:26.
[141] Meistad, *Mount*, 61-63, 147.
[142] Marquardt, *Social*, 93.

versal history' as 'the sphere of the operation of prevenient grace' and, on the other hand, 'special redemptive history' in which three uses of the law work for the restoration of the image of God in believers.[143]

However, whereas Luther, dividing between two kingdoms, excluded 'soteriology from creation', Wesley viewed 'the soteriological work of God ... in line with His work of creation', as 'the re-creation of the entire cosmos, including the created nature and human society, as well as the person'.[144] General history is understood as the object as well as the background of God's redemptive history. On the relationship between God's orders of creation and of salvation, Wesley had 'a perspective of development and actual change'.[145] Wesley's view of the relationship between prevenient grace as preliminary work of the law with which the process of salvation starts, and three uses of the law with which God gives convincing, justifying, and sanctifying grace, corresponds with his comprehensive view of salvation as 'the re-creation of humanity as well as the entire cosmos'.[146]

III. Dialectic vs. Correlation

Luther taught a dialectic between the law and the gospel, between human sins and God's forgiveness, between the impossibility of human merit and Christ's sufficient merit, or between imperfect human works and God's perfect grace. In this dialectic, the law helps sinners find Christ indirectly:

> The law with its function does contribute to justification – not because it justifies, but because it impels one to the promise of grace and makes it sweet and desirable. Therefore we do not abolish the law; but we show its true function and use, namely, that it is a most useful servant impelling us to Christ. After the law has humbled, terrified, and completely crushed you, so that you are on the brink of despair, then see to it that you know how to use the law correctly; for its function and use is not only to disclose the sin and wrath of God but also to drive us to Christ.[147]

To abolish the law is to abolish the gospel, since, as Lohse states, though the law is not 'the efficient cause' of justification, it is still re-

---

[143] Wilson, 'The Correlation of Love and Law in the Theology of John Wesley', 103.
[144] Meistad, *Mount*, 95, 110.
[145] Meistad, *Mount*, 99.
[146] Meistad, *Mount*, 93.
[147] LW 26:315.

quired as '*materialiter*'.¹⁴⁸ As an essential element that helps sinners accept Christ, the dialectic should remain.

Wesley agreed with Luther's dialectic. But, he taught a tension which Luther opposed, a tension between believers' present righteousness and the teleological end of Christian perfection. For Wesley, Christian love has the character of seeking more love, like 'an eternal debt, which can never be sufficiently discharged'. The teleological end of Christian perfection becomes an ever receding target that should always be pursued ever more vigorously.¹⁴⁹ Clarence L. Bence notes, in Wesley's soteriology, there is 'a dialectical tension between present attainment and future expectation throughout the entire order of salvation'.¹⁵⁰

Positively, this tension gives believers a good stimulus for continuous growth in grace. Negatively, the sense of 'an extreme unlikeness between God and us even after we have attained justifying faith' may cause in us 'heaviness' of heart which easily turns into an oppressive burden, as in the cases of many 'mystic authors' and 'plain people' in Wesley's times.¹⁵¹ In his sermon, 'Satan's Devices' (1750), Wesley warned that by blending together 'the natural tendency' of a believers' growth in sanctifying grace with 'the accidental abuse' of hypocrisy or despair, Satan endeavours to destroy the positive effects by the tension: firstly, he attacks the already received justification by the high standard of sanctification; secondly, he hinders the increase of holiness through 'our expectation of that greater work'.¹⁵²

Wesley's statement of the negative effects of the doctrine of Christian perfection reminds us of Luther's criticism of the same doctrine. To Luther, who regarded believers as forgiven sinners, believers' insistence on inherent righteousness is presumptuous as well as ungrateful. Since they are still sinful, on the basis of inherent righteousness they inevitably fall into either hypocrisy or despair. Luther solved this problem caused by the synergistic idea of inherent right-

---

¹⁴⁸ WA 39 I, 469, 13-19. 'The law is among the causes of things that work righteousness – this we contest. For justification is not among those things caused by the law, but rather death, damnation, horror and trembling, knowledge of sin [which] as I said above are [only] materially required [for justification]'. Quoted by Lohse, *Theology*, 181.
¹⁴⁹ ENNT Rom 13:8-10.
¹⁵⁰ Clarence L. Bence, 'John Wesley's Teleological Hermeneutic', (Ph.D. thesis, Emory University, 1981), 19.
¹⁵¹ S. Heaviness, III. 8.
¹⁵² S. Satan's, I. 1-14.

eousness monergistically through both Christ's atonement that gives justification, and the eschatological hope that God's grace will perfect a believers' own righteousness. In the present life in which believers remain still and always sinners, the dialectic between the law's accusation and the gospel's forgiveness is the best way of describing the state of believers.

For Wesley, the negative effect should not be overemphasized. Believers' 'clearer and fuller knowledge of our inbred sin ... after justification' does not necessarily 'occasion darkness of soul'. In proportion to the extent of sinfulness believers find in themselves, God's forgiving grace will be experienced; 'God may increase ... in the same proportion, the knowledge of Himself and the experience of His love'.[153] Further, by God's sanctifying grace, Wesley asserted, 'your own vileness ... shall be done away ... Like as the wax melteth at the fire, so shall this [every evil temper you feel] melt away before His face ... God of your salvation, who hath done so great things for you already ... will do so much greater things than these'.[154] Hypocrisy or despair is overcome not only by God's justifying grace that forgives, but also by His sanctifying grace that grants believers a real righteousness as the power of fulfilling God's law.

For Wesley, the sinful state of believers cannot be dealt with in isolation from the whole process of salvation in which there is 'the golden chain' of 'pardon, holiness, heaven', that is, a sequence of prevenient, justifying, sanctifying, and glorifying graces. Warning that to detach any stage of salvation from the whole may distort the very powerful and comprehensive works of God's grace, Wesley asserted, yearning for God's further grace should be done in sticking to the already received grace. Sanctifying grace should be sought in preserving and increasing justifying grace, and in hoping for the glorifying grace of the future. 'The golden chain' of God's graces must not be broken, and the order of each grace must not be changed.[155]

From Wesley's point of view, a tension between believers' present righteousness and the teleological end of Christian perfection cannot be solved by Luther's dialectic between the accusing law and the forgiving gospel. Luther's dialectic in which believers remain in their bondage to sin cannot exalt God's grace. As will be dealt with in more detail in Chapter 2, in many subjects that Luther described as a dialectic, Leon Hynson contends, 'Wesley, the man of superlative theo-

---

[153] S. Heaviness, III. 9.
[154] S. Satan's, II. 1.
[155] S. Satan's, II. 2-8.

logical gifts, wove a coherent synthesis of ... faith and reason, theology and anthropology, nature and grace, faith or ethics, divine initiative and human response, freedom and responsibility, law and grace, justification and sanctification'.[156] What solves the negative effects of the doctrine of Christian perfection is the very correlation between the law and the gospel; between God's requirement and His empowerment; and between the receding target of Christian perfection and God's sanctifying grace that makes believers reach it. For Wesley, what makes believers fall into despair or hypocrisy would not be the teaching of, but, to some extent, the objection to the doctrine of Christian perfection: 'If you press all the believers to go on to perfection and to expect deliverance from sin every moment, they will grow in grace. But if ever they lose that expectation they will grow flat and cold'.[157]

---

[156] Leon O. Hynson, *To Reform the Nation: Theological Foundations of Wesley's Ethics* (Grand Rapids: Francis Asbury Press), 23-24; see Wilson, 'The Correlation of Love and Law in the Theology of John Wesley', 110-115.

[157] Letters 6:66; see also Letters 6:54, 59, 74, 97, 103, 137, 240. The sources of citation are from Allan Coppedge, *John Wesley in Theological Debate* (Wilmore, KY: Wesley Heritage Press, 1987), 268.

Chapter 2:
God the Father and the Law

A. Martin Luther

I. God the Creator and the Law

Among various labels on Luther such as a protestant, a Reformer, a prophet, a hero, and etc, Dale Johnson's 'God-intoxicated thinker'[1] expresses well the character of both Luther and his theology. In his *"Preface to the Complete Edition of Luther's Latin Writings"* (1545), Luther testified that under the Roman Catholic Church he had been seized with the fear of the righteous God who crushes sinners 'by every kind of calamity by the law of the Decalogue'.[2] Against this dreadful image of God, Luther confessed, his Reformation breakthrough came with his encounter with the gracious God in the Bible who grants us His righteousness.[3] Luther's theology is the outcome of his new insight on God of the gospel as well as of the law.

While Luther's theology characteristically shows that 'God is God', for Luther being God meant being the Creator.[4] Relating God's divine attributes to being the Creator,[5] Luther taught that God the Creator 'works all in all',[6] making 'all things out of nothing'[7] or 'under the veil ... of its opposite':[8]

---

[1] Dale A. Johnson, 'Luther's Understanding of God', *LQ* 16:1 (Feb. 1964), 59.
[2] LW 34:336-337.
[3] LW 34:336-337.
[4] Althaus, *Theology*, 105; for sources and meanings of Luther's use of 'Creator', see Oswald Bayer, 'I Believe That God Has Created Me With All That Exists: An Example of Catechetical-Systematics', *LQ* (Summer 1994), 129-161.
[5] LW 37:59-60.
[6] LW 9:8, 205; LW 11:458; LW 14:301; LW 15:73; LW 19:112; LW 21:328; LW 33:140, 175, 189, 242; see Althaus, *Theology*, 105-115.
[7] LW 26:66; LW 1:17-18; LW 6:58-59, 102-103, 350-357; LW 7:105, 7:210-211; LW 8:37, 8:380; LW 18:376; LW 20:4-5, 49, 84; LW 46:250.
[8] Althaus, *Theology*, 119; see LW 21:297-358. God's creation 'out of its opposite' becomes the main theme throughout Luther's *The Magnificat* (1521).

> Just as God in the beginning of creation made the world out of nothing, whence He is called the Creator and the Almighty, so His manner of working continues unchanged. Even now and to the end of the world, all His works are such that out of that which is nothing, worthless, despised, wretched, and dead, He makes that which is something, precious, honorable, blessed, and living. On the other hand, whatever is something, precious, honorable, blessed, and living, He makes to be nothing, worthless, despised, wretched, and dying.[9]

'All things' include God's spiritual works of providence and salvation as well as His creation and preservation of the physical world. Justification was a special example of 'God's paradoxical creative activity' ; 'God enjoys bringing light out of darkness and making things out of nothing, etc. Thus He has created all things and thus He helps those who have been abandoned, He justifies the sinners, He gives life to the dead, and He saves the damned'.[10]

Luther represented God's words as 'Deed-Word' which effects what it signifies, distinguishing it from 'Call-Word' which names something which already exists;[11] 'God's works are His words; He speaks and it is done: because the speaking and the doing of God are the same'.[12] Luther said,

> When Scripture says that God speaks, it understands a word related to a real thing or action ... when He speaks ... indeed the whole earth is moved ... When the sun rises, when the sun sets, God speaks. When the fruits grow in size, when human beings are born, God speaks. Accordingly the words of God are not empty air, but things great and wonderful, which we see with our eyes and feel with our hands.[13]

The concept of Deed-Word teaches the directness of God's works in creation and 'continuous creation', which means that God created in the beginning and still creates, preserves, and rules His creation.[14] 'God has determined and preordained certain boundaries for all men, when they are to be born, when they are to die, what name they are to have, and what office they are to fill'.[15] God establishes 'king-

---

[9] LW 21:299.
[10] WA 40, III, 154. Quoted by Althaus, *Theology*, 120; LW 8:39.
[11] David C. Steinmetz, *Luther in Context*, 2nd ed. (Grand Rapids: Baker Book House, 2002), 115-116; LW 1:21-22 on Gen 1:3-5. See Johannes Schwanke, 'Luther on Creation', in *Harvesting Martin Luther's Reflections on Theology, Ethics, and the Church*, ed. Timothy J. Wengert (Grand Rapids: Wm. B. Eerdmans, 2004), 78-98.
[12] WA 3.152.7. Quoted by Forde, *Preached*, 64.
[13] LW 12: 32.
[14] LW 21:299; LW 22:26-29.
[15] LW 15:102.

doms and rulers' and determines their limits;[16] provides the great people such as David, Hannibal, and Alexander;[17] and gives individuals honour and blessings or disgrace and curses.[18] Luther related God's omnipresence to His being the Creator; 'If he [God] is to make and preserve all things everywhere, then his divine right hand, nature, and majesty must also be everywhere. He must surely be present if he makes and preserves them.'[19] God employs all human, angelic, or natural instruments as His masks. Where nonbelievers see only masks, believers grasp that God is working through them.[20] Whatever good believers receive from God's creatures, they receive them 'from God through them.'[21]

By asserting the omnipotence of God, His continuous creation, and the directness of His works behind masks, Luther endeavoured to foster in believers a living faith that believes God's words 'I am your God'[22] and confesses that 'I am a creature of God'[23] in both creation and salvation.[24] In this relationship, Luther's view of God is intrinsically associated with his understanding of the law. For Luther, 'the purpose of the law is something else than justification';[25] it teaches us that God is the source of everything, thus, all His human

---

[16] LW 17:36.
[17] LW 13:160-164.
[18] LW 21:299.
[19] LW 37:59-60.
[20] LW 3:166, 220; LW 6:257; LW 9:40; LW 35:162-163; Jaroslav Pelikan, *Luther the Expositor* (St. Louis: Concordia, 1959), 103-105.
[21] BC, 368.
[22] BC, 254; LW 5:233; LW 8:12; LW 14:87; LW 51:138-139; see Charles P. Arand, 'Luther on the God Behind the First Commandment', *LQ* 8 (1994), 400.
[23] BC, 412. 'I am a creature of God; that is, that He has given and constantly sustains my body, soul, and life, my members great and small, all the faculties of my mind, my reason and understanding ... my food and drink, clothing, means of support, wife and child, servants, house and home ... He makes all creation help provide the comforts and necessities of life — sun, moon, and stars in the heavens, day and night, air, fire, water, the earth and all that it brings forth, birds and fish, beasts, grain and all kinds of produce. Moreover, he gives all physical and temporal blessings — good government, peace, security. Thus we learn from this article that none of us has his life of himself ... nor can he by himself preserve any of them ... All this is comprehended in the word "Creator"'; BC, 514; LW 1:3; LW 40:96-98.
[24] For Luther, God being our God meant His being our Saviour as well. Because God is Creator, He can also give resurrection and eternal life. See LW 4:119-121; LW 5:233; LW 6:102, 359-365; LW 8:12, 37; LW 13:81-82; LW 14:87; LW 17:166; LW 21:291.
[25] WA 391, 213. Quoted by Althaus, *Theology*, 121; LW 31:49-50; Forde, *Cross*, 56-58; LW 34:117; see LW 25:190, 266, 342; LW 26:122.

creatures should do is to give all praise, thanks, and glory to God alone.[26]

Luther explained this correlation between God and the law in terms of the First Commandment. God in the First Commandment corresponds with God who works all in all[27] as 'the Creator, the Benefactor, the Promiser, and the Saviour',[28] to whom we owe everything; God of the First Commandment is 'is powerful, is all-sufficient of Himself, has power over everything, needs no one's help, and is able to give all things to all' .[29] Therefore, the First Commandment requires us to have 'fear of God, faith and love toward Him';[30] to have 'a hearty trust in Him for all blessings';[31] to 'call upon Him in trouble ... give thanks for deliverance'.[32] In the word 'faith' Luther inclusively summed up all proper attitudes toward God such as love, praise, thanks, obedience, and giving glory.[33] Faith that confesses that 'we are ... nothing and dust' and 'He is our God'[34] results in mortification of sinners' self-centredness and a new life under God.[35]

Because faith produces this fundamental change, the First Commandment's relation to the other commandments[36] can be summed up into superiority (and priority),[37] foundationality,[38] and unifying essence.[39] Faith that this supreme commandment deals with has

---

[26] LW 6:257; LW 14:114; LW 52:276; LW 21:297-358; Johnson, 'God', 68.
[27] Bayer, 'I Believe That God Has Created Me With All That Exists, 131.
[28] LW 3:116; LW 4:121; LW 6:102; LW 13:81-82; LW 47:89-90; LW 12:44; Arand, 'Luther on the God Behind the First Commandment', 397-423.
[29] LW 3:80.
[30] BC, 102; LW 51:138-139.
[31] BC, 365, 371
[32] LW 3:116; BC, 365-368, 412.
[33] BC, 102; 254; 412. 'The Creed is nothing else than a response and confession of Christians based on the First Commandment'.
[34] LW 4:68.
[35] LW 6:102-103, 350-357.
[36] See Arand, 'Luther on the God Behind the First Commandment', 397-423.
[37] LW21:69; LW 22:145-146. 'It is impossible to proclaim a more sublime worship of God'; LW 26:293. 'None ... could teach anything greater or more sublime than Moses himself, who laid down the supreme laws about the hightest and greatest things, such as the Decalog, especially the First Commandment'; LW 5:115, 124-125; LW 52:252.
[38] LW 34:154. 'Out of the Ten Commandments flow and depend all the other commandments and the whole of Moses ... He [God] has instituted so many different ceremonies or acts of worship. Through these He has interpreted the First Commandment and taught how it is to be kept'; LW 43:176.
[39] LW 17:52.

unique validity before God.[40] It sufficiently makes believers act in obedience toward His will.[41] As 'the chief source and fountainhead' of all the other commandments,[42] the First Commandment is inclusive of all the other commandments; 'This [the First] commandment is the very first of all commandments and the highest and the best, from which all others proceed, in which they exist and by which they are judged and assessed'.[43]

Luther showed a negative attitude toward doing any works on account of God's rewards. The children of God who acknowledge that they receive every blessing from God's grace 'do good with a will that is disinterested, not seeking any reward, but only the glory and will of God, and being ready to do good even if – an impossible supposition – there were neither a kingdom nor a hell'.[44] Since salvation pertains to God alone, those who deny their dependence on God and try to gain His favour by their efforts place themselves in His position.[45] Luther enumerated various sorts of idolatry against the First Commandment: imitating outward worship without true faith which is 'the kernel' of worship of God;[46] inventing their own ways of worship not prescribed by God;[47] loving greedily God's gifts more than God Himself;[48] or relying on something or someone 'for that which

---

[40] BC, 371. 'Let us ... learn the first commandment well and realize that God will tolerate no presumption and no trust in any other object ... it is the most important. For ... where the heart is right with God and this commandment is kept, fulfillment of all the others will follow of its own accord'; LW 44:40; Althaus, Theology, 131.
[41] LW 31:350; LW 40:86.
[42] BC, 409-410; LW 40:93; Bernd Wannenwetsch, 'Luther's Moral Theology', in McKim ed., The Cambridge Companion to Martin Luther, 121.
[43] LW 44:30; LW 51:141, 147; WA 1, 438, 7. 'The First commandment contains in itself all the other commandments. Whoever keeps it, keeps them all, and who does not keep it, neither keeps them'. Cited from Wannenwetsch, 'Luther's Moral Theology', 122.
[44] LW 33:153.
[45] Luther emphasized that salvation appertains to God alone. LW 26:257-259; LW 31:46. 'To trust in works ... is equivalent to giving oneself the honor and taking it from God ... this is ... to adore oneself as an idol'; WA 40, I, p. 404, 29ff. 'They ... by their own works to ... deliver themselves from sin and death, which is simply to deny God and set themselves in God's place. For all these are works of the Divine majesty alone'; WA 40, p. 405, 15. 'Whosoever seeks righteousness by works apart from faith, denies God and makes himself God, for he thinks thus ... I shall be victor over sin, death, the devil, the wrath of God and hell and shall attain eternal life ... this works ... belongs to God alone'. Quoted by Nygren, Agape, 702.
[46] LW 44:33; LW 4:327; Luther warned against inner idols in human hearts more than statues and images, opposing against Karlstad's iconoclasm. See LW 40:94-95.
[47] LW 9:85; LW 44:243-400.
[48] LW 11:69; LW 16:61. 'Greed is an idol in opposition to faith'.

should be sought and found in God alone'.[49] The First Command judges those idolaters to be robbers of God's glory.[50]

Luther's conception of the First Commandment is a re-assertion of *sola fide* in his soteriology in the context of his discussion of God. As 'a concise summary of the Christian faith', the First Commandment teaches 'the utter submission to God's grace',[51] confessing that not only faith[52] but also 'the good will, the merit, and the reward all come from grace alone'.[53] Luther contended that the Reformation was achieved by no other than establishing 'the true and certain doctrine regarding God ... from the First Commandment'.[54]

II. God the Saviour and the Law

God does not save sinners as a reaction to their meritorious works, but has the reason for their salvation within Himself, that is, love. Love was so important in Luther's view of God that he not only described God's nature as 'fire and passion ... of love' but also attributed love solely to God.[55] There exists a great difference between God's love and human love. Whereas human love 'comes into being through attraction to what pleases it', God's love 'does not first discover but creates what is pleasing to it'; '[sinners] are not loved because they are attractive', but they 'are attractive because they are loved' by God.[56] By initiative, unmotivated, and creative love, God makes sinners, fools, and weaklings righteous, wise, and strong.

From Luther's point of view, being ignorant of the nature of God's love, the medieval Catholic Church made three erroneous approaches toward God: the moralistic piety of popular Catholicism; the rational theology of Scholasticism; and the ecstatic religiosity of Mysti-

---

[49] LW 44:48; Luther dealt seriously with the idolatry of 'mammon', that is, money and possessions. See *The BC*, 365 and Luther's comments on Matthew 6:24-25 in LW 21:186-195; LW 6:49; LW 9:71; LW 10:395; LW 12:167; LW 14:240; LW 17:132; LW 20:276.
[50] *BC*, 365-368; LW 13:364-365; see Althaus, *Theology*, 145.
[51] LW 52:252.
[52] LW 43:24-25; *BC*, 102. Luther represented 'a surer knowledge of God, fear of God, trust in God, or at least the inclination and power to do these things' as God's gifts.
[53] LW 33:152.
[54] LW 6:228-231; Lohse, *Theology*, 209.
[55] WA 36, 424. 'If I were to paint a picture of God I would so draw him that there would be nothing else in the depth of His divine nature than that fire and passion which is called love... love is such a thing that it is neither human nor angelic but rather divine, yes, even God Himself'. Quoted by Althaus, *Theology*, 115-116.
[56] LW 31:57.

cism.[57] Against meritorious works, Luther asserted that even if fallen human beings do their best, they inevitably commit deadly sin.[58] Neither Scholastic speculations nor mystical contemplations can be the way to God, because human finitude cannot be equal with God,[59] and, worse still, we cannot stand before God's glory owing to our depravity.[60] Luther regarded those upward approaches toward God as harmful as well as impossible, seeing that by trying to reach the mysteries of God people put themselves on God's level, above their creaturely level.

Against this, Luther taught, God wants to turn human beings to their dependence on God's revelation. Christ is the only heavenly ladder through whom we have free access to God;[61] 'we must reflect ... on the incarnate Son ... there we shall really behold God, and there we shall look into His very heart'.[62] Luther's view of love of God is consistent with his teaching on the First Commandment: what God wants from sinners is only that they accept God's love in Christ through faith.[63]

There has been criticism that Luther destroyed Christian love, arguing that if a person is justified by faith alone, it devalues not only outward works of the law but also love which is the fulfilling of the law. However, Anders Nygren points out, for Luther faith was not a matter of rivalry between faith and love. He admitted that since faith can be produced only by God's love, 'love comes first'.[64] He even taught the superiority of love, contending that while faith makes us God's children, love makes us 'gods' since love is God's own nature; 'God's children are we through faith ... But we are gods through love, which makes us beneficent to our neighbour, for Divine nature is nothing else but pure beneficence and ... love towards man, which showers its blessings lavishly upon all creatures daily'.[65]

---

[57] Nygren, *Agape*, 681-682.
[58] LW 31:39-40. See Theses no. 1, and no. 13.
[59] Lohse, *Theology*, 197. For Luther, even before the fall, God's righteousness could not be judged by human standards; God is incomprehensible in both omnipotence and righteousness; LW 1:10-11.
[60] LW 1:11.
[61] Nygren, *Agape*, 705-709.
[62] LW 2:276
[63] Althaus, *Theology*, 127-129.
[64] LW 44:30.
[65] WA 10, I, I, p. 100, 17ff.; WA 36, 423, 22ff. love is 'that one, eternal unutterable good and supremest treasure which is God Himself ... he that abides in love, abides in God and God in him, so that he and God become one cake'. Quoted by Nygren, *Agape*, 719-720.

Luther's concern was not the contrast between faith and love, but the contrast between two fundamentally different conceptions of love; God's love (the Scriptural concept of unconditional love) and human love (the Hellenistic acquisitive love or the Judaic meritorious love). Abstracting the nature of Christian love from God's love, Nygren describes what Luther considered as God's love:

> Christian love is spontaneous in contrast to all activity with a eudaemonistic motive ... The fact that God's love for us is free and unmotivated carries with it the corollary that we love our neighbour also freely and without any selfish motivation.
>
> Christian love is also spontaneous in contrast to all legalism ... man is completely won for the good only when he does the good spontaneously from inward inclination, and would do it even if it were not commanded in the law.
>
> ... Christian love is by its very nature ... a lost love ... 'For it is of the nature of love to suffer betrayal'[66]... the love of God ... is in the highest degree a lost love.[67]

Luther removed human love from the context of justification because it depreciates love in two senses: first, it is to deny love in the sense of God's unmotivated, spontaneous love; second, a love governed by its end corrupts the purity of Christian love, being mixed with acquisitive love or with meritorious love. However, after justification, whoever receives God's unconditional love can love 'in a glad, peaceful, and confident heart ... with no thought of reward' without doubting and worrying how 'to do enough and to influence God with ... many good works'.[68] Living between God and their neighbours Christians receive God's love in faith and pass it on to their neighbours. In Christians who love others, God lives and works. With unconditional love, Luther asserted, Christians become a Christ to their neighbours.[69] Christ's law of love can be fulfilled only by Christians 'who are above every law and do more than the laws ordain' by God's love.[70] Though Luther ascribed love to God alone, he did not depreciate the value of Christian love. God's love becomes the source of Christian love; Luther's thought on God's love characterizes the nature of Christian love.

---

[66] WA 18, 652, 4ff.
[67] Nygren, *Agape*, 726-733.
[68] LW 44:26-28.
[69] Nygren, *Agape*, 733-737.
[70] LW 9:144.

III. The Hidden God and the Law

Luther's most radical affirmation of God being God is shown in his concept of the hidden God. In his *The Bondage of the Will* (1526) Luther asserted that 'God hidden in His majesty neither deplores nor takes away death, but works life, death, and all in all. For there He has not bound Himself by His word, but has kept Himself free over all things ... He does not will the death of the sinner according to His Word, but He does will this in His inscrutable will'.[71] Ascribing the inscrutability of the mysterious paradox between the revealed and the hidden God to the ontological difference between God and human beings,[72] Luther contended, until 'the light of glory' will reveal 'a God of most perfect and manifest righteousness', there is no other way to the hidden God except through the revealed God.[73]

Against this controversial assertion, Alister E. McGrath argues that if God's words may be refuted by the concept of the hidden God, it makes theology irrelevant.[74] Luther himself knew that the idea of the hidden God, especially the doctrine of predestination, is so abstruse and even dangerous that an improper understanding of it possibly destroys the gospel[75] and causes the loss of faith;[76] 'Who would not be offended? I myself was offended more than once, and brought to the very depth and abyss of despair, so that I wished I had never been created a man, before I realized how salutary that despair was, and how near to grace'.[77] Therefore, Luther advised believers to avoid thinking about the hidden God, or he warned that Christians should have passed several stages before they think about the hidden God: Christians should first cling to the revealed God; only

---

[71] LW 33:140.
[72] LW 33:290. 'The one true God... is wholly incomprehensible and inaccessible to human reason'.
[73] LW 33:292. Luther maintained that just like 'the light of grace' solved the problems of evil and injustice, which were insoluble 'in the light of nature', by the teaching of God's future reward and judgment, the light of glory will solve the paradox between the revealed and the hidden God. Until that time, we can only be admonished and confirmed about God's grace 'by the example of the light of grace'.
[74] McGrath, *Luther's Theology of the Cross*, 166-167; see Gerrish, 'Unknown', 133. Gerrish groups Luther interpreters into three according to the answers to the question whether 'the hidden and revealed Gods are antithetical (Theodosius Harnack, the two Ritschls, Reinhold Seeberg, Hirsch, Elert, and Holl), or identical (Kattenbusch, Erich Seeberg), or both (Althaus, Heim, von Loewenich). This book takes the 'both' side.
[75] LW 5:42.
[76] Gerrish, 'Unknown', 140.
[77] LW 33:190.

after they admit that they deserve the eternal death, and thank God for His free grace, they can bear the cross, bringing to death their arrogance, human-centred judgment, and doubt about God's trustworthiness; only then they can consider predestination without any harm.[78]

How can Luther's controversial assertion about the hidden God be understood properly? Introducing Luther's own principle of interpreting the Scriptures[79] as a good solution, Watson proposes that many contradictory statements of Luther can be understood if viewed from point of their motives.[80] In *The Bondage of the Will*, describing the question whether a human can cooperate with God in salvation as 'one half of the whole sum of things Christian', and the question whether everything occurs necessarily, as 'the other half of the Christian *summa*',[81] Luther insisted that God's grace is the sole source of salvation without any cooperation,[82] and everything occurs according to God's predestinating will. Luther taught if we are to believe God's promises, He must know, be able, and be willing to keep His words: there must be God's predestinating will first; according to this will He foreknows everything; finally, whatever happens occurs in consistent with this knowledge. Only this order can guarantee the trustworthiness of the gospel.[83] Forde summarizes Luther's argumentation:

> To question God's real transcendent control of what happens on earth would mean that what does actually happen on earth would not necessarily be the expression of His will. Then, the fact that Jesus came to a bad end in Jerusalem and that we have been baptized, received the sacrament, and heard the preaching of the Word, might be only an accident. If one questions God's ultimate control, then what happens here on earth has no real significance ... to insure the trustworthiness of the gospel, one must ... recognize that God is ultimately in control. Only then the death and resurrection of Christ is the revelation of His will and not an accident. The question of what God wills for you can be answered by what He actually does

---

[78] Althaus, *Theology*, 285-286.
[79] See W.M.L. V. 174. 'He who will understand what is said must see why or for what reasons it is said. Thus there are many sayings in the Scriptures which, if taken literally, are contradictory, but if the causes are shown, everything is right'. Quoted by Watson, *Let*, 7.
[80] Watson, *Let*, 7-8.
[81] LW 33:35-36.
[82] LW 33:35.
[83] LW 33:42-43.

... Luther believed that only on the basis of God's control over all things, the certainty of the gospel becomes secured.[84]

Luther's concern was to secure the foundation of the certainty of the gospel, for which he connected predestination and the cross, and sovereignty and grace of God, allowing no room for human works and casualty in this course. After establishing the gospel on the trustworthiness of God, Luther could challenge believers to trust God in spite of all unexpected, incomprehensible, or paradoxical situations in which God looks like a different One from the revealed God in the Bible.[85] As Lois Malcom observes, Luther's teaching of the hidden God is 'not descriptive but performative: to effect in his hearers or readers ... the very transformation he narrates'.[86] Presupposing that every believer may probably encounter the hidden God whether in destructive power of natural disasters, in unjust and evil events in history, or in predestination,[87] Luther made them have the most radical form of faith in God's grace; 'this is the highest degree of faith, to believe Him merciful when He saves so few and damns so many, and to believe Him righteous when by His own will He makes us necessarily damnable'.[88] His teaching of the hidden God is the strongest affirmation of the First Commandment.

The hidden God relates negatively to the First Commandment in another way.[89] We regard God as cruel or unrighteous when He abandons some people, not complaining when He saves unworthy sinners. In doing so, we not only judge God, not honouring Him but raising ourselves to His level, but also take God's grace for granted, demanding that God should save everyone.[90] For Luther, to trust God is quite different from daring to demand how God should be or what He should do under the pretext of faith in the gospel. Against this arrogance, the hidden God retains His majestic freedom in everything and sinners cannot take His grace for granted. Luther insisted, 'he [Paul] teaches of God's eternal predestination ... in order that our salvation may be taken entirely out of our hands and put in the hand of God alone'.[91] The hidden God is never indebted and Christians

---

[84] Forde, *Where*, 26-27.
[85] LW 33:62.
[86] Lois Malcom, 'A Hidden God Revisited: Desecularization, the Depths, and God's Sort of Seeing', in *Dialog* 40 (Sept. 2001), 185.
[87] Gerrish, 'Unknown', 138-140.
[88] LW 33:62.
[89] Althaus, *Theology*, 283-285.
[90] LW 33:290.
[91] LW 35:378.

cannot have Him under our control in arrogance and ingratitude.[92] Heiko Oberman properly contends that Luther's treatise *The Bondage of the Will* could much better have been called '*The Majesty of God*'.[93] The freedom of the hidden God prohibits believers from turning the majestic God into mere idols.

The majesty of the hidden God changes the law into a very existential one. Ebeling and Forde observe that for Luther the law does not exist as a mere collection of ideal requirements but, altering incessantly according to our changing relationship with God, it commands what God wants us to do now and here.[94] The law is defined by what it does to us rather than what information it contains. Forde contends:

> To talk of law, Luther says ... is not to speak about it 'technically or materially ... or grammatically ... it is and sounds in your heart, exhorting, piercing the heart and conscience until you do not know where to turn' ... The law is ... what it does to you. Law is that which accuses and terrifies and in a real sense, anything that does this functions ... it is the mark of man's existence in this age, from the rustling of the leaves to the agony of the cross. It is the voice, which for the sinner, never ends.[95]

The presence of natural disasters, sufferings from evil things, or the predestinating God possibly works as a dreadful threat to sinners, destroying any pride, self-trust, self-security in them.[96] Behind those things, Gustaf Aulén contends, the wrath of God always 'remains latent in and behind the Divine Love'.[97] As far as Christians are sinners, they are still in danger of various sins, haughtiness, and self-security, being deceitfully assured of their righteousness by false pretence of the gospel. By the concept of the hidden God, Luther reminded believers of the fearfulness of God.[98] When the hidden God seriously threatens the foundation on which we build up our life, idols in our hearts are broken; sinners, idolaters, and even believers try to find the true God for protection, salvation, and all true bless-

---

[92] Althaus, *Theology*, 283-285.
[93] Heiko Oberman, *Luther: Man Between God and the Devil*, tr. Eileen Walliser-Schwarzbart (New York: Image Books, 1992), 212.
[94] Gerhard Ebeling, *Word and Faith* (Philadelphia: Fortress, 1963), 277-278; Gerhard O. Forde, *The Law-Gospel Debate: An Interpretation of Its Historical Development* (Minneapolis: Augsburg Publishing House, 1969), 176-177.
[95] Forde, *Where*, 13-16; see Forde, *Preached*, 217-219; LW 6:399.
[96] Althaus, *Theology*, 283-284.
[97] Gustaf Aulén, *Christus Victor: An Historical Study of the Three Main Types of the Idea of the Atonement*, tr. A. G. Hebert (London: S.P.C.K., 1970), 115.
[98] LW 31:45-48.

ings. When the concept of the hidden God functions as the law, we truly cling to the revealed God as the gospel.[99]

The teaching of the hidden God, intended by 'untheoretical and pastoral concern', purifies Christians' faith from all arbitrary claims and all self-complacency.[100] After seeing the hidden God threatens and afflicts sinners' conscience, thus, our self-security, arrogance, and human-centred judgment are removed through the law of the hidden God, Luther represented the revealed God as a practical resolution to the law, that is, as the gospel.[101] In his *Lectures on Genesis* (1535-1545), leaving words which can be regarded as a kind of theological testament on the subject of the hidden God, Luther expressed his wish to be remembered as the advocate of the unity between the hidden and the revealed God.[102] The hidden God and the revealed God look to be contradictory in appearance, but in final analysis the two aspects of God are totally consistent with the complete outlook of Luther's theology which affirms the dialectic between the law and the gospel.

B. John Wesley

I. The Nature of God and the Law

Wesley understood the law from the perspective of the nature of God. The nature of God is 'the fountain whence it [the law] flowed'.[103] The law is not inconsistent with or alien to, but completely coincides with who God is. Because of its unity, God's law has the role of revealing God, like God's Son does,[104] making the incomprehensible nature of God visible and tangible to human perception; 'Yea, in some sense, we may apply to this law what the Apostle says of His Son: It is the streaming forth or out-beaming of his glory, the express image of His person'.[105] As the same 'picture of God' through which we can imitate God,[106] while Christ is a living example of the image of God, the law is a spoken or written example of the same image.[107] In

---

[99] Forde, *Where*, 27-29; Forde, *Preached*, 48-55.
[100] Althaus, *Theology*, 286.
[101] Gerrish, 'Unknown', 138-149; LW 24:64-73.
[102] LW 5:49.
[103] S. Law, III. 5; III. 10.
[104] S. Law, II. 6.
[105] See S. Mount (4), Intro. 1.
[106] S. Mount (3), IV.
[107] S. Mount (2), II. 2; S. Mount (4), Intro. 1; ENNT John 10:4.

his sermon, 'The Original, Nature, Properties, and Use of the Law', Wesley explained the unity between God and His law in various expressions: the law is a 'divine copy of [God] Himself'; 'a transcript of the divine nature'; 'the fairest offspring of the everlasting Father'; 'an incorruptible picture of the High and Holy One'; 'the face of God unveiled'; 'the heart of God disclosed to man'; and 'the express resemblance of God'. Teaching that the law is totally dependent upon God's will, Wesley affirmed in the strongest tone that the law of God is 'God Himself': 'None can doubt but God is the cause of the law of God. But the will of God is God Himself'.[108]

By calling the law 'God Himself' Wesley emphasized the homogeneity between the natures of God and of the law, but he did not mean that the law has a divine personality like Christ does. In his sermon, 'On Conscience' (1788), Wesley represented the natural law written in the human conscience as 'the Son of God' as well, in the sense that it functions as 'the true light, which enlighteneth every man that cometh into the world' like Christ does.[109] Collins distinguishes the law from 'God Himself' or from 'the Son of God' in Wesley's thought: while Christ is the eternally begotten Son of God, the law 'had its rise at the beginning of time since it was rooted in a *created* order'; though the source of the law was 'the uncreated mind from eternity',[110] the law itself 'took a particular form' in creation.[111]

The law contains God's holy love as its nature.[112] As God's 'reigning attribute', love is in itself the image of God.[113] Because of its holy nature, when the law confronts human sin, it has 'effects' of detecting and accusing sin.[114] As examined in the first chapter, Wesley's relating the law to God's nature opposed the confusion between the 'nature' and the 'effects' of the law, which caused Luther's 'coupling the law with sin, death, hell or the devil'.[115] Wesley asserted that the law's 'essentially holy' nature cannot be defiled. The law contains God's love within it.

---

[108] S. Law, III. 3-10.
[109] S. Conscience, I. 5.
[110] S. Law, II. 4.
[111] Collins, *Theology*, 97-98.
[112] S. Law, III. 1-3; S. Unity.
[113] S. Image, I. 2; S. Needful, II. 2; S. Love (2), Into. 2; Gregory S. Clapper, *John Wesley on Religious Affections: His Views on Experience and Emotion and Their Role in the Christian Life and Theology* (Metuchen: Scarecrow Press, 1989), 108.
[114] S. Mount (5), I. 1-2; S. Law, III. 2; III. 4.
[115] Journals, 2:467.

Viewing the law from the perspective of God's nature gave Wesley the clue to regard the law as a crucial way of recovering the image of God. While the end of religion is 'a participation of the divine nature, the life of God in the soul of man',[116] to obey each part of the law becomes a way though which we adapt ourselves to God's nature. Thus, Wesley represented the law as 'the only true way' to heaven and everlasting life;[117] 'It [the law] is God made manifest in our flesh, and bringing with him eternal life; assuring us by that pure and perfect love'.[118] By representing the law as the way of recovering the image of God, Wesley taught that though the law is not the basis of the relationship between God and humanity, it remains a standard of the relationship.[119]

II. The Works of God and the Law

The law relates to the way of God's works as well as God's nature. In his essay, *Thoughts upon God's Sovereignty* (1777), Wesley distinguished between the ways of God's working as Creator and as Governor.[120] For him, the doctrine of predestination, by erroneously applying God's sovereignty as Creator to God as Governor, abandons both human freedom and the role of God's law, ascribing everything to God.[121] Whereas God as Creator has acted with an absolute sovereignty, God as Governor does not rule merely by sovereignty. Having created humanity as free agents and given them His law, God rules His creation with His justice, goodness, and wisdom, making room for human freedom and the role of the law:[122]

> He [God] did not take away your understanding; but enlightened and strengthened it. He did not destroy any of your affections; rather they were more vigorous than before. Least of all did He take away your liberty; your power of choosing good or evil: He did not *force* you; but, being *assisted* by His grace, you ... *chose* the better part. Just so has He *assisted* ... without depriving any ... of that liberty which is essential to a moral agent.[123]

Wesley also taught the harmony between the works of God as Creator and as Governor in relation to the fundamental structure of

---

[116] S. Awake, II. 10; see Cunningham, 'Perceptible', 103-104.
[117] S. Mount (1), Intro. 3.
[118] S. Law, III. 12.
[119] Collins, *Theology*, 56-57.
[120] WW 10:361-363.
[121] WW 10:361-363; S. Heaviness, III. 7.
[122] WW 10:361-363; see S. Justification, IV. 8; S. Providence, 14; S. Law, I. 2; S. Heaviness, III. 7.
[123] S. Spread, 11.

the world. Employing Plato's concept of the 'chain of being', Wesley taught, all creatures of God not only have their particular values and positions in the order of creation, but also 'all the parts of it [God's creation] are admirably connected together', being 'conducive to the good of the whole'.[124] Creating humanity in the political image of God and placing them between the celestial and terrestrial hierarchies,[125] God made them co-workers with Him, who rule 'over' the other creatures and serve other people as mediators of His grace in loving relationships; 'the grand reason why God is pleased to assist men by men, rather than immediately by himself, is undoubtedly to endear us to each other by these mutual good offices, in order to increase our happiness both in time and eternity'.[126] Wesley explained:

> [Gratitude to our benefactors] ... will remain forever ... how much will that add to the happiness of those spirits which are already discharged from the body, that they are permitted to minister to those whom they have left behind ... He [God] is able, by His own immediate power, without any instruments at all, to supply the wants of all His creatures both in heaven and earth. But it is, and ever was, His pleasure, not to work by His own immediate power only, but chiefly by subordinate means, from the beginning of the world. And how wonderfully is His wisdom displayed in adjusting all these to each other! So that we may well cry out, 'O Lord, how manifold are Thy works! In wisdom hast Thou made them all'.[127]

Mutual responsibility and loving relationship are the keys to understand what the law is intended for. God who knows 'the inmost essence of everything' and 'all the connections, dependencies, and relations'[128] reflected in His law 'the nature and fitnesses of things, and ... their essential relations to each other',[129] and prescribed in it 'exactly what is right, precisely what ought to be done ... with regard to the Author of our being, with regard to ourselves, and with regard to every creature'. Thus, the law is harmonized with *all parties* and with *all circumstances.*[130] Wesley affirmed that the law is 'the everlasting fitness of all things that are or ever were created'.[131]

---

[124] S. Evil, Intro. 1-2; see S. Approbation, I. 11-14; Barry E. Bryant, 'John Wesley's Doctrine of Sin', (Ph.D. thesis, The University of London, 1992), 92-98.
[125] Natural Philosophy (1777), IV:110; see Bryant, 'John Wesley's Doctrine of Sin', 97-98.
[126] S. Good, II. 9-10; S. Deliverance, I. 3, II. 1; see Deschner, *Christology*, 126; Collins, *Theology*, 54.
[127] S. Faith (2), 11-13.
[128] S. Providence, 10-11; S. Law, III. 7.
[129] S. Law, III. 8.
[130] S. Law, III. 5.
[131] S. Law, II. 5.

Albert Outler points out that Wesley's sermons will be misread unless they are understood as 'restatements of vision of the Christian life'.[132] Applying God's law to our real life, Wesley wanted to establish Christian life on 'the everlasting fitness of all things' in loving relationship. Then, beyond the personal relationship, obeying the law becomes God's method of renewing His creation. As a mirror of the perfect unity between God, His law, and His creation before the fall,[133] the law reveals both how the world would be when the law is obeyed in an indicative way, and how the world should be in an imperative way. In Deschner's expression, 'We do not believe God's command because it confirms nature; we believe that what God commands is reaffirmation, a re-establishment of the nature we no longer see. There is a way from God's command to the praise of nature; there is no way from a knowledge of nature to an accreditation of God's command'.[134]

III. The Grace of God and the Law

Is the law for observance? Is it a moral ideal that cannot be kept? Or is it only an accuser of human sins? The answers relate to Wesley's thought on the correlation between the law and God's grace. Charles R. Wilson in his dissertation enumerated five ways Wesley correlated the law and God's love.[135] Firstly, God's love that saves sinners in Christ and the law are not 'opposites within the nature of God', but His love and His law have 'inner unity'. Originating from the same nature of God, the law contains in it God's love as its essence. Secondly, in the gospel God's love and the law are conjoined in a way that the law is fulfilled by His love-granting grace. God's love not only forgives sinners, but also gives what He wants from us, that is, Christian love. Thirdly, stating that both the law and God's love are revealed by the same Holy Spirit, Wilson suggests a correlation by the Spirit, but he does not develop this idea sufficiently, failing to explain how both are conjoined. As will be shown in more detail in the fourth chapter, Wesley taught, the Spirit makes believers understand the true meaning of the law, God's intention of giving the law, and the consequence of obeying the law, by witnessing God's love on the

---

[132] Outler's 'Introduction', 97. Quoted by Clapper, *John Wesley on Religious Affections*, 100.
[133] S. Approbation, Intro. 1-2, II. 1-2; S. Deliverance, III. 8-12.
[134] Deschner, *Christology*, 104.
[135] Wilson, 'The Correlation of Love and Law in the Theology of John Wesley', 110-115.

human heart. The Spirit's witness of the divine love teaches the meaning, the source, and the aim of the law. Fourthly, the law and God's love are conjoined in saving faith. Faith first receives God's love, and then establishes the law by producing our obedience. Faith reveals the divine origin of the law, and fulfils it. Lastly, the law and God's love are conjoined in Christian freedom, which means not only freedom from the guilt and the power of sin, but also freedom to love and to obey God's law.

The correlation not only exists in the concept of the 'covered promise',[136] but also is supported by the concept of God's providence. Wesley stressed, 'We will suffer no temptation to befall us but such as is proportioned to our strength'; God will increase believers' strength when they need God's help, lest the distress rise above their strength.[137] Wesley explained the reason why God limits believers' trials in terms of God's mercy, as well as His justice.[138]

For Wesley, there is no reason to think that 'any man *must* commit sin', or that we cannot fulfil God's law.[139] The sufficient grace of God not only enables us to escape from sins,[140] but also empowers us to fulfil the requirements of the law.[141]

C. Observations and Analysis

I. Believe in the Sovereign God vs. Imitate the God of Holy Love

Thoughts on God, including His nature, attributes, and the ways of His ruling and saving, became the foundation of the understanding of the law in both Luther and Wesley. How to understand the law already contains implications on who God is, what relationship He wants to establish between Himself and His human creatures, and what the most central command of the law is. From their different views of God, different understandings of the law flow, and vice versa. There are close correspondences or harmonies between the theologies of the law and of God.

What is characteristic in Luther's representation of God is that 'he did not give priority to the so-called divine attributes, but first of all

---

[136] S. Mount (5), II. 2-3.
[137] S. Temptation, II. 1-2.
[138] S. Temptation, II. 2, III. 8-10.
[139] S. Mount (9), 5.
[140] S. Perfection (1), II. 14.
[141] S. Law, IV. 7; S. Working, III. 2.

to the divine omnipotence'.¹⁴² The purpose of raising God's omnipotence above the other attributes was to emphasize the great differences between the sovereign Creator and His passive and dependent human creatures. In accordance with this, Luther thought that the law teaches us sheer trust in and total dependence on God as our foundational attitude toward God. In requiring faith, the law relates not only to the way in which human beings are saved anthropocentrically, but also to the way in which God is honoured and glorified theocentrically.¹⁴³ While 'there is no other honour equal to the estimate of truthfulness and righteousness', faith 'honours [God] ... with the most reverent and highest regard since it considers Him truthful and trustworthy'. Faith is understood as 'the very highest worship of God' that the law requires.¹⁴⁴

Whereas our trust in and dependence on God is the highest requirement of the law, the state of fallen humanity is no other than faithlessness itself.¹⁴⁵ Whereas faith receives everything as God's gift and gives all glory to God, faithlessness makes people 'robbers and thieves' of God's glory,¹⁴⁶ or idolaters who replace the true God with whatever they long for, or rely on.¹⁴⁷ The law that pertains to the sovereign God is the law of faith.

Like Luther, Wesley recognized the great difference between God the Creator and His human creatures,¹⁴⁸ and taught that our attitude toward God should be trust and fear as well as love.¹⁴⁹ However, Wesley's concern was more on the resemblance between the natures of God and of human beings than on the difference. Wesley regarded this resemblance as being through the moral image of God, which is carved in human nature by God as the fundamental element of the fellowship between God and humans.¹⁵⁰ The moral image of God is the holy love of God. After the fall, holy love is not only the causal instrument of God's recovering sinners to the image of God, but also

---

142 Lohse, *Theology*, 211-212. Lohse also mentions God's 'all-sufficiency' and 'freedom' as the characteristics of Luther's presentation of God, which will be dealt with in following sections.
143 Althaus, *Theology*, 44-46.
144 LW 31:350.
145 LW 1:163.
146 LW 13:358, 364-365.
147 Bornkamm, *Old*, 45-64.
148 S. Eternity, 20; S. Dream, 1; S. Mount (4), III. 7; S. Omnipresence, I. 1-II. 8; S. Unity, 2-7.
149 ENNT 2 Cor 7:1; S. Love (2), I. 3.
150 S. Justification, I. 1-4.

the teleological end of salvation. Holy love is both the root and fruit of human salvation.

While God's holiness – both His substantial excellence[151] and absolute moral purity[152] – results in our alienation from God, His love bridges 'the infinite distance' between God in 'His majesty and perfect holiness' and finite, weak, and depraved human beings.[153] Holy love is the content of Christ's revelation by His own life and teaching;[154] the medicine of our corrupted nature;[155] the end of our being born again;[156] the righteousness which God wants to cultivate in the believer;[157] and 'the spirit', 'the quintessence', and 'the fundamentals' of Christianity.[158] What God also uses for His providential works is the image of God in believers.[159]

Wesley emphasized that the major requirement of the law is for the believer to resemble God, to imitate Christ, to have the fruits of the Holy Spirit, and to have holy love toward God and neighbour. Though it is true that faith produces love toward God and neighbour out of our gratitude for God's love,[160] Wesley saw a very high probability that because faith enjoys the relief of being freed from the condemnation of the law by God's grace, it can have a more relaxed attitude toward demands of the law. In comparison, the eagerness of holy love to do good toward God and neighbour is more active and earnest.[161]

Negatively speaking, Wesley taught that the image of God contained in the law stands in direct opposition to the image of the Devil or evil tempers as countermeasures against it;[162]

---

[151] ENNT Rev 4:8. Wesley identified the divine holiness with the deity itself or with the divine glory.
[152] S. Unity, 7. God's moral purity separates Him infinitely far from 'every touch of evil'.
[153] ENOT Gen1:8; for the idea of God's love as bridge between holy God and sinners, see Young-Tae Han, 'The Trinity and Holiness in the Theology of John Wesley', (Ph.D. thesis [in Korean], Seoul Theological University, 1990), 46-106; Collins, *Theology*, 20-22; Yang, 'God', 124-129.
[154] S. Mount (4), Intro. I; S. Coming, III. 5.
[155] S. Original, III. 5.
[156] S. New (1), I. 1-4.
[157] S. Mount (2), II. 2.
[158] S. Mount (3), IV.
[159] S. Providence, 18.
[160] S. Unity, 16-17.
[161] Cobb, *Grace and Responsibility*, 61
[162] S. Coming, III. 2; S. Mount (2), II. 1; S. Mount (5), I. 3-4; S. Sin, II. 2.

> 'He [Satan] endeavours to inspire ... tempers which are directly opposite to 'the fruit of the Spirit'... unbelief, atheism, ill-will, bitterness, hatred, malice, envy, – opposite to faith and love; fear, sorrow, anxiety, worldly care, – opposite to peace and joy; impatience, ill nature, anger, resentment, – opposite to long-suffering, gentleness, meekness; fraud, guile, dissimulation, – contrary to fidelity; love of the world, inordinate affection, foolish desires, – opposite to the love of God'.[163]

The law that pertains to the God of holy love is to resemble His image; 'The most acceptable worship of God is to imitate Him'.[164]

II. The Law Unable to Influence God vs. The Law as a Medium for Divine Works

Another characteristic in Luther's teaching of God is the 'all-sufficiency' of God,[165] which means that God has the principle of His working in Himself, being not affected by human sins nor moved by human works in deciding our salvation. Luther admitted human beings' cooperation with God in a limited way in the secular sphere. Since God employs human beings for His works, Luther warned against the idea that we are to cease working because God works everything. Humans as masks of God should have sincerity and responsibility realizing their role as instruments of God's works;[166]

> God gives all good gifts; but ... you must work and thus give God good cause and a mask ... Make the bars and gates, and let Him fasten them. Labour, and let Him give the fruits. Govern, and let Him give His blessing. Fight, and let Him give the victory. Preach, and let Him win hearts. Take a husband or a wife, and let Him produce the children. Eat and drink, and let Him nourish and strengthen you. And so on. In all our doings He is to work through us, and He alone shall have the glory from it ... all this is said to refute those who tempt God, want to do nothing, and think God will give them whatever they desire without any work or diligence on their part ... God wants no lazy idlers. Men should work diligently and faithfully, each according to his calling and profession, and then God will give blessing and success.[167]

However, he rejected the idea of cooperation in salvation.[168] Even in God's secular kingdom, in that God works everything behind various masks,[169] the relationship between works of God and of humans is that human works are merely instrumental and God is effectual.

---

[163] S. Evil, II. 8.
[164] WW 10:68.
[165] Lohse, *Theology*, 211-212.
[166] LW 6:128; LW 33:155.
[167] LW 14:114.
[168] Lohse, *Theology*, 213.
[169] LW 6:257; Pelikan, *Luther the Expositor*, 103-105; Johnson, 'God', 67-68.

Luther's metaphor of 'a child's performance' implied God's superintending 'all things' of humans.[170] Luther made it the main motif of his theocentric theology that, regardless whatever masks He puts on, the absolute controller of all things is God.[171] In all things and events God's works have 'mediated immediacy', which means that God works directly but by using His instruments.[172]

Luther thought that human free will is not compatible with this all-sufficient God's way of working. A seeming freedom is not a real freedom, since in God's works, human beings are passive instruments;

> God's foreknowledge and omnipotence are diametrically opposed to our free choice, for either God can be mistaken in foreknowing and also err in action (which is impossible) or we must act and be acted upon in accordance with his foreknowledge and activity ... This omnipotence and the foreknowledge of God ... completely abolish the dogma of free choice.[173]

When whatever happens is ascribed to God, the divine authority of the ministries of God's people can be secured:

> When ... we teach the gospel, baptize, call men to the ministry of the word, and ordain ministers, we ourselves do not preach, we do not baptize, we do not ordain, but God is speaking through us. So it is called God's word, God's sacrament, God's ministry, and it is rightly said: 'God is speaking, God is baptizing' when He does it through ministers, since indeed all things are attributed to God which holy men have spoken.[174]

When God's perfect control over everything is fully accepted believers fulfil the First Commandment letting God be the King of all areas where they live and work in both secular and spiritual kingdoms.

Luther did not deny that God rewards believers' faithful service of God, and punishes disobedience. However, it cannot mean that we can bargain for God's favour by our works, prayers, and even faith.[175] When we recognize the all-sufficiency of God, depend entirely on His mercy, and give all glory to God, any work done in faith pleases God, however small or trivial it may be, 'even if it were so small a thing as picking up a straw'[176] But, any work done with human-centred motives to attain blessings and happiness is sinful and idolatrous, how-

---

[170] LW 14:114.
[171] Johnson, 'God', 68.
[172] Watson, *Let*, 79-80.
[173] LW 33:189.
[174] LW 6:257; LW 35:162.
[175] Watson, *Let*, 33-70.
[176] LW 44:25.

ever big and wonderful it may look.[177] Works of the law cannot be meritorious causes to move God.

Wesley also believed that God works 'all in all'[178] in creation, in preservation,[179] and especially in salvation.[180] God is 'the only Cause, the sole Creator of all things'; 'the Supporter of all the things ... for the continuance of it [their existence]'; 'the Preserver of all things' and 'the cement, of the whole universe' for their 'well-being'; 'the true Author of all the *motion* that is in the universe', 'the Redeemer of all the children of men'; 'the Governor of all things' and 'the ultimate End of all'.[181] Saying that 'all things are governed by the providence of God'[182] against casualism,[183] Wesley taught that even when God works through us, all glory should be given to God; 'He has always wrought by such instruments as He pleases: But still it is God Himself that doeth the work. Whatever help, therefore, we have, either by angels or men, is as much the work of God, as if He ... work without any means at all ... the same glory redounds to Him, as if he used no instruments at all'.[184]

He knew well the argument that if human beings have any 'free-will', 'God does not do the whole work' thus 'cannot have the whole glory'.[185] However, John Cobb observes that when Wesley dealt with the works of God, he was always concerned with the proper presentation of 'the relation of human responsibility to grace', seeing that people tend to either deny human responsibility on account of God's grace or regard human works as a more important factor than grace.[186] William Cannon maintains that the 'ultimate ground' of

---

[177] LW 44:26.
[178] ENOT 1 Chron 11:10; ENNT 1 Cor 3:7; 13:8; 15:28; Eph 4:13; 1 Pet 1:5; Rev 21:22; Journals, 4:117; 5:23; S. Means, II. 6; V. 4; S. Mount (3), I. 6; II. 6; WW 8:198; 8:469; 11:489
[179] S. Mount (6), III. 7. 'Every creature, visible and invisible ... could neither act nor exist, without the continual influx and agency of His almighty power'.
[180] WW 8:49. 'The author of faith and salvation is God alone. It is he that works in us both to will and to do. He is the sole Giver of every good gift, and the sole Author of every good work'.
[181] S. Worship, I.1-10
[182] S. Knowledge, II. 2.
[183] S. Knowledge, II. 1.
[184] S. Good, II. 3; II. 9.
[185] WW 10:229-230.
[186] Cobb, *Grace and Responsibility*, 9

God's works in Wesley's theology is 'the very nature and character of God'.[187]

Wesley related the ways of God's working together with humans to His holy love. God's holy love motivated His creating human beings.[188] God not only loves His creatures, but also wants His creatures to love each other.[189] To make human beings love each other, God gave them the law which is 'right, agreeable to the fitness of things, to the relation wherein they stand'.[190] The law teaches: a proper worship of God;[191] comparative values of every object and event;[192] due respect toward authorities such as political leaders, pastors, and parents; a balance between privileges and responsibilities;[193] a peaceful life among neighbours, believers and Churches, and nations;[194] and mutual service for looking after each other's souls for salvation.[195] Thus, the law helps enable loving relationships both between God and humans and between human beings themselves.[196]

In salvation we should first accept God's gift of salvation through faith passively.[197] Then, salvation, which was defined by Wesley as the knowledge of God's holy love and the recovery of it in human heart,[198] produces first our love with gratitude toward God and next our benevolent love toward our neighbours.[199] Wesley asserted that every process of God's saving each person, transforming societies,

---

[187] William R. Cannon, *The Theology of John Wesley* (New York: Abingdon-Cokesbury Press, 1946), 153.
[188] S. Established (2), II.3; S. Law, I.1-III.12.
[189] S. Love (2), I. 6.
[190] S. Law, III. 7-9.
[191] S. Law, I. 1.
[192] See S. Money; S. Steward; S. Riches (3); S. Riches (1); S. Dress; S. Sick; S. Riches (2); S. Lazarus; S. Inefficacy; S. Excellent Way; S. Folly; S. Dream.
[193] See S. Assize; S. Family; S. Children; S. Parents; S. Pastors; S. National.
[194] See S. Bigotry; S. Catholic; S. Speaking; S. Whitefield; S. Pleasing; S. Love (3); S. Schism.
[195] See S. Means; S. Manners; S. Reproving; S. World; S. Leave; S. Backsliders; S. Communion.
[196] S. Law, I. 2-3.
[197] See Collins, *Theology*, 20-22.
[198] WW 8:47-48.
[199] S. Mount (4), I. 1-9; Thomas C. Oden, *John Wesley's Scriptural Christianity: A Plain Exposition of His Teaching on Christian Doctrine* (Grand Rapids, Michigan: Zondervan Publishing House, 1994), 41.

and evangelizing the world will not be done solely by God's sovereignty, but together with holy love in believers' hearts and works.[200]

Human responsibility is required for God's providence as well.[201] By the concept of a threefold circle of divine providence, Wesley taught, God cares for all His creatures of the outer circle through Christians of the middle circle, and especially through the 'innermost' Christians.[202] In all of God's creation, salvation, and providence, God wants to make human beings active participants and fulfillers as well as passive recipients of God's holy love.

By the concept of God's masks, Luther focused on the idea that every human being confronts God as the ruler of everything directly, whereas people are related to each other indirectly through being employed as God's masks. But, in Wesley's view, God's works are not only direct, decisive, and single-acting, but also indirect, permissive, and synthetic, in which human beings are invited to participate more actively and to have more direct relationship with others, for the purpose of sharing holy love.[203]

For Wesley, between the works of God and of human beings, the law plays a very important role. For instance, in the case of the rich people, God entrusts them with money more than they need and also grants the law as guidance about how to use the surplus money; 'Together with that portion of His [God's] goods which He hath lodged in our hands He has delivered to us a writing, specifying the purposes for which He has entrusted us with them'.[204] That is, the law commands the rich 'to feed the hungry'.[205] Because of both the entrusted money and the given law, the rich have the responsibility to care for the needy, making good use of money as God's stewards and co-workers. At the same time, there exists danger that they may deprive poor people of God's money.[206] In cases of miseries and misfortunes in this world, whereas Luther ultimately ascribed them to the hidden God, Wesley contended that though we cannot understand

---

[200] S. Spread, 1-27; S. Manners, Intro. 1-V. 7; S. Question, III. 5; S. Pleasing, Intro. 1-II. 8; S. Sick, Intro. 1-III. 9; S. Inefficacy, 1-19; S. Mount (3), II. 5-6; S. Mount (7), IV. 7; S. Way (2), III. 9-10; S. Reward, I. 5.
[201] S. Mount (3), III. 5; S. Mount (6), III. 4-6; S. Enthusiasm, 29; S. Knowledge, IV; S. Temptation, II. 1-III. 10; S. Providence.
[202] S. Providence, 1-29; S. Faith (2), 13; S. Worship, I. 9; ENNT Mt 5:45, Col 1:24.
[203] S. Good, II. 10.
[204] S. Riches (1), I. 5.
[205] S. Riches (3), I. 12.
[206] S. Dress, 15.

the reasons perfectly, many result from the negligence and unfaithfulness of God's stewards who do not obey God's law.[207]

Whereas Luther emphasized that God is always the sole controller of all things, for Wesley the law is the instrument of God with which He rules and cares for the world indirectly through the obedience of believers. Whereas Luther employed the concept of God's masks to teach the all-sufficiency of God, Wesley's thought on God's works through the medium of the law supports the idea of evangelical synergism. On the basis of God's prevenient grace Wesley contended, 'God nevertheless may have all the glory' because 'the very power to "work together with Him" was from God'.[208]

III. The Hidden God Is the Law vs. Incomprehensibility Is the Law

The concept of the hidden God is Luther's radical assertion of the freedom of God.[209] His representation of the hiddenness of God was more highlighted in double predestination than in natural disasters and miserable events in history.[210] God hardened Pharaoh, and rejected Esau before he was born. To the question why some accept the gospel and not others, Luther answered that it is God who accepts or rejects as He pleases and we do not know why, and beyond that point we cannot go.[211] When Luther was seized by the terror of predestination, his way of insuring the trustworthiness of the gospel was to depend on God's ultimate control over everything and assert that what God wills is shown by what He actually does. Then, the declaration, 'I am a Christian', 'Christ died for me', 'I have been baptized!', or 'I received His body and blood in the sacrament', could settle his spiritual trials.[212] When the hidden God threatens and brings trials, believers should use those trials as a crucial challenge for their renewal of faith through contemplation of Christ as the mirror of God's heart.[213] Luther underlined that God does not lie.[214]

---

[207] S. Inefficacy, 1-19; S. Lord, Intro. 12; S. Mount (2), III. 18; S. Mount (8), 22-28; S. Established (2),I. 4-5; S. Zeal, Intro. 1; S. Excellent, Intro. 2; S. Iniquity, 1-36; S. Counsels, 14-20; S. Spread, 1-7.
[208] WW 10:229-230.
[209] Lohse, *Theology*, 211-212.
[210] Gerrish, 'Unknown', 134-140.
[211] Steinmetz, *Luther in Context*, 26.
[212] LW 5:48-49; Forde, *Where*, 26-27.
[213] Gerrish, 'Unknown', 138.
[214] LW 33:43, 185; Johnson, 'God', 64.

The terror of the hidden God can arise in various ways. Every believer is 'tempted concerning the wrath of God, predestination, and unbelief'.[215] When we are in trials, Satan tempts us to deny our faith in God.[216] In those situations, Luther's advice to escape to Christ can be a good practical solution, because we need to maintain a faithful attitude toward God to overcome severe crises and hardships in our lives. In many cases, though we cannot solve the problems by our reason, in all cases proper attitudes toward God help overcome trials without shipwreck of faith. Therefore, for Christians who live in the uncertainty of life, Luther's teaching on the hidden God has strategic advantages for evangelical theology, reminding us of both our finitude and God's majesty and, thus, making us encounter and overcome all trials by the hidden God through faith.

However, though escaping to Christ can be a practical resolution, the factor of divine determinism does not change. In insisting on divine determinism, Luther rejected the Catholic Church's view that human beings can control God by faith and works, affirming a position similar to what Allan Coppedge classifies as 'hyper-Calvinism'.[217]

For his part, Wesley believed that human beings cannot understand God 'to perfection' because 'only some of His attributes He hath been pleased to reveal to us in His word'.[218] Wesley acknowledged that 'the unsearchable depths of God's wisdom ... are far greater ... than that which is manifested. The secret wisdom of God is infinitely greater than that which is revealed to us by His word or works: the greatest part of what is known of God, is the least part of those perfections that are in Him'.[219] In Yang Jung's expression, 'what is not revealed of God is infinitely greater than what is revealed to us'.[220] Even the revealed truths of God are incomprehensible to human reason: His nature and attributes; His works of creation, providence, and grace; and the mystery of the Trinity.[221]

Among the unsearchable things of God Wesley included what Luther might have ascribed to the hidden God: the fall of nations by dreadful destruction with succession by more evil ones; miseries of countless poor people; the African slaves in the vilest bondage; cruel customs among savages; the poor state of the American Indians; the

---

[215] LW 6:148.
[216] LW 5:46.
[217] Coppedge, *John Wesley in Theological Debate*, 37-40.
[218] S. Unity, 2.
[219] ENOT Job 11:6.
[220] Yang, 'God', 13.
[221] S. Understanding, I. 1 - II. 3; S. Knowledge, I.1 - III. 5.

deplorable spiritual condition of people outside of Christianized Europe; wickedness in the Christian world; ill fortune of particular families and individuals; and a majority of people who do not have any chance to hear the gospel.[222] Wesley exclaimed, 'We know, "the Lord is loving unto every man, and His mercy is over all His works". But we know not how to reconcile this with the present dispensations of His providence'.[223]

Wesley explained the incomprehensibility of God from both the viewpoint of God and humanity.[224] On the human side, because of the ontological difference between the infinite Creator and finite human creatures, 'finite cannot measure infinite'.[225] Furthermore, the fall of humanity impaired and confined human knowledge of God 'within very narrow bounds'.[226] On God's side, the incomprehensibility of God is a result of God's deliberate 'hiding Himself from man'.[227] Wesley taught, God 'never designed us to be of His council, or privy to the secret springs of His conduct',[228] but, by shortening our knowledge of Himself, wants to lead us to more important things than knowledge: firstly, 'humility' that guards people from falling into pride and brings them 'more surely' to God;[229] secondly, 'faith' with which we trust the 'fact' of God's wisdom, goodness, and graciousness, though we cannot 'see and know' particular 'manner or reasons of God's acting';[230] thirdly, resignation of all things to God.[231] The incomprehensibility of God results from God's wisdom, goodness, and graciousness, as well as His power and sovereignty, not by divine determinism.[232]

From Wesley's viewpoint, Luther, trying to solve the inscrutable things of God by human reason, fell into the idea of predestination, entrapped by the seeming incompatibility between the biblical teaching on God's grace and providence, and miseries and even reprobation of many people in reality.[233] Comparing Luther's way of

---

[222] S. Knowledge, II. 1 - III. 1.
[223] S. Knowledge, II. 4.
[224] See Yang, 'God', 14-15.
[225] Letters 5:284.
[226] S. Knowledge, Intro. 2.
[227] S. Understanding, III. 2.
[228] S. Understanding, II. 3.
[229] S. Understanding, III. 1.
[230] S. Understanding, III. 1-2; S. Trinity, 15-16.
[231] S. Knowledge, IV.
[232] S. Understanding, III. 2.
[233] S. Knowledge, III. 2.

thinking to 'cutting the knot which we are not able to untie',[234] Wesley warned that the incomprehensibility of God should be left untouched, or, at least, any contemplation of it should not be done 'without having recourse to the oracles of God'.[235]

Wesley refuted the Calvinistic view of predestination first by the biblical fact of God's holy love and also by the necessary role of the law. Stating that if predestination is true 'God is now divided against Himself',[236] he underscored both the harmony of the nature and the attributes of God, and His approbation of the law that He has given human beings. Firstly, predestination distorts badly the nature and the attributes of God. For Wesley, the sovereignty of God the Creator is shown in His determining the way of salvation, not in predestination. The justice of God the providential Governor and the love of God the Father of human beings cannot be sacrificed.[237] From the viewpoint of the biblical presentation of the love of God who sacrificed Christ on the cross for us, the idea of a predestinating God blasphemes both God's love and Christ's deep compassion.[238] It looks impossible to reconcile 'vice and misery' in this world with 'the wisdom or goodness' of God.[239] But, however difficult it may be to understand mysteries of God, it cannot mean that 'God is not love, or His mercy is not over all His works'.[240] By reason that we cannot understand something, we should not 'make God a liar'.[241] Not to mention predestination, Wesley insisted that even a 'wilderness state' or a 'heaviness' in our soul cannot be resulted by 'the bare, arbitrary, sovereign will of God'. Such a supposition is 'inconsistent both with His justice and mercy'.[242]

Whereas reprobation is not compatible with God's love and justice, the idea of final perseverance is not compatible with God's holiness.[243] Wesley regarded both predestination and final perseverance as 'the direct antidote of Methodism, the doctrine of heart-holiness'.[244] God's sovereignty does not cause someone to sin, nor

---

[234] S. Spread, 10.
[235] S. Deliverance, Intro. 2.
[236] S. Free, 11.
[237] Coppedge, *John Wesley in Theological Debate*, 132.
[238] S. Free, 19-28.
[239] S. Spread, 1-8.
[240] S. Free, 26.
[241] S. Providence, 13; see S. Trinity, 16.
[242] S. Heaviness, III. 7; S. Wilderness, II. 1.
[243] Letters 3:96; WW 10:250-252; WW 10:297-299; Yang, 'God', 184
[244] WW 8:336; Yang, 'God', 184

does His love ignore our sins.[245] On behalf of God's holiness, Wesley stressed that believers may fall away.[246] Even in God's preserving grace, faith, love, and obedience are necessary as preconditions of it.[247]

Secondly, Wesley refuted predestination from the viewpoint of the law and human responsibility. In his sermon, 'On Divine Providence' (1786), stating that God cannot deny, counteract, or oppose Himself or His own work, Wesley taught that God who granted human beings both free will and the law, does not take away their liberty for the purpose of abolishing sin and pain out of this world. If God does such a thing, Wesley reasoned, God might be sovereign, but not wise nor good. God's wisdom and goodness as well as His power are demonstrated in His saving sinners dealing with them as free moral agents.[248]

---

[245] Yang, 'God', 187-188.
[246] WW 10:242-251.
[247] ENNT John 10:27-29.
[248] S. Providence, 15.

Chapter 3

Christ the Son and the Law

A. Martin Luther

I. The Person of Christ (Theology of Cross) and the Law

Luther regarded the doctrine of Christ as the essence and basis of all Christian faith.[1] In the preface to his *Lectures on Galatians* (1535) he wrote: 'In my heart there rules this one doctrine, namely, faith in Christ. From it, through it, and to it all my theological thought flows and returns, day and night'.[2] Althaus properly states that for Luther the doctrine of justification is no other than an application of the doctrine of Christ to humanity in need of salvation.[3] After examining the change and continuity in Luther's Christology, Marc Lienhard contends that what remained as the fundamental themes of Luther's Christology are the bond between Christ and justification by faith, the revelation of God in Christ, and theology of the cross.[4]

Luther's understanding of the law relates closely to all those themes. In this section, Luther's teaching that Christ, before revealing Himself as the gospel, works as the law in His incarnation or on the cross, will be examined in relation to Luther's concept of theology of the cross. Also, Luther's view of Christ's atonement will be examined in relation to a controversial subject on his position on the relationship between the imputed and inherent righteousness and between justification and sanctification. Finally, Luther's view of Christ's victory will be investigated, focusing on Luther's dualistic

---

[1] LW 33:26. 'Take Christ out of the Scriptures, and what will you find left in them?'; However, Luther's Christology has been given far less attention than his soteriology in the history of Luther research. See Lienhard, *Christology*, 11-13.
[2] LW 27:145.
[3] Althaus, *Theology*, 225-226.
[4] Lienhard, *Christology*, 254-255.

description of the conflict between Christ the conqueror on the one hand, and the law and the wrath of God on the other hand.

Luther thought that between the churches of the Reformation and of tradition there was no discord on the subject of Christ as both God and Man.[5] Luther regarded Christ's divinity as the foundation of Christianity[6] in that saving power appertains only to God,[7] and as the foundation of the trustworthiness of the gospel since the Trinitarian unity makes us confront with God in Christ.[8] Being coequal with the Father in glory and power,[9] Christ is 'God ... in the fullest sense'.[10]

However, Luther observed, Christ in His humanity was 'not always equally sweet and mild', but 'weak, tired, afraid, fled from dangers', and sometimes 'was filled with wrath and disgust', sadness, and angry, though He was sinless.[11] Luther saw that God reveals Himself in Christ in a very paradoxical way hiding 'His power only under weakness, His wisdom under foolishness, His goodness under austerity, His righteousness under sin, and His mercy under wrath'.[12] Refusing to separate Christ's humanity from His divinity Luther taught that in Christ's birth, ministry, and death, in the lowliness of the human Christ, the power of God operated.[13] While Christ's divinity relates to His qualification or competency for revelation and salvation, His humanity concerns God's way of revelation and salvation.

---

[5] LW 15:310. In 1543 Luther wrote concerning the Trinity and the Incarnation: 'This article of faith remained pure in the papacy and among the scholastic theologians, and we have no quarrel with them on that score'; his high evaluation of the first four ecumenical creeds as bearer of the Scriptural truth concerning the person of Christ is well represented in his treatise *On the Councils and the Church* (1539). LW 41:53-142; see also the introductory explanation in LW 41:5; cf. Lienhard, *Christology*, 308, 350.

[6] LW 26:282. 'Those who deny the divinity of Christ lose all Christianity'; the divinity of Christ is supported directly by the Scriptural texts where the title 'God' or 'Son of God' is used of Christ. Also, various indirect clues for Christ's divinity are such as Christ's being the object of faith: His assertion of the unity between God and Himself; His promise of answering believers' prayers; His offering eternal life to the faithful; and His sending the Holy Spirit. See LW 24:94-95; LW 41:105. Luther illustrated Luke 1:32, 2:11, John 20:28, Acts 20:28, Rom 9:5, Gal 4:4, I Cor 2:8, and Phil 2:6-7; Siggins, *Christ*, 192-198.

[7] LW 22:21; LW 24:108.

[8] Watson, *Let*, 102; Althaus, *Theology*, 181-185.

[9] LW 22:21.

[10] LW 23:365; Siggins, *Christ*, 195-197.

[11] LW 3:355; LW 52:147; LW 22:73; see Siggins, *Christ*, 38-39, 198-205.

[12] LW 25:370; see LW 29:111; Lienhard, *Christology*, 45, 137, 141.

[13] Siggins, *Christ*, 32-35; Lienhard, *Christology*, 250-255; WA 39II, 121. 'What Christ has suffered should also be attributed to God for they are one.' Cited from Althaus, *Theology*, 197.

Calling the true Christian faith that grasps God's purpose in this paradox, 'theology of cross', Luther asserted, it stands diametrically against 'theology of glory'.

By 'theology of glory' Luther meant the scholastic intellectual effort to penetrate God's glory, and moral effort to obtain God's favour by works. Both efforts presuppose that human reason can capture the glory of God and human works can manipulate God's grace.[14] What Luther saw problematic was that the theology of glory not only raises human beings to God's level,[15] but also seeks 'a God whose glory consisted in fulfilling what in fact are fallen human standards'.[16] Theologians of glory serve idols in which their projected desires and pride are worshipped; 'This is the way the wretched, perverse world acts, drowned in its blindness, misusing all the blessings and gifts of God solely for its own pride and greed, pleasure and enjoyment, and never once turning to God to thank Him or acknowledge Him as Lord and Creator'.[17]

Against this idolatrous and human-centred religion, Luther characterized his reformation theology as 'theology of cross'. For him, the cross, which is inclusive of all Christ's humiliation in His incarnation, His completely obedient life to God, and vicarious death on the cross, stands diametrically against haughty efforts to understand and manipulate God.[18] By theology of cross, he wanted to teach: firstly, the true God hides Himself from theologians of glory who pursue sinful desire and pride and, thus, continue to change God into mere idols.[19]

Secondly, the cross accuses theology of glory. In his treatise, *A Meditation on Christ's Passion* (1519), Luther asserted that, whoever contemplates Christ's passion properly considers it with a terror-stricken heart, because sinners learn from Christ's cross the sternness of the wrath of God against sin and sinners. Seeing that what tortured Christ on the cross were their sins, sinners should learn from Christ's death what they really deserve; 'The real and true work of Christ's passion is to make man conformable to Christ, so that man's conscience is tormented by his sins in like measure as Christ

---

[14] Kolb, 'Cross', 446-447.
[15] LW 31:47; Kolb, 'Cross', 448; Forde, *Cross*, 72-73; Forde, *Where*, 32-35.
[16] Kolb, 'Cross', 446.
[17] *BC*, 412-413.
[18] Lienhard, *Christology*, 141. In that Christ's Incarnation had the cross as its goal, Lienhard states, 'The cross only crowns the incarnation, or again, the incarnation is already the cross'.
[19] LW 10:444; LW 31:53-54.

was pitiably tormented in body and soul by our sins'.[20] In this identification with Christ, the cross plays the role of the law, revealing our state before God; 'We do not know ourselves and ... in what a shameful condition we are ... All things which Christ bore are therefore to be applied to our own being; thus as we can more clearly see Christ's suffering, we shall better see our own damnation'.[21] The cross which theologians of glory regard as the way to glory only judges them.

Thirdly, the cross is not only a sacrament by which our sins are removed but also an example after which old Adam in us must die.[22] As Forde states, Christ died 'ahead' of us as well as 'instead' of us, bringing the cross forward to us.[23] As long as believers are still sinners, cross, not glory, is their lot.[24] Crosses such as hardships, sufferings, or persecutions, are laid by God on true Christians for mortification of their flesh:[25]

The final cause of afflictions ... is ... mortification and getting rid of sins and ... the cleansing ... lest we snore and become dull because of the laziness and sluggishness of our flesh. For when there is peace and quiet, we do not pray. Nor do we meditate on the word, but we treat the Scriptures and all things that belong to God coldly or finally slip into fatal smugness.

Therefore we must be troubled and humbled ... through spiritual trials, sorrow, grief, and anguish of heart. Otherwise we shall perish in our sins. For the flesh is corrupt, filled with poison, leprous, and has need of a physician to counteract that rottenness by means of cross, martyrdom, sadness, confusion, and disgrace. These ... are the medicines with which God purges away sin.[26]

Harsh mortification gives liberation from sin.[27] Siggins states, 'the vicissitudes, trials, crosses, and duties of daily existence are means by which God effects our conformity to Christ'.[28]

---

[20] LW 42:7-14.
[21] WA 17I, 71. Quoted by Althaus, *Theology*, 204.
[22] Althaus, *Theology*, 214-215.
[23] Forde, *Where*, 35-38; Lienhard, *Christology*, 48 Lienhard explains this relationship in a similar way: 'It is has cross, unique because it is propitiatory; and it is ours because we participate in it'; see WA 2.141.501; WA 17I, 74 quoted by Althaus, *Theology*, 214.
[24] LW 6:236; LW 21:298.
[25] LW 6:146-152, 236.
[26] LW 8:7; see LW 30:117-118.
[27] LW 7:174-177.
[28] Siggins, *Christ*, 163.

The divine glory of Christ can properly be the object of true worship only after this cross removes theology of glory. Thus, before God reveals the glory of Christ, He first makes the cross 'the ultimate crescendo of the law' that kills sinners.[29] When sinners are mortified by the law of the cross, God reveals the glory of Christ.[30] The power with which believers can endure their own cross and win the victory over all hardships, sufferings, and persecutions comes only from God's promises of salvation and blessings.[31] Bearing their own cross with a humiliated heart, believers realize that God cares for the poor, despised, afflicted, miserable, forsaken, and those who are nothing, and that what makes them experience this love of God is the cross. The cross gives Christians chances of true speculation, the apprehension, and faith in the pure gospel.[32] Christians who accept the cross properly come to confess: 'I believe in God'.[33] The cross also helps Christians to endure and bear the sins of others. Therefore, Luther represented a life of suffering the cross as 'the best and most precious life'.[34]

II. Christ's Teaching and the Law

According to Siggins, Luther did not use the concept of 'the threefold office', which Calvin elaborated and spread wide, to describe Christ's mediatorial works. By the office of Christ, Luther 'almost always' meant Christ's role as preacher of the gospel.[35] Luther repeatedly stated that Christ is not a lawgiver but the redeemer from the law.[36] He not only contrasted Christ's office of the gospel with Moses' office of the law, but also described Christ's teaching of the law as His accidental or by-office.[37] Denying that Christ supplemented the law of Moses, Luther asserted, Christ's fulfilment of the law

---

[29] Forde, *Where*, 39.
[30] LW 42:186; LW 51:26; LW 8:6; Forde, *Where*, 40-44; see LW 21:299.
[31] LW 6:154; LW 6:360.
[32] LW 6:262; LW 21:301. 'For this reason God has also imposed death on us all and laid the cross of Christ together with countless sufferings and afflictions on His beloved children and Christians. In fact, sometimes He even lets us fall into sin, in order that He may look into the depths even more, bring help to many, perform manifold works, show Himself a true Creator, and thereby make Himself known and worthy of love and praise.'
[33] LW 6:360-361.
[34] LW 6:398.
[35] Siggins, *Christ*, 48-54.
[36] LW 26:72, 132, 178, 367-374; LW 27:11, 17-18.
[37] LW 12:41, 233; LW 17:230, 331; LW 22:145; LW 23:196; LW 35:120.

means only that He carried out the law of Moses perfectly 'in works and in life':

> The law [of Moses] is so rich and perfect that no one need to add anything to it; for the apostles themselves had to prove the gospel and the proclamation about Christ on the basis of the Old Testament. Therefore no one, not even Christ Himself, can improve upon the Law. What can you make up or teach that is higher than what the First Commandment teaches (Deut. 6:5): 'You shall love God with all your heart'? He does indeed go beyond law and doctrine when He gives His grace and Spirit to enable us to do and keep the law's demands, but that is not 'supplementing' the law.[38]

Compared with Christ's teaching of the law, Luther admitted that Christ made the gospel clearer than ever before; 'What had previously been taught through enigmas, as it were, Christ made clear and commanded to be preached in plain language'.[39] Luther's devaluation of Christ's teaching of the law was demonstrated in his attaching more importance to Christ as gift than Christ as example.[40] He reversed the tendency to 'make Christ into a Moses', correcting the order of Christ's coming us; Christ comes to us first as gift, then the same Christ changes into example to those who accepted the gift.[41] Owing to Luther's preference for Christ as preacher of the gospel, Siggins insists that Christ's role as a preacher of the law does not carry much 'doctrinal weight' in Luther's theology.[42]

However, by representing Christ as an example of Christian life, Luther embodied the nature of Christian life in a concrete form. The characteristic of love as cross-bearing, which surpasses human natural affection,[43] is most clearly illustrated by Christ's teaching and example:

---

[38] LW 21:69.

[39] LW 1:59.

[40] LW 27:34 'I will not let this Christ be presented to me as exemplar except at a time of rejoicing… in a time of tribulation I will not listen to or accept Christ except as a gift'; LW 26:352; Siggins, *Christ*, 159-161; LW 29:66-67. Christ's example cannot benefit, if He is not previously accepted as gift in faith, because those who are 'captive to sin cannot do anything'.

[41] LW 35:119 'The chief article and foundation of the gospel is that before you take Christ as an example, you accept and recognize him as a gift, as a present that God has given you and that is your own. This means that when you see or hear of Christ doing or suffering something, you do not doubt that Christ himself, with his deeds and suffering, belongs to you'; LW 30:117. Only those who first receive 'Christ as a gift through faith' can 'go forward and do as He does for us'.

[42] Siggins, *Christ*, 66.

[43] LW 27:353-356. For Luther, human natural affection has an ego-centered and a very limited love that 'loves, praises, does good, and speaks well as long as it has not been offended'. When it is offended 'its love falls away and turns to hatred, shouting,

Putting on Christ is... according to the Law (Rom. 13:14), "Put on the Lord Jesus Christ; that is: Imitate the example and the virtues of Christ. Do and suffer what He did and suffered". So also 1 Peter 2:21: "Christ suffered for us, leaving us an example, that we should follow in His steps." In Christ we see the height of patience, gentleness, and love, and an admirable moderation in all things. We ought to put on this adornment of Christ, that is, imitate these virtues of His.[44]

The cross is the 'touchstone' of Christian love that 'loves an enemy as well as a friend ... perseveres in the midst of trouble ... seeks the advantage of others, and is ready to give'.[45]

Luther's representing Christ as teacher of the gospel did not result from disregard of the law. His teaching was that Christ's teaching of the law is dependent on His gospel. Only believers who have accepted Christ's love as gift can imitate His love as the example of our love toward our neighbours;[46] 'After we have come to faith in Him [Christ] ... He places both Himself and His Father before our eyes as the noblest and most perfect examples'.[47]

III. Christ's Atonement and the Law

On the subject of atonement, more inclusively than Anselm who chose only satisfaction between the options of satisfaction and punishment,[48] Luther taught both: Christ suffered punishment in the place of sinners, and satisfied God by obeying His law perfectly.[49] Luther occasionally took Abelard's view of atonement.[50] The early

---

malice'. Human love is 'a friend, not of the neighbor but of the neighbor's goods and property' thus 'approves friendships on the basis of their usefulness; it seeks its own advantage and aims only at getting what is good'.

[44] LW 26:352; see LW 27:34.
[45] LW 27:353-356. In his treatise *Cur Deus Homo* ('Why God became Man?'), Anselm taught that between two choices to repair the damage done to His honor by humans' sins – punishment or satisfaction – God has chosen the way of satisfaction; Jesus as the God-man became the substitute payment to God. For Luther, Anselmic 'satisfaction' cannot exhaust all Christ's works, though it is an essential part of it.
[46] LW 31:300.
[47] LW 24:246-247.
[48] R. Larry Shelton, *Cross and Covenant: Interpreting the Atonement for 21st Century Mission* (Tyrone, GA: Paternoster, 2006), 176, 181; Forde, *Where*, 40-44; Althaus, *Theology*, 202-204; Siggins, *Christ*, 130.
[49] LW 31:297-298, 351; Althaus, *Theology*, 202-203; Shelton, *Cross and Covenant*, 181.
[50] Lohse, *Theology*, 227. However, according to McGrath, it is questionable, if not false, that Abelard was the originator of the so-called 'moral influence theory'. This subject needs further investigation. See, Alister McGrath, 'The Moral Theory of the

Eastern Church's view of Christ's work as victory was among the source traditions for Luther's view of atonement.[51] However, though 'characteristic themes of these different tendencies can be found in Luther', Marc Lienhard contends, 'he cannot be attached to any one of these systems'.[52]

The main distinctive of Luther's view of atonement is that Luther vigorously reminded sinners of their involvement and liability in Christ's death. For him, the doctrine of atonement can be easily converted into a mere theory which cannot afflict sinners or comfort believers, if it is not assimilated as a real event in which we participate. Viewed from this perspective, Anselm's teaching that Christ's atoning work aimed for the honour of God, exempts sinners from the affairs between God and Christ, missing the point that 'we are the obstacles to reconciliation, not God'. Abelard's view, presupposing sinners' openness toward God's demonstration of His unconditional love in Christ's cross, misses the point that sinners resist grace itself, wanting to control their life under their own power. In Aulén's thought, while Christ's work defeated the demonic powers such as sin, law, death, and devil, human beings are exonerated from the affairs between God and the demon.[53]

Against exempting sinners from their responsibility for Christ's death, Luther, before ascribing Christ's death directly to either wrath or love of God, stressed that not only the Jews in Christ's time but also we are joining in rejecting and killing Christ because of what Forde calls 'self-defense'.[54] Christ's cross was caused by our refusal to accept God's saving grace as well as by our breaking of God's law. In both sins, we are violating the First Commandment, trying to es-

---

Atonement: An Historical and Theological Critique', *Scottish Journal of Theology* 38 (1985), 205-220.

[51] See Aulén, *Christus Victor*.

[52] Lienhard, *Christology*, 177-179; Siggins contends the same thing. Siggins, *Christ*, 109. 'Luther's sermons abound in the motifs which figure in the historic atonement theories – patristic, classic, dramatic, or Western, Latin, and penal; objective or subjective. Shallow comparative study might suggest that Luther held all the great schemes – or that he was a confused thinker who really grasped none of them. In fact, Luther is not attempting what the theologians attempted for dogmatic or apologetic purposes, and it is impossible to equate his result with theirs. The logical structure of his doctrine differs from all of them and therefore may not be typed with any of them'.

[53] See Forde, *Radical*, 85-113; Lienhard, *Christology*, 176-179; Siggins, *Christ*, 108-113.

[54] Forde, *Radical*, 90-93. Sinners do not want to accept Christ, because it means giving up their own control over their life and surrendering to God's grace.

cape from the reign of God and of His grace. Only when our involvement in Christ's cross is revealed, Christ as the object of God's punishment turns into the self-sacrificial saviour and Christ's obedience changes into His salvific merit 'for us'.[55]

There have been debates among scholars on the ways how Christ 'for us' works. Tuomo Mannermaa, the leader of the Finnish Luther School, contends that Luther taught justification by *theosis* through 'communication of attributes'[56] between Christ and believers in union by faith; 'justifying faith does not merely signify a reception of the forgiveness imputed to a human being for the sake of the merit of Christ' but 'participation in God's essence in Christ'.[57] Though Christ is both God's grace and gift in Luther's view, faith and righteousness as gift affect grace, as the 'basis and prerequisite' of grace.[58]

However, Mannermaa's interpretation has not been generally accepted. R. Scott Clark notes that those who insist on justification by *theosis* do not consider Luther's chronological transition from his earlier view to mature one, making his material before 1521 definitive sources of their study.[59] Luther employed various dichotomies to distinguish between imputed and inherent righteousness: Christ as gift and as example; Christ as grace and faith as gift; and Christ as grace and the Holy Spirit as gift. The former ones designate the imputation of Christ's righteousness and the latter ones, a believers' own righteousness. From the standpoint of imputed righteousness, believers are fully righteous and fully sanctified since Christ's righteousness is perfect. From the angle of the believer, they are partly

---

[55] LW 17:221. 'His suffering was nothing else than our sin. These words, OUR, US, FOR US, must be written in letters of gold. He who does not believe this is not a Christian'; LW 35:121; LW 26:176-179; see Lienhard, *Christology*, 142.
[56] Tuomo Mannermaa, *Christ Present In Faith: Luther's View of Justification*, ed. Kirsi. Stjerna (Minneapolis: Fortress Press, 2005), 8.
[57] Ibid., 16-17.
[58] Ibid., 5.
[59] R. Scott Clark, '*Iustitia Imputata Christi*: Alien or Proper to Luther's Doctrine of Justification', in *CTQ* 70 (2006), 269-310; Mason Beecroft and J. Scott Horrel, 'Review of Union with Christ: The New Finnish Interpretation of Luther', *Bibliotheca Sacra* 157 (April-June 2000), 250-251; Ted Dorman, 'Review of Union with Christ: The New Finnish Interpretation of Luther', *First Things* 98 (December, 1999), 49-53; Dennis Bielfeldt and Klaus Schwarzwaller, 'Response to Sammeli Juntunen, Luther and Metaphysics' in *Union with Christ; The New Finnish Interpretation of Luther*, ed. Carl E. Braaten and Robert W. Jenson (Grand Rapids: Wm. B. Eerdmans, 1998), 161-166.

righteous, because they cannot subordinate their flesh to the Spirit perfectly, not being filled with the Spirit owing to the lack of faith.[60]

The former ones become the basis of the latter ones. Grace, favour, or Christ as gift becomes the basis of gifts of faith, the Spirit, or Christ as example.[61] Christian righteousness is based on Christ's perfect obedience to God imputed to them, not on the condition of inner renewal.[62] Contrasting between favours as God's giving grace and faith as the grace assimilated by believers, Luther warned repeatedly that putting one's trust even in faith is putting trust in ourselves as well.[63]

Luther taught that the imputation of Christ's righteousness occurs by a believers' union with Christ in faith.[64] However, though Christ is present in faith, the presence is not by a faith which is not perfect, but by God's perfect grace. What makes this 'imperfect' faith acceptable before God is God's sheer grace.[65] Further, the happy exchange which occurs in a believers' union with Christ does not mean a partial 'communication of attributes' but exchange between the whole righteousness of Christ and the whole sinfulness of sinners.[66] Justification is 'a matter, not of imitation' but of putting on the whole 'Christ Himself, that is, His innocence, righteousness, wisdom, power, salvation, life, and Spirit'.[67] This change is forensic, total, and objective, not progressive, partial, and subjective.

---

[60] LW 27:63-75; LW 31:358-359; LW 32:226-229; LW 35: 369-370.
[61] Timo Laato, 'Justification: The Stumbling Block of the Finnish Luther School', *CTQ* 72 (2008), 332, 337.
[62] Ibid., 338.
[63] WA 10.1.1:126,13-127,6. 'Rely not upon yourself, nor upon your faith. Flee to Christ; keep under His wings; remain under His shelter. Let His righteousness and grace, not yours, be your refuge. You are to be made an heir of eternal life, not by the grace you have yourself received, but, as Paul says here, by Christ's grace... true Christian faith does not take refuge in itself... but flees to Christ and is preserved under Him and in Him'. Quoted by Laato, Ibid., 333-334.
[64] LW 26:132-133, 166-170, 284, 356-357
[65] LW 26:229-236; LW 26:286. 'Although there are still remnants of sin in the saints because they do not believe perfectly, nevertheless these remnants are dead; for on account of faith in Christ they are not imputed'.
[65] LW 31, "Two Kinds of Righteousness"
[66] LW 31:297-298, 351; LW 27:219-222; LW 27:241 'Since he [a Christian] has all things in common with Christ. His sins are no longer his; they are Christ's. But in Christ sins are unable to overcome righteousness... Again, Christ's righteousness now belongs not only to Christ; it belongs to His Christian'; Shelton, *Cross and Covenant*, 182; Althaus, *Theology*, 212-213.
[67] LW 26:352-353.

Luther's view of sanctification is not different from this forensic view of justification. He reasoned that the imputation of Christ's righteousness is 'extremely necessary' as long as 'we are not yet purely righteous'.[68] As long as sins cling to believers, sanctification is not a possibility by a believers' own righteousness, but is given as 'alien purity' from without:

> How can we become 'purer than snow' even though the remnants of sin always cling to us? ... we have by faith obtained the blood of Christ, which is surely most pure. According to this purity ... the Christian is rightly said to be purer than snow, purer than the sun and the stars, even though the defilements of spirit and flesh cling to him. These are concealed and covered by the cleanness and purity of Christ ... We should note diligently that this purity is an alien purity, for Christ adorns and clothes us with His righteousness.[69]

Then, putting on Christ's imputed righteousness causes a real change in believers, because in faith we are united with Christ who 'lives and works in us, not speculatively but really, with presence and with power'; 'A new light and flame arise; new and devout emotions come into being, such as fear and trust in God and hope; and a new will emerges'.[70] As long as 'Christ is speaking, acting, and performing all actions' in believers, the flesh is in the process of being extinguished.[71] While inherent righteousness follows imputed righteousness, imputed righteousness works not only as the beginning point but the perpetual fountain of believers' inherent righteousness.[72]

However, Luther denied there could be full achievement of righteousness in this life. Since the Spirit 'begins' to subdue the flesh to a subordinate position 'increasingly', believers begin to subordinate their flesh to the Spirit, but they cannot do it perfectly.[73] Faith 'begins' to slay sin, but 'it has not yet become perfect'. Though the wounds of human sins are now 'bandaged and looked after', they are 'not yet' completely healed.[74] From the viewpoint of the law, faith is the beginning, but not a perfect fulfilment of the law.[75]

---

[68] LW 26:132-133.
[69] LW 12:366-367.
[70] LW 26:352-353; LW 26:357; LW 31:299-300.
[71] LW 26:170-172.
[72] For more detailed discussion, see Forde, *Radical*, 118-136.
[73] LW 27:63-75; LW 31:358-359;
[74] LW 30:118.
[75] Forde, *Radical*, 123.

IV. Christ's Victory and the Law

Luther often described Christ's work as victory over sin, death, the devil, hell, the law, and the wrath of God, grouping the law and the wrath of God into the same category of evil powers.[76] If viewed from a personal dimension, though the conflict between Christ and God's love on the one hand, and the law or the wrath of God on the other hand, has a dualistic outlook in Luther's dramatic description, the place of conflict is in the human conscience, not in the Being of God.[77] Siggins properly states:

> The conflict is man's ... The very list of 'tyrants' itself indicates the nature of Luther's metaphor. If this were a battle between God and His enemies, man would have to appear along with sin, the devil, and the world in the list of God's opponents: man is God's enemy ... The absence of man's name and the inclusion of God's wrath and His law establish that this cannot be God's battle ... the fact of man's sinfulness and his wilfulness are not at issue here but are presumed.[78]

The law and the wrath of God are counted among the enemies in the sense that they prevent the full realization of God's love in the human heart. Luther not only included the law among the enemies, but also considered it the chief of all, because, apart from their relation to the law, all the others would lose their powers.[79] Siggins explains: 'Sin has its tyranny from the law, which declares God's wrath and eternal condemnation, and thereby places man in bondage to death and hell and in thrall to the devil, prince of death and of this world. If, then, sin is forgiven, the tyrants are instantly overthrown'.[80]

If viewed from a cosmic dimension, Christ first won the victory over the enemies by conquering sin through His perfect obedience to God's will.[81] The devil was defeated by Christ in His weakness, not in demonstration of His power.[82] Especially, 'on the cross Christ was powerless; yet there He performed His mightiest work, conquering

---

[76] LW 26:10, 21, 26, 29, 48, 72, 147-150, 160-164, 167, 175, 26:287, 290, 293; LW 27:4; BC, 345, 414.
[77] See Aulén, Christus Victor, 108-116.
[78] Siggins, Christ, 139.
[79] Watson, Let, 118-119.
[80] Siggins, Christ, 140.
[81] WA 2, 691. 'He is the picture of God's grace against the sin which He has taken upon Himself and conquered through His invincible obedience'. Quoted by Althaus, Theology, 209.
[82] Siggins, Christ, 41-44.

sin, death, world, hell, devil, and all evil'.[83] In His person, Christ with His 'divine Power, Righteousness, Blessing, Grace, and Life' collided with and 'conquered, killed, and buried' all sins, death, and curses. Luther ascribed this victory to Christ's divinity, explaining that to conquer evil powers and to grant salvation pertain solely to 'the divine power'.[84] To describe this victory, Luther not only employed a patristic idea of the deception of the devil through Christ's humanity,[85] but also, as Gustaf Aulén notes, he used 'violent expressions, strong colours, realistic images'.[86] What proves that Christ's death is victorious is His resurrection.[87]

Believers' victory over evil powers are based on Christ's cosmic victory, through which Christ becomes their righteousness through faith.[88] By holding fast to Christ the Victor in faith, Christians also become conquerors over those powers.[89] Luther said:

> A Christian should steep himself in the thought of Christ's victory, in which everything is already done ... we can do nothing, cancel or crush the devil or overthrow death – they are all laid low already. Our suffering and fighting are not the real battle, but only a prize or morsel of the glory of this victory ... The battle must be already won and the victory achieved if I am to have comfort and peace. Christ says, 'I have done it already, just accept it and use the victory by singing about it, glorying and making a show of it – just be men of good cheer'.[90]

With such statements as His being our righteousness, His giving His victory to believers, and Christians' reception of Christ's victory in faith, Luther represented Christ's imputed righteousness through faith and forgiveness of sins as the way of Christian victory.

---

[83] WA 7, 586, 15. Quoted by Siggins, *Christ*, 44.
[84] LW 26:281-282.
[85] LW 5:150. 'He came into the world clothed in flesh and was cast into the water like a hook. After biting Him, the devil was suddenly pulled back out of the water by God, thrown on dry land, and crushed. This means that Christ presented to the devil His weak humanity, which covered that eternal and unconquerable majesty. Then the devil struck at the hook of His divinity, and by it all his power as well as the power of death and hell was overcome'; LW 26:267, n. 69.
[86] Aulén, *Christus Victor*, 103-104.
[87] Forde, *Where*, 35-38.
[88] LW 26:21, 290.
[89] LW 26:282; WA 10III, 356. 'Christ has conquered sin, death, hell, and the devil. This has also taken place in him who grasps this, firmly believes, and trusts; in Christ Jesus he becomes a conqueror of sin, death, hell, and the devil'; WA 36, 694 (Cruciger's edition). 'See, Christians must thus arm themselves with Christ's victory and beat back the devil with it'. Quoted by Althaus, *Theology*, 216.
[90] WA 46, 110, 24. Quoted by Siggins, *Christ*, 138.

Because of the elements such as the victory idea, the deception of the devil, and the imaginary and dramatic description, Aulén represents Luther's view of atonement as the victory type, after grouping various views of atonement into three: the 'classical' victory type, the 'Latin' legalistic type, and the 'ethical' type. Aulén properly observes that Luther viewed Christ's victory from the point of the victory of God's love over God's wrath and the law. Opposing the Latin type, Aulén insists that Luther's emphasis on Christ's victory over the law expresses his 'opposition to the moralism of Latin Christianity'.[91]

However, in the Latin type, God's wrath is regarded as God's strange work that serves His proper works of grace.[92] Consistently, the work of Christ does not create, but presupposes a gracious God. Christ's fulfilling the law and dying a sinner shows God's holy love that forgives at the cost of self-sacrifice, but does not compromise with sin. As long as God's wrath is not isolated from His love and God's love becomes the antithesis of legalism, Christ's satisfaction in the Latin type stands as the antithesis of legalism.[93] Luther's teaching on the victory motif asserts Christ's all-sufficiency.[94]

Althaus properly states that for Luther, the Latin type is more fundamental than the victory type, since 'the powers with which Christ struggled had their power and authority only through God's wrath'.[95] As long as Satan and the law are God's creatures, the ultimate object of reconciliation is not anything but God Himself.[96] Forde contends that looked at in this way there is no conflict between different views of the atonement. Jesus satisfied the wrath of God, bore the curse of the law, or suffered the punishment, and at the same time He won the victory over the law, sin, and death. Penal satisfaction and victory are all parts of Christ's works. Also, since His life, death, and resurrection are identified with ours, He becomes our example.[97]

---

[91] Aulén, *Christus Victor*, 111-116. Aulén contends that if satisfaction of the law is understood as the foundational element of the human relationship with God, it is moralism.
[92] Watson, *Let*, 124.
[93] Watson, *Let*, 124.
[94] Siggins, *Christ*, 140.
[95] Althaus, *Theology*, 220.
[96] Althaus, *Theology*, 222; Siggins, *Christ*, 137. Siggins asserts that for Luther, 'it is God only with Whom we have to deal'.
[97] Forde, *Where*, 40-44.

B. John Wesley

I. The Person of Christ and the Law

Wesley taught Jesus Christ is 'very God and very Man,' adhering to the Chalcedonian 'Definition of faith' and the Anglican Thirty-Nine Articles.[98] Christ's mediatorial works have foundation in the Trinitarian unity.[99] Christ's divine glory was shown forth 'through the whole series of His life': not only in His miracles and transfiguration, but also in His tempers, ministrations, conduct,[100] and even in His death.[101]

Wesley showed a tendency to stress His divine nature more than human nature, probably to avoid 'knowing Christ after the flesh'.[102] However, Christ's humanity is still very important in his understanding of the law.[103] Christ's incarnation meant that He was 'made under the law'.[104] Through His perfect fulfilment of God's law He was prepared to offer Himself as a sacrifice.[105] Thus, Christ's incarnation was 'an essential or integral part of the work of atonement'.[106] The neces-

---

[98] Charles R. Wilson, 'Christology', in Charles W. Carter, ed., *A Contemporary Wesleyan Theology* (Grand Rapids: Francis Asbury Press, 1983), 1:346; see WW10:81; Deschner, *Christology*, 5, 15; ENNT Phil 2:6, Heb 2:10, Lk 22:70.

[99] S. Mount (1), Intro. 2-3; Deschner, *Christology*, 84-85, 108.

[100] ENNT Jn 1:14.

[101] ENNT Luke 23:34, Heb 5:7. On the cross, Christ grieved over 'the dishonour that sin had done to so holy a God' and concerned for sinners' salvation, forgetting His own anguish and sufferings; ENNT MT 27:50. On the phrase 'No man taketh my life from me, but I ray it down of myself', Wesley commented, Christ neither chose to relieve His suffering by abandoning His body quickly nor continued to survive conquering even the greatest tortures on the cross; though He had power to chose either, He suffered enough and died voluntarily; ENNT Lk 23:40. The conversion of the thief put a peculiar glory on Christ 'in His lowest state'.

[102] In his editing Wesley omitted certain expressions on Christ's human nature. Editing the epistles of Ignatius, Wesley omitted passages that refer to Jesus as born 'of the race of David according to the flesh' in his Christian library. From the Anglican Thirty-nine Articles, he deleted the phrase 'of her [Mary's] substance' in his *The Twenty-five Articles*. Collins, *Theology*, 94-95; see Maddox, *Responsible*, 116; Deschner, *Christology*, 41, n. 41; S. Fresh, 1-16.

[103] Kenneth J. Collins, *A Faithful Witness: John Wesley's Homiletical Theology* (Wilmore, KY: Wesley Heritage Press, 1993), 39-43; see Deschner, *Christology*, 24-28, 61-62; Richard M. Riss, 'John Wesley's Christology in Recent Literature', *WTJ* 45:1 (Spring 2010), 108-129.

[104] ENNT Gal 4:4. 'Both under the precept, and under the curse, of it'; Lk 2:21.

[105] ENNT Heb 10:5-7.

[106] John R. Renshaw, 'The Atonement in the Theology of John and Charles Wesley' (Ph.D. dissertation, Boston University, 1965), 225.

sity of Christ's taking human nature can be understood in terms of the patristic idea of recapitulation of the fall of humanity through His perfect obedience to the law.[107] In His incarnation Christ became both a mirror of God's image and a teacher of the law.[108] Christ's incarnation provides believers with better knowledge of God, resulting in a deeper loving relationship with God in which they voluntarily obey the law.[109] Thus, the claims of Matthew Hambrick and Michael Lodahl that Wesley's Christology, downplaying Jesus' humanity and not allowing 'the dimension of human response its full and proper place in Jesus', conflicts with his soteriology which emphasizes the element of human responsibility,[110] cannot be accepted.

II. Christ the Prophet and the Law

For Wesley, prophecy meant declaring 'heavenly mysteries' or foretelling future things,[111] and mainly in the former sense, he called Christ a Prophet.[112] Wesley found the ground of Christ's prophetic office in Trinitarian unity. Because of this unity, Christ becomes 'the express image ... the character, the stamp, the living impression, of His [God's] person' in whom 'the children of men may herein see God'.[113] Also, because of the same unity, Christ has a unique authority and an infinite superiority over His human messengers in His teaching of the law.[114] Wesley explained Christ's fulfilling of the law in two senses: firstly, Christ obeyed the law perfectly; secondly, He explained the inner meaning of the law 'in its fullness'.[115] By the words, fullness, purity, and spirituality, Wesley represented the superiority of Christ's teaching of inner law.[116]

---

[107] ENNT Heb 2:17.
[108] S. Lord, I. 2; ENNT Heb 1:3, II Cor 4:4, Col 1:15; see Deschner, *Christology*, 27.
[109] S. Love (1), I. 1-16.
[110] Matthew Hambrick and Michael Lodahl, 'Responsible Grace in Christology? John Wesley's Rendering of Jesus in the Epistle to the Hebrews', *WTJ* 43 (Spring 2008), 95-96.
[111] ENNT Rom 12:6.
[112] Deschner, *Christology*, 84; ENNT MT 1:16; Heb 1:102, Mk 9:7, Rev 1:1, Phil 3:8, Heb 3:1, Lk 4:24, Ac 7:37, 3:22, Jn 17:3.
[113] S. Mount (4), Intro. 1.
[114] S. Mount (1), Intro. 2, 7-9. 'With what authority does he teach! ... Not as Moses ... not as any of the Prophets ... the Creator of all! A God, a God appears!'; see Deschner, *Christology*, 84-85, 108.
[115] S. Mount (5), I. 3-4; ENNT Matt 5:17.
[116] WW 11: 472.

Wesley took a serious view of human responsibility toward Christ's prophetic work in various ways.[117] Above all, to take into consideration the fact that Wesley represented both Christ and the law as the image of God, there exists a perfect unity between Christ's teaching of the law and the Person of Christ. Therefore, to 'imitate Christ', to have 'the mind which was in Christ', or to 'walk as Christ walked' is understood as the essential requirement of the law. Wesley asserted that 'the most acceptable worship of God is to imitate Him',[118] or that 'Christ formed in the heart' of believers is the end of Christian religion.[119]

Also, to make Christ's prophetic work not in vain, we should use all opportunities to hear His message.[120] When Christ gives the authentic teaching on 'true and solid doctrines', we should receive them as responsible interpreters.[121] Believers should become the living conveyors of Christ's teaching.[122]

III. Christ the Priest and the Law

What makes Christ's priestly office inevitable is God's wrath against violations of His law.[123] Against William Law's opposition to God's wrath, in his letter composed in 1756, Wesley said, God is 'mercy mixed with justice'.[124] The wrath of God is an expression of His justice toward sin.[125] While, as the central doctrine of Christianity, atonement becomes 'the distinguishing point' between Christianity and all heathenism,[126] justification by faith is the effect of 'the atonement of Christ actually applied to the soul of the sinner.'[127] Wesley's concern for the law was expressed in his presentation of Christ's atonement, focusing on the idea of the imputation of Christ's righteousness.

---

[117] Deschner, *Christology*, 88-92.
[118] WW 10:68.
[119] S. Awake, II. 10.
[120] S. Eye, I. 3; ENNT Matt 13:13.
[121] S. Mount (5), I. 4; ENNT Jn 8:43, 9:3, 14:23, 17:7-8, 18:37, I Cor 3:11-12, 8:2, Jn, I Cor 8:2
[122] ENNT Jn 4:37, Ac 20:32, Heb 1:2
[123] ENNT Rom 3:25, Gal 3:13, Mt 27:46.
[124] WW 9:485.
[125] WW 9:481. 'Whoever therefore denies God to be capable of wrath or anger, acts consistently in denying His justice also'.
[126] S. Original, III. 1; WW 13:34; Lindström, *Sanctification*, 55.
[127] S. Salvation, II. 7.

During a long debate with James Hervey (1714-1758), Wesley expressed a strong objection to the doctrine of Christ's imputed righteousness, though he eventually affirmed imputation, properly understood.[128] In his *Theron and Aspasio*[129] (1755) and *Eleven Letters* (1765),[130] Hervey attributed atonement to Christ's both active and passive obedience,[131] and insisted that sanctification is not possible for believers 'in themselves... but in Christ'.[132] In a letter to Hervey dated 15 October 1756, Wesley argued firstly that 'It [the law] required only the alternative, Obey or die'; those who obey the law will live, but disobeyers will die. Secondly, 'It [the law] required no man to obey and die too. If any man had perfectly obeyed, He would not have died'; the law does not require sinners to die and, at the same time, require them to obey. When punishment for sins was already executed in Christ, the law is already fulfilled by His substitutional death for sinners. Finally, Wesley said, 'Christ by His death alone ... fully satisfied for the sins of the whole world'.[133]

According to Herbert B. McGonigle's analysis, in his *A Treatise on Justification, Extracted from John Goodwin* (1765), Wesley also argued, firstly, Christ's perfect conformity to God's law qualified Him to become Redeemer. Secondly, justification is in essence forgiveness; therefore, imputed righteousness is not necessary for it. Thirdly, if God sees no sin in believers because of Christ's imputed righteousness, it is contrary to the teaching of the Scripture about fallen humanity. Fourthly, the doctrine of imputation confuses the covenant of works with the covenant of grace, making the gospel nothing more than God's assistance for fulfilling the covenant of works. However, the gospel promises that salvation will be given to all who repent and believe in Christ.[134] In 1772, in his *Some Remarks on Mr. Hill's*

---

[128] McGonigle, *Sufficient*, 236-239; Collins, *Theology*, 174-176.
[129] Full title, *Theron and Aspasio* 'Or a Series of Dialogues and Letters upon the most Important and Interesting Subjects', The Whole Works of the Late Rev James Hervey A. M.
[130] McGonigle, *Sufficient*, 217-219.
[131] While by Christ's active righteousness Hervey meant Christ's complete and wholehearted obedience to the law, by Christ's passive righteousness he meant Christ's absolute submission to the Father's will in relation to His death. See McGonigle, *Sufficient*, 221; cf. J Hervey, Works, 2:336-337. Quoted by McGonigle, *Sufficient*, 222.
[132] J Hervey, Works, 2: 163-164. Quoted by McGonigle, *Sufficient*, 223.
[133] Letters 3: 373.
[134] McGonigle, *Sufficient*, 233-234.

Review of All the Doctrines Taught by Mr. John Wesley, Wesley reaffirmed the same ideas.[135]

Wesley related Christ's fulfilment of God's law only to His being qualified for penal substitution for sinners, not to imputation of righteousness to believers. Also he disassociated the fulfilment of the law from justification, and attached instead repentance and faith to it, which means that Christ's perfect obedience to the law is not necessary for atonement.[136] Atonement is achieved only by Christ's penal substitution. Christ's righteousness does not replace a believer's righteousness. God does not regard believers righteous because Christ is righteous.[137] Against Hervey's insistence that the doctrine of imputation would humble sinners, Wesley objected that in practice it undermines Christian holy living; 'If the very personal obedience of Christ... be mine the moment I believe, can anything be added thereto? Does my obeying God add any value to the perfect obedience of Christ?'[138] If, as Hervey insisted, 'believers, who are notorious transgressors in themselves, have a sinless obedience in Christ', it makes sinners 'satisfied without any holiness at all ... It makes thousands content to live and die "transgressors of the law"', opening the door wide to antinomianism.[139]

In his sermon, 'The Lord Our Righteousness' (1765), accepting that in atonement both Christ's active and passive righteousness is imputed to believers as soon as they believe,[140] Wesley explained that his objection was against an antinomian tendency which misapplication of the concept of imputation may produce, rather than the concept itself.[141] However, Wesley's teaching of the imputation of Christ's righteousness was still much different from Hervey's. Collins notes that to emphasize a believer's own obedience to the law, quoting from Cranmer's 'Homily on Salvation' in his sermon 'The Lord Our Righteousness', Wesley omitted all references to Christ's fulfilling the law.[142] Also, he stressed Christ's passive righteousness

---

[135] WW 10:386.
[136] WW 10:312-315.
[137] S. Justification, II. 4.
[138] WW 10:315.
[139] McGonigle, *Sufficient*, 226.
[140] S. Lord, II. 1; see WW 8:277.
[141] S. Lord, II. 19-20; WW 10:315; McGonigle, *Sufficient*, 219.
[142] Collins, *Theology*, 112. What was omitted from Wesley's quotation is: 'He for them fulfilled the law in his life, so that now in him and by him every Christian may be called a fulfiller of the law, forasmuch as that which their infirmity lacked,

much more than His active righteousness, even after 1765 when he published his sermon 'The Lord Our Righteousness'. When Wesley employed the language of imputation in his writings, he related it only to justification, not to sanctification.[143] When he used the expression of imputed righteousness, he quickly emphasized the importance of accompanying inherent righteousness.[144] For Wesley, sanctification is not primarily a participation in Christ's righteousness, but inherent 'tempers', 'dispositions', 'affections', and 'intentions' in believers.[145] In the same context, Deschner observes, whereas Wesley taught that the ceremonial law is a 'type of Christ' which was fulfilled in Him, he declined to represent the moral law as the same sort of type of Christ which was fulfilled in Him, because 'it smacked of the imputed holiness of the antinomians.'[146]

Christ continues His priestly intercession after ascension to the right hand of God.[147] Since, from the perspective of 'the *strict justice* of God,' believers are 'still *worthy of death*' and 'still *deserve* punishment', Christ's intercession still interposes between them and condemnation; the atonement relates not only to justification, but to sanctification.[148] In Wesley's teaching of a threefold circle of divine providence, a believers' own righteousness was also emphasized. The atonement makes it possible for non-believers who receive only temporal blessings of God to enter into the middle circle of God's spiritual blessings, then, grow in grace toward the innermost circle of God's providence. While the 'innermost' Christians participate in God's providential works, the atonement becomes an attracting power to move people from the outermost to innermost circle. Christ's priestly work does not exempt believers from their duty. God's love produces a believers' love toward God and their neighbours.[149]

As a whole, Wesley's teaching of Christ's priestly office was guided by a twofold motive: on the one hand, he avoided any human merit in justification; on the other, he repudiated any antinomian tendency when inherent righteousness in believers is neglected. Wes-

---

Christ's [righteousness] hath supplied'; see Albert C. Outler ed., *John Wesley* (New York: Oxford University Press, 1964), 126.
[143] S. Lord, II. 10; Collins, *Theology*, 175; see S. Lord, II. 19-20.
[144] S. Lord, II. 12; see Collins, *Theology*, 176.
[145] Deschner, *Christology*, 105-106.
[146] Deschner, *Christology*, 115.
[147] S. Repentance, I. 16.
[148] S. Repentance, I. 16; III. 3.
[149] S. Worship, I. 9; ENNT Mt 5:45, Col 1:24; Deschner, *Christology*, 67-68.

ley's rejection of the idea of a fulfilment of the law by proxy was to make room for sanctification in the sense of a believers' own grace-enabled fulfilment of the law.[150]

IV. Christ the King and the Law

a. Christ the King as Lawgiver

Doubting if Wesley's remark that Christ the King is the giver of the law is his authoritative statement about Christ's kingly office, Deschner connects Christ's granting of the law only to His prophetic office. He insists that though Christ the King is once represented as a giver of laws in Wesley's sermon, 'The Law Established Through Faith (2)',[151] for Wesley, Christ's kingly office begins with resurrection. But, since the law plays a crucial role from creation, to assign the law to the kingly office would distort the continuity of the law in Wesley's thinking. By identifying Christ the King as the giver of laws, Wesley only wanted to emphasize the third use of the law for sanctification.[152]

However, Deschner passes over the other places where Wesley attributed giving of the law to Christ's kingship. Commenting on I Tim 1:9, Wesley, connecting the authority of the lawgiver to the Godhead,[153] ascribed it to Christ.[154] Also, in his sermon, 'Upon our Lord's Sermon on the Mount (1)', Wesley explained Christ's kingship in terms of His being Creator, Governor, and the great Lawgiver and Judge.[155] Christ's kingship is an eternal one rather than the one that began at a point after His incarnation.[156] Deschner is right when he connects Christ's kingship with sanctification. Yet, after dividing the stages of Christ's history in Wesley's view into three – His eternal glory, transient humiliation in incarnation, and re-exaltation through resurrection and ascension[157] – he fails to relate Christ's kingship to His eternal glory in which His kingship has a cosmic dimension.

---

[150] Lindström, *Sanctification*, 74-75.
[151] S. Established (2), I. 6.
[152] Deschner, *Christology*, 83.
[153] ENNT I Tim 1:9. 'They who despise the authority of the lawgiver violate the first commandment, which is the foundation of the law, and the ground of all obedience'.
[154] ENNT Mt 5:22, 7:29.
[155] S. Mount (1), Intro. 2.
[156] S. Mount (1), Intro. 2.
[157] Deschner, *Christology*, 45-60, 116-118; ENNT I Cor 15:24. 'The divine reign both of the Father and Son is from everlasting to everlasting'; ENNT MT 28:18. 'As God, He [Christ] had all power from eternity'.

Wesley distinguished between Christ's kingly office that originates the law as Creator, preserves it as ruler, and verifies it as judge, and His priestly office as the function of delivering or expounding the law that He has previously given. That is, what Christ the Prophet does is understood as re-proclamation of what Christ the King has already legislated and inscribed in human hearts.[158] Christ the King is not the Lawgiver in the sense that He proclaims or delivers God's law, which Christ the Prophet does, but the Lawgiver in the sense that He Himself has made the law and given it to all human hearts from the beginning. Wesley especially referred to Christ's divine origin and the superiority of His authority and wisdom, when he emphasized the originality, the authority, and the propriety of the law.[159]

b. Christ the King as Lord of Believers

Christ's kingship relates to both His and His people's victory over their enemies such as Satan, sin, and death.[160] His victory is understood as the repression of a rebellion rather than the conquest of a new territory.[161] Christ's being King means that believers come to obey Christ in their 'every temper, and thought, and word, and work'.[162] Because Satan rules over sinners, Christ's kingship is accepted only by believers. In that way, Wesley distinguished between Christ's eternal and actual kingship. Though Christ has been the 'rightful Master' from the beginning, His kingship can be truly realized only in His 'mediatorial kingdom', that is, in sanctified believers who obey God's law.[163] In sanctified believers, Christ's kingship is demonstrated by His inscribing 'the true, full, spiritual meaning' of His law to their hearts and by their obedience to Him from their hearts on the foundation of His working in them.[164]

Christ's victory has three stages; in the atonement, in sanctification, and in the last day. Christ breaks Satan's dominion, first by re-

---

[158] S. Mount (1), Intro. 2.
[159] S. Mount (1), Intro. 2-9.
[160] S. Sin, III. 8; S. Coming, III. 1-4; ENNT Rev 11:15, Eph 1:10, I Jn 3:8; Deschner, *Christology*, 128. Deschner notes that ENNT I Cor 15:26, 25, 28 indicate that Christ participated in the everlasting reign of the Father, even while carrying out His mediatorial works.
[161] Deschner, *Christology*, 116; ENNT Rev 11:15. 'This province has been in the enemy's hands: it now returns to its rightful Master'.
[162] S. Repentance, III. 4.
[163] ENNT I Cor 15:24; Rev 11:15.
[164] ENNT Heb 8:10-12; S. Law, I. 6; S. Mount (5), II. 3.

moving from sinners their guilt in justification, next by removing the power of sin in sanctification, and finally by removing the being of sin in glorification.[165] Though decisive, the victory of Christ is not complete until the last day.[166] It is in tension between the 'already' and the 'not yet' in the understanding of Christ's kingdom. Christ's victory does not guarantee our salvation. Therefore, sanctified believers must win their own victory for final justification. Through the tension of the 'already' and the 'not yet' in Christ's victory, Wesley wanted to prevent believers from being negligent.[167]

c. Christ the King as Judge

On the last day Christ the king will judge every person either to eternal life or to eternal destruction in the final judgment.[168] In that judgment, Wesley repeatedly emphasized, Christ will use the law as 'the rule whereby He will judge the world'.[169] In his sermon, 'On the Wedding Garment', (1789) Wesley taught that a believers' own righteousness, not Christ's righteousness, will be their wedding garment for their final justification.[170] Active obedience to the law by believers themselves will verify their acceptance with God.[171]

How then can Christ's judgment according to the law be harmonized with the doctrine of justification by faith? Wesley distinguished between present and final justification by explaining that while in the former only faith in Christ is required, in the latter Christ considers obedience to the law as the evidence for faith.[172] Though sanctification is not a condition of present justification, it is a condition of final justification.[173] In his pamphlet, *A Letter to a Gentleman at Bristol* (1758), that Wesley wrote 'to guard them from seeking salvation by works on one hand, and antinomianism on the other', he contended that the inward and outward fruits of the Spirit do not

---

[165] ENNT Jn 14:30, Col 1:14, I Cor 15:26; Deschner, *Christology*, 121-122.
[166] S. Coming, III. 1-4; ENNT Eph 1:10; I Cor 15:26; I Jn 3:8.
[167] Deschner, *Christology*, 118-126.
[168] S. Assize, II. 1. God's commitment of all judgement to Christ is regarded as exalting His Son as a reward for Christ's perfect obedience to the Father.
[169] S. Law, IV. 8; ENNT Rev 22:12; Rom 2:11; Heb 10:37; Mt 12:37. 'For by thy words (as well as thy tempers and works) thou shalt then be either acquitted or condemned.'
[170] S. Garment, 7-10.
[171] S. Lord, II. 12.
[172] ENNT Mt 12:37.
[173] ENNT I Tim 6:19; Lindström, *Sanctification*, 124-125.

merit justification but they prove their justification.[174] For Wesley, like obedience to all the commandments prepare believers for receiving God's grace of entire sanctification by faith,[175] in final judgment, obedience to the law will prepare them for their acceptance with God as the evidence of their true faith which is the only condition of final justification.

C. Observations and Analysis

I. Christ as the Law (Theology of Cross) vs. Christ the Teacher of the Law

Luther taught that Christ's teaching of the law cannot surpass the Decalogue, which is the best representation of God's law.[176] Christ did not add anything to the superior teaching of the law of Moses in terms of the content of the law. This means that the law in the Old Testament already contains rich spiritual and inner implications. Heinrich Bornkamm shows that Luther regarded the Old Testament believers as mirrors of present believers in the realm of the spiritual world as well as in the political world.[177] Especially in the Psalms Luther found the best expressions of spirituality.[178] The Old Testa-

---

[174] WW 10:307.
[175] WW 11:402-403.
[176] WA 18, 81:26ff. 'What can be a better proclamation than the Ten Commandments? Nothing can be said that is higher than the First Commandment. It is impossible to invent a more excellent doctrine after Moses; to worship, to praise, and to give thanks to God is the highest and most excellent doctrine that can be handed on. The Decalogue, therefore, is the highest doctrine!... This is the ancient [doctrine]: believe in God, love him as much as you love yourself. No more perfect law can be handed on'; WA 40I, 15:25. 'It is ridiculous to make Christ the giver of the law and to see in him the promise of another law. Since nothing can be higher in heaven and on earth than the law of Moses for man to understand, to do so is hardly possible'.Quoted by Bornkamm, *Old*, 132.; LW 12:44.
[177] Bornkamm, *Old*, 1-44. The spiritual world relates to faith, doubt, and spiritual trials, and the political world covers civic affairs, labor, household, marriage, and education.
[178] LW 35:255. 'Where does one find finer words of joy than in the psalms of praise and thanksgiving? There you look into the hearts of all the saints, as into fair and pleasant gardens, yes, as into heaven itself. There you see what fine and pleasant flowers of the heart spring up from all sorts of fair and happy thoughts toward God, because of His blessings. On the other hand, where do you find deeper, more sorrowful, more pitiful words of sadness than in the psalms of lamentation? There again you look into the hearts of all the saints, as into death, yes, as into hell itself. How gloomy and dark it is there, with all kinds of troubled forebodings about the wrath of God! So, too, when they speak of fear and hope, they use such words that no

ment believers' experience of the wrath of God in severe spiritual trials reflects the spiritual implications of the Old Testament law. When Luther taught about the law's spiritual nature, he did not distinguish between the Old and the New Testament laws.[179]

When Luther represented Christ as the law, his focus was not on the contents of the law, but on the way of declaring the law. Luther's ascribing the law to Moses does not mean that the law was properly received and functioned as it was intended to do. God's repeated declaration of the law in creation, through Moses and prophets, and through Christ was caused by human sins that disregarded or abused the law. What is needed to correct sinners' misuse of the law is not to declare the same content of the law, but to declare the law in a shockingly impactful way; by representing the law in a way that directly deals with sinners' pride and desire on the pretext of theology or worship of God. It is to make Christ Himself whom sinners claim as the vindicator of their theology and their use of the law, refuter against them. Christ Himself should become the most dreadful law of God.

For Luther, theology of cross attacks theology of glory. Christ in His humiliation stands against humans idolizing themselves. His death on the cross rebukes sinners' self-justification. Christ's incarnation and death can be understood properly by those who humble themselves before God, thus, theology of cross contains, in itself, an element of judgment against human pride and greed. Though Luther did not teach the so-called third use of the law, he taught a believers' progressive change through mortification.[180] Christ works as the law more for mortification than for imitation. The contents of the law do not change, but in Christ the law becomes radically applied to sinners.

---

painter could so depict for you fear or hope, and no Cicero or other orator so portray them'.
[179] LW 35:365-380; John M. Headley, *Luther's View of Church History* (New Haven: Yale University Press, 1963), 130-143; Bornkamm, *Old*, 124-135.
[180] S. Denial, Intro. 3. Wesley admitted that the Reformers taught that believers can be progressively renewed through mortification. 'So many Ministers of Christ, in almost every age and nation, particularly since the Reformation of the Church ... have wrote and spoke so largely on this important duty [of self-denial] ... They knew both from the oracles of God, and from the testimony of their own experience, how impossible it was not to deny our Master, unless we will deny ourselves; and how vainly we attempt to follow Him that was crucified, unless we take up our cross daily'.

Because of Christ as the law, sinners come to rely on Christ as the gospel. Then, what Christ did for us as the gospel changes again into Christ as example for us to follow in our relationship with our neighbours. Christ becomes our example neither by His teaching of the law nor by His setting an example of obeying the law, but by giving Himself to us as the gospel. In Luther's Christology, Christ does all in all; He Himself becomes the most powerful law of accusation, the gospel, and the most beautiful example of Christian life in turn. The so-called third use of the law is transferred to the role of Christ as the example of love. Christ demonstrated what God's law commands, recovering humanity both into fundamental dependence on God and into self-sacrificial love toward neighbours.

Wesley's view on Christ's teaching of the law is much different from Luther's. He ascribed the complete teaching of the law not to Moses but to Christ whose teaching supplemented and surpassed the law of Moses. Like Luther, Wesley taught that there is a homogenous character of several kinds of the law.[181] However, he observed that the Jews criticized Christ as 'a teacher of novelties, an introducer of *a new religion*' and rejected Him, which shows a great difference between Christ's teaching and the Jews' understanding of the law.[182] In this difference, Wesley found the necessity for Christ's teaching of the law.[183] In the meaning of fulfilment of the law Wesley included Christ's full exposition of the meaning of the law as well as His perfect obedience to it, paraphrasing Christ's declaration, 'I am not come to destroy, but to fulfill' as 'I am come to establish it [the law] in its fullness ... to place in a full and clear view whatsoever was dark or obscure therein ... to declare the true and full import of every part of it; to show the length and breadth, the entire extent of every commandment contained therein, and the height and depth, the inconceivable purity and spirituality of it in all its branches'.[184]

Wesley harmonized Christ's introducing a religion as old as creation and His supplementing of the defect of the law by the concept of

---

[181] S. Law, I. 1-4; III. 11. It is the same law that 'God gave at first, and has preserved through all ages'; S. Mount (5), I. 2.

[182] S. Mount (5), Intro. 1 - I. 4. Wesley contended that before Christ's teaching of the law, the Jews knew 'nothing but outside worship, nothing the form of godliness'.

[183] S. Mount (5), I. 4. The law was 'never so fully explained, nor so thoroughly understood till the great Author of it Himself condescended to give mankind this authentic comment on all the essential branches of it'.

[184] S. Mount (5), I. 3.

dispensations.[185] Collins affirms that the relation between the laws in the two Testaments is not one of contradiction but of development.[186] The superiority of the Christian dispensation relates to the revelation of inner religion, while the old law related to 'a bare outward service'.[187] Christians build their house obeying God's law from their inner heart.[188] Regarding the Scribes and Pharisees as 'sincere' observers of the law under the Jewish dispensation, Wesley contended that Christians are superior to them because of inner observance of God's law:

> The righteousness of a Christian exceeds all this righteousness of a Scribe or Pharisee, by fulfilling the spirit as well as the letter of the law; by inward as well as outward obedience ... The Pharisee 'cleansed the outside of the cup and the platter'; the Christian is clean within. The Pharisee laboured to present God with a good life; the Christian with a holy heart. The one shook off the leaves, perhaps the fruits, of sin; the other 'lays the axe to the root' ... to do no harm, to do good, to attend the ordinances of God (the righteousness of a Pharisee) are all external ... poverty of spirit, mourning, meekness, hunger and thirst after righteousness, the love of our neighbour, and purity of heart (the righteousness of a Christian) are all internal.[189]

Like Luther Wesley described the First Commandment as 'the foundation of the law, and the ground of all obedience'.[190] However, Christ's teaching of the law deals with not only such fundamental sins as pride and unbelief, but also, more inclusively, various degrees and sorts of 'the bondage of sin and Satan';[191] 'omission or commission ... inward or outward sin'; 'any sinful temper, passion, or affection; such as pride, self-will, love of the world, in any kind or degree; such as lust, anger, peevishness; any disposition contrary to the mind which was in Christ'.[192] All of Christ's temper, deeds, and death have profound implications as the law. Christ's fulfilling the law by His own obedience becomes the object of a believers' *imitation*. Deschner states, 'The active obedience, so far as it has a positive role, has the character of a teaching ministry, closely related to the pro-

---

[185] S. Perfection (1), II. 11; see Scott J. Jones, *John Wesley's Conception and Use of Scripture* (Nashville: Kingwood Books, 1995), 53-58.
[186] Collins, *The Scripture Way of Salvation*, 52.
[187] S. Law, Intro. 2; WW 11:472. 'The glory of the whole Mosaic dispensation was chiefly visible and external; whereas the glory of the Christian dispensation is of an invisible and spiritual nature'.
[188] S. Mount (13), II. 1-4.
[189] S. Mount (5), IV. 11.
[190] ENNT Tim 1:9.
[191] S. Wilderness, Intro. 1; II. (I.) 1-10.
[192] S. Sin, II. 2.

phetic office. It reinforces the law's authority in both sanctification and the last judgment'.[193] Christ as the teleological end of imitation remained an unchanged element in Wesley theology before and after the Aldersgate.[194] Obeying Christ's teaching of the law and imitating Him are all essential parts of salvation.

II. Christ as Imputed Righteousness vs. Christ for Inherent Righteousness[195]

Concerning Christ's atonement, different views of Luther and Wesley were contrasted in the debate between Nicolaus Ludwig von Zinzendorf (1700-1760) and Wesley. Wesley accepted Luther's teaching on justification by faith through the Moravians.[196] However, after visiting Herrnhut in the summer of 1738 Wesley suffered from a troubled spirit, being influenced by what he later identified as the Moravian errors of mixing justification and sanctification, and of associating full assurance with justification.[197]

The conflict between Zinzendorf and Wesley in London on 3 September 1741 shows clearly the points of disagreements. Concerning the normal state of believers, Wesley said 'true Christians are not miserable sinners', but Zinzendorf denied; 'the best of men are miserable sinners till death'. Whereas Wesley represented Christian perfection as a believers' own righteousness, contending that 'Christ's own Spirit' works inherent righteousness and believers have the image of God in their own love of God and neighbors, Zinzendorf refuted Wesley's contention by Luther's teaching of believers as simultaneously saints and sinners, approving only of forensic sanctification by imputation of Christ's righteousness: 'I know of no such thing as inherent perfection in this life. This is the error of errors ... Christ is our only perfection. Whoever affirms inherent perfection denies Christ ...

---

[193] Deschner, *Christology*, 153.
[194] Geordan Hammond, 'John Wesley and "Imitating" Christ', *WTJ* 45:1 (2010), 197-212.
[195] By 'inherent righteousness' Wesley meant a believers' own righteousness or holiness following their acceptance by God through faith. See S. Lord, II. 12; WW 8:369; WW 10:272, 274.
[196] Frederick Dreyer, *The Genesis of Methodism* (Bethlehem, PA: Lehigh University Press, 1999); Dreyer, 'Pietist', 72-73. The Moravians' influence on Wesley was so great that Dreyer contends, by the year 1740 when Wesley's second Journal was published, Methodism could be regarded as an English version of the Moravianism; S. Lord, Intro. 4.
[197] Collins, *John Wesley: A Theological Journey*, 99-102.

Christian perfection is entirely imputed, not inherent ... [the full *imago Dei*] is mere legal'.[198] Whereas Wesley related progressive sanctification to various levels of faith, love, or being filled with the Holy Spirit, Zinzendorf denied degrees of faith and of sanctification: 'the event of sanctification and justification is completed in an instant. Thereafter, it neither increases nor decreases'; 'a babe-in-Christ is as pure in heart as any father-in Christ. There is no difference'.[199]

In his Journal for 15 June 1741, Wesley expressed his thought that his real adversary in this dispute was Luther.[200] However, whether Zinzendorf was faithful to Luther's teaching should be examined. Concerning the degrees of faith, Wesley had already known of the *Bußkampf* controversy between two German Pietistic groups who were influenced respectively by Zinzendorf and by August Hermann Francke.[201] Francke, classifying believers into three – children, young men, and fathers – taught degrees of sanctification.[202] For him, in the process of conversion, first comes the *Bußkampf*, or penitential struggle and, then, the *Durchbruch*, breakthrough by saving grace. However, Zinzendorf, dividing people into two classes – the dead and the awakened – rejected any possibility of growth in holiness after awakening. Missing the *Bußkampf* in his conversion experience, he thought that it was not the *Bußkampf* which directs peoples' attention to the wrong things such as the law and guilt, but the doctrine of atonement that should be the point where conversion ought to begin and end. One must start joyful with the knowledge of redemption and only afterwards

---

[198] Outler ed., *Wesley*, 368-371; Peter Vogt, '"No Inherent Perfection in This Life": Count Zinzendorf's Theological Opposition to John Wesley's Concept of Sanctification', *Bulletin of the John Rylands University Library of Manchester* 85:2-3 (Summer-Autumn 2003), 297-307.
[199] Outler ed., *Wesley*, 370-371; Dreyer, 'Pietist', 77-79.
[200] Journals 2:467. 'Here (1 apprehend) is the real spring of the grand error of the Moravians. They follow Luther, for better or worse'; see Journals 3:409. Later, on 19 July 1749, Wesley criticized Luther's 'rough untractable spirit and bitter zeal for opinions, so greatly obstructive of the work of God'.
[201] Karl Zehrer, tr. James A. Dwyer, 'The Relationship Between Pietism in Halle and Early Methodism', *MH* 17:4 (July 1979), 211-224; see J. Steven O'Malley, 'Pietistic Influence on John Wesley: Wesley and Gerhard Tersteegen', *WTJ* 31:2 (Fall, 1996), 127-139; Dale W. Brown, 'The Wesleyan Revival from a Pietist Perspective', *WTJ* 24 (1989), 7-17.
[202] Dreyer, 'Pietist', 76-77.

proceed to contrition, remaining confident in the efficacy of the atonement.²⁰³

In that faith upholds Christ as righteousness, Zinzendorf's view looks similar to Luther's. However, Luther admitted both degrees of inherent righteousness and of faith,²⁰⁴ though he denied the full achievement of inherent righteousness in this life. Conversion without the *Bußkampf* deviated from Luther's own experience that occurred in the *Bußkampf* pattern.²⁰⁵ On the subject of faith Luther would not have agreed with Zinzendorf, but rather at least in part with Wesley who taught degrees of faith; justifying faith can be marked by both doubt and fear, and justification may occur apart from assurance.

However, on the matter of sanctification by imputation, Zinzendorf faithfully followed Luther. For Luther, both justification and sanctification are given through imputation of Christ's righteousness. Since Christ's righteousness cannot be divided, justification and sanctification are perfected by the imputation of the whole.²⁰⁶ Christians being both saints and sinners means that they are totally holy and totally sinful simultaneously; they are holy because of Christ's righteousness, though they remain sinful in their nature.²⁰⁷ Wesley's criticism of Luther on account of the Moravian errors was half right and half wrong. In distinguishing between Luther and Zinzendorf, he should have been more careful.

Wesley's objection against Luther's teaching of imputation might be that Christ's obedience cannot replace a believers' obedience.

---

²⁰³ Dreyer, 'Pietist', 79-81.
²⁰⁴ LW 21:310; LW 30:154-155; LW 33:62; Althaus, *Theology*, 234-242; Kleinig, 'Holiness', 77-78.
²⁰⁵ Dreyer, 'Pietist', 81-84. Luther firstly recognized that he was damned and then discovered that he was saved.
²⁰⁶ LW 32:228. 'They [wrath and grace] are poured out upon the whole ... he who is under wrath is wholly under the whole of wrath, while he who is under grace is wholly under the whole of grace ... He whom God receives in grace, He completely receives ... He is angry at the whole of him with whom He is angry. He does not divide this grace as gifts are divided, nor does He love the head and hate the foot, nor favour the soul and hate the body'.
²⁰⁷ LW 32:228-229. 'It [the gift] works so as to purge away the sin for which a person has already been forgiven ... As far as its nature is concerned, sin in no way differs from itself before grace and after grace; but it is indeed different in the way it is treated ... it is treated as non-existent and as expelled. Despite this, it is truly and by nature sin. Indeed, it is ingratitude and injury to the grace and gift of God to deny that it truly is sin'.

Christ's perfect obedience works only for His qualification for being a vicarious sacrifice, but not for imputation: imputation taught in such a way may result in antinomian negligence toward a believer's own fulfilment of the law. In Wesley's view, while entire sanctification is given instantaneously by God's grace though faith,[208] gradual growth in grace before and after entire sanctification depends on a believers' use of the law.[209] Wesley asserted, '[The mighty power of God] can work a complete deliverance; His grace is sufficient for you. But not unless you are a worker together with Him'.[210] Lindström notes that the former is dependent on the latter to some extent. Even in the instantaneous work of God's grace, believers would not be altogether passive because it requires a total surrender of the believers' heart to God.[211] In addition, when Wesley discussed instantaneous sanctification given by God's grace, he did not relate it to imputation, but to faith. Thus, in various ways Wesley did not diminish the human role in sanctification. Wesley's emphasis on Christ's teaching of the law is logically connected with another emphasis on human responsibility.

Luther explained Christ's fulfilment of the law in terms of His perfect obedience to God's law, denying a fulfilment through representation of its full meaning. Whereas Christ's full exposition of the law relates to human responsibility to obey the law, His perfect obedience emphasizes the characteristic of the grace of imputation. Thus, in Luther's teaching, Christ's perfect obedience is connected with the imputation of His righteousness, which demonstrates the God-centredness of his theology.

Against Wesley's criticism that the doctrine of imputation may cause an antinomian negligence, Luther would reply that only imputation of Christ's righteousness makes possible true fulfilment of the law through voluntary obedience to God's law from the inner heart, doing away with a believers' guilt and causing voluntary love toward God. As mentioned earlier, if Christian righteousness can be completed by believers' own works of the law, it inevitably means that Christians are always accused by the law of hypothetic perfection which is not possible in this life. Consequently, the idea of sanctification by a believers' inherent righteousness results in either hypocri-

---

[208] S. Way (2), III. 3, 14-17. 'We are sanctified ... exactly as we are justified by faith ... Faith is ... the only condition of sanctification, exactly as it is of justification'.
[209] Letters 5:112-13.
[210] S. World, 18.
[211] Lindström, *Sanctification*, 132.

sy or despair.[212] Paradoxically, Christ's being the end of the law and His giving freedom from the law makes possible the true fulfilment of the law. On the basis of imputed righteousness, a true righteousness of believers starts.

By teaching both characters of *simultaneity* that believers are at the same time saints and sinners, and of *commencement* that a believer's inherent righteousness starts but cannot be perfected in this life, Luther guarded against the idea of salvation by human works. Luther's teaching of simultaneity and commencement implies the defectiveness of human righteousness as well as the perfectness of God's grace. Luther solved the problem of lack of real righteousness by reinforcing believers' present faith from the viewpoint of the eschatological hope that their righteousness will be perfected by God's grace, since until the time believers receive the future grace, they are regarded as already perfect from the perspective of the future grace, on the foundation of God's promise:

> We are not yet perfectly righteous. Our being justified perfectly still remains to be seen, and this is what we hope for. Thus our righteousness does not yet exist in fact, but it still exists in hope ... You must hope that you are righteous in the sight of God. That is, your righteousness is not visible, and it is not conscious; but it is hoped for as something to be revealed in due time. Therefore you must not judge on the basis of your consciousness of sin, which terrifies and troubles you, but on the basis of the promise and teaching of faith, by which Christ is promised to you as your perfect and eternal righteousness.[213]

The eschatological hope continually influences believers, leading to a real change in them, though there is no perfection in this life.

In contrast, Wesley's teaching of the important role of the law for sanctification is shown in his teaching of Christ's offices. Christ's priestly work becomes the basis on which His prophetic and kingly offices through the law work, changing the role of God's law from accusation into guidance and indication of a possible goal through the help of the Holy Spirit.[214] Christ's priestly office motivates a believers' obedience to the law through responsive, voluntary, and 'filial love' to the initiative, creative, and sacrificial love of God, dispelling a 'servile fear' of punishment and making the 'evangelical principle' of love by far a more powerful motive for achieving the law than the legal one of fear.[215]

---

[212] LW 26:344-345.
[213] LW 27:20-27; Forde, *Preached*, 214-221.
[214] See Lindström, *Sanctification*, 164-165.
[215] S. Established (1), III. 3-4; ENNT I John 4:18; Deschner, *Christology*, 98.

The kingly office of Christ transforms the law into a 'covered promise' as well.[216] Wesley ascribed inscription of the law and recovery of the image of God in a believers' heart to the kingly office of Christ.[217] Christ reigns over all believers' hearts through the Holy Spirit, empowering them to do what the law commands. The accomplishment of the law commanded through the prophetic works becomes real through the kingly works of Christ.[218]

For Wesley, all three offices of Christ remain very important elements in sanctification, in that believers may commit sins. Christ the Prophet continues to convince believers of the remaining sin in their hearts and lives, to keep them close to Christ the Priest for His blood to cleanse their transgressions, and to make them benefit from the enabling power for achieving the law. The interactions among Christ's three offices continue in the process of sanctification.[219]

III. Christ's Victory over the Law vs. Christ's Victory through the Law

In the midst of the controversy with the Moravians, Wesley criticized Luther because of his negative representation of the law:

> How blasphemously does he speak of good works and of the law of God; constantly coupling the law with sin, death, hell, or the devil; and teaching, that Christ delivers us from them all alike. Whereas, it can no more be proved by Scripture that Christ delivers us from the law of God, than that He delivers us from holiness or from heaven ... who art thou that 'speakest evil of the law, and judgest the law?'

Believing that the error of coupling the law with evil powers originates from misapprehending Paul's statement in Rom. 7:5, 'the motions of sins, which were by the law', Wesley explained that the law arouses sins in the sense of 'searching' or exposing sins that have been working in unrecognized ways, with which Luther would have agreed.[220] However, it cannot mean that 'the law of God is either sin itself, or the cause of sin'. Though sin becoming 'far more odious' is 'accidentally occasioned' by those who are 'carnally minded', God's law remains 'an irreconcilable enemy to sin'.[221]

---

[216] S. Mount (5), II. 2-3.
[217] S. Established (2), I. 6.
[218] S. Law, I. 6; IV. 4.
[219] S. Law, IV. 4.
[220] See LW 1:163-164.
[221] ENNT Rom 7:5; S. Law, Intro. 3; III. 4.

Wesley regarded the law as God's instrument for human salvation. Two different roles of the same law – either accusation or teaching – depend on who becomes the recipient of the law – a sinner or a saint. Wesley limited the violent reaction of sin toward the law only to 'the person of one who was convinced of sin, but not yet delivered from it', denying that it is a normal state of believers.[222] For believers Christ the King transcribes the 'holy, just, and good' nature contained in the law in their heart and life so that the law in its nature works as 'enmity to sin'.[223] Through sanctifying grace, Christ the King makes believers 'more than conquerors over sin'.[224] Since '[Christ] empowers them to do what His law commands',[225] every Christian, even a babe in Christ, is so far perfect, as to overcome sins.[226]

Thus, Christ Who first won His victory over sin by obeying God's law perfectly, continues to win through a believers' obedience to the law, not through believers overcoming the law. If Christ's teaching of 'every jot and title' of the law is written in the heart of believers, Christ can rule as the King, putting all the sins the law convicts a believer of under His feet.[227] This victory over sin is the privilege of the Christian dispensation.[228]

Concerning his negative presentation of the law, Luther illustrated that Paul spoke 'very insultingly about the law' calling it 'weak and beggarly elements' (Gal. 4:9). Though to use such names for the law looks like a blasphemy, 'it is no longer the holy law of God' if it just accuses and produces despair, but does not indicate the promises and grace gospel. Distinguishing between awakened sinners who seek God's grace terrified by the law, and hypocrites who boast of their righteousness against the law, Luther taught that Paul applied the law as 'weak and beggarly elements' only to the latter hypocrites.[229] Calling his acrimonious description of the law 'a lovely depreciation', Luther employed various metaphors to describe the impotence of the law in giving salvation:

---

[222] S. Law, III. 4.
[223] ENNT Rom 7:5; S. Law, Intro. 3; III. 3.
[224] S. Perfection (1), II. 11.
[225] S. Law, IV. 4.
[226] S. Perfection (1), II. 11, 20-21. Wesley related the superiority of the Christian dispensation not only to sanctification but also to justification.
[227] S. Law, III. 10.
[228] S. Perfection (1), II. 8; II. 13.
[229] LW 26:402.

> It [the law] makes men weaker and more beggarly ... as though someone suffering from epilepsy were to catch the plague in addition ... he who falls away from faith and follows the law is like the dog in Aesop ... trying something that he can never achieve ... laying a burden upon someone who is already oppressed to the point of collapse, trying to spend a hundred gold pieces and not having even a pittance, taking clothing away from a naked man, imposing even greater weakness and poverty upon someone ... sick and needy.[230]

Luther justified this negative description by Paul's own phraseology, saying 'if Paul had not done it first, I would not have dared use such a name for the law but would have regarded it as the height of blasphemy'.[231] For Luther, justification and sanctification are not achieved by the law, but by Christ Who overcomes and wins the victory over the law for us. His view of the law was expressed explicitly: 'the Law cannot be fulfilled except in Christ'.[232]

The fact that human salvation becomes possible by the three offices of Christ in justification and sanctification shows that Wesley's Christology is based on Reformation theology. However, in that in any salvation process, the law's relation to Christ's offices is explicit, Wesley's concern against antinomian tendencies is demonstrated. David Rainey observes that Wesley related Christ's active obedience not to Christ's priestly office but to His prophetic office or kingly office to avoid the antinomian tendency.[233] Wesley regarded a laxity of morality and lack of love among Luther's followers after the Reformation as an inevitable consequence of their turning back 'from the holy commandment', meaning that without proper teaching on the law, that is, without a believer's inherent righteousness and with imputation only, mere reformed doctrines and modes of worship cannot change believers' 'hearts and lives ... tempers and practice'.[234]

---

[230] LW 26:402-407; see LW 13: 396.
[231] LW 26:407; LW 26:147.
[232] LW 29:202.
[233] David Rainey, 'John Wesley's Doctrine of Salvation in Relation to His Doctrine of God', (Ph.D. thesis, University of London, 2006), 147-148.
[234] S. Counsels, 10.

Chapter 4
The Holy Spirit and the Law

A. Martin Luther

I. The Person of the Holy Spirit and the Law

Luther constantly represented the Holy Spirit either as the Sovereign Saviour or as a gift of salvation.[1] The crucial position he attributed to the Holy Spirit is shown in his 1520 exposition of the third article of the Apostles' Creed:

> The Holy Spirit is the only true God together with the Father and the Son ... apart from the operation of the Holy Spirit, no one can come to God, nor receive any of the blessings effected through Christ, His life, cross, and death, and whatever else is ascribed to Him ... Through the Holy Spirit, the Father and the Son rouse, call, and draw us; and, through and in Christ, give us life and holiness, and make us spiritually-minded. Thus the Holy Spirit brings us to the Father, for He it is by whom the Father, through Christ and in Christ, does all things, and gives life to all.[2]

Teaching the *Filioque*,[3] Luther taught that the Holy Spirit mediates all activities of God and Christ in creation and in the Church.[4]

---

[1] Lohse, *Theology*, 239; LW 24:298. 'He is the same true and only God, since He is to perform works that God alone performs, such as illumining the hearts inwardly and bringing them to the true knowledge of God; kindling, creating, and strengthening faith in them; and comforting consciences and keeping them undismayed in the face of the terrors of devil and all creatures, etc.'

[2] Martin Luther, 'A Short Exposition of the Decalogue, the Apostles' Creed and the Lord's Prayer', in *Reformation Writings of Martin Luther*, tr. Bertram Lee Wolff (London: Lutterworth Press, 1952), 1:87. Quoted by Gary D. Badcock, *Light of Truth and Fire of Love: A Theology of the Holy Spirit* (Grand Rapids: Wm. B. Eerdmans, 1997), 91; *BC*, 419. 'We could never come to recognize the Father's favour and grace were it not for the Lord Christ, who is a mirror of the Father's heart. Apart from him we see nothing but an angry and terrible Judge. But neither could we know anything of Christ, had it not been revealed by the Holy Spirit'.

[3] LW 1:57-59; LW 2:227; LW 24: 297-298, 365.

Lohse properly states that a formula, 'Through the Holy Spirit Alone', appropriately paraphrases Luther's thought.[5] Especially, commenting on John 16:13, 'Whatever He [the Holy Spirit] hears He will speak', Luther taught that from inner relationship in the Godhead – God the Father is the Speaker, Christ the Son is the Word, and the Spirit is the Listener – the Holy Spirit economically becomes 'Preacher' of God's word for human beings.[6] As the real and active subject of all occurrences in the world and in human hearts, the Holy Spirit reveals the wrath and the grace of God, changes the death or the resurrection of Christ into a believers' experience in faith, and works as the law or the gospel to sinners through all things.[7]

II. The Holy Spirit and Revelation of the law or the gospel

Luther did not disregard the freedom of the Spirit. The Holy Spirit decides when and how He will work, sometimes working after a gap of more than ten year subsequent to the proclamation of God's word, or sometimes not working at all despite the preaching of God's word.[8] The freedom of the hidden God even from His words and any means may be equally applicable to the Spirit. However, as Won Yong Ji states, such an idea has no practical value. Luther emphasized the link between the work of the Spirit and the word far more than the Spirit's freedom.[9] Calling God's word 'the bridge, the path, the way, the ladder ... by which the Spirit might come',[10] Luther asserted, 'He could of course do without the Word, but He does not will so to do'.[11]

Luther's close linkage between the Holy Spirit and God's word was intended to refute the claims of both Catholics and enthusiasts.[12]

---

[4] Lohse, *Theology*, 235. The work of the Holy Spirit, being not limited to the sphere of the church and believers, comprises 'a universal activity' through which He rules and controls every creatures of God; *BC*, 415-420.
[5] Lohse, *Theology*, 237.
[6] LW 24:362-365.
[7] LW 24:111. 'We may truly recognize the Holy Spirit and feel His comfort ... everything ... will cause Christians to fear, be sad, and despair'.
[8] LW 22:302; LW 14:62; WA 31I, 100; WA 39I, 370; WA 38:205; WA 30III, 180. Quoted by Althaus, *Theology*, 39-40.
[9] Won Yong Ji, 'The Work of the Holy Spirit and the Charismatic Movement, from Luther's Perspective', *CJ* 11:6 (Nov. 1985), 206.
[10] LW 40:147; LW 18:401.
[11] LW 33:155.
[12] *BC*, 312-313. 'God gives no one his Spirit or grace except through or with the external Word which comes before. Thus we shall be protected from the enthusiasts ... who boast that they possess the Spirit without and before the Word ... Münzer did

Against the papists who boasted 'the church, the church!' insisting that the Catholic Church is the only Church who, as the apostles' successors, has the Holy Spirit along with the God's word, the Popes, and sacraments, Luther argued that the main office of the Holy Spirit is to preach Christ, therefore, the Reformation Church, which preaches Christ properly, has the true sign of the presence of the Holy Spirit.[13] Though the Church can be regarded as 'the mother that begets and bears every Christian', the authority of the Church is dependent on the work of the Spirit through the word: 'Where Christ is not preached, there is no Holy Spirit to create, call, and gather the Christian church'.[14]

Against the enthusiasts such as Karlstadt and Münzer who, repeating 'Spirit, Spirit, Spirit',[15] alleged to have learned directly from the Holy Spirit 'without an external Word', he stressed that 'God will not deal with us except through His external Word and sacrament'.[16] Teaching both the precedence of the word and the Spirit's working 'with and through it', Luther affirmed, '[the Holy Spirit] ... never goes beyond the word'.[17]

The link between God's word and the Holy Spirit relates to the concept of the letter and the spirit. Luther usually identified the law with the letter in that the law written in letters cannot improve human life, but identified the gospel with 'the spirit' since the Holy Spirit grafts it into believers' hearts as a living word which motivates them to fulfil God's law.[18] What distinguishes the law and the gospel is not only the contents of the word, but also the inspiration of the Holy Spirit. Without the Holy Spirit, even the word which is the obvious gospel inevitably becomes the law from which human beings draw ethical implications, and Christ turns into an object of historical knowledge or an ideal of imitation, since human reason is bound to the natural law.[19] Without the Holy Spirit, the obvious law cannot influence human conscience either, because sinners excuse them-

---

this ... The papacy, too, is nothing but enthusiasm, for the pope boasts that "all laws are in the shrine of his heart"'.
[13] LW 24:124-129, 294-295. 'To testify of Me [Christ] ... is the Holy Spirit's own specific office; by means of it one must discern all other doctrine'; LW 51:291-299.
[14] *BC*, 415-420.
[15] See LW 40:147.
[16] LW 40:195; *BC*, 312.
[17] WA 21, 469. Quoted by Ji, 'The Work of the Holy Spirit and the Charismatic Movement, from Luther's Perspective', 206; LW 24:362-365.
[18] LW 39:182-183; LW 27:188; LW 11:161; Prenter, *Spiritus*, 58-59.
[19] Prenter, *Spiritus*, 114-122; *BC*, 521-526.

selves, perverted by pride and self-justification. Only the Holy Spirit, being 'intent on' showing the spiritual nature of the law[20] changes the law a living word that makes sinners realize their depravity and inability to obey God.[21]

The Holy Spirit, accompanying the external word, changes it into the internal word in the human heart. By Him, as Gerhard Ebeling contends, the 'alien, remote, and external' word changes into 'something alive in the heart, which takes possession of man'.[22] While the external word is the resource which the Holy Spirit uses, 'the real teacher' of the word is the Holy Spirit.[23] The Holy Spirit makes the law a thunderbolt or a hammer,[24] and the gospel, the open gate to paradise.[25]

Luther's view of the Holy Spirit as the worker of mortification by the law and vivification by the gospel had a distinctive character compared to the popular Catholic view. In his early work *Lectures on Romans* (1515-1516), distinguishing 'the law of the Spirit' in believers' hearts from the natural law in all human hearts, Luther explained the former in terms of 'God's love' which 'has been poured into our hearts through the Holy Spirit'.[26] Prenter notes that though the young Luther used an Augustinian and scholastic expression of the infusion of love,[27] his view was decisively different from the neoplatonic teaching that we can love God above all things because we

---

[20] LW 26:315.
[21] LW 25:188; LW 35:365-368.
[22] Ebeling, *Luther: An Introduction to his Thought*, 98.
[23] WA 17II, 459 f. Cited from Althaus, *Theology*, 37.
[24] BC, 303-310; LW 34:171-174; LW 26:315.
[25] See LW 34:337.
[26] LW 25:67, 185-187.
[27] W. A., LVI, 203, 8. 'The sentence "let the law be written in their heart" says the same thing as "Love is infused into the heart through the Holy Spirit". It is in the same sense both the law of Christ and the fulfillment of the law of Moses'. Quoted by Prenter, *Spiritus*, 3.

can love His creature.[28] Luther asserted that human sinful love of the creature and themselves stands as an antithesis to our love of God:[29]

> To love is to hate oneself, to condemn oneself, and to wish the worst, in accord with the statement of Christ: 'He who hates his life in this world will keep it for eternal life' ... He who loves himself in this way truly loves himself ... not in himself but in God, that is, in accord with the will of God, who hates, damns, and wills evil to all sinners, that is, to all of us. For what is good for us is hidden ... so deeply that it is hidden under its opposite. Thus our life is hidden under death, love for ourselves under hate for ourselves, glory under ignominy, salvation under damnation, our kingship under exile, heaven under hell, wisdom under foolishness, righteousness under sin, power under weakness.[30]

The infused love by the Holy Spirit makes believers recognize themselves as depraved sinners and deny themselves along with their sinful judgment of good and evil. This love already has in itself the implication that believers, on the foundation of the Spirit's revelation, apply the judgment of the law to themselves. The concept of the infused love by the Holy Spirit has the essence of the Reformation dialectic between the law that judges a believers' sinful love and the gospel that recovers their love to God.[31] Even in his earlier work, *First Lectures on the Psalms* (1513-1515), commenting on Psalm 1:2, Luther contended that while believers keep God's law 'with a cheerful and free will ... by the bonds of love', this love cannot come 'out of us apart from the Spirit of God'.[32] Prenter states that the infused love through which the Spirit produces a 'spontaneous and happy will' to obey God's law 'does not take place at the initiative of

---

[28] Prenter, *Spiritus*, 3-27; see LW 2:112-124. 'Of the same sort is the statement of Scotus that as a result of his natural endowments man is able to love God above all things ... He reasons thus: A man loves a girl, who is a creature. But he loves her so desperately that he risks himself and his life for her. A merchant loves riches, and indeed so passionately that he undergoes a thousand perils provided he can make some profit. Therefore if there is such love for creatures, who rank far beneath God, how much more will man love God, who is the highest good? Hence God can be loved on the basis of the natural endowments alone ... such a great theologian does not know what it means to love God'.
[29] LW 31:9-15; LW 2:124. 'Our nature is so corrupt that it no longer ... cannot love God ... it loves an idol and the dream of its heart ... it is so completely bound up in its love for the creatures that even after it has learned to know God from the Word, it still disregards Him and despises His Word'.
[30] LW 25:382.
[31] See WA 56, 366, 14; Prenter, *Spiritus*, 6-8.
[32] LW 10:13-15.

man ... Such a will is always forced',[33] underlying the theocentric character of Luther's Pneumatology.

Luther's theology of the cross is firmly based on his view of the Holy Spirit. Differently from the mystics who represented the historical Jesus as the ideal of imitation, Luther contended that the conformity to Christ cannot be achieved by imitation as human-initiated works, but by a believers' identification of Christ's death and resurrection with their own punishment and new life in faith. Further, Luther taught that not only faith but also fruits of faith (or fruits of the Spirit) 'certainly testify that the Holy Spirit is present' because 'such things do not come into being in the heart by human powers; nor ... by any exercises or efforts'.[34] Refuting the mystics' contention that imitation is preparation for receiving the Holy Spirit, Luther explained it as 'the direct result of the Holy Spirit's activity'.[35]

By ascribing both faith and the fruits of faith to the Spirit, Luther contradicted the imitation piety of the scholasticism in which human beings become an active subject and Christ remains the object of human striving. He recovered the Holy Spirit to the position of the active 'subject of the self-condemnatory act' and of the believers' voluntary obedience to God. For Luther, the Holy Spirit is a living, redemptive reality that first kills sinners as the law and next saves believers as the gospel.[36]

III. The Holy Spirit and Sanctification

Luther titled his exposition on the third article of the Apostles' Creed in *the Large Catechism* (1530) 'Sanctification' contending that it portrays the nature and the office of the Holy Spirit.[37] For Luther, the word holiness pertains solely to God.[38] If a believer can be called holy, it is only 'on the basis of what He effects'.[39] Since the holiness of God and His activating of holiness through the Holy Spirit become

---

[33] Prenter, *Spiritus*, 8.
[34] LW 26:374-380.
[35] Arnold E. Carlson, 'Luther and the Doctrine of the Holy Spirit', *LQ* 11 (May, 1959), 137-142; Prenter, *Spiritus*, 10-11, 28.
[36] Prenter, *Spiritus*, 3-27, 49-53, 60-64.
[37] *BC*, 415; LW 30:6. 'Nothing is holy but the holiness that God works in us'; Kleinig, 'Holiness', 76-77.
[38] LW 16:70. 'All holiness in the whole earth must be ascribed to God alone'; LW 12:325. 'It is a fictitious expression to speak of a "holy man", just as it is a fictitious expression to speak of God's falling into sin; for by the nature of things, this cannot be'.
[39] LW 16:10; Forde, *Preached*, 226.

the centre of the subject of sanctification, Luther affirmed that 'the other things we have, such as gifts, intellect, good habits, our best endeavours' should be removed from the discussion of sanctification.[40]

Luther based sanctification above all on the Spirit's repeated affirmation of the 'forgiveness of sins'.[41] The sanctifying work by the Spirit is primarily continuous assimilation of the fact of justification into believers' perceptions.[42] Also, as John W. Kleinig observes, Luther, being loose in the terminology of sanctification, sometimes identified sanctification with the beginning of a believer's inherent righteousness.[43] The Holy Spirit subdues desires of the flesh in them so that 'the Spirit rules and the flesh is subordinate',[44] then, believers can 'repress' their corrupt flesh, inclination toward sin, and unholy tempers.[45] Positively speaking, the Spirit 'forms the true shape of the Christian mind' or 'creates new attitudes' in them by producing faith in God's fatherly love and, thereof, their love toward other people.[46]

If viewed from the human side, Luther was emphatic that 'Christian holiness' or 'Christian righteousness' is passive. Whereas he regarded the righteousness of the law as 'active' righteousness that 'can be achieved by us', he thought of 'faith, grace, the forgiveness of sins or Christian righteousness' as passive righteousness for which human beings 'work nothing' but 'only receive and permit someone else to work in us, namely, God'.[47] Active holiness achieved by believers is based on passive holiness.[48] Even 'the righteousness of the law or of the Decalogue' cannot be totally an active one in that its fulfilment depends on passive righteousness acquired by faith:

> Christian holiness is not active but passive. Therefore let no one call himself holy on the basis of his way of life or of his works – fasting, prayer, flagellation, almsgiving, or the consolation of the sad and afflicted ... Such works, of course, are holy, and God strictly demands them of us; but they do

---

[40] LW 16:70.
[41] *BC*, 417-418; LW 26:293.
[42] *BC*, 415-420; Forde, *Preached*, 226.
[43] Kleinig, 'Holiness', 77-78.
[44] LW 27:70.
[45] LW 27:96-97; LW 12:327-331.
[46] LW 26:430; LW 27:98. 'He changes men who are vainglorious, wrathful, and envious into men who are humble, gentle, and loving. Such men seek not their own glory but God's. They do not provoke and envy one another; they yield to one another and outdo one another in showing honour'.
[47] LW 26:4-6.
[48] LW 26:6. Passive holiness meant for Luther 'the righteousness of Christ and of the Holy Spirit, which we do not perform but receive, which we do not have but accept'.

not make us holy. You and I are holy; the church, the city, and the people are holy – not on the basis of their own holiness but on the basis of a holiness not their own, not by an active holiness, but by a passive holiness. They are holy because they possess something that is divine and holy, namely, the calling of the ministry, the Gospel, Baptism, etc., on the basis of which they are holy.[49]

To synthesize Luther's view of sanctification and his Pneumatology, the Holy Spirit makes believers holy through forgiveness and renewal, or through passive and active holiness; the latter is dependent on the former. Luther connected these two ways of sanctification by the Spirit to the abolition of the law for believers. The law is abolished in two ways: 'by works and by the forgiveness of sins'. 'By the forgiveness of sins', Luther taught, the law is abolished because it no longer has 'the right to accuse' believers even though they cannot perform what the law requires. By 'works' Luther meant that the law is abolished in the sense that it is no longer needed to require believers to do something, because believers do 'more than the law requires' producing fruits of the Holy Spirit 'spontaneously, without any legal constraint'. By the Spirit believers become those who live as though they 'had need of no law to admonish, urge, and constrain'.[50]

Luther's teaching of the Spirit's abolition of the law shows his Pneumatological transition that moves the role of leading a holy life from the so-called 'third use of the law' to the Holy Spirit. By ascribing a believers' active righteousness to the Holy Spirit Luther could oppose righteousness by human works. By representing 'the law of Christ' as 'the law of mutual love', Luther did not mean that those who love can attain enough righteousness to meet the requirement of God's law. On the contrary, Christ's commandment of love reflects the reality that 'there are faults in every station of society and in all men'. In this state, to love each other implies 'to bear and overlook ... faults and sins, which we commit in such great numbers every day'.[51] Further, though love is 'the fulfilling of the law', believers cannot love perfectly because of their flesh and sin that cling to them, which only the Holy Spirit suppresses.[52] What is needed for believers to live a

---

[49] LW 26:4, 25; see Kleinig, 'Holiness', 78-79.
[50] LW 27:93-96.
[51] LW 27:113-114.
[52] LW 27:63-70. 'We should keep the law and be justified by keeping it; but sin gets in the way ... from this it does not follow: "this is written, and therefore it is done; the law commands love, and therefore we love" ... When he [Paul] commands them to walk by the Spirit, he clearly denies that works justify ... you are not justified by love'.

holy life is not to keep the law but to 'follow the Spirit'. Therefore, sanctification for Luther is sanctification by the Holy Spirit or by faith, not by the law. Whereas Luther employed the term 'the law' negatively, teaching that even believers cannot keep the law, he described walking by the Spirit positively, explaining that believers who follow the Spirit fulfil the requirements of the law, which shows that Luther replaced the law by faith and the Holy Spirit.[53]

IV. The Holy Spirit and Experience

In *Table Talk*, Luther once mentioned the importance of experience in Christian faith: 'Experience alone makes the theologian'.[54] In his *Preface to the Complete Edition of Luther's Latin Writings* (1545) he described his own 'Tower Experience' through which he confessed he came to have a new understanding of the gospel.[55] Won Yong Ji observes that by experience Luther meant 'experience which is put in God's hand, and experience expressed through the Word of God'.[56] What are the crucial elements of the Christian experience to which Luther attached a great importance?

Christian experience by the Holy Spirit through the word is twofold. Firstly, believers experience a severe spiritual trial ('*Anfechtung*') by the Spirit's coming as the law. This spiritual trial is not a psychologically abnormal state or a mental disease, but a common condition of sinners in whom the Holy Spirit works.[57] Prenter states that by the concept of spiritual trial, Luther modified the mystic concept of resignation to hell. Whereas mystic resignation to hell was an imaginary event useful for mortification and preparation for the coming of the Holy Spirit, to Luther *Anfechtung* related not to an imaginary but to the real judgment of the hell that torments sinners' conscience, and also *Anfechtung* meant that the Holy Spirit is already present. The Spirit does not wait until sinners become qualified for receiving the Spirit by sufficient mortification, but initiates to open sinners' eyes to see and experience the wrath of God and the torment

---

[53] Luther identified faith with receiving the Holy Spirit, grouping faith and the Holy Spirit together when his discussion was focused on a believers' active holiness. LW 26:170-172, 202-216, 253-268, 26:374-380; LW 27:20-22, 86.
[54] LW 54:7.
[55] LW 34:336-337; see LW 12:313; LW 22:145-146.
[56] Ji, 'The Work of the Holy Spirit and the Charismatic Movement, from Luther's Perspective', 208-209.
[57] WA 9, 508, 11; Prenter, *Spiritus*, 14.

of the hell in their conscience; *Anfechtung* is not an active, human-initiated work, but a state of passive suffering of God's work.[58]

Secondly, to those who are in the torture of the hell in their conscience, the Holy Spirit is experienced as Comforter. In his exposition on John 14:16-17, 15:26, and 16:13, Luther frequently referred to the Holy Spirit as Comforter and Spirit of truth. The roles as Comforter and as Spirit of truth are interactive. To comfort believers who inevitably become feeble and weak by the terror of God, because of their sins, the Spirit reminds and re-establishes the truth of the gospel continuously, counteracting against all attacks and accusations of the law by the world, the Devil, and a believers' own conscience.[59]

The Holy Spirit not only moans and prays for believers in spiritual trial, but also supports them to endure all their sufferings until God begins His proper work. Sinners' experience of the Spirit as Comforter becomes the source of their love to God.[60] As a result of the works of the Holy Spirit, Luther contended, those who really come to love God 'would not desire even to be saved nor would he refuse to be damned', but 'willingly and happily submit to damnation for the sake of God' as Christ did. Both resignation to hell and conformity to Christ cannot be human works of preparing for receiving the Holy Spirit, but the results of the Spirit's grace.[61] Viewing Christian experience of the Holy Spirit by way of *Anfechtung* and comfort is a Pneumatological interpretation of the dominating elements of Luther's theology of the law and the gospel along with the dialectic between the alien and the proper work of God, and between the cross and resurrection of Christ.

---

[58] Prenter, *Spiritus*, 15-19; Carlson, 'Luther and the Doctrine of the Holy Spirit', 138-140.
[59] LW 24:110-117, 290-298, 357-365; *BC*, 415-420. 'Forgiveness is needed constantly, for although God's grace has been won by Christ ... we are never without sin ... The Holy Spirit must continue to work in us through the Word, daily granting forgiveness'.
[60] LW 25:74-78, 364-370; Prenter, *Spiritus*, 15-19.
[61] LW 25:381-382; see LW 33:62; Prenter, *Spiritus*, 11-12.

B. John Wesley

I. The Person of the Holy Spirit and the Law

Concerning the Person of the Holy Spirit within the Trinity, Wesley, accepting the *Filioque* clause following the Western orthodox and the Church of England,[62] ascribed all attributes and works of God the Father and the Son to the Holy Spirit.[63] As the presence of God the Father and the Son, the Spirit works in both orders of creation and redemption.[64]

Wesley's emphasis on the role of the law is expressed in his exposition of the works of the Holy Spirit. The Spirit not only created humanity in the image of God,[65] but also, after the fall, restores reason and moral or religious senses in every human being through prevenient grace.[66] On the basis of His universal works in creation, the Holy Spirit furthers His salvific works; opening spiritual senses in human hearts, witnessing God's fatherly love to sinners, and renewing believers in God's image. According to Outler, being influenced by the Eastern Orthodox emphasis on dynamic interaction between divine and human will, in which the Spirit leads but does not coerce human will, Wesley taught that the works of the Holy Spirit are compatible with human freedom.[67] In Wesley's Pneumatology, Maddox notes, the important role of the law presupposed in human freedom 'is not to weaken God's power but to determine its character'.[68] Wesley often said that God works 'strongly and sweetly'.[69] The Holy Spirit works 'powerfully, but not irresistibly' through 'empowerment, rather than ... overpowerment'.[70] The Spirit uses the law as an integral part of His salvific works; as a crucial element in both the Spirit's

---

[62] ENNT John 15:26; WW 7:514; ENNT Rom 8:10; Starkey, *Spirit*, 24-38; Collins, *Theology*, 144.
[63] S. Unity, 21; see Cunningham, 'Perceptible', 89-93.
[64] Starkey, *Spirit*, 39-62.
[65] See S. Unity, 21.
[66] WW 14:301; ENNT Acts 4:19. Wesley took Socrates as an example of the Spirit's universal inspiration; see Starkey, *Spirit*, 40.
[67] Outler, *Wesley*, 9-15; BE 1:74-76. Outler contends that Wesley's consistent distinction between God's irresistible sovereignty in creation and the resistibility of the Spirit's works after creation found its source in the Eastern Church's notion of a synergism between God and human beings.
[68] Maddox, *Responsible*, 55.
[69] ENNT Rom 8:28; S. Assize, II. 10; S. Signs, II. 9; S. Omnipresence, II. 1; Letters 6:345.
[70] Maddox, *Responsible*, 55.

preparatory works by prevenient grace and His redemptive works.⁷¹ Our recognition of and obedience to the requirements of the law functions as accepting, sustaining, and advancing deeper works of the Spirit. Wesley's teaching on the Spirit as the presence of God the Father and the Son and His interaction with human beings through the law, being consistent with his axial theme of holy love and free/co-operative grace, sheds light on Wesley's theology of the law.

II. Inspiration of the Holy Spirit and the Law

Wesley believed that God's prevenient grace has the potential to lead human beings to salvation on the condition that 'man did not hinder'.⁷² However, it has a limitation in enabling salvation of sinners since it is hindered by the dullness of human reason and stubbornness of human conscience.⁷³ The consequences are: the spiritual senses in a sinner are closed, 'having no inlets for the knowledge of spiritual things', a sinner becomes 'a stranger to the law of God' and remains 'a willing servant of sin'.⁷⁴

Wesley defined 'inspiration' in a broad way as the 'inward assistance of the Holy Ghost which "helps our infirmities, enlightens our understanding, rectifies our will, comforts, purifies, and sanctifies us"'.⁷⁵ While the Holy Spirit 'reveals, testifies, and defends the truth'⁷⁶ to lead sinners to salvation, what He employs to cure defective senses which cannot 'reach beyond the bounds of this visible world'⁷⁷ is faith that perceives the Spirit's inspiration concerning in-

---

[71] S. Working, II. 1, III. 4; ENNT John 16:8, Rom. 2:14; WW 10:229-230; see Lindström, *Sanctification*, 47; Starkey, *Spirit*, 41, 130. Starkey notes that the law relates to a continuity in the Spirit's works in both orders of creation and redemption; the Spirit is given to all human beings in a 'preliminary' way, and to believers in 'fulfillment'.

[72] S. Working, II. 1. Prevenient grace includes 'the first wish to please God, the first dawn of light concerning his will, and the first slight transient conviction of having sinned against him. All these imply some tendency toward life; some degree of salvation; the beginning of a deliverance from a blind, unfeeling heart, quite insensible of God and the things of God'; ENNT John 1:9. 'This light, if man did not hinder, would shine more and more to the perfect day.'

[73] Collins, *Theology*, 122-123; WW 9:455 'The natural man is unholy, and loves to be so; and therefore "resists the Holy Ghost"'; S. Adoption, II. 1; S. Reason, I. 1 – II. 10; see Charles Wesley's S. Awake, I. 3.

[74] S. Adoption, I. 1-7; S. Working, III. 4.

[75] Letters 4:39.

[76] ENNT Luke 24:45, John 14:17.

[77] S. Discoveries, 3.

visible heavenly truths.[78] Faith defined in a comprehensive way as 'a divine evidence and conviction of things not seen ... particularly ... of God, and of the things of God'[79] can be distinguished into two: faith of a servant 'who feareth God, and worketh righteousness', and faith of a child of God who has the witness of the Spirit concerning their being a child of God.[80] Wesley related both to the Spirit's activity: faith of a servant to the Spirit's illumination of the law; and faith of a child of God to His witness of God's salvific love.

Faith of a servant is worked by the Holy Spirit's 'convincing grace' by which the Spirit convinces sinners of their sins.[81] This grace is no other than the Spirit's illumination of 'the inward, spiritual meaning of the law of God'.[82] To make sinners convinced of their sin, the Holy Spirit can work in various ways: 'without any means at all, or by whatever means it pleaseth Him': 'by some awful providence, or ... by an immediate stroke of His convincing Spirit'; by 'hearing, reading, meditating, praying, and partaking of the Lord's supper'; and even through the message of the gospel that 'God was in Christ, reconciling the world unto Himself'.[83] The sovereign Holy Spirit has freedom to decide whether to work mediately by the law or immediately without it.[84] However, Wesley did not deny the peculiar role of the law. In teaching God's will, while the Holy Spirit can be understood as the teacher, the law can be compared to the textbook with which Christians can 'examine all, real or supposed, revelations'.[85] For convincing the world of sin, the law is 'the ordinary method of the Spirit of God'.[86] Through it the Holy Spirit 'pierces through all the folds of a deceitful heart ... flashes conviction on every side'.[87]

In the revelation of the law, the respective roles of each Person in the Trinity are distinguished: God the Father is the origin of the law; Christ the Son taught the law by preaching and by His own example;

---

[78] Cunningham, 'Perceptible', 101-140; Letters 5:209. Faith is 'spiritual sight.'
[79] S. Faith (1), Intro 1.
[80] S. Faith (1), I. 11-13.
[81] S. Working, II. 1. Convincing grace brings to sinners 'a larger measure of self-knowledge, and a farther deliverance from the heart of stone'.
[82] S. Adoption, II. 1-2.
[83] S. Law, IV. 1; S. Means, V. 1; S. Adoption, II. 1.
[84] Starkey, *Spirit*, 127. Starkey points out, 'There is no necessary relationship between the Spirit and the means divinely appointed for his use, which would place the Spirit at the disposal of men'.
[85] See Letters 2:117; S. Mount (5), II. 4. Wesley explained the Spirit as guide, and Scripture as rule of all truth.
[86] S. Law, IV. 1.
[87] S. Law, IV. 1; S. Adoption, II. 1-10; S. Way (1), II. 1-7.

the Holy Spirit changes the law into an inward voice in human hearts.[88] However, in the Spirit's existence and works, the Father and the Son are present. What makes the law the Spirit's means of convincing grace is that the Holy Spirit is no other than the presence of God who is the origin of the law,[89] and the 'inward manifestation of [Christ] Himself' who is the teacher of the law;[90] in the law 'applied with the demonstration of his [God's] Spirit', sinners are confronted with God Himself with His holy nature, and feel 'a lively sense of the wrath of God'.[91]

III. The Witness of the Holy Spirit and the Law

To those who properly react to the law's accusation and ask for God's favour, the Holy Spirit gives the faith of a child of God by showing the 'love of God, in the face of Jesus Christ',[92] which Wesley explained as the witness of the Holy Spirit. The direct witness of God, that is, the 'inward impression on the soul' of God's love reveals to believers not only the gospel[93] but also the essence of God's law. Commenting on Heb. 8:12, Wesley said, 'For I will justify them, which is the root of all true knowledge of God. This, therefore, is God's method. First, a sinner is pardoned: then he knows God, as gracious and merciful then God's laws are written on his heart: he is God's, and God is his'.[94] Wesley identified the event of believers experiencing God's pardoning love with God's law being written on a believer's heart. In God's love through the sacrifice of His Son, believers recognize that God is 'gracious and merciful'. Without encountering this love first, the nature of God's law – holy love – remains hidden. To know God by experiencing His love in Christ is the prime meaning of the law being inscribed on believers. In that sense, the Holy Spirit witnesses to the holy love of God as the origin of the law itself. Witnessing to God's love, the Holy Spirit also reveals that His commandments have sprung from His love. The witness of the Spirit to

---

[88] See ENNT John 9:5.
[89] S. Adoption, II. 1-2.
[90] For the Holy Spirit as the presence of Christ, see Cunningham, 'Perceptible', 89-93; S. Coming, II. 7; ENNT Jn 9:5, Eph 4:21.
[91] S. Adoption, II. 1-6.
[92] S. Adoption, II. 10, III. 1-3.
[93] S. Witness (1), I. 7. 'The testimony of the Spirit is an inward impression on the soul, whereby the Spirit of God directly witnesses to my spirit, that I am a child of God; that Jesus Christ hath loved me, and given Himself for me; and that all my sins are blotted out, and I, even I, am reconciled to God'.
[94] ENNT Heb 8:12.

God's love opens believers' eyes: to the true spirit of the law; to the motive that moved God to give them the law; and to the way they can respond to God's love, that is, to obey His law.

To write the law in the heart of believers does not mean that there is a different sort of law than Christ's teaching of the law, but that there exists a radical change in the believer's heart. Before justification and regeneration, the law, being alien to sinful nature, could not be assimilated into a nonbeliever's heart. There was enmity and hostility between the law and sinners: the law condemns sinners; sinners abhor the law. However, to those who have experienced God's love through Christ, the law is accepted, favoured, and appreciated as the expression of the same holy love of God.

In this change, the Holy Spirit works neither as an impersonal power nor as a divinely-originated product which overrides human freedom, but as the personal Presence of God the Father and the Son.[95] The Holy Spirit produces the believers' love toward God by witnessing to His initiating, sacrificing, and pardoning love. In the process of producing this loving relationship, the witness of the Spirit has, in Starkey's expression, 'the persuasive nature' with which He motivates a believers' volition, enlightening their rational and emotional faculties.[96]

IV. Empowerment through the Holy Spirit and the Law

Wesley represented the fulfilment of the law through the empowerment of the Holy Spirit as the end of salvation, in which believers are renewed in the image of God and the whole creation is recovered to the original pure order of creation.[97] Empowerment through the Holy Spirit is very important in Wesley's concept of the grace of God: 'The Grace of God ... means that power of God the Holy Ghost which worketh in us both to will and to do of His good pleasure ... we can perform, through God, what to man was impossible. Now we can order our conversation aright. We can do all things in the light and power'.[98] Maddox points out that, between aspects of God's grace as pardoning of sins and as empowerment for fulfilling the law,[99] the

---

[95] Maddox, *Responsible*, 120.
[96] Starkey, *Spirit*, 134.
[97] S. Scriptural; see Hoo-Jung Lee, 'The Doctrine of New Creation in the Theology of John Wesley', (Ph.D. thesis, Emory University, 1991), chapter 2-3.
[98] S. Witness (3),15.
[99] See S. Means, II. 6.

aspect of empowerment was more definitive for Wesley.[100] Joseph Cunningham in his doctoral thesis (2010) demonstrates that the Holy Spirit, grace, and power are very closely conjoined in Wesley's Pneumatology.[101] Hoo-Jung Lee contends, 'Wesley centred his spirituality and theology in the transforming work of the Holy Spirit'.[102]

Human inability to keep God's law was caused by their own fall, not by the law which is beyond human capacity. Nevertheless, God 'could not mock his creatures, by requiring of them what He saw it was impossible for them to perform',[103] but He 'hath engaged to give whatsoever He commands'.[104] The grace of God works as 'the power of His Holy Spirit, which alone worketh in us all that is acceptable in His sight',[105] 'enabling us to believe and love and serve God'.[106] Wesley's concept of the law as a covered promise is firmly based on the Spirit's empowering grace. Wesley identified the fruits of the Holy Spirit with fulfilment of the law in believers' hearts as an accomplishment of the promise: 'I will put my laws in their minds ... and write them on their hearts'.[107] Then, the fruits of the Spirit, being not merely emotions but also holy tempers, dispositions, or affections, produce all that the law requires of believers: holy thoughts, words, and lives.[108] As long as the holy tempers are truly fruits of the Spirit's empowering Presence, not inherent human possessions, they are dependent on God's free grace:

> 'All merit is in the Son of God, in what He has done and suffered for us, so all power is in the Spirit of God. And therefore every man, in order to believe unto salvation, must receive the Holy Ghost. This is essentially necessary to

---

[100] Maddox, *Responsible*, 120, especially see endnote no. 5.
[101] Cunningham, 'Perceptible', 85-89.
[102] Hoo-Jung Lee, 'Experiencing the Spirit in Wesley and Macarius', in *Rethinking Wesley's Theology for Contemporary Methodism* (Nashville: Abingdon Press, 1998), 200; see Lee, 'The Doctrine of New Creation in the Theology of John Wesley', 154-209.
[103] WW 1:128; S. Perfection (2), II. 5.
[104] S. Mount (5), II. 3.
[105] S. Steward, I. 8.
[106] *Instructions for Children*, 10. Quoted by Maddox, *Responsible*, 120.
[107] ENNT Heb 8:10.
[108] S. Fruits, I. 6. 'These are they who indeed "walk after the Spirit". Being filled with faith and with the Holy Ghost, they possess in their hearts, and show forth in their lives, in the whole course of their words and actions, the genuine fruits of the Spirit of God, namely, "love, joy, peace, long-suffering, gentleness, goodness, fidelity, meekness, temperance", and whatsoever else is lovely or praiseworthy. "They adorn in all things the gospel of God our Saviour"; and give full proof to all mankind, that they are indeed actuated by the same Spirit "which raised up Jesus from the dead"'; Maddox, *Responsible*, 132.

every Christian, not in order to his working miracles, but in order to faith, peace, joy, and love - the ordinary fruits of the Spirit ... All true faith, and the whole work of salvation, every good thought, word, and work, is altogether by the operation of the Spirit of God'.[109]

However, representing Christian life as reciprocal breathing between the Spirit and the believer,[110] Wesley gave emphasis to 'the absolute necessity' of believers' re-action toward the Spirit's grace by continual fulfilment of God's law, saying that 'He will not continue to breathe into our soul unless our soul breathes toward Him again'.[111] In believers' responsibility toward the Spirit's grace through obedience to God's law, the Holy Spirit with His power to conquer sin, the world, and the devil is not 'given all at once, as if they had a stock laid up for many years; but from moment to moment'.[112]

C. Observations and Analysis

I. Preacher of the Word of God vs. Presence of the Nature of God

In Luther's Pneumatology, whereas the Spirit is represented as Sovereign Saviour or as the gift of salvation, human beings are regarded as passive recipients; either being inevitably led by the Spirit to obey God's law or being aroused to accept Christ as Saviour. The reality of Christ's death and resurrection as believers' own mortification and vivification is grasped only through the Spirit's revealing activity. Either *Anfechtung* or comfort comes from outside, not by believers' readiness or yearning but by the Spirit's presence.

The theocentricity of Luther's Pneumatology relates also to the way the Spirit sanctifies believers. Luther stressed that the Holy Spirit uses not only the external word but especially external preaching as important methods of saving sinners. Roland Bainton says, 'The Reformation gave centrality to the sermon ... Luther held that

---

[109] WW 8:49; Maddox, *Responsible*, 132;
[110] S. Privilege, III. 2. 'The life of God in the soul of a believer is ... the continual inspiration of God's Holy Spirit; God's breathing into the soul, and the soul's breathing back what it first receives from God ... an unceasing presence of God, the loving, pardoning God, manifested to the heart, and perceived by faith; and an unceasing return of love, praise, and prayer, offering up all the thoughts of our hearts, all the words of our tongues, all the works of our hands, all our body, soul, and spirit, to be a holy sacrifice, acceptable unto God in Christ Jesus'.
[111] S. Privilege, III. 3.
[112] S. Repentance, 17.

salvation is through the Word ... but the Word is sterile unless it is spoken'.[113] For Luther, whereas the study of the written word may be regarded as human work that is bound to the natural law, preaching highlights the aspect of the otherness of God's word that is given from the outside. The preached word conveys new reality of either the law or the gospel from the outside.[114]

The Scriptural text does not merely inform the objects of Christian experience, but affects them:[115] 'God's works are His words; He speaks and it is done: because the speaking and the doing of God are the same'.[116] J. Mark Beach explains how salvation is given to believers through preaching:

> The work of the cross does not ... impart the grace accomplished there ... Christ distributes and imparts this accomplished work 'through the Word' – that is, through the preaching of the gospel. 'He has won it once for all on the cross. But the distribution takes place continuously, before and after, from the beginning to the end of the world. For inasmuch as He had determined once to achieve it, it made no difference to Him whether He distributed it before or after, through His Word ...'[117] ... for Luther, the preaching and teaching of the Word is a key element in the divine work of redemption.[118]

When Christ's cross is preached, the Holy Spirit first condemns sinners, working as the law. Through the preaching of Christ's resurrection the Holy Spirit makes believers resurrected, working as the gospel.[119] Not only the effects of preaching but also the activity of preaching itself is the Spirit's work through His Church.[120] The Holy Spirit not only effects real things through what He preaches, but also gives listeners faith that believes the achievement by the preaching as reality.[121] Thus, the Holy Spirit justifies, sanctifies, and gives faith through external preaching and inward illumination. The Spirit works all in all for justification and sanctification.

According to Gary D. Badcock, late medieval theology, being influenced by the nominalists' emphasis on the individual, turned its attention to 'the effects of grace' in the moral life of the justified, ne-

---

[113] Bainton, *Here I Stand*, 348.
[114] Prenter, *Spiritus*, 101-130.
[115] Forde, *Preached*, 60-68; WA 3.152.7.
[116] WA 3, 152, 7. Quoted by Forde, *Preached*, 64.
[117] LW 40:214.
[118] J. Mark Beach, 'The Real Presence of Christ in the Preaching of the Gospel: Luther and Calvin on the Nature of Preaching', *Mid-America Journal of Theology* 10 (1999), 78-83.
[119] Prenter, *Spiritus*, 101-130.
[120] Beach, 'The Real Presence of Christ in the Preaching of the Gospel', 83-87.
[121] Prenter, *Spiritus*, 56-57, 118.

glecting the fact that justifying grace is just free grace. Criticizing this tendency as Pelagian, Luther endeavoured to move the main attention of theology away from the believer to the grace of God, putting the matter of the effects of grace in a secondary place. Badcock contends, this resulted in a profound change in Luther's view of the work of the Holy Spirit in Christian life, that is, an inevitable 'displacement of the Spirit from the centre of the scheme of salvation'. Consequently, 'rather than being the agent of renewal by which we are made righteous, the Spirit becomes the means by which we come to Christ, who alone justifies, and only secondarily the agent of moral renewal – a moral renewal that is located only at the periphery of soteriological theory'.[122] Luther's narrowed focus of sanctification on forgiveness or passive righteousness is consistent with his theocentric Pneumatology that maximizes the role of the Holy Spirit in salvation, but denies any merit in human works.

For Wesley, the Holy Spirit sanctifies, like Luther taught.[123] Consistent with Luther's emphasis on grace, Wesley explained sanctification as well as justification, above all, in terms of free grace.[124] However, Outler notes, 'in Wesley's view ... grace is always interpreted as something more than forensic pardon'.[125] Whereas by sanctification Luther meant mainly application or consolidation of forgiveness given in justification, Wesley's concept of sanctification was more focused on a believer's inherent righteousness. In his sermon, 'The Means of Grace' (1746), Wesley wrote:

> So little do they understand that great foundation of the whole Christian building, 'By grace are ye saved': Ye are saved from your sins, from the guilt and power thereof, ye are restored to the favour and image of God, not for any works, merits, or deservings of yours, but by the free grace, the mere mercy of God, through the merits of His well beloved Son: Ye are thus saved, not by any power, wisdom, or strength, which is in you, or in any other creature; but merely through the grace or power of the Holy Ghost, which worketh all in all.[126]

Also, differently from Luther's representation of the works of the Holy Spirit as the otherness that comes from outside of believers,

---

[122] Badcock, *Light of Truth and Fire of Love*, 96-97.
[123] ENNT Col 1:10; Journals 4:69; S. Perfection (2), III. 7; S. Patience, 14; WW 11:218.
[124] WW 8:49. 'The author of faith and salvation is God alone ... He is the the sole Giver of every good gift, and the sole Author of every good work ... All true faith, and the whole work of salvation, every good thought, word, and work, is altogether by the operation of the Spirit of God'; ENOT 1 Chron 29:16; S. Evil, II. 9.
[125] Outler, *Wesley*, 33.
[126] S. Means, II. 6.

Wesley taught that the work of the Holy Spirit is implanted in the nature of believers as the fulfilment of God's gracious promise in Jer. 31:33 (along with Deut. 30:6 and Ezek. 36): 'I will put My law in their inward parts, and write it in their hearts'.[127] In the new birth the Holy Spirit results in 'a qualitative change' in a believers' nature, by implanting His holy love into their hearts. He becomes really 'a constitutive part of' the new nature of believers, being resident in their hearts 'in a distinctive way'.[128] Wesley's teaching of 'this divine presence, tabernacling among believers, along with the attendant dispositional transformation' shows a significant advance in sanctification in the sense of a believer's inherent and active righteousness, compared to Luther's concept of sanctification as 'alien righteousness ... instilled from without'.[129] Collins explains, 'Not wanting believers to repeat the first works of sin and repentance afresh, in a cycle of rising and falling, Wesley maintained that the work of the Spirit in adjusting the disposition of the heart to their proper end results in the habituation of holy tempers, over time, that are not only long-lived but also not easily shaken'.[130] As inherent righteousness of believers imparted by the Holy Spirit, the new nature saves believers 'from pride, self-will, passion; from love of the world, from foolish and hurtful desires, from vile and vain affections'. 'Holiness of conversation' follows 'holiness of heart'.[131]

The joint working of the Holy Spirit's initiative of free grace and a believers' voluntary response from their new nature forms Wesley's teaching of the 'evangelical synergism'.[132] Though Wesley ascribed all holiness to the Holy Spirit, he quickly added that He works not in the way of laying aside, but of supporting, correcting, or strengthening human faculties such as reason, will, and spiritual senses.[133] Differently from Luther who ascribed not only the preaching activity but also its effects to the Spirit, Wesley regarded the role of human

---

[127] S. Law, I. 6; Laurence W. Wood, 'Exegetical-Theological Reflections on the Baptism with the Holy Spirit', *WTJ* 14:2 (Fall 1979), 60.
[128] Collins, *Theology*, 124-126; see Cobb, *Grace and Responsibility*, 47.
[129] LW 31:297.
[130] Collins, *Theology*, 127.
[131] S. Heaviness, IV. 5.
[132] Starkey, *Spirit*, 116-123.
[133] WW 10:82; see S. Steward, I. 8. 'I believe the infinite and eternal Spirit of God ... to be ... the immediate cause of all holiness in us; enlightening our understanding, rectifying our wills and affections, renewing our natures, uniting our persons to Christ, assuring us of the adoption of sons, leading us in our actions; purifying and sanctifying our souls and bodies, to a full and eternal enjoyment of God'.

free will and human reason as important factors in accepting the works of the Holy Spirit.[134] Whereas for Luther the preached text itself achieves what the Spirit intends to fulfil, for Wesley, the Scripture teaches just 'a general rule' that 'the will of God is our sanctification', and the Holy Spirit makes believers participants in God's nature 'in the highest degree whereof we are capable'.[135]

According to Badcock, the Anglican Protestant tradition which was a deep influence on Wesley had 'an explicit tendency to emphasize the importance of works, moving away from justification by faith alone, even in the Reformation era between the theologies of Cranmer and of Hooker'.[136] However, in Wesley's emphasis on good works and imitation of Christ, the presence of the Holy Spirit was necessarily prerequisite. Therefore, Starkey maintains, Luther's strong criticisms of those who pursued imitation piety by human works 'do not apply to Wesley' who always asserted 'the necessary priority and continuing sustenance of ... the power of the Spirit' to make sanctification possible.[137]

II. Realism of Sin vs. Optimism of Grace

In describing the state of believers as both saints and sinners, Luther was consistently two-sided. The Holy Spirit is described as the Victor over sin and the flesh in believers. However, if Luther's focus moves from the Spirit to believers, believers themselves are sinners who make no progress in improving their nature. In his comments on Gen. 8:21, stating that 'not even the saints are excluded' from the Scriptural diagnosis that 'the imagination of the human heart is evil', Luther contended that believers are 'by nature no better' than nonbelievers except the fact that they resist sin 'through the Holy Spirit, who is given for the purpose of contending against this wickedness of nature and overcoming it'. Believers, 'too, are evil', but the reason why they are 'not altogether evil' can be found only in 'the Holy Spirit, through whom they contend against what is evil'.[138]

When God forgives believers, their sin becomes 'dead sin, harmless sin' or 'sin without wrath, without the law', and the Holy Spirit starts to 'purge away the sin for which a person has already been forgiven'. Nevertheless, believers are still sinners. Luther empha-

---

[134] S. Enthusiasm, 24-25.
[135] S. Enthusiasm, 23.
[136] Badcock, *Light of Truth and Fire of Love*, 106.
[137] Starkey, *Spirit*, 108.
[138] LW 2:118-119.

sized, 'as far as its nature is concerned, sin in no way differs from itself before grace and after grace'; 'it is called sin, and is truly such in its nature', though after justification it is regarded 'as non-existent and as expelled'.[139]

Though Lennart Pinomaa insists that it is an 'absurd charge' to say that believers in Luther's thought remain slaves to sin, Luther showed a clear tendency to describe believers in themselves as mere sinners, whereas he represented them as saints when he explained the works of the Holy Spirit in them. Though forgiven sin can no longer accuse, it, remaining latent in believers, produces its fruits. Though Christ's righteousness was imputed to believers and their old nature in them began to be mortified, they inevitably live in 'continuous warfare [against the devil and against the sins which beset us] rather than peace and rest'.[140] In this warfare, Luther set the limit to which believers can go; their resistance against sin and the flesh or, at best, obtaining from the Holy Spirit not continual conquest but occasional suppression over them:

> It is impossible for you to follow the Spirit as your guide through everything without some awareness of hindrance by the flesh. Your flesh will be an obstacle, the sort of obstacle that will prevent you from doing what you would. Here it is sufficient if you resist the flesh and do not gratify its desires, that is, if you follow the Spirit rather than the flesh, which is easily disturbed by impatience, which seeks revenge, grumbles, hates, bites back, etc.[141]

Because of the remaining great discrepancy between the Scriptural account of believers as saints and believers' own experience as sinners, Pinomaa contends, 'the real battle line in sanctification is to be found in the tension between the state of sin and the righteousness of Christ'.[142] In this battle, the major anthropological locus in which the Holy Spirit works is the believer's conscience, not their will. The battle line in Luther's thought does not move forward enough to ensure a believers' constant victory or inherent righteousness, but repeats advance and retreat centring on the certainty of justification.[143] Since believers are sinners, the object that the Spir-

---

[139] LW 32:229-230.
[140] Lennart Pinomaa, *Faith Victorious: An Introduction to Luther's Theology*, tr. Walter J. Kukkopen (Philadelphia: Fortress Press, 1963), 62-64.
[141] LW 27:72.
[142] Pinomaa, *Faith Victorious*, 69-73.
[143] *BC*, 417. 'Forgiveness is needed constantly, for although God's grace has been won by Christ, and holiness has been wrought by the Holy Spirit through God's Word ... we are encumbered with our flesh we are never without sin. Therefore everything in the Christian church is so ordered that we may daily obtain full

it continuously deals with in the believer's conscience is the condemnation of the law.[144] This battle is an unceasing process of sanctification in this life.

By ascribing believers' occasional victory over sin and the flesh, and the beginning of inherent righteousness to the work of the Holy Spirit, Luther could oppose human merit in sanctification as well as in justification. However, by denying a change of human nature by the Spirit's sanctifying work, Luther upheld realism regarding human sin even in his Pneumatology. The optimistic hope comes only from the eschatological perspective, not from sanctification in this life:

> In the life to come, when we shall be completely cleansed of all our faults and sins and shall be as pure as the sun, we shall love perfectly ... But in this present life such purity is hindered by our flesh, to which sin will cling as long as we live. And thus our corrupt love of ourselves is so powerful that it greatly surpasses our love of God and of our neighbor ...
>
> If we were pure of all sin, and if we burned with a perfect love toward God and our neighbor, then we would certainly be righteous and holy through love ... That does not happen in this present life but must be postponed until the life to come. We do indeed receive the gift and the first fruits of the Spirit here (Rom. 8:23), so that we do begin to love; but this is very feeble.[145]

Wesley thought that Luther did not assign a proper position to sanctification. In his sermon, 'On God's Vineyard' (1779), which shows Wesley's mature view of Luther, Wesley expressed his favourable view of Luther on the doctrine of justification. However, he criticized severely his doctrine of sanctification:

> Who has written more ably than Martin Luther on justification by faith alone? And who was more ignorant of the doctrine of sanctification, or more confused in his conceptions of it? In order to be thoroughly convinced of this, of his total ignorance with regard to sanctification, there needs no more than to read over, without prejudice, his celebrated comment on the Epistle to the Galatians.[146]

'Whether Wesley ever thoroughly read Luther's writings or not', Leo G. Cox contends, 'Wesley never considered that Luther taught sanctification nor urged a complete change in peoples' lives ... He liked him for as far as he went but it was just not far enough. Wes-

---

forgiveness of sins through the Word and through signs appointed to comfort and revive our consciences as long as we live'.
[144] See Randall C. Zachman, *The Assurance of Faith: Conscience in the Theology of Marin Luther and John Calvin* (Minneapolis: Fortress Press, 1993), 2.
[145] LW 27:64-65.
[146] S. Vineyard, I. 5.

ley's task, he thought, was to carry on to perfection'.[147] Wesley agreed with Luther that although believers are forgiven, they are still sinners.[148] However, Wesley separated from Luther, by contending that although 'by all the grace which is given at justification we cannot extirpate them [both outward and inward sin]', when Christ our Lord speaks 'to our hearts again ... "Be clean": And then only the leprosy is cleansed. Then only the evil root, the carnal mind, is destroyed; and inbred sin subsists no more'.[149]

Wesley's doctrine of Christian perfection stands as an antithesis to Luther's teaching on believers as both saints and sinners. Denying the insistence that it is enough if believers resist sins though they are inevitably sinners until death, Wesley taught that 'Christians are saved in this world from all sin, from all unrighteousness; that they are now in such a sense perfect, as not to commit sins and to be freed from evil thoughts and evil tempers'.[150]

Saying that 'holiness is the work of God'[151] and that 'the things impossible with men, are possible with God',[152] Wesley took seriously that 'the presence of the Holy Spirit means the presence of a power sufficient to translate noble intentions into good affections, words, and works'.[153] He contended, whereas sin could have dominion over believers under 'a dispensation of terror and bondage, which only shows sin', 'under the merciful dispensation of the gospel ... everyone who is under the powerful influences of the Spirit of Christ' is given the power for 'complete victory over it [sin]'.[154] 'Fathers' in Christ are cleansed from 'inbred sin',[155] being filled with 'love excluding sin'.[156] 'Young men', who 'are strong in the Lord', are freed 'from evil thoughts and evil tempers'.[157] Even those 'who are born again in

---

[147] Leo G. Cox, 'John Wesley's View of Martin Luther', *Bulletin of the Evangelical Theological Society* 7:3 (Summer 1964), 86-88.
[148] S. Sin, V. 2. 'Although we are renewed, cleansed, purified, sanctified, the moment we truly believe in Christ, yet we are not then renewed, cleansed, purified altogether; but the flesh, the evil nature, still remains, (though subdued) and wars against the Spirit'; S. Repentance, I. 3-20.
[149] S. Repentance, I. 20; cf. LW 32:229-230.
[150] S. Perfection (1), II. 28; see Lindström, *Sanctification*, 129-132.
[151] S. Spread, 13.
[152] S. Perfection (2), II. 8; S. Riches (1), II. 20.
[153] Starkey, *Spirit*, 106-107.
[154] ENNT Rom 6:14.
[155] S. Perfection (1), Poem 16; S. Repentance, I:20.
[156] S. Way (2), I. 9.
[157] S. Perfection (1), II. 1, 21.

the lowest sense', are 'so far perfect as not to commit sin'[158] in the sense of a 'voluntary transgression of the law'.[159]

Explaining the Christian life under the Christian dispensation pneumatologically, Wesley employed 'three basic phrases': 'receiving the Holy Ghost', 'baptized with the Holy Ghost', and 'filled with the Holy Ghost'.[160] The first two phrases apply to all Christians. Without exception, all Christians were 'baptized with the Holy Ghost' or '"received the Holy Ghost" when they were justified'.[161] However, Wesley related the same phrases, in the sense of receiving the Holy Spirit in fullness, to entire sanctification as well, asserting that 'sanctifying graces' not only were given 'on the day of Pentecost', but also will be given to those who 'pray and expect' that their own 'Pentecost may fully come'.[162] When Wesley used the third phrase, he usually explained it with the words descriptive of entire sanctification: per-

---

[158] S. Perfection (1), II. 2-3, 11; *Plain Account*, 12.
[159] S. Privilege, II. 2.
[160] Collins, *Theology*, 137-140; see Herbert McGonigle, 'Pneumatological Nomenclature in Early Methodism', *WTJ* 8 (Spring 1973), 61-72; Wood, 'Exegetical-Theological Reflections on the Baptism with the Holy Spirit', *WTJ* 14:2 (Fall 1979), 51-63; William M. Arnett, 'The Role of the Holy Spirit in Entire Sanctification in the Writings of John Wesley', *WTJ* 14:2 (Fall 1979), 15-30; George Allen Turner, 'The Baptism of the Holy Spirit in the Wesleyan Tradition', *WTJ* 14:1 (spring 1979), 60-76; Alex R. G. Deasley, 'Entire Sanctification and the Baptism with the Holy Spirit: Perspectives on the Biblical View of the Relationship', *WTJ* 14:1 (Spring, 1979), 27-44; Mildred B. Wynkoop, 'Theological Roots of Wesleyan Understanding of the Holy Spirit', *WTJ* 14:1 (spring 1979), 77-98; Robert W. Lyon, 'Baptism and Spirit Baptism in the New Testament', *WTJ* 14:1 (spring 1979), 14-26; Joseph McPherson, 'Historical Support for Early Methodist Views Of Water and Spirit Baptism' (Paper Presented at the Wesleyan Studies Summer Seminar at Asbury Theological Seminary, June 2011), 1-10.
[161] ENNT Acts 1:5; WW 8:106-107, 184; Journals 2:361; Letters 5:215; ENNT Rom 8:9.
[162] ENNT Acts 8:15, 19:2; Letters 6:221. In his letter to John Fletcher (30 May 1776), 'The generality of believers in our Church (yea, and in the Church of Corinth, Ephesus, and the rest, even in the Apostolic age) are certainly no more than babes in Christ; not young men, and much less fathers. But we have some, and we should certainly pray and expect that our Pentecost may fully come'; Journals 4:532. 'Many years ago my brother frequently said, "Your day of Pentecost is not fully come; but I doubt not it will: and you will then hear of persons sanctified, as frequently as you do now of persons justified". Any unprejudiced reader may observe, that it was now fully come. And accordingly we did hear of persons sanctified, in London, and most other parts of England, and in Dublin, and other parts of Ireland as frequently as of persons justified'; ENNT Mt 3:11. 'He shall fill you with the Holy Ghost, inflaming your hearts with that fire of love ... And this was done ... on the day of Pentecost'.

fected love of a 'father',[163] 'scriptural Christianity', 'the mind which was in Christ ... fruits of the Spirit',[164] and restoration to the image of God.[165] But, he did not use the third phrase to refer exclusively to entirely sanctified Christians, applying it to 'all true believers'.[166]

According to Collins, by relating all three pneumatological phrases to justification and regeneration as well as to entire sanctification, Wesley implied that 'the ministry of the Spirit is richly enjoyed by those who are justified ... and born of God'.[167] McGonigle agrees that in his pneumatology, Wesley endeavoured to emphasize entire sanctification as the teleological end of Christian faith and, at the same time, not to devalue justification and regeneration that he described as such an efficacious transformation as to make believers conquerors over sin. Wesley set his emphasis against the antinomian excuse that the merely justified inevitably commit sins.[168] McGonigle also notes that in his sermon, 'Christian Perfection' (1741), and in his tract on entire sanctification, *A Plain Account of Christian Perfection* (1777), Wesley focused on fruits, effects, or changes of believers by the Spirit, barely mentioning the Holy Spirit Himself,[169] which also can be understood as Wesley's intention to defend the important position of Christian holiness against any sort of enthusiasm which may

---

[163] Letters 5:229. Wesley wrote to Joseph Benson (9 Mar. 1771), 'A babe in Christ ... has the witness sometimes. A young man ... has it continually. I believe on that is perfected in love, or filled with the Holy Ghost, may be properly termed a father. This we must press both babes and young men to aspire after – yea, to expect. And why not now?'; WW 8:191 'Active, patient, spotless love of God and man'.
[164] S. Scriptural.; S. Spread, 18-20; S. Counsels, 7.
[165] S. Iniquity. 8-11; S. Bigotry, I. 13.
[166] WW 8:107. 'They [Christians] do doubtless now "receive", yea, are "filled with the Holy Ghost" in order to be filled with the fruits of that blessed Spirit. And he inspires into all true believers now, a degree of the same peace and joy and love which the Apostles felt in themselves on that day, when they were first "filled with the Holy Ghost"'; Letters 5:215. In his letter to Joseph Benson (28 Dec. 1770) Wesley wrote, 'An entire deliverance from sin, a recovery of the whole image of God, the loving God with all our heart, soul, and strength ... a second change, whereby they shall be saved from all sin and perfected in love. If they like to call this "receiving the Holy Ghost", they may: only the phrase in that sense is not scriptural and not quite proper; for they all "received the Holy Ghost" when they were justified. God then "sent forth the Spirit of His Son into their hearts, crying, Abba, Father"'; ENNT Acts 1:5. 'Ye shall be baptized with the Holy Ghost – And so are all true believers to the end of the world'
[167] Collins, *Theology*, 138.
[168] McGonigle, 'Pneumatological Nomenclature in Early Methodism', *WTJ* 8 (Spring 1973), 70; Arnett, 'The Role of the Holy Spirit in Entire Sanctification in the Writings of John Wesley', 23.
[169] McGonigle, 'Pneumatological Nomenclature in Early Methodism', 63-66.

result in antinomian tendency on the pretext of special inspiration by the Spirit.[170]

III. Faith against Experience vs. Experimental Christianity

In his *The Magnificat* (1521) Luther, using a metaphor of three virgins,[171] distinguished believers into three: the 'impure and self-seeking spirits' whose faith is based on their self-centred feelings of enjoyment, comfort, and blessings; 'the spirits that make a beginning of serving God ... but [are] not ... free from all self-seeking and enjoyment', whose faith is dependent on an occasional 'smile' of God; and the true brides of Christ who love nothing but God Himself and totally trust in His goodness, even though they continually experience things contrary to it. Luther passed incisive criticism on the first two kinds of believers who rely on sensation or feeling, but do not believe in God's love regardless of their feeling.[172]

For Luther, that God's goodness, righteousness, wisdom, and all good things of God may be hidden to believers' senses and experiences, gives them a great trial, testing and training their true faith in God.[173] Even to those who pass the test by showing their constant faith in God, the good things they ascribe to God may continue to be hidden.[174] In Luther's thought, the hidden God Who does not limit

---

[170] Starkey, *Spirit*, 73-77.
[171] LW 21:310. 'During the Mass, a beautiful boy leaped from the altar, and approaching the first virgin in a most friendly manner, lavished caresses upon her and smiled lovingly in her face. Then he approached the second virgin, but was not so friendly with her; he did not give her a caress, though he did lift her veil and give her a pleasant smile. But for the third virgin he had not a friendly sign, struck her in the face and tore her hair, thrust her from him and dealt most ungallantly with her. Then he ran swiftly back upon the altar and disappeared'.
[172] LW 21:307-311. 'The impure and perverted lovers, who are nothing else than parasites and who seek their own advantage in God, neither love nor praise His bare goodness, but have an eye to themselves and consider only how good God is to them, that is, how deeply He makes them feel His goodness and how many good things He does to them. They esteem Him highly, are filled with joy and sing His praises, so long as this feeling continues. But just as soon as He hides His face and withdraws the rays of His goodness, leaving them bare and in misery, their love and praise are at an end. They are unable to love and praise the bare, unfelt goodness that is hidden in God'.
[173] LW 21:336. 'He tries you to see whether you will dispense with your right for His will's sake, be in the wrong and suffer wrong, endure shame for Him, and cleave to Him alone'.
[174] LW 21:334-336. 'To confess the right and good is one thing, to obtain it is another ... To you is committed the confession, the obtaining God has reserved to Himself'.

Himself to His word, the theology of cross that teaches that God works contrary to sinners' expectations, and the external, transcendent character of the imputation of Christ's righteousness are all logically connected to the nature of faith that overcomes the hindrances of rational or sensational judgment:

> 'But I am not conscious of having righteousness, or at least I am only dimly conscious of it!' You are not to be conscious of having righteousness; you are to believe it. And unless you believe that you are righteous, you insult and blaspheme Christ, who has cleansed you by the washing of water with the Word (Eph. 5:26) and who in His death on the cross condemned and killed sin and death, so that through Him you might obtain eternal righteousness and life. You cannot deny this, unless you want to be obviously wicked, blasphemous, and contemptuous of God, of all the divine promises, of Christ, and of all His benefits. Then you cannot deny either that you are righteous.[175]

Because the spiritual reality that faith holds is not always consistent with a believers' experience, Luther taught, 'in reality it [faith] is a profound art'.[176] Faith is neither dependent on nor consistent with but overcomes experiences.

The trans-experiential nature of faith was represented in Luther's Pneumatology. Luther admitted that the work of the Holy Spirit can be recognized by 'the testimony of our conscience' through indirect, external signs such as: 'a new judgment, new sensations, and new drives ... in us'; 'spiritual motivation'; 'our very ability to judge, our speech, and our confession'; 'the testimony of our conscience, by which we know as a certainty that it is a divine gift when we not only believe in Jesus Christ but proclaim and confess Him openly in the presence of the world'; attitude of doing 'ordinary works' such as running the household, tilling the field, and 'serving neighbors' in 'faith, a joyful spirit, obedience, and gratitude toward God'; experience of love toward the Word through enjoying 'hearing, speaking, thinking, lecturing, and writing about Christ'; and forsaking wife, children, property, and life because of their confession of faith, Christ, and His Word.[177] He also explained faith itself as 'the internal testimony' by which believers are assured that they are given the

---

[175] LW 27:26.
[176] LW 23:179. Luther continued, 'Temptation and experience ... constrains us to say that it is far harder and more difficult to adhere to God's word and fortify the heart against the terrors of sin and death ... than observing all the rules of Carthusian and monastic orders'. Here Jeffrey K. Mann's translation is partly cited from his 'Luther and the Holy Spirit: Why Pneumatology Still Matters', *Currents in Theology and Mission* 34:2 (2007), 112.
[177] LW 26:374-380.

Holy Spirit, contending that believers can see their own faith if they really have it. Both faith (the internal testimony) and fruits of faith (the external testimony) are 'not a work of human will or reason but a gift of the Holy Spirit'. Since it is impossible for these things to happen without the Holy Spirit, faith and the fruits of faith give great consolations to a believers' conscience.[178]

However, Luther explained that when the Holy Spirit is sent 'through the Word... into the hearts of believers', 'this happens without a visible form'. That 'it is not evident ... that we have the Holy Spirit' makes believers uncertain of their receiving the Holy Spirit. Furthermore, in spite of the fact that believers have faith and live holy lives, believers continue to 'experience the opposite feelings, namely, fear, doubt, sorrow, etc.' Therefore, in believers, there must be a battle between faith and doubt.[179] Forde contends, for Luther 'sanctification is God's secret, hidden ... even from the sanctified'.[180] Luther clearly expressed that imputed righteousness is not an experiential reality, but in its nature 'a righteousness hidden in a mystery' that believers should hold in faith.[181]

Whereas believers' spiritual trials show their struggles with existential anxiety which comes from the discrepancy between imputed righteousness and their sinfulness, the solution is that the Spirit arouses faith in God's word concerning God's forgiveness and their being children of God. This means that the witness of the Spirit is not a direct but an indirect and mediated work through faith and the word, lacking the aspect of His direct witness.[182]

Wesley's theology shows significant differences from Luther's on the subject of Christian experience. In the preface to his standard sermons, Wesley wrote,

> I have endeavoured to describe the true, the Scriptural, experimental religion, so as to omit nothing which is a real part thereof, and to add nothing thereto which is not ... to guard those who are just setting their faces toward heaven ... from formality, from mere outside religion, which has almost driven heart-religion out of the world; and ... to warn those who know the

---

[178] LW 26:374-380; *BC*, 148.
[179] LW 26:374-380.
[180] Forde, *Preached*, 226-227.
[181] LW 26:5.
[182] LW 25:71. 'The Holy Spirit, who is given to us, *who bears witness*, by strengthening our faith in God, *with our spirit that we are the children of God*. For we are and have only as much as we believe'.

religion of the heart, the faith which worketh by love, lest ... they make void the law through faith, and so fall back into the snare of the devil.[183]

Here Wesley expressed his thought that the Scriptural Christian experience ('the Scriptural, experimental religion') means heart religion together with Christian holy life, standing as an antithesis to both pharisaism and antinomianism (or solifidianism).

He also presented his 'theocentric doctrine of Christian experience'[184] against deism and rationalism. By Christian experience Wesley meant inner and outer holiness achieved by both the Spirit's transcendent work of grace and the believer's responsive work of the law. Lindström properly asserted that 'Christian experience played a most important role in his theology', which can be described as 'a theology of experience'.[185]

The experimental aspect also relates to Christian assurance.[186] Christian assurance includes both the direct witness of the Spirit and the indirect witness of our own spirit. In his sermons, 'The Witness of the Spirit' (1746 and 1767), Wesley represented the witness of the Spirit not as a sort of '*extraordinary* gift' like those that belonged to the apostolic age, but as 'the privilege of *ordinary* Christians'.[187] For Wesley, the 'impression on the soul' by the Spirit is neither 'the result of reflection or argumentation' nor, as Arthur S. Yates notes, what is 'necessarily applied to the heart by texts of Scripture', but 'immediate and direct' testimony by the Spirit:[188] 'Suppose, for instance, you are employed in private prayer, and God pours His love into your heart. God then acts *immediately* on your soul; and the love of Him which you then experience, is as *immediately* breathed into you by the Holy Ghost'.[189] Whereas Luther criticized any assertion of the direct witness of the Holy Spirit as enthusiasm or as theology of glory, Wesley accepted influences from various traditions and approved of their teaching concerning the immediacy of the witness of

---

[183] WW 5:4.
[184] Lindström, *Sanctification*, 3.
[185] Ibid., 1-6.
[186] In his early years after Alderstage experience, Wesley regarded assurance as essential to salvation under the influence of the Moravians. Later, he admitted that there may be 'exempt cases' and that there are degrees in faith and assurance. For more detailed analysis on modification of Wesley's teaching of assurance, see. Collins, *Theology*, 131-136; Arthur S. Yates, *The Doctrine of Assurance: With Special Reference to John Wesley* (London: The Epworth Press, 1952), 72-73.
[187] S. Witness (1), Intro. 2.
[188] S. Witness (2), III. 4.
[189] Works 8:107.

the Holy Spirit: 'Wesley's own Anglican tradition' through those such as 'Hooker, Donne, Pearson, and Barrow'; 'the religious empiricism of continental Pietism' through the Moravians; seventeenth-century English nonconformity such as Richard Baxter; and, to a limited extent, religious radicals such as George Fox.[190]

The direct witness corresponds with the free grace of God that forgives sinners and gives them God's fatherly love. Wesley contended that 'Everyone ... who denies the existence of such a testimony, does in effect deny justification by faith';[191] 'to ground the assurance only on the fruit is to go back to justification by works'.[192]

The direct witness produces the indirect witness. God's holy love produces holy love in believers' hearts and holy 'conversation'. While the witness of the Spirit contains in it the Spirit's revelation of God's holy love, the witness of our own spirit means in our 'consciousness' we are conformed to God's law.[193] This indirect testimony of our conscience is 'the result of reason, or reflection ... a conclusion drawn partly from the word of God, and partly from our own experience'.[194] Wesley illustrated the process of reasoning: 'Those who have these marks are children of God: But we have these marks [a conscience void of offense, faith, hope, love, keeping the commandments of Christ, fruits of the Spirit, etc.] Therefore we are children of God'.[195]

When Wesley distinguished degrees of faith or assurance into three – 'faith ... mixed with doubts and fear', 'the full assurance of faith, a full conviction of present pardon', and 'a full assurance of hope ... a full conviction of their future perseverance'[196] – his emphasis on the importance of the law is explicit in each level of assurance.[197] Firstly, the direct witness produces the indirect witness, but without the latter which is works of the law, the direct witness cannot be sustained.[198] Secondly, against the Calvinistic doctrine of per-

---

[190] Starkey, *Spirit*, 124-130.
[191] S. Witness (2), III. 8.
[192] Lindström, *Sanctification*, 115; see Letters 5:8.
[193] S. Witness (1), I. 2-6; II. 6-14.
[194] S. Witness (2), 6; S. Witness (1), I. 4; I. 11; see Collins, *Theology*, 129.
[195] S. Witness (1), I. 4; I. 11. 'He that now loves God, that delights and rejoices in Him with an humble joy, and holy delight, and an obedient love, is a child of God: But I thus love, delight and rejoice in God; Therefore, I am a child of God'; Collins, *Theology*, 129.
[196] Letters 3:305.
[197] See Collins, *Theology*, 129-142.
[198] Yates, *The Doctrine of Assurance*, 79; John Wesley, *Wesley's Standard Sermons*, ed. E. H. Sugden (London: Epworth, 1951), 2:343. When believers consciously break

severance of the saints, Wesley limited the full assurance of faith given through sanctifying grace as not 'an assurance of what is future, but only of what now is'. This assurance is what the Holy Spirit gives 'from hour to hour' to those who continue in sanctification;[199] 'A natural man has neither fear nor love; one that is awakened, fear without love; a babe in Christ, love and fear; a father in Christ, love without fear'.[200] The full assurance of hope that 'excludes the possibility of doubting' concerning future glory 'cannot subsist any longer', if believers give way to 'anything unholy', even though God may give full assurance even to the regenerated but not to all sanctified believers.[201]

Experimental Christianity relates to another important aspect, that is, happiness. In his sermon 'On Love' (1737), Wesley wrote: 'By happiness I mean, not a slight, trilling pleasure, that perhaps begins and ends in the same hour; but such a state of well-being as contents the soul, and gives it a steady, lasting satisfaction'. Such a 'well-being' state of happiness is twofold. Christian happiness relates to happiness in the future life. Also, it is 'our present happiness' that comes from holy love that we are receiving from and return to God and our neighbours; 'without love nothing can so profit us as to make our lives happy'.[202] Whereas evil tempers result in misery, the way of increasing happiness is to obey God's law that perfects our nature and entitles to future reward.[203]

Concerning Wesley's accusation of Luther's *Comment on the Epistle to the Galatians* as being 'deeply tinctured with mysticism throughout, and hence often dangerously wrong', Leo G. Cox explains that it was not Wesley's 'mature judgment' but his 'first impression' being affected by his controversy with the Moravians on their teaching of quietism.[204] However, the difference between Luther and Wesley as expressed in Wesley's criticism is a more fundamental one; it is highly probable that Wesley's focus of criticism was laid on what Mildred B. Wynkoop classifies as 'the apocalyptic interpretation of Christian experience':

God's commandments, they inevitably lose both witnesses altogether; 'not only by the commission of any outward sin, or the omission of known duty, but by giving way to any inward sin; in a word, by whatever grieves the Holy Spirit'.

[199] S. Free, 16; *Plain Account*, 94, 114.
[200] ENNT 1 John 4:18.
[201] WW 13:81.
[202] S. Love (3), III.
[203] S. Law, I. 2; see S. Speaking, III. 5.
[204] Cox, 'John Wesley's View of Martin Luther', 86-87.

In this view, crisis experience 'happens' but cannot be made to mesh with life prior to the experience. There is a total qualitative disjunction between God and man, grace and human nature, supernature and nature. What God does to us, or in us, is thought to be a divine invasion cutting across our existence as rational beings, unrelated to our understanding and responsibility, resulting either in a new status in God's sight, or in some mutation of human nature below the level of consciousness.[205]

For Wesley Christian religion is an experimental religion that entails holiness as a believer's inherent righteousness; assurance of the Holy Spirit and salvation through both the witness of the Spirit and the witness of our own spirit; and happiness through obedience to God's law and its future rewards. All three aspects of Christian experience – holiness, assurance, and happiness – relate closely to Wesley's emphasis on obedience to the law.

---

[205] Wynkoop, 'Theological Roots of Wesleyan Understanding of the Holy Spirit', 84.

Chapter 5
Faith and Works in Soteriology

A. Martin Luther

I. Fulfilment of the Law

Though Luther related the law mainly to accusation of sinners, he did not deny that the law is in its nature the will of God.[1] What God wants is that His law is obeyed in a way that it is loved from the human heart.[2] If the law is loved, it is already fulfilled inwardly, even though believers are still struggling with sins outwardly. No matter how perfect they look outwardly, works of the law done without a willing heart are 'hypocritically said to have been fulfilled', that is, 'with a hatred for the law'.[3]

What makes human hearts love God's law is faith. Jeha Lee points out that for Luther, *Iustitia Dei* (the righteousness of God) as the 'controlling motif' of Pauline theology, and *caritas Dei* (the love of God) as the main motif of Johannine theology, do not teach different things; God's granting righteousness is the other side of His love.[4] By stating that 'love comes first' or that love 'comes at the same time as faith', Luther taught not only that God's love is recognized through faith, but also that God's love produces our faith.[5] From the relationship between God's love and faith, Lee represents Luther's view of

---

[1] LW 22:143.
[2] LW 9:278. 'The law demands an inner nature which loves it and has pleasure in it; thus it is satisfied and fulfilled if it is loved'.
[3] LW 27:233.
[4] Jeha Lee, 'Love or Theosis? A Critique of Tuomo Mannermaa's "New Paradigm" of Luther's Concept of Love in his Commentary on The First Epistle of John (1527)', (Ph.D. thesis, Boston University, 1991), 118-120.
[5] LW 44:30.

Christian faith in the formula *'fides formata Caritate Dei'* (faith is formed by God's love).[6]

To speak in Christological language, faith is formed by Christ. Christ is not only 'the object of faith' but also 'the One who is present in the faith'. If 'faith takes hold of Christ', Christ becomes 'the form that adorns and informs faith as colour does the wall'. Through faith 'believers are 'cemented to Christ ... into one flesh and one bone'.[7] Since 'nothing but Christ alone' is 'the form of faith', Christian love cannot replace Christ as its form; faith justifies 'without love and before love'.[8]

Pneumatologically, Luther, using the terms of 'infused faith' by the Holy Spirit, taught both the divine originality of faith and its substance as a sort of quality in the human heart.[9] Luther explained this faith in terms of infused love, which denotes a transition that God's love received through faith changes into a believer's own love toward God and neighbours.[10] When faith becomes 'satisfied with the fullness' of God's love, it expresses its returning love through works of the law 'cheerfully and lovingly done'.[11] By the Holy Spirit 'Who fashions a man after the law', believers acquire 'a desire for the law ... out of a willing heart'.[12] Since this desire obeys God's will, Luther represented faith as 'the fulfilment of the law ... a law reaching far beyond everything that a written law commands'.[13]

Faith affects the willingness of the heart intellectually as well as volitionally. It, denying the value judgment of human reason that highly estimates things great and glorious in sinners' eyes, realizes that the value worthy of obedience originates from God Himself.[14] Even if believers cannot understand God's will, faith, surrendering their judgment to God's wisdom, righteousness, and goodness, allows believers' lives to be ruled by His will:

> It [faith] honours Him [God] whom it trusts with the most reverent and highest regard since it considers Him truthful and trustworthy... When this is

---

[6] Jeha Lee, 'A New Interpretation of Faith Active in Love in Martin Luther', *Mission and Theology* 21 (2011), 57-60. Though Luther did not use this expression, it correctly represents his thought.
[7] LW 26:129-130, 168.
[8] LW 26:88-89, 137. Christian love is not included in justifying faith, only divine love.
[9] LW 27:28-31; LW 26:144-147, 269-270.
[10] LW 27:233; LW 25:187.
[11] LW 31:365; see LW 27:336.
[12] LW 35:367.
[13] LW 25:187.
[14] LW 2:77-80; LW 4:102-107; LW 24:220-221.

done, the soul consents to His will. Then it hallows his name and allows itself to be treated according to God's good pleasure for... it does not doubt that He who is true, just, and wise will do, dispose, and provide all things well.

Is not such a soul most obedient to God in all things by this faith? What commandment is there that such obedience has not completely fulfilled? What more complete fulfilment is there than obedience in all things? This obedience, however, is not rendered by works, but by faith alone.[15]

Faith means a fundamental change of intellect, emotion, and volition for obeying God's will. As 'a divine work in us [believers]' as well as 'for us', faith 'makes us altogether different men, in heart and spirit and mind and powers'.[16]

Faith encompasses every facet of salvation in it: 'the fulfilment of all the law, the righteousness for all time ... the mortification of the flesh, the reviving of the spirit, the victory over the world, over the flesh, and over hell', therefore, it is the fulfilment of Christ's salvific work and the 'eternal life itself'.[17] If we have faith, Luther taught, it replaces the role of the law in teaching God's will.[18] Furthermore, faith is not only 'the understanding of the law' or the fountain of all obedience to the law,[19] but also, replacing the obedience to the law, faith becomes the obedience itself. 'Faith is the new law';[20] '"Obey me", that is, "Believe that I am your God and that this is the way I want you to know me when I show mercy and help you, for I do not need your sacrifices"'.[21] Luther emphasized that what God searches for from human beings is this faith, not just outer works of the law; 'faith bring about righteousness that is hidden in God ... Therefore the whole substance of the new law and its righteousness is that one and only faith'.[22] Faith fulfils the law that sinners cannot fulfil with their works.[23] Luther asserted that faith becomes 'absolutely all in all' both in justification and in the Christian life.[24]

---

[15] LW 31:350.
[16] LW 35:370-371.
[17] LW 14:328-329; LW 31:359; LW 35:370-371.
[18] LW 44:26.
[19] LW 27:221.
[20] LW 17:81.
[21] *BC*, 254.
[22] LW 29:123.
[23] LW 23:28.
[24] LW 27:221.

II. Faith Working Through Love

To emphasize the certainty of the fact that faith produces love and good works, Luther used the expression, 'it is impossible'. Faith is 'a living, busy, active, mighty' reality in believers, therefore, 'it is impossible for it not to be doing good works incessantly ... it is impossible to separate works from faith';[25] 'it ... brings with it good works and is irresistible ... just as a living person ... move, eat, drink';[26] 'it is impossible for him who worships in accordance with the First Table not to keep the Second Table ... This is the clear and unfailing result';[27] 'faith is followed by works as the body is followed by its shadow'.[28]

To explain the relationship between faith and love, Luther, employing metaphors such as a person and works,[29] a tree and fruits,[30] an artisan and tools,[31] and Christ's divinity and humanity,[32] attributed an active, powerful, and controlling character to faith, but a passive, limited, and negative character to love. Faith as a person or a tree, and love as works or fruits, mean that love cannot produce faith, but vice versa. Faith as Christ's divinity and love as Christ's humanity teach both the self-sufficiency of faith and the dependence of love on it;

> 'The Infant lying in the lap of His mother created heaven and earth' ... the humanity does not create. Nevertheless, it is said correctly that 'the man created', because the divinity ... is incarnate with the humanity ... the meaning of the passage, 'Do this, and you will live', is 'You will live on account of this faithful "doing"; this "doing" will give you life solely on account of faith' ... Everything that is attributed to works belongs to faith ... let faith always be the divinity of works, diffused throughout the works in the same way that the divinity is throughout the humanity of Christ ... faith is the 'do-all' in works.[33]

---

[25] LW 35:370-371.
[26] WA 12. 559, 20-31. Quoted by Gerhard Ebeling, 'Faith and Love', in Helmut Gollwitzer ed., *Martinus Luther: 450th Anniversary of the Reformation* (Bad Godesberg: Internationes, 1967), 70.
[27] LW 1:329.
[28] WA 25, 324, 1. Quoted by Forell, *Faith Active in Love*, 56.
[29] WA 17, 2, 97-98. 'Faith and love must be distinguished in such a way that faith is referred to the person and love to works'; 'faith remains the doer, and love remains the deed'. Quoted by Ebeling, 'Faith and Love', 69.
[30] LW 1:329; 26:209-211, 255-256.
[31] LW 27:28-29.
[32] LW 26:264-268.
[33] LW 26:264-268

Faith is in itself a perfect quality for salvation whether love is already produced by it or not yet, as Christ's divinity is perfect regardless of His incarnation.

In contrast, Christian love is excluded from justification.[34] It is both unnecessary and harmful in the context of salvation. Only after salvation is Christian love necessary as the proof of faith, and helpful for believers to overcome sin and continue in faith.[35] As hope can preserve faith that has already begun in hardships by the world, the flesh, and the devil,[36] love can protect believers from falling into licentiousness on the pretext of Christian freedom; from becoming 'slothful ... in presenting the word, praying, doing good works, enduring evil'; from looking for 'comfortable way of life ... suitable to our flesh'; and from the consequence that they finally 'lose ... faith in Him [Christ]'.[37]

This does not mean that love supplements faith because faith alone is not enough, but that faith 'arouses and motivates good works through love'. Representing love as 'the tool through which faith works', and faith as 'the artisan who works with it [love]', Luther made faith the lord of love. Love 'has its power, movement, and action, not from itself but from' faith that 'works with it'.[38] Faith preserves and strengthens itself by employing love as a servant.[39] Faith is 'the beginning, middle, and end' of love, not vice versa.[40]

Luther agreed that 'love is the fulfilling of the law'; however, he denied the argument that 'if love is the fulfilling of the law, then ... if we love, we are righteous'. For Luther, it is 'completely fallacious' to conclude that because something is commanded, we can do it. Such a conclusion does not consider that 'sin gets in the way', and human corruption 'greatly surpasses our love of God and of our neighbour'. Even the most devout believers' love is too 'tiny and weak' as well as 'imperfect and impure' to achieve 'the perfection of righteousness'.[41] 'Therefore', Luther concluded, 'it is a great error to attribute justification to a love that does not exist or ... is not great enough'.[42] If righteousness is attributed to love, it is to make love, good works, or

---

[34] LW 26:88.
[35] LW 27:48-50; LW 30:274.
[36] LW 27:20-27.
[37] LW 27:48-50; LW 30:274.
[38] LW 27:28-31.
[39] LW 44:32. 'Faith ... brings along with it hope and love'; LW 31:360.
[40] LW 35:82.
[41] LW 27:64, 68; LW 25:342; LW 2:120.
[42] LW 27:64.

the law an antithesis to faith, Christ, grace, and the gospel;[43] then, 'Christ is denied and faith is abolished'.[44]

III. The Third Use of the Law?

Among Luther scholars there has been much debate on whether Luther taught the so-called third use of the law. What was Luther's position and how can it be supported? In the whole of Luther's writings there are two passages that seem to teach the third use of the law. However, according to Werner Elert and Gerhard Ebeling, the one in *The Second Disputation Against the Antinomians* (1538)[45] is a later interpolation by a pupil of Melanchthon.[46] The expression 'threefold use of the law' in *the Christmas Postil* (1522) does not indicate the uses of the law such as the civil, the theological, or the third use, but three responses toward the law – to disregard, to keep outwardly, or to keep both inwardly and outwardly. Luther's teaching in this context is that believers do not need the law; for them, there is 'no Moses, but Jesus Christ, who leads by faith and fulfils all that is commanded by Moses'.[47] Therefore, the threefold use here does not support but refutes the concept of the third use of the law.[48]

Essential arguments that support the third use of the law in Luther's theology are based on the law's prescriptive role for the believers' life, and on Luther's connecting the believers' life to the fulfilment of the law. It is undeniable that, as Althaus notes, though Christ frees believers from the law as 'the power to force, to accuse, to damn', the law as 'God's good will for men, remains unchanged'.[49] The law, whether it is the law of Christ, the Decalogue, or the natural law, has the prescriptive role of teaching believers in their lives and vocations:[50] 'God's commandments provide me with the correct di-

---

[43] LW 21:285-294.
[44] LW 26:143.
[45] WA 39. 1. 485, 16-24. 'The law is to be retained so that the saints know what works God commands, in which they can exercise obedience toward God'. Quoted by Lohse, *Theology*, 183.
[46] Ebeling, *Word and Faith*, 62; Lawrence M. Vogel, 'A Third Use of the Law: Is the Phrase Necessary?', *CTQ* 69:3-4 (2005), 193. Vogel corrects Ebeling's dating of Melanchthon's first reference to the third use from the *Loci* of 1535 to the *Scholia* of 1534; see Lohse, *Theology*, 183.
[47] WA 10. 1. 1. 458. 8-11. Quoted by Ebeling, *Word and Faith*, 64.
[48] WA 10. 1. 1. 456. 8 - 458. 13; Ebeling, Ibid., 62-64.
[49] Althaus, *Theology*, 266.
[50] See Grobien, 'Natural Law', 211-229.

rectives for life; they supply me with abundant information about righteousness ... the law serves to indicate the will of God'.[51]

However, Luther did not identify either prescription or fulfilment of the law, with the third use of the law. Firstly, in spite of the prescriptive role of the law, Luther did not ascribe the power of fulfilling God's will to the law. 'It [the law] resembles a hand which ... gives me the proper direction', but 'feet, a wagon ... or horses' that bring believers to the place the hand points out, are 'illumination by the Holy Spirit ... and our faith in Christ'.[52] Luther ascribed a prescriptive role to the law, but its fulfilment only to faith.

Consistently Luther admitted that love fulfils the law externally,[53] only if believers do all 'their duty ... on the basis of the command ... of God' and abstain from 'the desires and vices of the flesh'.[54] However, differently from faith that 'covers the countless sins' perfectly before God, love cannot 'check' the flesh and sins completely.[55] Inevitably, love 'belongs under the law', that is, under the theological use.[56]

Secondly, in spite of the prescriptive role of the law, what makes God's will contained in the law understood as intended by God is faith: faith is 'the understanding of the law'.[57] He distinguished between 'the spiritual use of the law' and 'the spiritual law'. The former is the theological use, but the latter is the law understood spiritually; whereas the former pertains to 'those who are to be justified' to lead them to Christ, the latter pertains to the justified who live 'above and beyond any law'.[58] For Luther, faith, the fulfilment of the law, the spiritual law, and the gospel are all identical. They all describe the state of believers who understand, love, and obey God's law.[59] Though all spiritual meanings of the law are already revealed by Moses, without faith, they cannot be accepted properly.[60]

Thirdly, a believer's fulfilment of the law is not identical with the third use. To use the distinction between 'a process' and 'an

---

[51] LW 22:143.
[52] LW 22:143-144.
[53] LW 27:96, 223. The internal 'fulfilment of the law produces works ... fulfilment of the law [in the heart] come first, before works are done'.
[54] LW 27:82.
[55] LW 30:274; LW 54:234.
[56] LW 54:234.
[57] LW 27:221.
[58] LW 26:344.
[59] LW 10:401; WA 4:134.20. 'The spiritual law and the gospel are identical'. Quoted by Heckel, *LEX*, 358.
[60] LW 2:15.

achievement' by which Luther explained that mortification of believers is in process but cannot be achieved in this life,[61] Luther applied the term 'faith' to the process in which believers begin to obey the law. However, when he explained the 'achievement' of faith, he used the phrase, the fulfilment of the law. In the 'process' of fulfilling the law only faith works, however, to explain the achievement of faith, the terminology of 'the law' is used. While faith is perception of God's will, and the motif and the dynamic to fulfil it, the outcome is the fulfilment of the law.

Without the distinction between the 'process' through the terminology of faith, and the 'achievement' through the terminology of the law, the debate on the third use cannot be solved. Faith is in itself self-sufficiently inclusive, informative, and prescriptive of God's will. Luther averred, 'a Christian man living in this faith has no need of a teacher of good works, but he does whatever the occasion calls for, and all is well done'.[62] However, 'the law finds man not only unwilling but also unable to do what the law demands'.[63] The active worker who fulfils the law is the Holy Spirit on God's side, and faith on the human side.[64]

In sum, Luther attributed all of understanding, loving, and achieving the law to faith. Then, can it be proper to say that the law is still valid in instructing and conducting God's will, when faith does everything and the law does nothing except accusing sinners? Positively speaking, the law is not only 'ratified' as God's will through faith that understands its full meaning, but also 'grounded on' faith that fulfils it.[65] Negatively speaking, those who have faith as the new law die to the old law,[66] because faith, working 'far above and beyond any law', replaces the law.[67] 'The law does not rule and is not over those who fulfil it ... The fulfilment of the law is the death of the law'.[68] Whether the law is established or replaced by faith, Luther taught the same thing. Faith fulfils God's law when 'it has no laws' or when it 'has all

---

[61] LW 9:186.
[62] LW 44:26.
[63] LW 9:179.
[64] LW 35:368-369.
[65] LW 25:67.
[66] LW 17:81.
[67] LW 26:344.
[68] LW 10:405.

laws'; faith obeys God's will perfectly either with or without the law.[69]

When God's will is revealed through the law, there are three responses toward the law – to disregard, to keep outwardly, or to keep both inwardly and outwardly. What makes the difference is neither contents nor uses of the law, but the presence of faith and the Holy Spirit.[70] Only faith that knows Who God is, perceives correctly His will in the law. Faith that receives God's love produces love which is commanded by the law: 'Consequently, you do not have to demand good works at length from someone who has once believed. For faith teaches him everything, and everything that he does is well done'.[71] To argue that there is no third use in Luther's theology of the law is not because the law does not have prescriptive role, but because the law cannot help sinners to understand or fulfil it. In Luther's theology the law leads non-believers to faith and sustains believers in faith by always accusing their sins. The law is valid only for the civil and the theological uses.

B. John Wesley

I. Fulfilment of the Law

Wynkoop, calling Wesley 'a modern Apostle of love', states, 'no matter which door one enters into his thinking – holiness, sanctification, perfection, cleansing, faith, man, God, salvation, or any other – not only does each of these begin to flow together and intertwine with the others, but the whole is channelled inevitably into love'. Wesley explained all aspects of God's nature, Christ's atonement, holiness, faith, and Christian ethics in relation to love.[72]

Wesley's theology of the law can be viewed from the dynamic relationship between God's love, the believers' love of God, and their love of neighbours and the other creatures of God: God's love is causal;[73] the believers' love of God is responsive;[74] and their love of

---

[69] LW 9:70. 'The fulfilling of the law is love from a good heart and from faith that is not feigned, which uses law lawfully when it has no laws and has all laws'.
[70] LW 35:368-369.
[71] WA 12. 559, 20-31. Quoted by Ebeling, 'Faith and Love', 70.
[72] Mildred Bangs Wynkoop, *A Theology of Love: The Dynamic of Wesleyanism* (Kansas City: Beacon Hill Press, 1972), 10-31.
[73] S. Justification, III. 2. 'There is no love of God but from a sense of His loving us'.
[74] S. Way (1), II. 12. 'Dost thou now believe? Then "the love of God is" now "shed abroad in thy heart". Thou lovest Him, because He first loved us'; S. Love (2), I. 3.

neighbours and other creatures are consequent on both.[75] God's love not only gives its recipients the most powerful motive to return their love to God,[76] but also implants a new nature which takes after His love in their hearts.[77] Believers love others and other creatures not merely as a means of repaying God's love, but they love in a more natural way suitable to their new nature; their wholly renewed Christian nature.

Believers fulfil the requirements of the law in relation to three objects: to love God;[78] to love neighbours; and to love God's creatures.[79] In relation to God, love becomes 'the pure, clean, unpolluted worship of God'.[80] In relation to neighbours, love does what the golden rule requires.[81] By loving the other creatures of God, believers not only follow the example of God's love toward His creatures,[82] but also please God, since 'God ... hath commanded us ... to love many of His creatures ... to delight in them, to enjoy them'.[83]

Since the state of salvation can be described as loving relationship between God, human beings, and the other creatures, Wesley regarded love as the very goal, the very blessing, or the content of religion itself.[84] The highest grace that believers receive in this life is the gift of 'pure love ... governing the heart and life, running through all our tempers, words, and actions'.[85] Wesley contended, though 'there are many [commandments] in the law', 'if this [love] be rightly performed ... it discharges all the rest'.[86] He appraised love very highly:

This love is a twofold love of delight and of gratitude toward God. While love of delight means to love 'what He is in Himself', love of gratitude means to love 'what He is to us'. In the former His divine attributes become the reason of our love of God. In the latter His salvation and blessings become the reason; we love God because He first loved us.

[75] S. Love (2), I. 8; S. Love (3), II. 4-8; III. 1. After explaining the nature of Christian love according to the biblical exposition in 1 Cor. 13, Wesley asserted that such love becomes possible 'by the love of God shed abroad in our heart'; S. Scriptural, I. 5. 'He that thus *loved* God could not but love his brother also'.
[76] S. Witness (1), II. 7; ENNT Rom 13:8-10.
[77] ENNT Heb 8:12; S. Established (2), III. 3.
[78] S. Love (3), II. 2; S. Love (2), I. 5.
[79] S. Love (3), II. 3.
[80] S. Law, III. 2; S. Mount (9), 4-5.
[81] S. Way (1), I. 9; S. Mount (10), 23-24.
[82] S. Love (2), I. 6.
[83] S. Love (3), II. 3.
[84] S. Question, III. 2.
[85] WW 11:397.
[86] ENNT Rom 13:8-10.

'The heaven of heavens is love'. There is nothing higher in religion ... if you look for anything but more love, you are looking wide of the mark, you are getting out of the royal way ... from the moment God has saved you from all sin, you are to aim at nothing more, but more of that love described in the thirteenth of the Corinthians. You can go no higher than this, till you are carried into Abraham's bosom.[87]

The essential requirement of the law, the nature of the law, the possibility of fulfilling the law, and the end of the law for Wesley is love.[88] Affirming that love is 'the sum of all Christian righteousness',[89] Wesley stressed, 'the love of God and man ... is all in all', without which 'whatever we do ... profits us nothing'.[90]

II. Faith Working Through Love[91]

When Wesley taught that God's love is the cause of Christian love, the role of faith is presupposed, since God's love is received through faith. Without faith, Christian love cannot exist or subsist.[92] On the foundation of the close connection between faith and love, Wesley could employ the principle to 'know the cause from its effects!'[93] as a hermeneutic of real faith and love. He related Scriptural teachings on Christian duties of love to their source, faith, or, Scriptural teaching of faith to its effect, love. In the Sermon, 'On Working Our Own Salvation' (1785), Wesley did not say that salvation takes place through faith. Intentionally he asserted that it takes place 'in the holy, humble, gentle, patient love of God and man', and that it grows in the same love.[94] Reversely, Wesley explained believers' works of love such as feeding the poor, visiting the sick, and welcoming a stranger (Matt. 25:35-36) in terms of true faith.[95] Wesley's ways of tracing love or good works to faith, and explaining salvation on the foundation of love, is based on his view of faith as the basis of Christian love.

However, by teaching that Christian love is dependent on faith, did Wesley elevate faith over love? Certainly not! Wesley argued that

---

[87] *Plain Account*, 102-103.
[88] Young Tae Han, *The Trinity and Holiness* (Seoul: SeungKwang Press, 1992), 209.
[89] S. Way (1), I. 7-9; S. Mount (10), 23-24.
[90] S. Mount (4), III. 2.
[91] ENNT I Cor 7:19; Jam 2:14; S. Privilege, III. 1-4; S. Signs, II. 4; S. Dissipation, 17; S. Original, III. 3.
[92] S. Salvation, I. 4-5; S. Almost, II. 1-6.
[93] S. Bigotry, I. 7.
[94] S. Working, II. 1.
[95] S. Reward, Intro. 3.

faith exists for love or good works, just like a tree has the reason of its existence from its fruits:

> Good works are ... the perfection of religion ... works springing from this love are the highest part of the religion. Of these our Lord Himself says, 'Hereby is my Father glorified, that ye bring forth much fruit'. Much fruit! Does not the very expression imply the excellency of what is so termed? Is not the tree itself for the sake of the fruit? By bearing fruit, and by this alone, it attains the highest perfection it is capable of, and answers the end for which it was planted. Who, what is he then, that is called a Christian, and can speak lightly of good works?[96]

Placing faith in the position of a means, Wesley raised up love as the goal of faith. While 'love is the end of all the commandments of God',[97] faith serves as 'the most direct and effectual means' of restoring love to believers.[98] For the purpose of serving love, faith will exist only temporarily from the time love was lost by the fall until they are recovered to perfect love in heaven.[99] As 'the great temporary means which God has ordained to promote that eternal end' of love, 'all the glory of faith ... arises hence, that it ministers to love'.[100] Though love receives its existence from faith, by value judgment love is superior to faith. Against those who ascribe the highest supremacy to faith, Wesley maintained,

> Faith ... was originally designed of God to re-establish the law of love. Therefore, in speaking thus, we are not undervaluing it ... but on the contrary showing its real worth, exalting it in its just proportion, and giving it that very place which the wisdom of God assigned it from the beginning. It is the grand means of restoring that holy love wherein man was originally created ... it is the only means under heaven for effecting it [love].[101]

Therefore, for Wesley faith cannot be a substitute of love, but 'only the handmaid of love'.[102] As the fruits for which faith exists, love, good works, and holiness are the touchstone of the true Christian faith.[103] Love that fulfils both the negative law by doing no evil and the positive law by doing good works is the lord of faith.[104]

---

[96] S. Reward, I. 6.
[97] S. Established (2), II. 1.
[98] S. Established (2), III. 2.
[99] S. Established (2), 1-5.
[100] S. Established (2), II. 2.
[101] S. Established (2), II. 6.
[102] S. Established (2), II. 1.
[103] S. Mount (13), III. 5; S. Established (2), III. 4.
[104] S. Established (2), II. 1; III. 3.

III. Faith and Works in the Order of Salvation

In his sermon, 'The Scripture Way of Salvation' (1765), Wesley defined salvation in a broad sense as that 'the entire work of God, from the first dawning of grace in the soul' by prevenient grace 'till it is consummated' by glorifying grace, not narrowing its meaning to 'the soul's going to paradise' after death.[105] In another sermon, 'On Working Our Own Salvation' (1785), Wesley described the order of salvation as a sequence of the works of God's grace: prevenient grace, convincing grace, justification, and sanctification.[106] Though each work of grace is given instantaneously, before and after those instants, 'gradual' growth in grace is necessary for obtaining further grace:

> All experience, as well as Scripture, shows this salvation to be both instantaneous and gradual. It begins the moment we are justified ... It gradually increases ... till, in another instant, the heart is cleansed from all sin, and filled with pure love to God and man. But even that love increases more and more, till we 'grow up in all things into Him that is our Head'; till we attain 'the measure of the stature of the fullness of Christ'.[107]

Wesley's views of the role of the law and of the relationship between God's grace and human works in salvation are examined in two works of Kenneth Collins. In his dissertation, 'John Wesley's Theology of Law' (1984), Collins explains the Wesleyan order of salvation in terms of a rotation between 'law pauses' and 'law remains'. The 'law pauses' at the instantaneous moments when God gives prevenient, justifying, or sanctifying grace as a free gift. However, for those who received each grace, the 'law remains' an imperative with which they should keep and increase the already received grace until they obtain a further grace.[108]

In his more recent book, *The Theology of John Wesley* (2007), Collins observes several 'key conjunctions in Wesley's theology' in the process of salvation in which 'law pauses' and 'law remains' take turns one after another: between views of salvation as 'the sole activity of God', and as co-operant works of God and a human in an evangelical synergism; between views of grace as 'undeserved favour of God' and as 'the power of the Holy Ghost to enable people in the ways of God'; between views of the human role in salvation as 'receiving ... the gifts of God alone' and as a duty of responding to grace;

---

[105] S. Way (2), I. 1-2.
[106] S. Working, II. 1.
[107] S. Working, II. 1; see Collins, *Theology*, 73-82.
[108] Collins, 'Law'.

and between 'instantaneous elements' of salvation by 'grace as the favour of God' and the elements of 'process' through human works of the law. Tracing the former factors to the influences by 'the Protestant heritage of Reformation Anglicanism and the insights of Moravians and German Pietists', and the latter, to 'a broader Arminianism' or to the 'broad catholic tradition (Anglican, Roman, and Greek)', Collins contends that Wesley synthesized both aspects of divine grace and human response in a way that in each state of salvation, we receive before we respond; the former precedes and gives foundation to the latter, and the latter, after receiving the former as gifts, preserves and increases the former.

As 'a species of free grace', prevenient grace 'irresistibly' restores the law erased from the human hearts owing to the fall back to every human heart in a limited way.[109] Human beings come to have the responsibility to proceed to the realization of their sinful state.[110] Since this grace is free gift, Collins states, 'the first movement towards salvation is by God and ... human initiative is precluded. But because God has acted, human response is possible. Prevenient grace ... supports the notion of synergism'.[111]

Convincing grace is a sort of prevenient grace. But, while prevenient grace is 'the objective re-inscription' of the law into every human heart irresistibly by God, convincing grace is 'a subjective re-inscription' of the law 'by the human instrumentality of preaching'.[112] Since 'the generality of men stifle' the benefit by prevenient grace,[113] God gives this grace as a supplement of prevenient grace for the purpose of giving them self-knowledge that they are 'not subject to the law of God':[114]

> The inward, spiritual meaning of the law of God now begins to glare upon him. He perceives 'the commandment is exceedingly broad', and there is 'nothing hid from the light thereof'. He is convinced, that every part of it relates, not barely to outward sin or obedience, but to what passes in the secret recesses of the soul, which no eye but God's can penetrate ... And so much the more, because he is conscious to himself of having neglected so great salvation; of having 'trodden underfoot the son of God', who would

---

[109] Collins, *Theology*, 73-82.
[110] Collins, 'Law', 83-100; Collins, *Theology*, 73-82; S. Working, III. 4; S. Way (2), I. 2.
[111] Collins, 'Law', 99.
[112] Collins, 'Law', 101.
[113] S. Way (2), I. 2.
[114] S. Way (1), II. 1; S. Way (2), III. 2;

have saved him from his sins, and 'counted the blood of the covenant an unholy', a common, unsanctifying thing.[115]

After receiving this convincing grace instantaneously and 'irresistibly',[116] the cooperative and gradual aspect of human works is required; not only as fruit of repentance, but also as preparation for justifying grace.[117] They are 'of the utmost necessity', though they are required only when circumstances permit, like in the case of the thief on the right side of Christ's cross.[118]

In the moment of justification, the law pauses, since works of the law are not required for justification which can be defined as 'the forgiveness of sins', and forgiveness presupposes sinfulness and ungodliness, not sanctity.[119] The law pauses not only with respect to human beings because by works of the law nobody is capable of being justified, but also with respect to Christ since He suffered a penal substitution for sinners, which implies that His positive fulfilment of the law is not necessarily related to atonement.[120] Agreeing with the Church of England, Wesley taught that three things required for justification are: On God's part, God's grace and Christ's satisfaction of God's justice; on human part, faith in Christ.[121]

However, in regeneration which occurs instantaneously at the same instant as justification, Wesley underlined that at the moment when God's love is manifested to the newly born again through faith, the enabling power of the Holy Spirit 'to will and to do His [God's] pleasure' is given.[122] To avoid any antinomian implication of the 'law pause' in justification, Wesley taught, on the foundation of regenerating grace that gives both freedom from the power of sin and freedom to obey God's law,[123] believers should respond toward the grace through works of the law; 'God works; therefore you *can* work. Secondly, God works, therefore you *must* work'.[124] Being an inception of the gradual process of sanctification, regeneration is not only 'a spe-

---

[115] Sermons, "The Spirit of Bondage and of Adoption," II. 2.
[116] Journals 3:85.
[117] However, Wesley denied that works meet for repentance are absolutely necessary as condition of justification. See WW 8:57; WW 8:275-276; Collins, 'Law', 107-108; Collins, *Theology*, 155-160.
[118] S. Way (2), III. 2; see Collins, 'Law', 102-111.
[119] Collins, *Theology*, 147, 160-172; S. Justification, II. 5; S. Way (2), I. 3; Lindström, *Sanctification*, 87.
[120] Collins, 'Law', 150-151.
[121] WW 8:54.
[122] S. Witness (3), 15; Collins, *Theology*, 195-199.
[123] Collins, 'Law', 180-193.
[124] S. Working, III. 2.

cies of free grace',[125] but also has an aspect of synergism between God's transforming grace and believers' cooperation through the law.[126] Except in the instant of justification and regeneration when grace alone works, the 'law remains':

> God does not continue to act upon the soul, unless the soul re-acts upon God ... He first loves us ... calls us to Himself, and shines upon our hearts. But if we do not then love Him who first loved us; if we will not hearken to His voice; if we turn our eye away from Him, and will not attend to the light which He pours upon us; His Spirit will not always strive: He will gradually withdraw, and leave us to the darkness of our own hearts.[127]

In sanctification, which Wesley explained in terms of both *perfecting* perfection[128] and *limited* perfection,[129] instantaneous experience and gradual process are combined: 'Gradual sanctification may increase from the time you were justified; but full deliverance from sin, I believe, is always instantaneous'.[130] While the instantaneous work of sanctifying grace is received in a moment by faith,[131] gradual sanctification concerns a believers' use of the law in 'the grace which is already given' through the works of the law that include both works of piety before God and works of mercy toward people.[132] As Lindström states, to some extent, the former is dependent on the latter.[133] Wesley maintained, 'the blessing depends on our works, alt-

---

[125] Collins, *Theology*, 82.
[126] Collins, 'Law', 193; S. Means, II. 7-8; S. Way (2), III. 5.
[127] S. Privilege, III. 3.
[128] S. Perfection (2), I. 3. 'The *highest* perfection which man can attain, while the soul dwells in the body'; BE 2:98. Explaining the different nuances of perfection between the Greek *teleiotes* which is dynamic and allows further development and the Latin *perfectus* which is static and allows no further improvement, Outler contends that perfection in Wesley's thought, who was working constantly out of the Greek text, assumed the Greek notion of a perfecting perfection, as found in the pre-Augustinian Eastern church writers; ENNT Phil 3:12. Wesley taught that Paul's statement that he is 'not perfect' though he was 'already perfect' supports a perfecting perfection; Oden, *John Wesley's Scriptural Christianity*, 320.
[129] S. Perfection (2), I. 4. 'The perfection of which man is *capable* while he dwells *in a corruptible body*'.
[130] Letters 8:190; see Letters 7:222. If someone entirely sanctified contends that it was wrought gradually in them, Wesley explained, it is because they did not perceive the particular moment when sin ceased to be; S. Way (2), III. 18.
[131] S. Way (2), III. 3-5, 14-17; Letters 5:315; 7:317; 7:322; see Collins, *Theology*, 287.
[132] Letters 5:112-13; *Plain Account*, 64.
[133] Lindström, *Sanctification*, 132.

hough immediately on simple faith'.[134] Even after the entire sanctification, believers are required to grow in sanctification.[135]

C. Observations and Analysis

I. Justification as the Whole of Salvation vs. Justification as a Door of Salvation

In Wesley's adoption of the doctrine of justification by faith, Luther's theology played a crucial role through the Moravians' influence on Wesley.[136] Against Outler's insistence that Wesley's major source of the doctrine of justification by faith was 'the reformers (Anglican) of the sixteenth century', Collins maintains that Wesley could not 'understand the radicality of *sola fide*' before he met the Moravians. Though Wesley later came to find a rich fountain of the doctrine of justification by faith within the Anglican tradition, '*initially* the doctrine of justification which Wesley embraced' came from Luther's teaching.[137]

However, on the subjects of the law and good works, there exist great differences between the views of Luther and Wesley. In his Journal dated on 24 January 1738, Wesley described Luther's theology as solifidianism:

> But before God's time was come, I fell among some Lutheran and Calvinist authors, whose confused and indigested accounts magnified faith to such an amazing size that it quite hid all the rest of the commandments. I did not then see that this was the natural effect of their overgrown fear of Popery; being so terrified with the cry of merit and good works, that they plunged at once into the other extreme. In this labyrinth I was utterly lost; not being able to find out what the error was, nor yet to reconcile this uncouth hypothesis either with Scripture or common sense.[138]

---

[134] Letters, 4:71; Way (2), III. 2; Letters 5:200. 'To use the grace given is the certain way to obtain more grace. To use all the faith you have will bring an increase of faith. But this word is of very wide extent: it takes in the full exercise of every talent wherewith we are entrusted. This comprises the whole compass both of inward and outward religion'; WW 3:204. 'It is impossible that any should retain what they receive, without improving it'.
[135] *Plain Account*, 118.
[136] Journals 1:110, 440, 442, 436, 465-447, 457.
[137] Collins, 'Law', 117-130.
[138] Journals 1:419.

In his journal of 4 April 1739, he criticized Luther's reference to St. James' Epistle as 'an epistle of straw'.[139] On 15 June 1741, after reading Luther's *Comment on the Epistle to the Galatians*, Wesley wrote that Luther 'is quite shallow ... muddy and confused almost on all ... how blasphemously does he speak of good works and of the law of God'.[140] In his sermon, 'On God's Vineyard' (1787), Wesley showed his mature view on Luther, writing, 'Who has wrote more ably than Martin Luther on justification by faith alone? And who was more ignorant of the doctrine of sanctification ...? In order to be thoroughly convinced of this ... there needs no more than to read over, without prejudice, his celebrated comment on the Epistle to the Galatians'[141]

It is probable, as Leo G. Cox supposes, that because of his bad experience with the Moravians, Wesley, 'a busy man', has scanned quickly, rather than perused, Luther's commentary on the Galatians, searching 'one thing, namely, Moravian errors' in it, in order to find the seeds of their errors in Luther. Consequently, Wesley's acquaintance with Luther's theology could have been very limited.[142] Admittedly, as Gordon Rupp states, Luther 'disposed of antinomians and mystical quietists in phrases more violent than had any place in John Wesley's genteel vocabulary'.[143]

However, 'if Wesley could have read all of Luther's works', would Wesley's view of Luther's theology have been different? Cox aptly answers 'No', arguing that there exists a 'fundamental difference' on the views of salvation between Luther and Wesley. Cox says, 'Wesley never considered that Luther taught sanctification nor urged a complete change in peoples' lives. It is at this point he sees the weakness of the Reformation and the strength in the Revival ... He liked him as far as he went but it was just not far enough. Wesley's task, he thought, was to carry on to perfection'.[144] Concerning their different views of justification, William Cannon writes:

> It is possible to consider the nature of the Christian conception of justification in one of two ways. Either it may be viewed as the means whereby a sinner, who stands in condemnation before the righteous law of God, is actually converted into a righteous person, and is thereby enabled to meet the standards of divine holiness and in a manner consistent with

---

[139] Journals 2:174; see LW 35:360-362.
[140] Journals 2:467.
[141] S. Vineyard, I. 5.
[142] Cox, 'John Wesley's View of Martin Luther', 87.
[143] Gordon Rupp, *The Righteousness of God: Luther Studies* (London: Hodder and Stoughton, 1953), 46.
[144] Cox, 'John Wesley's View of Martin Luther', 88; see S. Former, 14.

absolute justice to merit the right of eternal fellowship with God, or it may be interpreted solely as divine mercy which even in spite of sin claims the sinner and pardons him for Christ's sake and accepts him into the everlasting fellowship of the redeemed. The former of these alternatives leads to a limitation of the extent of the justification in the process of salvation as a whole, and makes it, not the sum total or even the final goal of religion, but merely the start. The second of these alternatives, on the other hand, extends the bounds of justification until it comes to include almost the whole of the Christian life and makes it synonymous with salvation itself.[145]

Cox states, for Luther 'what God does and continues always to do in pardon and acceptance is final, and all moral and spiritual effects in life and character are manifestations of the one fundamental act of forgiveness, which is the end as well as the beginning of man's religious life'. For Wesley, 'what God does in pardon and acceptance is relative to its consequences, and the act of forgiveness is not in itself ultimate, but is a means to a more glorious end'. Whereas Luther had an 'all inclusive concept of justification', Wesley had 'less inclusive concept of justification'.[146]

In Luther's theological system, sanctification is not the goal of justification, but both are identical. The justified can worship God properly, obey His law, and produce good works through faith. Justification, being inclusive of sanctification, becomes the source of those works. In Forde's words, the progress in salvation is 'not from the partial to the whole, but always from the whole to the partial': from change of being to change of doing; from change of the tree to the change of its fruits; or from faith to works.[147] 'The whole' of salvation, not only forgiveness but also mortification of the old being, good works, and Christian love, is included in justification. 'The total crisis' of the whole of salvation occurs by the loss of faith.[148]

What made Luther regard justification as the whole of salvation is his understanding of the law. Since believers are in themselves not perfectly righteousness, the law accuses.[149] The only way out is to revisit God's forgiving grace. 'To advance' in grace 'is always a matter of beginning anew',[150] 'forgetting what is before them'.[151] Philip Watson states,

---

[145] Cannon, *The Theology of John Wesley*, 244-245.
[146] Cox, 'John Wesley's View of Martin Luther', 89; Lindström, *Sanctification*, 91-92.
[147] Forde, *Radical*, 126.
[148] Forde, *Radical*, 127.
[149] Forde, *Radical*, 119-125.
[150] LW 25:478-479.
[151] LW 11:541.

To be always beginning again seems hardly the best way to advance! But what is the beginning of which he speaks? It is nothing else but repentance and faith – the faith that is centred in God and His grace, His promises, His power and love, and not in anything of our own. Luther knows how easy it is for us to slip away from this centre and to rely for our salvation on the change that takes place in ourselves, so that we either pride ourselves on our Christian virtues or despair because of our lack of them. But true Christian virtues can grow only on the ground of repentance and faith, so that if we leave it we lose them. That is why we can make progress only as we begin ever anew. Repentance and faith form the permanent basis of the Christian life.[152]

Luther contended, 'Because we always lose, we always sin, we always die ... we always have need for Him to give and for us always to begin anew'.[153] Continuous practice of justifying faith is the key of Christian life.[154] Therefore, justification is 'not a mere beginning point that can be allowed to recede into the background' but 'the perpetual fountain, the constant power' of salvation and Christian life.[155]

The reason Luther identified salvation with justification is to show the radical nature of grace as the sole source of salvation.[156] Luther taught that even the numerous Scriptural 'passages about reward and merit' do not support the idea of a believers' cooperation with God for salvation. God's reward toward good works reveals a further aspect of God's grace, not only because believers' works are done by faith supernaturally given, but also because God's rewards are intended to *comfort* believers who persevere hardships and persecutions in faith.[157] God's grace is perfect for the justified; their works can neither increase nor decrease God's grace, just like 'the same sun shines on the poorest beggar and on the greatest king'.[158]

In contrast to Luther, Wesley regarded justification as a part of salvation that comprises the whole process of 'the total restoration of the deformed image of God in us'.[159] He regarded justification as

---

[152] Philip Watson, 'Wesley and Luther on Christian Perfection', *Ecumenical Review* 15 (1963), 299. On this matter Wesley was consistent with Luther. See S. Mount (13), III. 4.
[153] LW 11:425.
[154] See Lindström, *Sanctification*, 92.
[155] Forde, *Radical*, 126.
[156] LW 21:287.
[157] LW 21:290.
[158] LW 21:285-290.
[159] Albert Outler and Richard Heitzenrater, eds., *John Wesley's Sermons: An Anthology* (Nashville: Abingdon Press, 1991), 69.

'the door' of religion, but sanctification as 'religion itself'.[160] Sanctification is not only the teleological end of salvation,[161] but also becomes 'the determining factor' for understanding all other doctrines hermeneutically.[162] For Wesley, faith working by love is 'aimed at holy living', and pardon aims at participation.[163]

As Robert Rakestraw teaches, Wesley understood God's grace in a threefold way: firstly, God's free love and unmerited favour 'by which I a sinner, through the merits of Christ, am now reconciled to God'; secondly, 'power of God the Holy Ghost, which "worketh in us both to will and to do of His good pleasure"';[164] finally, 'the fruit, virtue, character, or temper produced in a Christian life' including '"passive graces" ... such as patience, meekness, and long-suffering' as consequence of both favour and empowerment.[165] For Wesley, God's justifying or forgiving love is a part of His grace as it is all of 'love, power, and virtue'.[166] Therefore, Wesley taught that, as a pair of justification, regeneration pertains to all three aspects of grace,[167] and made sanctification the goal of justification.[168]

Wesley's emphasis on sanctification relates to his belief that, in Charles R. Wilson's words, 'there exists between God and man an essential relation based on the nature of things'. Wesley made this 'essential nature of things' the starting-point for his religious inquiry.[169] Since Christian religion depends on 'the nature of God and the nature of man, together with their mutual relations', salvation that restores 'the due relations between God and man' cannot be done without human nature taking after God's nature.[170]

---

[160] Letters 2:268.
[161] Lindström, *Sanctification*, 122.
[162] Bence, 'John Wesley's Teleological Hermeneutic', 18
[163] Outler, *Heritage*, 93-94.
[164] S. Witness (3), 15.
[165] Robert Vincent Rakestraw, 'The Concept of Grace in the Ethics of John Wesley', (Ph.D. thesis, Drew University, 1985), 130-138; Outler, *Wesley*, 253.
[166] Rakestraw, 'The Concept of Grace in the Ethics of John Wesley', 137.
[167] Mitsuru Samuel Fujimoto, 'John Wesley's Doctrine of Good Works', (Ph.D. thesis, Drew University, 1986), 172-179.
[168] Lindström, *Sanctification*, 120-124.
[169] Wilson, 'The Correlation of Love and Law in the Theology of John Wesley', 56.
[170] WW 8:12.

II. Monergism vs. Evangelical Synergism

Different views of salvation in Luther and Wesley relate to their thoughts on the roles of grace and works in salvation. To understand Luther's repudiation of human works as a means of salvation, it is necessary to understand the medieval scholastics' teachings on grace and works. Augustine (354-430), whose theology was dominant for the whole span of the medieval period,[171] had an ambivalent view on salvation. On the one hand, grace was emphasized as the source of salvation in his views on predestination; God's unmerited grace, and His absolute control over everything;[172] 'the depravity of man ... and the necessity of grace for morally good acts';[173] and God's agape demonstrated in Christ.[174]

On the other hand, a seemingly opposite emphasis on the human role in salvation is shown. Whereas the fall of humanity resulted in a state of servitude to sin, by infusing love into the believer, the Holy Spirit changes the human will that sinfully loves the world (*cupiditas*) into a righteous love toward God (*caritas*).[175] Grace does not take away the human will, but changes it 'from bad to good' and assists it 'when it is [already] good' through conversion.[176] '[God] operates ... without us, in order that we may will; but *when we will* ... He co-operates with us'.[177] God does not just give salvation, but rewards it by His grace, as Johann Heinz states.[178] This ambivalence of Augustine's theology 'laid foundation of further construction of the teaching of merit' that reached its climax in the later scholastics.[179] McGrath regards the medieval theology as 'a series of Augustinian syntheses' in which 'certain elements in his thought became emphasized and combined with other views to produce a plurality of medi-

---

[171] Heiko Oberman, *Forerunners of the Reformation: The Shape of Late Medieval Thought* (New York: Holt, Renehart and Winston, 1966), 123; Jaroslav Pelikan, *The Growth of Medieval Theology* (Chicago: University of Chicago Press, 1978).
[172] Johann Heinz, *Justification and Merit: Luther vs. Catholicism* (Berrien Springs, MI: Andrews University Press, 1981), 124-131.
[173] McGrath, *Luther's Theology of the Cross*, 67.
[174] Nygren, *Agape*, 468-475.
[175] Augustine, *De civitate Dei* (City of God), XV. 7. 604, *NPNF*. vol. II; Augustine, *De civitate Dei*, XV. 22; Augustine, *De Trinitate* (On the Trinity), VIII. 1. 5, *NPNF*. vol. III; Augustine, *Confessions*, X. 27. 38, *NPNF*. vol. II; Ibid., X. 29. 40; Ibid., X. 43. 70; Christopher Kirwan, *Augustine* (London, New York: Routledge, 1989), 90.
[176] Augustine, *On Grace and Free Will*, 41, *NPNF*. vol. V.
[177] Ibid., 33.
[178] Heinz, *Justification and Merit*, 131.
[179] Ibid., 133.

eval viewpoints within the Roman Catholic Church'.[180] However, upon Augustine's legacy the medieval Roman Catholic Church tended to develop its theology in a way that increased more and more the importance of human works in salvation, rather than of faith that highlights the aspect of the divine grace.

Thomas Aquinas (1225-1274), who is regarded as the most influential theologian among the medieval scholastics and whose theology was affirmed as the 'normative theology' of the Roman Catholic Church at the Council of Trent,[181] defined justification as the whole process of the movement from a state of injustice to the state of justice.[182] The process starts with faith by instantaneous infusion of grace, with which human free will immediately begins to detest sin and turn toward God.[183] However, faith is not perfect unless it is supplemented by love; therefore, 'love is infused' in order to counteract sin.[184] For Aquinas, faith is not only an intellectual act that holds truth, but also it has an element of the will that should be perfected by the believers' own volition. What helps believers' wills to work to perfection is love. In this sense, 'faith works by love'.[185] Employing the Aristotelian concepts of matter and form, Aquinas explained that since 'the act of faith is made perfect and brought to its form through love', 'love is accordingly said to be the form of faith'.[186] In justification human free will cooperates with grace through love.[187] Calling conversion by faith 'imperfect conversion', Aquinas taught that love should make conversion perfect;[188] 'an act of faith is not meritorious unless faith works by love'.[189]

The relationship between faith and love relates to the concepts of congruous merit and condign merits. Viewed from an absolute equality, God's reward toward human merit cannot exit, since human beings owe every good thing to God. However, God graciously sanctions their works as meritorious.[190] Though human works can-

---

[180] Alister E. McGrath, *Iustitia Dei*, vol. 1 (Cambridge: Cambridge University Press, 1986), 38.
[181] Ibid., 145.
[182] ST Ia IIae q. 113 a. 1; ST Ia IIae q. 113 a. 6.
[183] ST Ia IIae q. 113 a. 7; ST Ia IIae q. 113 a. 2.
[184] ST Ia IIae q. 113 a. 4.
[185] ST IIa IIae q. 4 a. 2.
[186] ST IIa IIae q. 4 a. 3.
[187] ST Ia IIae q. 113 a. 5.
[188] ST Ia IIae q. 113 a. 10.
[189] ST Ia IIae q. 114 a. 4; see LW 26:88, 268.
[190] ST Ia IIae q. 114 a. 1.

not be condignly meritorious, they are regarded as congruously meritorious because God rewards them with the excellence of His grace.[191] In receiving eternal life, while the mercy of God is the first cause, human merit is the secondary cause, for which love becomes an essential element.[192]

Gabriel Biel (1420-1495)[193] went further than Aquinas in stressing the importance of human works in salvation.[194] Contending that 'Whoever ... does what he can will receive forgiveness of sins from God',[195] Biel taught that if human beings endeavour to desist from approving of sin by their 'purely natural powers', that is, without any help of grace, God will graciously remit their sin as a reward for their efforts.[196] In this contention, Biel shared the view of covenantal causality with Ockham who employed a metaphor of small lead coins to explain God's reward for human works. Like lead coins which have a 'negligible inherent value' come to have a 'greater ascribed value' when they are used as currency according to the declaration of the king, human works that do not have a considerable 'inherent moral value' are regarded as having a greater 'meritorious value' according to the divine covenant between God and human beings.[197]

Further, Biel taught that, as Johann Heinz summarizes, 'a person is able in his own strength to love God supremely, to avoid sin, and, out of the force of the free will, to merit the grace *de congruo*'.[198] Insisting that the merits of Christ are not the sole meritorious cause, but only the 'chief and principal' one for salvation, Biel maintained, 'if our merits would not complete those of Christ, the merits of Christ would be insufficient, yes, nihil'.[199] This statement, as Oberman anal-

---

[191] While the merit of congruity means imperfect merits according to works done 'in accordance with the law of God', the merit of condignity means perfect merits not according to 'the work itself' but to 'the character of the work ... performed in a state of grace'. See LW 2:123-124.
[192] ST Ia IIae q. 114 a. 3.
[193] Biel was a representative theologian of the nominalism of the *via moderna*, distinguished from the realism of the *via antiqua*. See MaGrath, *Cross*, 27-40, 53-63.
[194] LW 26:214; LW 54:391-392.
[195] Gabriel Biel, 'The Circumcision of the Lord', in Oberman, *Forerunners of the Reformation*, 173.
[196] LW 54:391-392; LW 26:130-131; Sun-Young Kim, 'Luther on Faith and Love: The overriding thematic pair in the dynamics of Christ and the law in the 1535 Galatians Commentary', (Ph.D. thesis, Princeton Theological Seminary, 2008), 97; McGrath, *Luther's Theology of the Cross*, 61; Heinz, *Justification and Merit*, 136-153.
[197] McGrath, *Luther's Theology of the Cross*, 59-60.
[198] Heinz, *Justification and Merit*, 141-142.
[199] Biel, Sermones de Festivitatibus Christi, II G., Quoted by Oberman, "*Iustitia Christ*" and "*Iustitia Dei*", 16.

yses, means that without human beings' complementary works of the law, the salvific works of Christ fall short of securing them of their final salvation.[200] Doing one's best or doing what lies in a person is necessary in order that they receive God's final acceptance.[201]

McGrath insists that since God Himself graciously opened the real possibility of salvation by establishing the covenant between Himself and human beings, 'God alone ... takes the initiative in man's salvation', therefore, Biel's view of justification is not Pelagian but 'actually strongly anti-Pelagian'.[202] Oberman agrees with McGrath that Biel's theology has the aspect of 'by grace alone', saying that 'if God had not decided to adorn man's good works with created and uncreated grace, man would never be saved'. However, he quickly adds that Biel, at the same time, emphasized the aspect of 'justification by works alone' more than 'by grace alone', since under the covenant human beings 'have to produce the framework or substance for this adornment' to which God 'is committed, even obliged to add ... infused grace and final acceptance'. Oberman properly argues that Biel's doctrine of justification is 'essentially Pelagian' in the sense that if a person has done his/her very best, God's rewards follow 'automatically'; what decides justification are the merits of human works.[203] Oberman's view of Biel is consistent with Luther's, who criticized Biel's teaching of congruous merit:

> If this is true, then it necessarily follows that Christ died to no purpose. For what need would a man have of a Christ who loves him and gives Himself for him when without Christ, by the merit of congruity, he is able to obtain grace and eventually to do good works and to merit eternal life by the merit of condignity, or surely to be justified by performing the law? ... why is Christ born, crucified, and dead? ... Simply to no purpose at all if the meaning of justification which the sophists set forth is true, because I find righteousness in the law or in myself, outside grace and outside Christ.[204]

Placing 'too much confidence' in the natural power of human will originates from 'a false assessment of the scope of the requirements of the law for justification and of the seriousness of sin and its power', which makes inevitable the 'duel between the law and Christ'.[205]

---

[200] Oberman, Ibid.
[201] Heiko Oberman, *The Harvest of Medieval Theology: Gabriel Biel and Late Medieval Nominalism* (Grand Rapids: Wm. B. Eerdmans Publishing Co., 1967), 176.
[202] MaGrath, *Luther's Theology of the Cross*, 61-62.
[203] Oberman, *The Harvest of Medieval Theology*, 175-178, 196.
[204] LW 26:181-182.
[205] Kim, 'Luther on Faith and Love', 98-108, 135; LW 26:124-125, 371; LW 27:63-64.

Likewise, Luther criticized Aquinas as 'the fountain and foundation of all heresy, error, and the obliteration of the gospel (as his books prove)'.[206] For Luther, the term 'infused faith' is acceptable. Nevertheless, he denied the argument that love should supplement faith. Such false insistence arises from the depreciation of faith that makes it a mere intellectual function or, at best, as a desire of the heart, usurping the power of justifying sinners in front of God from faith. They made Christian faith 'a useless and formless material'.[207] From this, the scholastics ascribe what is lacking in faith to the superiority of love. However, Sun-Young Kim properly contends, to Luther, 'human love is not pure. Even when it loves God, it seeks its own benefits. It loves not out of purity but out of fear of punishment or expectation of reward. Given this view of fallen human love, Luther is very reluctant to employ "love" to define the character of the disposition of human ... toward God'.[208] Theoretically, the scholastics distinguished between grace and works. However, Luther saw that 'in practice' they taught 'the very opposite', by ascribing the roles of perfecting faith and, thus, of securing salvation to love.[209] To Luther, this is nothing but mixing grace with works, or the gospel with the law, changing God's grace into human works.[210] Against Aquinas' mixing grace with works, Luther affirmed that 'Christ alone is our merit of congruity and condignity'[211] and that 'where they speak of love, we speak of faith'.[212]

Against Augustine's insistence that a perverted will of sinners is changed into good through infused love by the Spirit, Luther maintained that the change of human nature is possible not by love but only by faith. In his discussion of the change of human nature, Luther excluded Christian love, relating it only to faith and the Holy Spirit.[213] Commenting on 1 Pet. 1:4, Luther rarely admitted that, in a limited way in this life, believers receive the divine nature itself as blessings, defining the divine nature as 'whatever can be called good' including 'eternal truth, righteousness, wisdom, everlasting life, peace, joy,

---

[206] WA 15:184. Cited from Michael Root, 'Aquinas, Merit, and Reformation Theology after the Joint Declaration on the Doctrine of Justification', *Modern Theology* 20:1 (January 2004), 5.
[207] Kim, 'Luther on Faith and Love', 98.
[208] Kim, 'Luther on Faith and Love', 107.
[209] LW 26:144.
[210] LW 26:142-145; LW 26:130.
[211] LW 26:375; Kim, 'Luther on Faith and Love', 109.
[212] LW 26:129.
[213] LW 25:67-68.

happiness', and etc. However, the means to become a partaker of the divine nature is only faith.[214]

Not only from the viewpoint of faith, but also from the doctrine of original sin, the scholastic teaching of human works and merit cannot be supported.[215] Luther stressed that in Scripture, the depravity by original sin is described as a 'generic term' that is inclusive of 'imagination of the human heart ... wisdom ... reason, together with all their powers', from which 'not even the saints are excluded'.[216] However, Luther observed, the scholastics' positive view of human nature or human works originated from erroneous interpretation of the Scriptural text that the human heart is 'inclined to evil' rather than is really evil, or that the natural reason or natural endowment of humanity 'remained unimpaired' in spite of spiritual corruption. From such false opinions that 'belittle original sin', they fell into the trap of Pelagianism:[217] 'This is what they teach: "Faith in Christ does indeed justify, but at the same time observance of the commandments of God is necessary ... Here immediately Christ is denied and faith is abolished, because what belongs to Christ alone is attributed to the commandments of God or to the law'.[218]

For Luther, 'grace and merit ... are mutually exclusive'; what saves sinners is grace, not merit, whether it is congruous or condign.[219] Supernaturally given faith by God is everything needed for salvation. Luther affirmed, 'Faith is the beginning, middle, and end of all works and righteousness'; faith is the sole means of *sola gratia*.[220]

In Wesley's theology, what makes believers' works of the law, love, or good works an important element of Christian religion is not a Pelagian confidence in the goodness of human nature and in their ability to merit salvation by works as insisted on by some scholastics, but deep trust in God's grace as taught by Luther.[221] Wesley's views of original sin and of total depravity were consistent with Luther's. Wesley taught that faith is the sole condition of both justification and sanctification, on the foundation of Luther's Reformation

---

[214] LW 30:154-155.
[215] LW 2:119-120.
[216] LW 2:119-120.
[217] LW 2:118-123.
[218] LW 26:143.
[219] LW 21:285.
[220] LW 35:82.
[221] Starkey, *Spirit*, 116-123.

theology.222 Thanks to the Reformation insights, Wesley could penetrate the Roman Catholics' 'anti-Scriptural and anti-Christian ... utterly false and erroneous ... doctrines as well as ... practice ... gross superstition as well as idolatry ... in numberless innovations, without any warrant either from antiquity or Scripture'.223 Wesley criticized that though it would be 'endless to attack, one by one, all the errors', 'salvation by faith strikes at the root' of 'the Romish delusion', describing the Roman Catholicism as a religion of the law, but not of the gospel.224

However, at the same time Wesley admitted that among them 'undoubtedly there are many' true Christians who 'rest on Christ alone, both unto present and eternal salvation', though they cannot explain well their faith doctrinally.225 Though the Roman Catholics, especially at the Council of Trent, added many 'new Articles' of faith, both unnecessary and unscriptural, they did not abolish 'any of the ancient Articles' 'once delivered to the saints'.226 Further, after finishing his translation of *Martin Luther's Life*, on 19 July 1749, a day after he wrote the *Letter to a Roman Catholic* in which his catholic spirit is expressed, Wesley lamented Luther's 'rough untractable spirit and bitter zeal for opinions, so greatly obstructive of the work of God'.227

As Michael Hurley analyses, Wesley's generosity to the Roman Catholic Christians probably reflected his pastoral circumstance that among audiences who listened to his sermons, there were many Roman Catholics, for whom he felt a pastoral responsibility.228 However, the more fundamental reason that Wesley was so broadminded toward the Roman Catholics was that he believed 'many of them ... still retain (notwithstanding many mistakes) that faith that worketh by love'.229 In Wesley's judgment, whereas Luther, being 'ignorant of the doctrine of sanctification', taught justification by

---

[222] S. Way (2), I. 9; III. 14-17; S. Witness (3), 8. '[By] faith alone ... we "see the wondrous things of God's law", the excellency and purity of it; the height, and depth, and length, and breadth thereof'; In faith sinners can receive God's love, which produces their returning love toward God and neighbours. See Way (2), II. 2; S. Witness (1), I. 8; S. Witness (2), III. 5.
[223] S. Bigotry, II. 5; S. Zeal, III. 5-6; S. Inefficacy, 5; S. Attending, 14-15; S. Iniquity, 27-28.
[224] S. Salvation, III. 8-9.
[225] S. Lord, II. 15; S. Trinity, 1; see S. Lazarus, I. 5.
[226] S. Faith (1), I. 7; S. Church, 19.
[227] Journals 3:409; Michael Hurley, S.J. ed., *John Wesley's Letter to a Roman Catholic* (London: Geoffrey. Chapman, 1968), 32.
[228] Michael Hurley, Ibid., 33-34.
[229] S. Faith (1), II. 3.

faith, 'the Romish Church', though 'entirely unacquainted with the nature of justification', preserved strong Scriptural doctrine of sanctification. God's unique commitment to the Methodists, Wesley believed, was 'a full and clear knowledge of each, and the wide difference between them'.[230] In this regard, Outler states that Wesley was best characterized as 'the most important Anglican [*via media*] theologian of the eighteenth century' who connected 'the evangelical principle with the catholic substance of Christianity', integrating 'the antithesis of faith alone and holy living' and avoiding 'the equally unacceptable extremes of moralism and solifidianism'.[231]

Wesley was 'bred up' in the climate of 'the old English Protestantism – older than Dort and Arminius, older than Henry VIII', whose message can be understood as 'a gospel of moral rectitude' through 'faith working by love leading to holiness'.[232] The sources of the doctrine of the Church of England reflected in 'the Homilies' Wesley read[233] can be traced back to Cranmer, Martin Bucer, Cranmer's father-in-law Andreas Osiander, Erasmus, 'the free-will traditions of English nominalism', and 'the holy living mysticisms of Richard Rolle and Juliana of Norwich'.[234] Outler regards Wesley as especially an 'heir to a tradition that ran back through central Anglicanism, through the Oxford nominalists, back to a late-patristic slogan ... "He who lives up to what is truly his best, God will not deny him a measure of graces" (*facientis quod in se est, Deus non denegat gratiam*)'.[235] Whereas the nominalist teaching of '*in se*' was denounced by the reformers 'in Protestant Europe', 'it survived in England' in a way that it supplied 'the Anglican Reformation its most distinctive theology':[236]

> Nominalism had deep roots in England and especially in Oxford. Scotus was an Oxford man; his major work is aptly titled *Opus Oxoniense* [the Oxford Lectures]. Ockham was trained at Oxford, and four of the five identifiable targets of Thomas Bradwardine's *De cause Dei contra Pelatium* were English and Oxonian. As a philosophy, nominalism was the fibrous root of what became 'British empiricism' ... its theological residues fertilized the special brand of "faith *and* good works" that became the hallmark of the central Anglican tradition in which John Wesley's mind was formed. All this suggests ... that there was a native-born tradition of Christian synergism in Europe

---

[230] S. Vineyard, I. 5.
[231] Outler, *Heritage*, 78-79, 200.
[232] Outler, *Heritage*, 82-83, 91-92.
[233] Journals 2:101.
[234] Outler, *Heritage*, 86-87.
[235] Outler, *Heritage*, 181.
[236] Outler, *Heritage*, 199.

and England long before Arminius and the Synod of Dort – and that it was *this* tradition that nourished Wesley.[237]

In his own way of seeking 'a third alternative', Wesley not only accepted 'the nominalists' distinction between God's sovereignty in creation (*potentia absoluta*) and God's accommodations to human freedom (*potentia ordinata*)'[238] and 'the medieval tradition of *in se est*',[239] but also fused 'the Protestant article on justification by faith (imputed righteousness) with the Catholic insistence on the impartation of actual righteousness in *the process* of Christian maturation (from regeneration to sanctification)'.[240] Wesley synthesized and integrated between: the Protestant emphasis on 'God's unmerited mercy in our justification' and the catholic emphasis on 'our active participation in working our own salvation'; the Protestant theology of cross and the catholic theology of glory; and the catholic eudemonistic ideal combined with holiness and the Protestant conception of faith as the way to it.[241]

Whereas Luther and Wesley had 'the deep affinities' concerning 'the gospel of faith', Outler contends, they 'stood poles apart' in regard to 'evangelism, Christian nurture, and holiness', and 'the polarity was focused' on the issue of 'the human *in se*'.[242] From Luther's point of view, Wesley's evangelical teaching of justification by faith would be 'nullified by his overgenerous allowance for the human *in se*'. Luther would have denounced Wesley's theology as 'being virtually Pelagian'.[243] In contrast, Outler maintains, Wesley's synergism by 'the human *in se*' is 'God's doing', since it is founded on God's creation in which humanity became free agents, and whoever lives according to the '*in se*' is sanctioned by His grace.[244] Randy Maddox says, 'in Wesley's work' there is 'an abiding concern to preserve the vital tension between two truths that he viewed as co-definitive of Christianity'; 'without God's grace, we *cannot* be saved; while without our (grace-empowered, but uncoerced) participation, God's

---

[237] Outler, *Heritage*, 199.
[238] See WW 10:361-63; Oberman, *The Harvest of Medieval Theology*, 30-37.
[239] Oberman, *The Harvest of Medieval Theology*, 129-45; S. Working, III. 6-7; S. Signs, II. 10; S. Spread, 9; S. Knowledge, 1; S. Schism, 21; see LW 54:392.
[240] Outler, *Heritage*, 64-65.
[241] Outler, *Heritage*, 67-68.
[242] Outler, *Heritage*, 202.
[243] See Outler, *Heritage*, 181, 202-203; Kim, 'Luther on Faith and Love', 93, 111.
[244] Outler, *Heritage*, 182-183.

grace *will not* save. I have chosen to designate this as a concern about "responsible grace"'.[245]

Further, concerning Aquinas' teaching of faith formed by love, Wesley accepted Luther's concept of faith formed by God's love,[246] teaching that God's love produces our faith, and faith is the sole condition of salvation, and, accordingly, denying that love supplements faith which alone is not sufficient for salvation. Differently from Aquinas, for Wesley, love is not infused when believers respond to infused faith properly, but at the same instant that saving faith is given. When God's love is felt through faith, a new nature that loves God and others is implanted in believers, all of which occur instantaneously by the sheer grace of God. No human response intervenes between infused faith and infused love, though the former precedes the latter logically. As Wesley taught that 'in proportion to the strength and clearness' of faith, believers can love and become holy,[247] love cannot be detached or isolated from faith, but is always dependent on it. Even if faith already fulfilled its end by producing love, love is still and always dependent on faith.[248]

However, Wesley was consistent with Aquinas in contending that faith cannot be the end of salvation, and that 'grace perfects, not destroys, nature'.[249] Similarly to Aquinas, Wesley defined sanctification as a 'habitual disposition of the soul'.[250] Holy tempers in Wesley's teaching 'are analogous to virtues' of Aquinas, as essential elements of Christian holiness, toward which both theologians taught God will reward 'fully in the life to come and imperfectly in this life'.[251] For both, Christian life was regarded as ascending from the lowest to the highest state of grace with the eudemonic goal of the blending of holiness and happiness.[252]

On the subjects of original sin and total depravity, following Augustine and Luther, Wesley refuted the view of Aquinas who taught that the first principle of morality in human beings, that is, the dic-

---

[245] Maddox, *Responsible*, 19.
[246] S. Circumcision, II. 4; S. Family, I. 1-3.
[247] S. Satan's, I. 8; see S. Wilderness, I. 1-2; S. Heaviness, IV. 5; S. Reason, II. 8-10; S. Riches (2), I. 2.
[248] S. Salvation, III. 1-2.
[249] Long, *Moral*, 129-130.
[250] S. Circumcision, I. 1.
[251] Edgardo A. Colón-Emeric, *Wesley, Aquinas, and Christian Perfection: An Ecumenical Dialogue* (Waco: Baylor University Press, 2009), 137-138; Sermon, 'The Circumcision of the Heart', I. 1.
[252] Colón-Emeric, *Wesley, Aquinas, and Christian Perfection*, 135-138.

tum 'do good and avoid evil', was not affected by the fall of humanity.[253] Nevertheless, Wesley agreed with Aquinas that 'grace perfects nature', which signifies that Aquinas also thought that 'what is natural is not in itself sufficient'. Wesley's teaching of humility and repentance is in agreement with Aquinas' contention that infused virtue by God's grace, not 'human achievement ... through our own powers', is 'the essence of moral life'. D. Stephen Long maintains, 'This is a clear Thomistic inheritance mediated through persons such as Malebranche, Norris, and Cudworth'.[254] Wesley 'did not construct' but inherited and advanced 'already well-established' teachings of virtue in the Christian tradition, especially from Aquinas.[255]

Compared with Luther's criticism of Augustine's teaching that believers can cooperate with God for salvation, Wesley's criticism was laid on the very opposite side of Augustine's view, that is, on his denial of Christian perfection as well as his teaching of predestination.[256] Augustine taught that 'the old nature' that remains in spite of 'the new nature', cannot be 'cured completely' in this life, whereas for Wesley, the cure of human will can be 'accomplished now and here'.[257] Whereas Luther criticized Augustine's idea of synergism in salvation, Wesley criticized that Augustine did not teach enough about human capacity of moral perception and of moral decision. From this, in contrast to Augustine's harsh attitude toward both Pelagius and Donatus, Wesley praised both as advocates of Christian perfection.[258]

Wesley's favourable view on scholastic theology and his Protestant conception of faith synthesized the Catholic conception of co-operative grace that perfects human nature, and the Protestant emphasis on free grace. Starkey states, 'the uniqueness' that distinguishes Wesley's theology from both Luther and the scholastic exists in 'the way he accounts for the freedom of the will within the framework of a doctrine of man which is essentially Reformation in make-

---

[253] See Long, *Moral*, 143-144.
[254] Long, *Moral*, 129-130.
[255] Long, *Moral*, 145-146.
[256] John C. English, 'References to St. Augustine in the Works of John Wesley', *Asbury Theological Journal* 60:2 (Fall 2005), 9-15.
[257] Seung-An Im, 'John Wesley's Theological Anthropology: A Dialectic Tension Between the Latin Wesletn Patristic Tradition (Augustine) and The Greek Eastern Patristic Tradition (Gregory of Nyssa)', (Ph.D. thesis, Drew University, 1994), 286-302.
[258] English, 'References to St. Augustine in the Works of John Wesley', 5-24.

up'.[259] Outler notes that the distinctiveness of Wesley's teaching is found in the 'style of integrating the evangelical stress on God's sovereign grace and the catholic accent on human agency in salvation'.[260]

As a consequence, Wilson notes that in Wesley's teaching there exists a tension 'between the love of God as sufficient for salvation and the law of God as requiring obedience in the continuance of salvation'. Wesley thought that this tension was already inherent in the covenant of grace.[261] The third way is realized by God's giving prevenient grace.[262] By prevenient grace, Colin Williams says, Wesley could have two different attitudes toward original sin. In an 'absolute' sense 'original sin is total; under these terms no man can ever cease to be a sinner'. At the same time, every human being, being free from original sin understood in the absolute sense, is already on the way to salvation.[263] For Wesley, God's grace operates 'at an earlier point' in the order of salvation than Luther taught.[264] It restores human will to the extent that sinners can respond God's salvific works not as mere passive reaction coerced by God's arbitrary decision but as voluntary response with a grace-enabled free will. Further, through the law restored in the human heart, prevenient grace causes a measure of 'active faith' that produces works meet for repentance, though it is faith of a servant.[265]

Human beings are, in Michael T. Burns' words, already 'graced' beings[266] by prevenient grace which gives the freedom of choice to repent and 'to receive additional gifts of grace'.[267] The freedom 'to accept [justifying] faith or refuse it' has been given in 'the restored faculties of prevenient grace'.[268] Further grace of sanctification is also partly dependent on their good use of freedom restored by preve-

---

[259] Starkey, *Spirit*, 117, 119.
[260] Outler, *Heritage*, 191, 194; see Starkey, *Spirit*, 117, 119.
[261] Wilson, 'The Correlation of Love and Law in the Theology of John Wesley', 100-101; WW 8:289.
[262] Collins, *The Scripture Way of Salvation*, 39.
[263] Collin W. Williams, *John Wesley's Theology Today* (Nashville: Abingdon Press, 1960), 42-44.
[264] Collins, 'Law', 112-114.
[265] Collins, Ibid.
[266] Michael T. Burns, 'John Wesley's Doctrine of Perfect Love as a Theological Mandate for Inclusion and Diversity', (Ph.D. thesis, University of Manchester [Nazarene Theological College], 2009), 121.
[267] Charles A. Rogers, 'The Concept of Prevenient Grace in the Theology of John Wesley', (Ph.D. thesis, Duke University, 1967), 8.
[268] Collins, *Theology*, 81; Williams, *John Wesley's Theology Today*, 41, 54.

nient grace. In that sense, James C. Logan says, 'the prevenient grace ... continues to operate even though one may experience justifying and sanctifying grace'.[269] By the concept of prevenient grace, Wesley overcame 'the wholly negative evaluation' of human capacity to respond to the law and the gospel,[270] keeping total depravity and avoiding 'the accusation of Pelagianism and semi-Pelagianism'.[271] McGonigle adds that by prevenient grace, Wesley could 'subscribe to a near-Augustinian understanding of original sin, yet deny unconditional election on one hand and universalism on the other'.[272] Prevenient grace made it possible that Wesley could 'hold together the three motifs of total depravity (apart from God's prevenient grace), salvation by grace, and the offer of salvation to all',[273] supporting the necessity of human works in salvation. Rogers says that with prevenient grace, Wesley could avoid 'predestination, stillness, antinomianism and human self-determination, while at the same time maintaining both the doctrine of *sola gratia* and a place for human participation'.[274] Collins affirms that 'the inclusion of prevenient grace in Wesley's theology implied that salvation is not, "the arbitrary breaking through of God upon man's passivity", but that "it is the reciprocal work of God and man"... But again, even in this synergism there is the primacy of grace, for it is God who initiates and humanity which responds'.[275]

In Wesley's holding of the conception of prevenient grace, the influence from the theological tradition of the Church of England was essential,[276] as he appreciated his inheritance from 'the English writers such as Bishop Beveridge, Bishop Taylor, and Mr. [Robert] Nelson' in his Journal dated on 24 January 1738.[277] Rogers in his dissertation shows that the main 'sources of Wesley's concept of prevenient grace' included the Scripture texts,[278] ancient and medieval theology, the *Thirty-Nine Articles* and *The Book of Common Prayer* of the

---

[269] James C. Logan ed., *Theology and Evangelism in the Wesleyan Heritage* (Nashville: Kingswood Books, 1994), 18.
[270] Collins, 'Law', 112-113.
[271] Burns, 'John Wesley's Doctrine of Perfect Love', 37.
[272] McGonigle, *Sufficient*, 193.
[273] Collins, 'Law', 85.
[274] Rogers, 'The Concept of Prevenient Grace in the Theology of John Wesley', v.
[275] Collins, 'Law', 113.
[276] Rogers, 'The Concept of Prevenient Grace in the Theology of John Wesley', 25-58.
[277] Journals 1:419.
[278] Especially Rom. 1:19, 2:12-14, 8:32, John 1:9; Rogers, 'The Concept of Prevenient Grace in the Theology of John Wesley', 26.

Church of England, and Anglican theologians such as Dr Robert Barnes (1495-1540), Thomas Rogers (d. 1616), Richard Hooker (1554-1600), Bishop William Beveridge (1637-1708), Bishop Gilbert Burnet (1643-1715), Bishop John Pearson (1612-1686), the Puritan Samuel Annesley (1620-1696), Susanna Wesley's father, and Dr William Tilly.[279]

III. Faith as Lord of Love vs. Faith as Handmaid of Love

Leon Hynson argues that Luther and Wesley were not that much different in their teachings on 'faith working by love', except that Luther's emphasis was laid on faith, and Wesley's, on love. He states,

> Luther is especially anxious about the danger of works righteousness, and rigorously argues for the sola fide (faith alone) position ... John Wesley particularly worries about faith divorced from love (antinomianism). Faith alone justifies, but it also renews and sanctifies... Luther seeks to guard the doctrine of faith, without denying love. Wesley guards the doctrine of love, declaring the prior work of faith.[280]

Hynson's view is acceptable, though, beyond different emphases on either faith or love, there are fundamental differences in their views of salvation, of the ways of salvation, and of the extent of salvation in this life.

For Luther, while faith represents the fundamental relationship between God and human beings, the relationship between faith and love can be explained in terms of cause (God's love, faith, justification) and result (Christian love). Collins notes, for Luther, 'the process of salvation is a movement from the law to gospel ... and should not entail the contrary movement of gospel back to law'.[281] Elert states, 'it is not the gospel that serves the law, but the law which serves the gospel'.[282] The law serves the gospel firstly by leading sinners to Christ through its accusation, and also by explicit commandment to have faith in God, but the gospel does not serve the law. It is by far superior to the law, being in itself self-sufficient, working perfectly with or without the law, and giving incomparably better things than love. It replaces and abolishes the law. Calling faith 'all in all', Luther attributed to faith what Wesley ascribed to love: fulfilment of

---

[279] Rogers, 'The Concept of Prevenient Grace in the Theology of John Wesley', 43-58
[280] Leon O. Hynson, *To Reform the Nation: Theological Foundations of Wesley's Ethics* (Grand Rapids: Francis Asbury Press, 1984), 53-54.
[281] Collins, 'Law', 184.
[282] Elert, *Law*, 48.

the law, righteousness, vivification in the Spirit and mortification of the old nature, and victory over sin, the flesh, and the world.[283]

Wesley added another element to the relationship between faith and love, that is, a means and the end: 'I regard ... faith itself, not as an end, but a means only. The end of the commandment is love ... Let this love be attained, by whatever means, and I am content; I desire no more. All is well'.[284] 'The theological reason' that Wesley regarded faith as an instrument for holy love, Tore Meistad analyses, is that 'faith is not in itself *imago dei* but leads to it. Love is *imago dei*'.[285] While, as Runyon says, 'renewal of the *imago Dei* in humanity ... is the indispensable key to Wesley's whole soteriology',[286] Burns contends, 'love for Wesley was ... a love imitative of' God.[287] 'Faith working by love' and sanctification are identical.[288]

Luther regarded the expression 'faith without works' as a 'mere vanity and a dream of the heart' or 'a false faith',[289] since faith will certainly produce love and works. In this sense, Sun-Yong Kim states that for Luther, 'works is already inherent in faith' or 'love already exists in faith'.[290] Luther always excluded Christian love from the context of justification. In his teaching, whereas faith is a divine work, since God's love produces faith, the love that faith produces is a human work, though it depends indirectly on the divine grace. Whereas Luther represented the nature of Christian love positively when he related it to its source, that is, the love of God, he described the effect of Christian love negatively, since, as long as love is located in believers, Christian love is limited and hindered by sin and the flesh. Nevertheless, for 'genuine' believers, to commit sins 'out of weakness, not out of deliberate wickedness' 'does not hinder their holiness at all', since 'by faith they return to Christ' and 'obtain forgiveness'. What makes them 'stand or fall' before God is not love, good works, or 'morals', but faith.[291] Justifying faith is the foundation on which the whole of Christian life stands; Christian life is the battle for keeping this faith.

---

[283] LW 14:328-329.
[284] WW, 12:79.
[285] Meistad, *Mount*, 111.
[286] Theodore Runyon, *The New Creation: John Wesley's Theology Today* (Nashville: Abingdon Press, 1998), 60.
[287] Burns, 'John Wesley's Doctrine of Perfect Love', 60.
[288] Ibid., 43; WW, 14:321.
[289] LW 26:155.
[290] Kim, 'Luther on Faith and Love', 152.
[291] LW 27:82.

For Wesley, the power of Christian love given through God's regenerating grace or sanctifying grace cannot be regarded as a natural affection or a natural power of human will, since this love is motivated and empowered supernaturally by God's grace. Like saving faith given instantaneously by grace, this love is given supernaturally. Sanctifying grace is no other than God's giving 'pure love; love expelling sin, and governing both the heart and life of a child of God'.[292] Faith in God's love and Christian love as the fruit of faith are given in the same instance. Christian love is always a pair of true faith, and both are the divine works.

Since Luther was consistently positive concerning the effect of justifying faith on love or good works, he thought that only a false faith distorts God's words 'in a fleshly way', transforming 'the freedom of the spirit into the freedom of the flesh'.[293] Wesley would agree with Luther; what makes the difference between a true believer who rejoices to obey God, and a 'presumptuous pretender' who thinks that God's love gives 'liberty to disobey, to break, not keep, the commandments of God', is whether or not they have a true faith that accepts the love of God witnessed in their hearts by the Holy Spirit.[294] However, for Wesley, even a true faith may turn into 'practical antinomianism', which makes believers 'less obedient to God'; 'less zealous of good works: less careful to abstain from evil ... less earnest to deny himself, and to take up his cross daily'.[295] Believers who came to love God and neighbours, if they do not increase their love in a constant obedience to God's law, cannot continue to overcome sin and the flesh, and produce love and good works.[296] Lack of love, opening door to 'some sin of omission' or 'some inward sin', may result in 'the loss of faith', and 'the loss of faith' may result in 'committing outward sin'.[297] In contrast to this vulnerable faith, love cannot be satisfied with a loose standard in keeping God's law; it endeavours to 'keep the whole law' and not to 'offend in one point', preserving believers on the firm foundation of a loving relationship with God.[298]

Intellectually, it is not easy even for true Christians to explain correctly their justifying faith with doctrinal exactness. However, in

---

[292] WW 12:432.
[293] LW 27:48.
[294] S. Witness (1), II. 6-7.
[295] S. Established (1), II. 1, 4-8; S. Witness (1), II. 7.
[296] S. Privilege, II. 7.
[297] S. Privilege, III. 1; S. Wilderness.
[298] *Plain Account*, 18.

Theodore Runyon's words, even when true believers cannot express exactly their 'orthodoxy' ('right belief'), Wesley thought that their 'orthopraxy' ('right practice') and 'orthopathy' (holy tempers or dispositions) may verify their true faith, and that orthodoxy apart from orthopraxy and orthopathy is 'insufficient'.[299]

Thus, for Wesley, though faith is sufficient for receiving justifying and sanctifying grace, the peculiar role of human works still remains in preserving and improving the already received grace. By faith Wesley meant not only an intellectual assent, but also 'a disposition of the heart',[300] which is inclusive of sinners' humbleness and readiness to accept God's grace[301] and of 'a sure trust and confidence' in 'the favour of God'.[302] True believers, being 'sincere of heart', do not continue in sins on the pretext of the rich grace of God.[303] In order not to 'halt with God, through an inconstant, wavering faith', believers support faith by reminding themselves of already received favour.[304] Thus, both in preparing for faith beforehand and in preserving saving faith, a human role of assuming a proper attitude before God is required. Vindicating only 'faith unfeigned',[305] Wesley emphasized, believers fulfil God's law through faith working through love:

> He loves God, so he 'keeps His commandments'; not only some, or most of them, but all ... He is not content to 'keep the whole law and offend in one point', but has in all points 'a conscience void of offense towards God, and towards man'. Whatever God has forbidden, he avoids; whatever God has enjoined, he does. 'He runs the way of God's commandments'... All the commandments of God he accordingly keeps.[306]

---

[299] Runyon, *The New Creation*, 147-149; Theodore Runyon ed., *Sanctification and Liberation* (Nashville: Abingdon Press, 1981), 45; S. Lord, II. 15; S. Trinity, 1; Letters 5:264.
[300] S. Salvation, I. 4-5; see S. Almost, II. 1-6; S. Way (1), I. 6; II. 10; S. Circumcision, I. 7; S. Marks, I. 3; S. Mount (3), I. 6-11; S. Mount (9), 4-8; S. Without, 15.
[301] S. Justification, IV. 8.
[302] S. Almost, II. 5; S. Scriptural, I. 1-2; S. Justification, IV. 2;
[303] S. Salvation, II. 1-7; III. 4; see S. Justification, IV. 8-9; S. Righteousness, III. 3; S. Fruits, II. 1-8; S. Sin, IV. 12; S. Circumcision, I. 8; S. Backsliders, II. 10 (6).
[304] S. Justification, IV. 3.
[305] S. Mount (4), III. 2.
[306] *Plain Account*, 18.

Chapter 6

Humanity and the Law

A. Martin Luther

I. Humanity in Creation

In Luther's theology, the subjects of God and of salvation are closely interrelated in his theological anthropology. Luther thought that we can know who we are when we see ourselves in our 'origin which is God'.[1] And, this makes us understand the nature of salvation from the viewpoint of humanity 'in its primal perfection as God created it, in its fall into sin ... and as freed through Christ'.[2] In this sense, Luther represented his view of humanity in three stages: creation, the fall, and salvation.[3]

Luther sought to investigate the nature of humanity by examining the Scriptural teaching of the image of God in innocent humanity.[4] Kristen E. Kvam points out that, for Luther, the image of God had 'a variety of facets ... from a number of different angles'.[5] Nathan Jastram notes, in describing the image of God, Luther employed 'not only, but also' language.[6]

From the viewpoint of the natural endowments, Luther thought, Adam's were incomparably superior to those of present human be-

---

[1] LW 34:138.
[2] Althaus, *Theology*, 9-10.
[3] LW 34:138. 'Man is a creature of God consisting of body and a living soul, made in the beginning after the image of God, without sin, so that he should procreate and rule over the created things, and never die. But after the fall of Adam, certainly, he was subject to the power of the devil, sin and death, a twofold evil for his powers, unconquerable and eternal. He can be freed and given eternal life only through the Son of God, Jesus Christ (if he believes in Him)'.
[4] LW 1:60.
[5] Kristen E. Kvam, 'Luther, Eve, and Theological Anthropology: Reassessing the Reformer's Response to the "Frauenfrage"', (Ph.D. thesis, Emory University, 1992), 24.
[6] Jastram, 'Image', 12.

ings; 'his inner and ... outer sensations were all of the purest kind. His intellect was the clearest, his memory was the best, and his will was the most straightforward'.[7] To Adam's superior qualities Luther included the 'most beautiful and superb qualities of body' which surpassed those of 'all the remaining living creatures'; 'his eyes ... surpassed those of the lynx and eagle. He was stronger than the lions and the bears ... he handled them the way we handle puppies'.[8] Stating that 'the loveliness and the quality of the fruits he used as food were also far superior to what they are now', Luther also implied that before the fall of Adam, human beings were blessed with excellent and superb qualities of God's creation in an ecological harmony.[9] However, most importantly, Theo M.M.A.C. Bell correctly notes, Luther thought that the image of God represents 'the right relationship of a person to God'.[10] Luther said, 'the image of God is ... that he not only knew God ... he also lived in a life that was wholly godly; that is, he was without the fear of death or of any other danger, and was content with God's favour'.[11] Both spiritual and physical qualities 'make up and produce the sort of man in whom ... the image of God is reflected'.[12] Jastram summarizes Luther's 'definitions of the image of God' as follows:

> Luther had several explanations of what the image of God included, usually expressed as trinities: knowledge of God, belief that God is good, and holiness of life; justice, wisdom, and happiness;[13] 'to feel, think, and want exactly what God does';[14] righteousness, holiness, and truth; eternal life, freedom from fear, everything that is good; glory and prestige; domination and dominion; immortality.[15] Most of his statements stress the spiritual dimension of the image of God, but he did not deny that a non-spiritual dimension is included in the image.[16]

What was the life of humanity in the image of God like? As will be examined in more detail in the next chapter, Luther taught that the earth is the locus of human life; not merely for physical life but also for spiritual life. Forde points out that Luther thought that human

---

[7] LW 1:62.
[8] LW 1:62.
[9] LW 1:62.
[10] Theo M.M.A.C. Bell, 'Man Is a Microcosmos: Adam and Even in Luther's *Lectures on Genesis* (1535-1545)', *CTQ* 69:2 (April, 2005), 163-164.
[11] LW 1:62.
[12] LW 1:63-64.
[13] WA 42:51.
[14] LW 26:431.
[15] LW 34:177; WA 42:65; LW 1:69, 84.
[16] Jastram, 'Image', 12.

beings were not created as 'quasi-divine' beings but 'strictly *creaturely*' beings. Although they had considerable knowledge of God, their intellectual and spiritual faculty was for living a creaturely life in faith, gratitude, and praise of God, and in love for neighbours. For him, 'man is man and not God. Man is a creature and is to remain a creature ... The perfections which man possessed when he was originally created ... were *creaturely* perfections'.[17]

Robert Kolb notes, the heart of the creaturely life can be described as the life of 'trusting God'.[18] Luther asserted, the words, 'man is justified by faith', exactly 'sums up the definition of man'.[19] The image of God is not 'some secret spiritual faculty now lost', but rather a capacity to live a peaceful life with God, with other people, and with the other creatures of God.[20] The role of God's law towards this humanity was, James Arne Nestingen properly states, to 'set out the requirements of creaturely life, incumbent by creation'.[21] In the image of God or in original righteousness,[22] Adam lived 'at peace with his Maker, with himself and with his world';[23] loving God and the other creatures with the greatest joy; without any lust, evil inclination, or sin.[24]

Denying that if there was no fall human beings could live eternally in their natural power, Luther believed that human beings were dependent on God for their eternal life. Even though they were 'created for an immortal and spiritual life', their physical life which was dependent on 'food, drink, and procreation', 'would have been translated to the eternal and spiritual life'[25] 'without death after living in Eden' for the time being.[26]

II. Humanity after the Fall

Because of the fall of Adam, the innocent state of humanity in the image of God has become 'something unknown' to present humanity,

---

[17] Forde, *Where*, 53-54.
[18] Kolb, 'Cross', 459-460.
[19] LW 34:139.
[20] Forde, *Where*, 54.
[21] James Arne Nestingen, 'The Lord's Prayer in Luther's Catechism', Word & World 22:1 (Winter 2002), 39.
[22] *BC*, 102-103; Jastram, 'Image', 15-18.
[23] Forde, *Where*, 54.
[24] LW 1:113.
[25] LW 1:56.
[26] LW 1:104.

about which we can hear only in Scripture.[27] Nevertheless, from this original state we can understand the nature of the fall and of salvation. When the fall is thought of as degradation from the state suitable to who we are, the purpose of Christ's coming can properly be understood as the recovery of the lost state.[28]

Luther thought that Adam and Eve's temptation was 'the greatest and severest of all temptations', since the serpent attacked their 'most excellent powers in the uncorrupted nature' and 'the highest form of worship itself', that is, their faith in 'the Word and the good will of God'.[29] The process of Adam's fall is 'the pattern of all the temptations of Satan'; 'he first puts faith to trial and draws away from the Word'. Then, the other sins such as 'disobedience ... fear, hatred, and avoidance of God follow unbelief'.[30]

Unbelief is to Luther the supreme sin which can be identified with unrighteousness itself.[31] Luther also described ingratitude as 'the most shameful vice and the greatest contempt of God'.[32] Likewise, human nature 'has been so deeply curved in upon itself' that, even when it seeks God, it does so 'for its own sake'.[33] Mary E. Lowe correctly points out, 'Luther identified the basic forms of sin as unbelief and pride and *curvatus in se* in which the human puts her/himself in the place of God'.[34]

Original sin together with its unbelief, pride, and self-centredness has brought to Adam both the loss of the spiritual dimension and the marring of natural and physical dimensions of the image of God.[35] It caused human beings 'a lack of a certain quality in the will ... in the mind ... in the memory'; 'a total lack of uprightness ... of body and soul' or 'of original righteousness'.[36] Original sin affected the ecological environments, since 'God's practice has always been this: whenever He punishes sin, He also curses the earth'.[37] From 'the deprava-

---

[27] LW 1:63.
[28] LW 1:164-166.
[29] LW 1:146.
[30] LW 1:163, 171; *BC*, 302.
[31] LW 25:319.
[32] LW 14:51.
[33] LW 25:291.
[34] Mary E. Lowe, 'Sin from a Queer, Lutheran Perspective', in Mary J. Streufert, ed., *Transformative Lutheran Theologies: Feminist, Womanist, and Mujerista Perspectives* (Minneapolis: Fortress Press, 2010), 77.
[35] Jastram, 'Image', 15-18; *BC*, 102-103.
[36] LW 25:299-300; LW 2:65.
[37] LW 1:99; LW 2:65

tion and the curse of the creation',[38] 'all the remaining creatures derive their shortcomings'.[39] Human beings have lost their physical strength as well as their intellectual capacity; beasts have become disobedient; and the land has lost its previous fertility.[40] Describing original sin as 'the very tinder of sin', 'the tyrant', 'the original sickness', Luther stressed that original sin is an active power, not merely 'the weakness of our nature' or 'the loss of health'.[41] Being dominated by original sin that works through 'the imagination of the human heart, namely, industry, wisdom, and, and human reason, together with all their powers', the human heart 'is always opposed to God's law ... it cannot be freed of this evil by its own powers'. Therefore, the scholastic teaching of 'the human *in se*' based on the hypothesis of 'unimpaired natural endowments' cannot be accepted:[42]

> If the natural or carnal free will of St. Paul and other regenerated persons wars against the law of God even after their regeneration, the will of man prior to his conversion will be much more obstinately opposed and hostile to God's law and will. From this it is evident... that the free will by its own natural powers can do nothing for man's conversion, righteousness, peace, and salvation, cannot cooperate, and cannot obey, believe, and give assent when the Holy Spirit offers the grace of God and salvation through the Gospel. On the contrary, because of the wicked and obstinate disposition with which he was born, he defiantly resists God and His will unless the Holy Spirit illuminates and rules him.[43]

To subdivide Luther's view of the effects of original sin, as Jastram summarizes,[44] firstly, original righteousness was absolutely lost, so that in human beings 'nothing spiritually good remains'. Secondly, natural endowments and faculties were greatly marred. Though human beings are still superior to the other creatures which lack the knowledge of God, their knowledge of God also became 'almost completely obliterated'.[45] Similar to the way the original world and Paradise disappeared but left its trace,[46] the image of God in human be-

---

[38] LW 1:77-78.
[39] LW 1:64.
[40] LW 1:78; LW 2:65; Bret Stephenson and Susan Power Bratton, 'Martin Luther's Understanding of Sin's Impact on Nature and the Unlanding of the Jew', *Ecotheology* 9 (2000)85-89.
[41] LW 25:299-300.
[42] LW 2:119-126; LW 34:139.
[43] *BC*, 524.
[44] Jastram, 'Image', 13.
[45] LW 1:19.
[46] LW 1:90. Luther thought that the trace of Paradise was present in the beautiful landscape of 'the land of Canaan', where he believed 'Paradise was situated'. See LW 2:204; Stephenson and Bratton, 'Martin Luther's Understanding', 86-87.

ings left 'remnants that are corrupted or marred ... on account of sin'.[47]

The effects of original sin upon natural endowments can be distinguished again into its effects on human reason and on the will. Firstly, though God did not 'take away this majesty of reason', it knows 'almost nothing' about its Creator. Its knowledge is limited to 'exceedingly material' things. It 'is subject to error and deception'. Further, since human reason after the fall 'remains under the power of the devil', its judgment is 'impiously in opposition to theology'.[48] At best, by way of reason human beings can obtain some 'objective' knowledge of God, but fail to find out His will 'for me':[49]

> Natural reason is aware that ... Godhead is something superior to all other things ... it regards God as kind, gracious, merciful, and benevolent ... However, it manifests two big defects: first ... reason believes in God's might ... but it is uncertain whether God is willing to employ this in our behalf ... The second defect is this: Reason ... knows that there is a God, but it ... never finds the true God, but it finds the devil or its own concept of God ... honouring their own delusion and their own fancy as God.[50]

The consequence is that they try to reach to God's glory intellectually, or that they seek to merit God's favour, for which they are uncertain, by pursuing vain things which look great by the judgment of human reason.[51]

Secondly, 'free choice is allowed to man only with respect to what is beneath him',[52] that is, 'in the ordinary affairs of life'.[53] However, 'in relation to God', Luther asserted, 'a man has no free choice, but is a captive, subject and slave either of the will of God or the will of Satan'.[54] In those matters, free will is 'a mere title, an empty name, with no reality'.[55] Concerning the effects of original sin upon the will, Cameron A. MacKenzie notes, Luther taught: '(1) all human beings are sinful; (2) every person is sinful in every part; (3) sin puts people

---

[47] Jastram, 'Image', 14.
[48] LW 34:137-139.
[49] Althaus, *Theology*, 10-11, 15-16
[50] LW 19:53-55.
[51] LW 3:276-277.
[52] LW 33:70.
[53] Gerhard O. Forde, *The Captivation of the Will: Luther vs. Erasmus on Freedom and Bondage* (Grand Rapids: Wm. B. Eerdmans, 2005), 49.
[54] LW 33:70.
[55] Forde, *The Captivation of the Will*, 47-49; LW 31:40 (Theses 13-18 of *Heidelberg Disputation*).

under the power of Satan; and (4) even after Baptism, man remains a sinner'.[56]

On the first aspect of the universal depravity, Luther wrote, 'from this man [Adam], thus corrupted, all [human beings] are born ungodly'.[57] Consequently, 'they do nothing but what deserves wrath and punishment, because they are all ungodly and wicked'.[58] The second point means that 'there is no part of man that is not sinful'.[59] Commenting on Rom. 3:20, Luther asked, if 'the best and noblest' people who are zealous to keep God's law and to do good works, together with 'the best and noblest parts of themselves' such as 'their reason and will', have become 'condemned for ungodliness and ... declared to be flesh in the sight of God, what is there now left in the whole race of men that is not flesh and not ungodly?'[60]

On the third point, Luther taught that 'Satan reigns ... all who are not snatched away from him by the Spirit of Christ ... the Spirit of God'.[61] Then, 'as long as he reigns the human will is not free ... but is the slave of sin and Satan, and can only will what its master wills'.[62] To explain this Luther employed a metaphor of a beast and two riders; 'If God rides it [the will], it wills and goes where God wills ... If Satan rides it, it wills and goes where Satan wills; nor can it choose to run to either of the two riders or to seek him out, but the riders themselves contend for the possession and control of it'.[63] Concerning the state of sinners affected by original sin, Heckel well expresses, 'Human reason has no insight into the meaning of the law, and human will has not the smallest propensity to fulfil it'.[64]

However, even though human beings are bound to sin under the effects of original sin and under the reign of Satan, Luther, representing the image of God as 'both lost and present at the same time' or both 'disappearing and yet remaining in a marred condition',[65] contended that 'God wants us to show respect for this image in one an-

---

[56] MacKenzie, 'The Origins and Consequences of Original Sin in Luther's Bondage of the Will', *CJ* 31:4 (Oct. 2005), 386.
[57] LW 33:174.
[58] LW 33:247.
[59] MacKenzie, 'The Origins and Consequences of Original Sin in Luther's Bondage of the Will', 387.
[60] LW 33:257-258.
[61] LW 33:287.
[62] LW 33:238.
[63] LW 33:65.
[64] Heckel, *LEX*, 18.
[65] Jastram, 'Image', 13-14.

other' since 'it can be restored through the Word and the Holy Spirit'.[66] The fourth point is represented in Luther's teaching of believers as saints and sinners.

III. Humanity after Salvation

Luther represented very confidently and positively the fruit and power of faith in Christian life, asserting that 'he who does right, shows this with fruits, and no longer sins against his neighbour is born of God. And he who does not do right to his neighbour is a false Christian'.[67] However, in his view of Christians, such a positive tone was diminished. Luther stated, 'Now, is he perfectly righteous? No, for he is at the same time both a sinner and a righteous man; a sinner in fact, but a righteous man by the sure imputation and promise of God that He will continue to deliver him from sin until He has completely cured him'.[68] Luther also said, 'he sins in the same act because of the will of the flesh; he does not sin because of the contrary will of the spirit'.[69]

In Luther's teaching of believers as both saints and sinners, three seeming contradictions can be discerned. Firstly, believers are saints 'apart from' themselves and 'in Christ', whereas we are sinners 'in and by myself apart from Christ'.[70] Secondly, believers are 'righteous in hope' since God's promise will certainly be fulfilled in the eschatological future, whereas presently we are still sinful.[71] Thirdly, believers are righteous in the Holy Spirit who works in our life, whereas we repeat sins in our flesh. Commenting on the Apostle Paul's confession, *'For I know that nothing good dwells within me, that is, in my flesh'* (Rom. 7:18), Luther explained:

> See how he attributes to himself flesh which is a part of him as if he himself were flesh ... Because of his flesh he is carnal and wicked ... because of the spirit he is spiritual and good ... the words 'I want' and 'I hate' refer to the spiritual man or to the spirit, but 'I do' and 'I work' refer to the carnal man or to the flesh. But because the same one complete man consists of flesh and spirit, therefore he attributes to the whole man both of these opposing qualities which come from the opposing parts of him. For in this way there

---

[66] LW 2:141.
[67] LW 30:264.
[68] LW 25:260.
[69] LW 31:62.
[70] LW 38:158.
[71] LW 25:258.

comes about a communication of attributes, for one and the same man is spiritual and carnal, righteous and a sinner, good and evil.[72]

Negatively speaking, in reality not in faith in God's promise, in believers themselves not in Christ, or in flesh not in spirit, as Lowe properly expresses, Christians are mere 'justified sinners' who 'sin repeatedly and are forgiven continually' rather than 'being forgiven and never sinning again'.[73] They cannot be freed from the effects of original sin, though they are forgiven of the guilt of it; 'original sin has been taken away in baptism' not in the sense that it does not exist any longer, but that 'God no longer imputes it to us'.[74]

For Luther, the flesh is an inclusive word that covers not only 'the desires' or 'the coarse drives of the flesh' such as 'sexual desire, anger, impatience', but also 'the spiritual ones' such as 'doubt, blasphemy, idolatry, contempt and hatred of God, etc'.[75] McGrath points out that for Luther, flesh does not indicate a human's 'lower nature' but 'the entire' person 'in its irrepressible egoism and its radical alienation from God', whereas spirit refers to the entire person in 'openness to God and the divine promises'.[76] Because of the flesh, Luther contended, a Christian 'is always a sinner, always a penitent, always righteous'.[77] Believers live 'in sins', being 'daily ... either justified or ... more polluted'.[78] However, 'since the noblest, best and most important part of man, the spirit, remains by faith godly and righteous', Luther argued, 'God does not charge the sin which remains in the lesser part, the flesh, toward his condemnation'.[79] In this life, 'the flesh [will] continue, and consequently ... sin [will] continue'. All that believers can do is to 'restrain it' with the power of the Holy Spirit.[80]

---

[72] LW 25:331-332, 336.
[73] Lowe, 'Sin from a Queer, Lutheran Perspective', 77.
[74] WA 17, II, 285. Cited from T. A. Noble, 'Doctrine of Original Sin in the Evangelical Reformers', *European Explorations in Christian Holiness* 2 (2001), 71.
[75] LW 27:69.
[76] McGrath, *Luther's Theology of the Cross*, 133.
[77] LW 25:434.
[78] LW 34:140.
[79] LW 32:21.
[80] LW 27:68-69; LW 7:234-235.

B. John Wesley

I. Humanity in Creation

Wesley found the essence and the value of human beings not from the body which he called 'a house of clay', not merely from the intellectual or the volitional faculty, but from the 'immortal spirit ... made in the image of God' to which he ascribed 'infinitely more value ... than the whole material creation'.[81] For Wesley, the fact that human beings are made in God's image has profound implications for their relationship with God, with neighbours, and with the other creatures of God. While Wesley's theology is soteriological in character, his discussion of salvation is focused on the states of the image of God in them: the original, the lost, and the restored.

On the original state of human beings before the fall, Wesley wrote in his sermon, 'The New Birth' (1760): 'God created man ... in His *natural image*, a picture of His own immortality; a spiritual being, endued with understanding, freedom of will, and various affections ... in His *political image*, the governor of this lower world ... chiefly in His *moral image*; which ... is "righteousness and true holiness"'.[82] For Wesley, all images are of some help toward the characteristic of human beings as free agents in determining their destiny.

In the category of the natural image, Wesley included such faculties that give human beings the 'power of self-motion' as 'understanding, will, and liberty'.[83] Though not an infinite or an omniscient knowledge, Adam had 'a power of distinguishing truth from falsehood' by intuition or by reasoning.[84] Illustrating Adam's naming of the animals, Wesley explained the characteristic of his understanding as: 'just' in the sense that 'everything appeared to him according to its real nature'; 'clear' without 'error and doubt'; 'swift in its motion' and 'extensive' in boundary.[85]

For Wesley, as a 'far greater and nobler' endowment than understanding[86] the 'will' relates to 'passions and affections', rather than to 'the traditional understanding of free-will'.[87] Adam's will was 'steadily and uniformly guided by the dictates of his unerring understand-

---

[81] S. Man (1), II. 5; see Cannon, *The Theology of John Wesley*, 179.
[82] S. New (1), I. 1.
[83] S. Deliverance, I. 1.
[84] BE 4:293
[85] BE 4:293-294.
[86] BE 4:294.
[87] Kim, 'Anthropology', 32.

ing; embracing nothing but good'.[88] Wesley contended, 'he had but one [affection]: man was what God is, love. Love filled the whole expansion of his soul ... his heart'.[89]

By liberty, Wesley meant 'freedom of choice',[90] 'a self-determining principle',[91] teaching that 'without this, both the will and the understanding would have been utterly useless'.[92] Wesley taught that Adam had an 'entire freedom either to keep or change his first estate'.[93] Liberty is what makes it possible for human beings to be partners with God's covenant.[94] Without it human beings cannot be 'a *free agent*', since 'where there is no liberty, there can be no moral good or evil, no virtue or vice'.[95]

The political image relates to the role of human beings as 'God's vicegerent upon earth' through whom 'all the blessings of God flowed ... to the inferior creatures'.[96] The political image represents human status and responsibility to care for other people and other creatures.[97] In the political image human beings are superior to the other lower creatures in that they are 'capable of knowing, loving, or obeying God', whereas 'the inferior creatures' can only have 'a loving obedience to man'.[98]

The 'principal image of God'[99] or the 'essence of the *imago Dei*'[100] is the moral image, which is inclusive of 'righteousness and true holiness' after God's moral image[101] and 'love, reverence, resignation to His Father; humility, meekness, gentleness; love to lost mankind, and every other holy and heavenly temper' after the moral image of the Incarnate Christ.[102] Collins explains three reasons why the moral image is principal: firstly, it 'distinguishes humanity from the rest of creation'; secondly, it becomes 'the context for the very possibility of sin'; thirdly, this image validates the use of the moral law as a norm

---

[88] S. Deliverance, I. 2.
[89] BE 4:294.
[90] S. Deliverance, I. 1.
[91] WW 10:468.
[92] S. Coming, I. 4; see S. Man (2), 11.
[93] BE 4:295, n. 12.
[94] Collins, *Theology*, 53.
[95] S. Coming, I. 4-6; S. Fall, II. 6; S. Deliverance, I. 1.
[96] S. Deliverance, I. 3; II. 1.
[97] Collins, *Theology*, 54.
[98] S. Deliverance, I. 4-5; Kim, 'Anthropology', 29, 42.
[99] Kim, 'Anthropology', 44-46.
[100] Collins, *Theology*, 56.
[101] S. Coming, I. 7; I. 10.
[102] S. Lord, I. 2; S. Mount (4), Intro. 1; II. 2; S. Justification, I. 1.

of the God-human relationship, since the moral law is a conveyor of the same moral image of God.[103]

The natural and political image serves this essential and principal image. While the political image locates human beings in the relationship in which they exercise the moral image, the natural image provides them with a 'fundamental faculty' which is prerequisite for exercising the moral image.[104] Young Taek Kim summarizes the imperatives of God's law which reflect all three images of God as: 'to glorify God'; 'to love God'; and 'to reflect God in the world'.[105] The third imperative has as its objects not only other people[106] but also all other creatures in the ecological environment.[107] Maddox aptly maintains:

> Wesley's anthropology recognized four basic human relationships: with God, with other humans, with lower animals, and with ourselves. A holy (and whole!) person is one in whom all of these relationships are properly expressed. The proper relationship to God is knowing, loving, obeying, and enjoying God eternally (i.e., participation). The proper relationship to other humans is loving service. The proper relationship to all other animals is loving protection. When each of these relationships is properly expressed, we will also have a proper relationship to ourselves of self-acceptance.[108]

II. Humanity after the Fall

'Whence came evil and why?', according to Barry E. Bryant, were questions from Wesley's 'long interest in theodicy' which he regarded as an enquiry into 'God's ability to extract good out of evil'.[109] Wesley found the answers from two possible sources of evil. Firstly, Wesley never ascribed any part of evil to God, advocating both 'the moral attributes of justice and goodness' of God and the goodness of His creation which has been created as 'best possible world' 'without evil and sin'.[110]

Secondly, Wesley taught, the misuse of liberty resulted in not only 'the heavenly revolt' by Satan, who Wesley described as 'the first sinner in the universe; the author of sin; the first being who ... intro-

---

[103] Collins, *Theology*, 55-57.
[104] Kim, 'Anthropology', 42-44, 52.
[105] Kim, 'Anthropology', 49-58.
[106] S. Children, 4; Collins, *Theology*, 54-55;
[107] Runyon, *The New Creation*, 200-207; Cobb, *Grace and Responsibility*, 50-55; Kim, 'Anthropology', 51-58.
[108] Maddox, *Responsible*, 68.
[109] Barry E. Bryant, 'John Wesley on the Origins of Evil', *WTJ* 30:1 (Spring 1995), 111-112; S. Mourning, 6.
[110] Bryant, 'John Wesley on the Origins of Evil', 111-120.

duced evil into the creation', but also the earthly revolt by Adam and Eve.[111] In 1782, Wesley wrote, 'Why is there *pain* in the world ...? Because there is sin ... why is there sin in the world? Because man was created in the image of God ... not mere matter ... but ... a being endued ... with ... understanding ... will ... liberty ... He chose evil. Thus "sin entered into the world", and pain of every kind'.[112] Whereas Satan, being self-tempted, 'gave way first to pride, then to self-will', human beings, being tempted externally by Satan, fell into unbelief so that 'unbelief begot pride... it begot self-will'.[113] For human beings, 'unbelief is the parent of all evil'.[114] Collins outlines the different sequences of the fall of Satan and of Human beings according to Wesley:

Satanic Evil

Self-Temptation → Pride → Self-Will → Evil Tempers and Affections

Human Evil

External Temptation → Unbelief → Pride → Self-Will → Evil Tempers and Affections[115]

The fall of human beings resulted in physical and spiritual death. Physically, Adam's body 'became corruptible and mortal'.[116] 'The sentence of death' not only passed upon Adam, but also 'overwhelmed his posterity' who 'had not, like him, sinned against an express law'; 'even ... infants who had never sinned'.[117] Further, the death was 'not only temporal, but spiritual, and (without the grace of God) eternal'.[118] Collins explains that the soul of human beings is dead 'in a metaphorical sense'; though 'it continues to exist', it is 'separated from God',[119] and 'deprived of the favour of God, but also of His image'.[120]

The effects of both physical and spiritual death affected the image of God in humanity. Firstly, the moral image of God was lost: 'He lost

---

[111] S. Coming, I. 8-10; S. Deceitfulness, I. 1; Bryant, 'John Wesley on the Origins of Evil', 120-133.
[112] S. Fall, Intro. 1.
[113] S. Coming, I. 8-9.
[114] ENNT Heb 3:12.
[115] Collins, *Theology*, 58-59.
[116] S. Justification, I. 5.
[117] BE 4:297; ENNT Rom 5:14-16.
[118] WW 9:291.
[119] Collins, *Theology*, 60-61; S. Justification, I. 5.
[120] S. Love (1), Intro. 1.

the whole moral image of God, righteousness and true holiness. He was unholy ... Thus was his soul utterly dead to God! And in that day his body likewise began to die; became obnoxious to weakness, sickness, pain'.[121] In the room of God's image, sinners had 'the very image of the devil' such as 'pride and self-will', and also 'the image of the beasts' such as 'sensual appetites and desires'.[122] Though Wesley described unbelief as the parent sin, he did not belittle those diabolic or brutal tempers and passions, since hence 'the inexhaustible flood of evils' came into this world.[123]

Secondly, the political image stopped working properly. The unity, harmony, and order of the chain of being were obscured:

> As man is deprived of *his* perfection, his loving obedience to God; so brutes are deprived of *their* perfection, their loving obedience to man. The far greater part of them flee from him; studiously avoid his hated presence. The most of the rest set him at open defiance; yea, destroy him, if it be in their power. A few only, those we commonly term domestic animals, retain more or less of their original disposition, (through the mercy of God,) love him still, and pay obedience to him.[124]

The 'communication between the Creator and the whole brute creation' was 'cut off', since the fall has made human beings 'incapable of transmitting' God's blessings to His creation.[125] The tragic result was that 'the whole creation' fell into 'disorder, misery, death ... in consequence of which the whole creation now groaneth together'.[126]

Thirdly, the natural image was seriously marred. Adam's will after the fall became 'seized by legions of vile affections' and 'earthly, sensual, and devilish passions' such as grief, anger, hatred, fear, and shame.[127] His liberty has gone 'away with virtue'.[128] Adam's intellectual power also became so weak that 'it mistook falsehood for truth, and truth for falsehood. Error succeeded and increased ignorance'.[129] Being affected by a disordered body, the operation of the soul came to be hindered, thus, ignorance, mistakes, infirmities, and tempta-

---

[121] S. Coming, I. 10.
[122] S. New (1), I. 2; S. Love (1), Intro. 1; S. Evil, I. 4.
[123] S. Deceitfulness, I. 1; S. Evil, II. 8; see S. Deceitfulness, I. 1; S. Coming, I. 8-9; S. Evil, II. 6.
[124] S. Deliverance, II. 2.
[125] S. Deliverance, II. 1.
[126] S. Approbation, II. 3.
[127] S. Image, II. 3.
[128] S. Image, II. 4.
[129] S. Image, II. 2.

tions became unavoidable.[130] Especially on spiritual matters, 'he is utterly ignorant of God ... He is totally a stranger to the law of God'.[131] As a related consequence of being ignorant of God, 'he is utterly ignorant of himself', being confident of his blamelessness but not having 'understanding enough to fear'.[132]

Describing the doctrine of original sin as 'the *shibboleth*' or 'one grand fundamental difference' that distinguishes Christianity and heathenism,[133] Wesley taught, consequences of Adam's fall are transmitted to all human beings: 'sinful Adam then "begat a son in his own likeness" ... "there is no difference"'.[134] Collins points out that as his reproduction of the Ninth Article of the Anglican Thirty-nine Articles in his *Sunday Service* demonstrates, in his presentation of this doctrine Wesley emphasized 'the transfer ... of a *corrupt* nature' more than 'the transfer of *guilt*'.[135]

III. Humanity after Salvation

Wesley understood salvation as the restoration of the image of God. Outler properly states that 'the recovery of the defaced image of God is the axial theme of Wesley's soteriology'.[136] In his sermon, 'Original Sin' (1759), Wesley wrote, 'the great end of religion is, to renew our hearts in the image of God, to repair that total loss of righteousness and true holiness which we sustained by the sin of our first parent'.[137] In another sermon, 'The End of Christ's Coming' (1781), he taught the 'Christian religion' as 'a restoration of man ... not only to the favour, but likewise to the image of God'.[138] Theocentrically speaking, 'the image of Him [God] that created us',[139] Christologically, 'the image of Christ',[140] or anthropologically, the image 'wherein we were at first created',[141] is the goal of salvation.

---

[130] S. Image, I. 1; S. New (1), I. 1; S. Treasure, II. 1; S. Fall, II. 2; II. 6; S. Perfection (1), I. 3; S. Coming, I. 3; *Plain Account*, 21-22.
[131] S. Adoption, I. 1.
[132] S. Adoption, I. 2-4.
[133] S. Original, III. 1-2.
[134] S. Original, Intro. 4.
[135] Collins, *Theology*, 64. Wesley omitted the phrase focused on the guilt; 'it deserveth God's wrath and damnation'.
[136] BE 2:185, n. 70.
[137] S. Original, III. 5.
[138] S. Coming, III. 5; see Kim, 'Anthropology', 94-97.
[139] WW 12:68.
[140] WW 8:471.
[141] S. Perfection (2), II. 4.

What initiates the process of restoration is the prevenient grace of God, which partially restores the image of God as well as forgives the guilt of original sin.[142] The restoration of the image of God is carried on, through 'convincing grace ... *repentance;* which brings a larger measure of self-knowledge',[143] by the combined process of 'justification-regeneration-sanctification'.[144] Seung-An Im points out, 'conviction of the illness of fallen humanity is "only one step" toward recovery of the original humanity, and "often no step at all; since every conviction is not a lasting one"',[145] since 'repentance must lead to faith in order for a penitent to be renewed'.[146]

In terms of the restoration of the moral image, the combined process of salvation produces a believer's growth in love from the moment of justification, in which 'It [Love] is the only kind of holiness ... in various degrees'. The difference in the process 'properly lies in the degree of love'.[147] As 'two aspects of one event',[148] justification is a believer's experience of God's holy love through forgiveness, while regeneration is their participation in the same holy love.[149] Wesley described the new birth as 'a change from inward wickedness to inward goodness; an entire change of our inmost nature from the image of the devil (wherein we are born) to the image of God'.[150] Furthermore, sanctification is 'the full renewal of humankind in the [moral] image of God'.[151] While the state of regeneration 'is alloyed with sinful inclinations', Lindström correctly distinguishes, 'entire sanctification is seen more clearly as a distinct stage of love', that is, 'a love unmixed with sin, a pure love'.[152]

In terms of the natural image, by prevenient grace alone, human senses can perceive 'no information at all concerning the invisible world',[153] nor can human reason 'know God in a relational sense' in spite of a limited knowledge of divine things.[154] As 'the supernatural

---

[142] Maddox, *Responsible*, 87-88.
[143] S. Working, II. 1.
[144] Kim, 'Anthropology', 111.
[145] BE 4:312.
[146] Im, 'John Wesley's Theological Anthropology', 190.
[147] S. Patience, 10.
[148] Runyon, *The New Creation*, 71.
[149] S. Privilege, Intro. 2.
[150] Journals 2:275-276; S. Vineyard, I. 9.
[151] Kim, 'Anthropology', 138.
[152] Lindström, *Sanctification*, 141-142.
[153] S. Discoveries, 3.
[154] Cunningham, 'Perceptible', 111.

evidence of things invisible',[155] justifying and regenerating faith gives believers 'spiritual sight'.[156] Faith illumines a believer's reason to understand numerous things which 'the Holy Scriptures declare'; 'the being and attributes of God ... His eternity and immensity; His power, wisdom, and holiness ... His method of dealing with the children of men; the nature of His various dispensations, of the old and new covenant, of the law and the gospel ... repentance ... faith ... justification ... new birth ... holiness'.[157] Then, the enlightened understanding 'immediately directs us to reform our will by charity'.[158] 'The more we advance in the knowledge and love of God', Wesley taught, 'the more do we discern of ... the necessity of our being entirely renewed in righteousness and true holiness', knowing 'our alienation from God'.[159] Being closely interwoven, the natural faculties influence each other.[160] Most of all, liberty 'not only from guilt ... but from sin' is restored to believers.[161] Since a fruit of faith is the 'power over outward sin ... and over inward sin',[162] the regenerated are 'delivered from the bondage of corruption into the glorious liberty of the sons of God'.[163]

However, Wesley taught that there is a limitation in the restoration of the natural image in spite of sanctifying grace.[164] Cox notes that Wesley taught that the moral likeness to God is recovered for the entirely sanctified, but not the natural image which includes rational power.[165] Enumerating many kinds of infirmities, Wesley contended that 'from such infirmities ... none are perfectly freed till their spirit returns to God; neither can we expect till then to be wholly freed from temptation'.[166] Infirmities are not only 'found in the best of men', but also 'it is as natural for a man to mistake as to

---

[155] BE 11:46.
[156] Letters 5:209; Letters 3:174.
[157] S. Reason, I. 6.
[158] S. Image, III. 2.
[159] S. Mount (1), I. 13.
[160] Im, 'John Wesley's Theological Anthropology', 202.
[161] S. Adoption, III. 5.
[162] S. Marks, I. 4.
[163] S. Image, III. 3.
[164] S. Perfection (2), I. 3-4.
[165] Leo G. Cox, *John Wesley's Concept of Perfection*, (Kansas City: Beacon Hill Press, 1964), 148-149.
[166] *Plain Account*, 21-22. 'The weakness or slowness of understanding, dullness or confusedness of apprehension, incoherency of thought, irregular quickness or heaviness of imagination... the want of a ready or retentive memory... slowness of speech, impropriety of language, ungracefulness of pronunciation'.

breathe'.[167] In this state, humans could not fulfil the demands of the law perfectly, as innocent Adam did.[168] Even the entirely sanctified cannot get to the point where it is impossible to sin.[169] Believers can experience temptations even because of perfected Christians' infirmities.[170] So Wesley advised believers 'to expect temptation ... in an evil world ... capable of all evil'.[171] However, the entirely sanctified are those who will be guarding continually against the subtleties of temptations and seeking to gain early victory over each temptation to sin as it arises.[172]

C. Observations and Analysis

I. Humanity as Creatures of God vs. Humanity with Divine Nature

For Luther, while the image of God represents 'the right relationship of a person to God', rather than 'an active human power',[173] the relationship is based on the creatures' faith in their Creator.[174] The activities of innocent Adam in Paradise were not exceptionally spiritual ones, but 'activities of physical life – like eating, drinking, procreating, etc.'[175] God's commandment toward Adam and Eve was no other than to exercise the image of God by becoming 'the rulers of the earth, the sea, and the air' and by making 'use of the creatures' as they wish 'for [their] physical life'.[176] When those things were used and all physical activities were done in faith and gratitude, they 'would have been a service pleasing to God'.[177] Therefore, after 'he lived in this physical life ... in obedience to God', Luther contended, God will give him 'a spiritual life, in which he would neither make use of physical food nor do the other things which are customary in this life but would live an angelic and spiritual life'.[178]

---

[167] *Plain Account*, 84.
[168] S. Righteousness, II. 5.
[169] S. Perfection (1), I. 8.
[170] S. Temptation, I. 6.
[171] S. Wilderness, III. 14.
[172] S. Privilege, III. 1.
[173] Bell, 'Man Is a Microcosmos', 163.
[174] Kolb, 'Cross', 459-460.
[175] LW 1:56.
[176] LW 1:66-73.
[177] LW 1:56.
[178] LW 1:65; LW 1:57.

Adam's life in Paradise was characteristically a physical life in dependence on and in obedience to God. Forde points out, 'man's relationship to God in Paradise was comprehended entirely by *faith*. That is to say that even in Paradise man lived from day to day by trusting God. He "knew" God, to be sure, but only as a creature knows his Creator. He did not know God in any more immediate or direct sense'.[179] On the essence of creaturely life as created by God, Luther wrote:

> God has created me and all that exists ... He has given me and still sustains my body and soul, all my limbs and senses, my reason and all the faculties of my mind ... He provides me ... with all the necessities of life, protects me from all danger, and preserves me from all evil. All this He does out of His pure, fatherly, and divine goodness and mercy, without any merit or worthiness on my part. For all of this I am bound to thank, praise, serve, and obey Him.[180]

The reason why Luther represented the activities of innocent Adam in Paradise mainly as physical ones, is not different from the reason he was decisively opposed to sinners' upward approach to God through either intellectual contemplation or meritorious good works;[181] that is, he wanted to avoid any hint of 'the distortion of the human creatureliness into self-glorification'.[182]

Further, Luther's view of humanity as God's earthly creature is based on his positive appreciation of God's creation itself. As Larry Rasmussen observes, for Luther, both 'the biblical witness to God' and a believers' confession of faith begin with God's creation.[183] As shown in such as 'the First Article of the Creed, his writings on the sacraments, the lectures on Genesis, and the doctrine of creation itself', in Luther's view, 'earth is crammed with heaven because God has chosen to be present *to* creation *in* creation *through* and *as* creation'.[184] Luther wrote, 'God in His essence is present everywhere, in and through the whole creation in all its parts and in all places, and so the world is full of God and He fills it all, yet He is ... at the same time beyond and above the whole creation'.[185] Human beings can recognize God's glory and goodness, and worship Him in a very crea-

---

[179] Forde, *Where*, 54.
[180] *BC*, 345.
[181] See Forde, *Cross*, 12, 58.
[182] Oswald Bayer, *Luthers Theologie*, 19. Quoted by Theo A. Boer, 'Is Luther's Ethics Christian Ethics?', *LQ* 21:4. (2007), 411.
[183] Larry Rasmussen, 'Luther and a Gospel of Earth', *Union Seminary Quarterly Review* 51:1-2 (1997), 2.
[184] Ibid., 2-3.
[185] LW 37:59.

turely way without viewing 'the Christian life as one of progressive ascetic ascent' toward God.[186]

Even after the fall, God saves sinners not in a way that abandons His depraved creation, but by reaffirming His creation by reconciling it with Him in Christ. Luther thought that 'God – especially in the person of Jesus Christ – involves Himself with people where they are'.[187] Therefore, Eric W. Gritsch points out, Luther's view of creation is not 'worldly in a hedonistic sense' but 'worldly in the sense in which he understood God to be worldly'.[188] Because of the fall of humanity 'we do not even have insight into that fullness of joy and bliss which Adam derived from his contemplation of all the animal creatures'.[189] In Christ, believers are returned to the lost state in which we enjoy creation as God's gift and blessing.[190] Consistently, Gritsch observes that 'Luther's use of rather earthly language increased with age', that is, according to the gradual development of his theological thoughts, Luther appraised creation more and more positively.[191]

In Luther's view, while human beings can be defined as creatures of God who worship God and care for His creation, living in the boundary of creaturely life, God's law is understood as the command to live a creaturely life as His creatures. Luther's anthropology not only emphasizes the difference between God the Creator and His human creatures, but also teaches that the locus of human life is this world. The law commands Christians to live as human beings, not to be like God.

Quite differently from Luther, Wesley viewed the essence of human beings in terms of their similitude to God's nature, and viewed human life from the point of fellowship based on the similitude. Whereas for Luther peaceful life on earth without any fear and anxiety, which he regarded as the image of God, comes from faith, Wesley ascribed such life to love, which is the moral image.[192] Wesley understood the essence of true humanity as love. Saying that 'man was what God is, Love',[193] he taught that the whole content of the law

---

[186] Rasmussen, 'Luther and a Gospel of Earth', 3.
[187] Eric W. Gritsch, 'The Worldly Luther: Wholistic Living', *Word & World* 3/4 (1983), 362.
[188] Ibid., 361.
[189] LW 1:66.
[190] Forde, *Radical*, 149.
[191] Gritsch, 'The Worldly Luther: Wholistic Living', 355-363.
[192] S. Needful, II. 2.
[193] S. Image, I. 2.

which God gave to Adam was to love God; 'love is the very image of God' and 'to this end was man created'.[194]

Doubting that 'faith ... had any place in paradise', Wesley contended that innocent Adam probably was blessed with a rather direct face-to-face fellowship with God, walking with Him 'by sight and not faith', contrasting with Luther's view that the human relationship to God was a mediated fellowship through faith, not a direct one in love and by sight.[195] From Wesley's point of view, for the purpose of magnifying faith, Luther sacrificed not only the loving relationship which God established between Himself and human beings, but also the very spiritual capacity God has granted to humanity, that is, to see and have a direct fellowship with God.[196] The sin Luther wanted to avoid by limiting the boundary of human life to the earth, such as pride and self-glorification, is rejected by Wesley's view of the image of God; the political image that refers to a proper order in the chain of being with celestial and terrestrial hierarchies; and also the moral image that is inclusive of pious affections and attitudes toward God such as humility, thankfulness, and righteousness. For Wesley, to avoid sinners idolizing themselves, no part of the image of God, either the natural or the moral, needs to be sacrificed.

Luther rarely admitted human beings becoming 'partakers of the divine nature' and possessing virtues such as 'eternal truth, righteousness, wisdom, everlasting life, peace, joy, happiness'. He believed that only in a limited sense believers receive these virtues passively from God through faith, just in the same way that we receive the imputed righteousness of Christ in faith.[197] However, Wesley did not hesitate to teach that human beings are 'partakers of the divine nature'.[198] Human beings are, in a sense, divine beings as well as creaturely beings: 'a little world, consisting of heaven and earth, soul and body';[199] a 'wonderful mixture ... of greatness and littleness, of nobleness and baseness'.[200] He contended that 'man's [Adam's] nature resembled the divine nature more than that of any of the creatures of this lower world'.[201] Because of the unity of the natures

---

[194] S. Needful, II. 2.
[195] S. Established (2), II. 4.
[196] S. Established (2), II. 3-4.
[197] LW 30:154-155.
[198] ENNT II Peter 1:4; S. Awake, II. 8; S. Mount (10), 17; S. Children, 3.
[199] ENOT Gen 2:4-7.
[200] S. Treasure, Intro. 1.
[201] ENOT Gen 5:1-2.

of God and human beings, Wesley stated even that 'by love man is not only made like God, but in some sense one with Him'.[202]

Therefore, the essence of worship of God does not exist in making human beings unable to properly contemplate God's glory or to make any decision concerning their own destiny, but in the fact that they 'offer Him a free and willing service' in obeying His law *through* or *in spite of* all their spiritually and physically superior powers and faculties God has granted them. The law commands human beings to live a life suitable to their divine nature.[203]

II. Sin is to Be Like God vs. Sin is to Be Unlike God

In Luther's view, the essence of the fall of humanity is that sinners fail to 'fear, love, and trust in God', refusing 'to let God rule and to be God'.[204] Adam's fall was caused by not believing God's words and being seduced by Satan. Failing to have faith, a fundamental sin that tempted him was 'to become like God'.[205] All sinners after Adam similarly commit sin, tempted by pride, refuting their creaturehood, refusing to live in their earthly boundary, and trying to reach something that belongs to the divine realm. Rasmussen properly observes that for Luther, 'trying to rise above nature is, for earthbound creatures like us, the essence of sin'.[206] For Luther, 'the essence of sin' is pride. Forde maintains:

> Sin is located not primarily in the body, but rather precisely in our spiritual pretensions and ambitions. It is our god-like aspirations that destroy our life and seduce us to make life miserable for our fellow men. This is the basic understanding from which Luther started in developing his understanding of man ... If he attempts to step beyond the limits of his creaturehood, as did Adam, he commits the prime sin.[207]

Whereas 'the baser lusts of the flesh' can be discerned quite easily and obviously, sinners' arrogance and their idolatrous self-worship, which Forde calls 'the lusts of the spirit', are not easily detected.[208] Taking very pious masks such as intellectual pursuit of God or good works that aim to please God, what sinners do is try to be like God, by penetrating God's sovereignty or seeking salvation by themselves,

---

[202] S. Needful, II. 2.
[203] S. Law, I. 1-3.
[204] Kolb, 'Cross', 459-460; Watson, *Let*, 64.
[205] Forde, *Where*, 53.
[206] Rasmussen, 'Luther and a Gospel of Earth', 3.
[207] Forde, *Where*, 53-54.
[208] Forde, *Where*, 106.

not depending on His sheer grace and disregarding His absolute otherness from us.

What is closely connected to Luther's view of the fall and sin is his understanding of God's law. Luther represented the prime role of God's law as disclosing 'the depth of our own sinfulness', that is, our self-centredness, pride, or self-glorification. Robert Kolb maintains, 'until sinners recognize their failure to trust in the true God … they are blind to the depth and the root cause of their troubles in this world. The law crushes sinful pretensions to lordship over life … it focus[es] their understanding clearly enough to see that the original, root, fundamental sin that perverts and corrupts life lies in this lack of trust'.[209]

In contrast, Wesley viewed the essence of the fall as the loss of loving relationship. The effects of the fall are not only that sinners who enjoyed their loving relationship with God came to enjoy worldly things in place of God, but also that they are depraved into the image of the devil or brutes. Wesley's view of sin has dual focuses on unbelief and unholy tempers or affections. Firstly, describing unbelief as 'the very quintessence of atheism', which he defined as 'the art of excluding Him [God] … out of the world He has created … out of the minds of all His intelligent creatures', Wesley taught that it is 'one of the choicest instruments of destroying immortal spirits'.[210] The loss of faith brings the loss of love, joy, peace, and the power which they possessed before.[211] Unbelief 'blots out all religion at one stroke, and levels man with the beasts that perish'.[212]

Secondly, Satan and evil angels, after depraving human beings with unbelief, contracted all evil tempers to them.[213] Though it is not necessary, even believers may wander in the spiritual wilderness state.[214] Their wander does not always originate from unbelief. It can come from various degrees and sorts of 'the bondage of sin and Satan':[215] 'any sinful temper, passion, or affection; such as pride, self-will, love of the world, in any kind or degree; such as lust, anger, peevishness; any disposition contrary to the mind which was in Christ'.[216] Like he described unbelief as 'the parent of all evil',[217] Wes-

---

[209] Kolb, 'Cross', 459-460.
[210] S. Walking, 20-21.
[211] S. Wilderness, I. 1-5.
[212] S. Walking, 21.
[213] S. Evil, I. 4; S. Love (1), Intro. 1; S. Deceitfulness, I. 1.
[214] S. Wilderness, Intro. 1-2; II. (I.) 1-10.
[215] S. Wilderness, Intro. 1; II. (I.) 1-10.
[216] S. Sin, II. 2.

ley called evil tempers 'the true origin of evil',[218] 'the hindrances of true religion',[219] or 'roots of bitterness'.[220] Evil tempers are 'a kind of practical atheism', since, like unbelief, they also separate humanity from God.[221]

Not only on the essence but also on the effects of the fall upon natural endowments, Luther and Wesley held different views. Firstly, on human free will, Luther disavowed any freedom of choice in sinners:[222] 'Original sin ... leaves free choice with no capacity to do anything but sin'.[223] In his proof of Thesis 14 of the *Heidelberg Disputation*,[224] Luther contended that dead people can have life only in their 'passive capacity', that is, only when the Lord raises them up.[225] He insisted that even before the fall Adam 'received the ability to act' from God only in his 'passive capacity'.[226] Also, when Luther approved of some limited freedom 'with respect to what is beneath him', he quickly added that 'even this is controlled by the free choice of God alone'.[227] Both before and after the fall, Luther described human beings strictly as 'creatures who lived by faith ... and not their own power'.[228] 'As for the person who does not' depend on God for everything, Luther affirmed, 'not only are all his sins mortal, but even his good works are sins'.[229]

Wesley also denied that sinners can 'return to God' with their natural ability.[230] Denying that sinners have 'natural free-will'[231] like Luther did, Wesley taught that sinners are 'by nature totally destitute of righteousness and subject to the judgment'.[232] Luther and

---

[217] ENNT Heb 3:12.
[218] S. Deceitfulness, I. 1; S. Coming, I. 8-9. Here Wesley reverses the order; first, pride and, next, self-will.
[219] S. Mount (2), II. 1.
[220] S. Mount (11), I. 3; S. Evil, II. 6-8
[221] S. Mount (3), I. 11.
[222] For Luther's reasoning in the Heidelberg Disputation which starts with the subject of the law's condemnation of human works (Theses 1-12), then, proceeds to the subject of free will (Theses 13-18), see LW 31:39-40; Forde, *Cross*, 23-67.
[223] LW 33:272.
[224] LW 31:40. 'Free will, after the fall, has the power to do good only in a passive capacity, but it can always do evil in an active capacity'.
[225] LW 31:49.
[226] LW 31:50.
[227] LW 33:70.
[228] Forde, *Cross*, 57; LW 31:49.
[229] LW 27:76.
[230] Williams, *John Wesley's Theology Today*, 47-48.
[231] WW 10:229.
[232] Cannon, *The Theology of John Wesley*, 200.

Wesley agreed with each other in their teaching of both 'the universality of condemnation and the inability of humanity apart from God to do anything to rectify this situation'.[233]

However, Wesley differed from Luther by teaching that thanks to God's prevenient grace, even after the fall every human being has some portion of liberty.[234] It makes human beings in a sense '*response-able*' for making proper decisions for their salvation.[235] Without some portion of liberty, Wesley believed not only that God cannot condemn sinners for what they are not enabled to do,[236] but also that coerced worship or obedience is neither 'rewardable in itself' nor acceptable to God.[237] Wesley said:

> If man were not free ... he would not be capable either of reward or punishment; he would be incapable either of virtue or vice, of being either morally good or bad. If he had no more freedom than the sun, the moon, or the stars, he would be no more accountable than them ... it would be as absurd to ascribe either virtue or vice to him as to ascribe it to the stock of a tree.[238]

Whereas in Luther's view, there is no liberty in nonbelievers, but only in believers, in Wesley's view, there is no person without liberty. Where there is sin, 'there is more or less concurrence of his [sinner's] will'.[239]

Secondly, on the subject of human reason, Wesley, after reading Luther's *Commentary on Galatians*, criticized Luther's irrationalism in his journal of 15 June 1741: 'How does he (almost in the words of Tauler) decry reason, right or wrong, as an irreconcilable enemy to the gospel of Christ! Whereas, what is reason ... but the power of apprehending, judging, and discoursing?'[240] According to Wesley's criticism it seems that Luther seriously devaluated human reason in the matter of religion. Has Wesley properly understood Luther's view of human reason? Certainly not. Wesley was only partly right in that concerning spiritual matters, Luther took a very gloomy view of sinners' reason. Luther, calling reason ironically as 'Madam Reason'[241]

---

[233] Collins, 'Law', 82.
[234] S. Man (2), 11.
[235] Collins, *Theology*, 77-82.
[236] S. Fruits, II. 9.
[237] S. Law, I. 1-3.
[238] S. Predestination, 6.
[239] S. Fruits, II. 11; S. Temptation, II. 2.
[240] Journals 2:467.
[241] LW 33:122; LW 33:206.

or as 'Frau Hulda',[242] who is 'a capricious elfin creature in Germanic mythology',[243] criticized it severely as 'the devil's prostitute', 'archprostitute', 'the devil's bride' or 'the lovely whore'.[244]

Inho Choi characterizes Luther's view of an unbeliever's reason in spiritual matters in terms of 'ignorance, misguidance, and rebellion': 'it is (1) powerless because of ignorance, (2) false because of misguidance, and (3) absolutely wicked because of its rebellious rejection of God'.[245] The reason of depraved human beings does not ascribe to God what they have and have achieved, but to themselves, glorifying themselves.[246] Even though reason has some 'ethical and religious' knowledge on the basis of the natural law, it, being 'trapped in moralism', cannot 'understand the gospel', but seeks to 'measure God according to the law'.[247] It cannot understand spiritual things such as the Trinity and incarnation, regarding them 'absurd, unbelievable, and impossible things'.[248]

However, the gloomy aspects of reason were not everything that Luther taught. In creation, he believed, human beings have received reason as a very noble gift from God.[249] In all areas of earthly things such as 'all law, science, economics',[250] reason worked, having 'perfect knowledge', though their knowledge was limited concerning heavenly things.[251] After the fall, human reason has become 'very much impaired', however, it has remained, especially in earthly affairs.[252] In spite of the fact that there are distortions which the fall caused upon reason, the essence of reason remains. Therefore, if it is illuminated through faith by the Spirit, 'reason's God-given essence' can be 'brought to life and regenerated' again.[253] Then, 'reason enlightened by the Spirit helps us to understand the Holy Scripture ... Reason, insofar as it is enlightened, serves faith in thinking about

---

[242] LW 40:174, 192, 193, 195, 202, 208, 215, 216.
[243] A. Skevington Wood, *Captive to the Word: Martin Luther: Doctor of Sacred Scripture* (London: Paternoster, 1969), 159.
[244] LW 40:174; LW 51:374; *BC*, 345.
[245] Inho Choi, 'Historical Studies on Ratio in Luther: Comparison and Analysis of Luther's Two Commentaries on Galatians of 1519 and 1535', (Ph.D. thesis, Luther Seminary, 2004), 113-128.
[246] Althaus, *Theology*, 65-66; Gerrish, *Reason*, 76-78.
[247] Althaus, *Theology*, 67-69; Gerrish, *Reason*, 84-99.
[248] Althaus, *Theology*, 66-70.
[249] *BC*, 345.
[250] WA 40 III, 222. Quoted by Althaus, *Theology*, 65, fn. 5.
[251] Forde, *Where*, 54; LW 1:42; LW 1:63; Althaus, *Theology*, 65.
[252] LW 1:64.
[253] Althaus, *Theology*, 70-71.

something ... Enlightened reason receives all of its thoughts from the Word'.²⁵⁴ Laying what Inho Choi calls 'the epistemological bridge' between reason and faith,²⁵⁵ Luther represented a believer's reason very positively:

> Before we come to faith and the knowledge of God, our reason is darkness; in believers, however, it is a most useful tool ... Faith then is aided by reason, rhetoric, and language which were such great obstacles before [we had] faith. Enlightened Reason which is incorporated into faith receives gifts from faith ... Reason in godly men is something different since it does not fight with faith but rather aids it.²⁵⁶

Luther appraised human reason both before the fall and after salvation very positively. In his reading of Luther, Wesley failed to recognize Luther's distinctions not only between the roles of reason in the earthly affairs and in spiritual affairs, but also between reason as a gift in creation, a sinners' reason after the fall, and a believer's reason illuminated by faith.²⁵⁷ While, as Inho Choi points out, 'reason can be either good or bad, depending on how it is used', what Luther criticized was improper use of reason, not reason itself.²⁵⁸ Gerrish points out that in Luther's negative representation of reason, the presuppositions such as without illumination of faith or 'without the leading of the Holy Spirit', are presupposed.²⁵⁹

In reality, Wesley's view of reason was not much different from Luther's view. Certainly he valued the role of reason very highly, stressing that 'to renounce reason is to renounce religion ... religion and reason go hand in hand; and ... all irrational religion is false religion',²⁶⁰ and opposing the insistence that reason is not only 'of no use in religion' but is 'a hindrance to it'.²⁶¹ Asking, 'What can reason do in religion?', he answered, 'it can do exceeding much, both with regard to the foundation of it, and the superstructure ... reason (assisted by the Holy Ghost) ... enables us to understand what the Holy Scriptures declare'.²⁶²

Like Luther, Wesley taught that the reason of unbelievers is impotent in spiritual affairs: it is powerless in producing faith, hope, and

---

[254] WA, TR 3, 2938. Quoted by Althaus, *Theology*, 71.
[255] Choi, 'Historical Studies on Ratio in Luther', 135.
[256] WA, TR 3, 2938. Quoted by Althaus, *Theology*, 71.
[257] Althaus, *Theology*, 64; Forde, *Where*, 9-10.
[258] Choi, 'Historical Studies on Ratio in Luther', ii, 120; Gerrish, *Reason*, 84.
[259] Gerrish, *Reason*, 167.
[260] WW 14:354.
[261] S. Reason, Intro. 1.
[262] S. Reason, I. 6.

love, and, consequently, in making people happy.[263] As Rex Dale Matthews notes, Wesley warned that 'reason may be abused, and confidence in it may be misplaced'.[264] When Wesley cautioned believers to 'beware of the reasoning devil', or to 'vehemently resist the reasoning devil', which, as Matthews points out, is similar to Luther's devil's 'whore',[265] he meant that even believers may fall into unbelief when they fail to use their reason properly,[266] just like Luther taught that the 'consequence of allowing reason to trespass in the province of faith is unbelief'.[267]

If Wesley would have understood Luther's view of reason properly, he might have not criticized Luther's depreciation of an unbelievers' reason, but rather his too high evaluation of a believers' reason, since in contrast to Wesley's view, Luther ascribed more to a believers' reason. As Siegbert W. Becker notes, Luther, defining faith as 'right thinking of the heart about God', equated faith and 'the activities of reason in the human soul'.[268] Ascribing the role of recognizing God's will mainly to faith, Luther even insisted that believers 'do not need the law', or that a Christian 'needs no law to teach him to live a good life' since they are lead through faith by the Holy Spirit.[269] Sometimes Luther gave so much credit to human reason, especially to a believer's reason as to insist that the law is not needed in judging properly in civil affairs as well as in spiritual affairs, to which Wesley would not have agreed:

> If the ruler is wise, he will govern better by a natural sense of justice than by laws. If he is not wise, he will foster nothing but evil through legislation, since he will not know what use to make of the laws nor how to adapt them to the case at hand. Therefore, in civil affairs more stress should be laid on putting good and wise men in office than on making laws; for such men will themselves be the very best of laws, and will judge every variety of ease with a lively sense of equity. And if there is knowledge of the divine law combined with natural wisdom, then written laws will be entirely superfluous and harmful. Above all, love needs no laws whatever.[270]

---

[263] S. Reason, II. 1-10.
[264] Rex Dale Matthews, 'Religion and Reason Joined: A Study in the Theology of John Wesley', (Th.D. Dissertation, Harvard University, 1986), 163.
[265] Ibid., 181; see LW 33:122, 206; LW 40:174, 192, 193, 195, 202, 208, 215, 216; LW 51:374; *BC*, 345. Wood, *Captive to the Word*, 159.
[266] WW 12:369, 517; Letters 2:230.
[267] Gerrish, *Reason*, 78.
[268] Siegbert W. Becker, *The Foolishness of God: The Place of Reason in the Theology of Martin Luther* (Milwaukee: Northwestern Publishing House, 1999), 87-91.
[269] LW 27:96, 378; LW 44:34-35; LW 45:94.
[270] LW 36:98.

For Wesley, no one can be as wise as not to need the law in recognizing God's will.

III. Believers as Simul Justus Et Peccator vs. Believers Sanctified in Finitude

Luther explained salvation in terms of restoration of the image of God which was lost after the fall. However, he limited the extent of restoration in this life. A believer's own righteousness which has begun 'cannot attain perfection' because of the flesh. When Luther related the impossibility of perfect righteousness of believers to their flesh, by the flesh he did not mean simply 'a pejorative reference to the body', but 'human condition'.[271] Commenting on Gal. 2:16, Luther wrote:

> In Paul 'flesh' does not, as the sophists suppose, mean crass sins; for these he usually calls by their explicit names, like adultery, fornication, uncleanness, etc. (Gal. 5:19 ff.). But by 'flesh' Paul means here what Christ means in John 3:6: 'That which is born of the flesh is flesh'. Therefore 'flesh' means the entire nature of man, with reason and all his powers... For Paul, therefore, 'flesh' means the highest righteousness, wisdom, worship, religion, understanding, and will of which the world is capable.[272]

The flesh meant 'anything untouched and unredeemed by the Spirit' or 'whatever is outside of Christ'.[273] Gerrish points out: '[Luther] does not take the terms [flesh and concupiscence] in the narrow and specific sense which the Scholastics attached to them ... concupiscence is "self-love" or "egocentricity", and the flesh is the "whole man apart from Christ" ... The man of faith, on the other hand, lives his life towards the spiritual realm, and his centre is in Christ'.[274] In believers this self-centred sinful nature and the Spirit struggle against each other.[275] This makes a believer's perfect righteousness impossible.[276]

From Wesley's viewpoint, what was astonishing in Luther's teaching is that he taught God does not remove the sinful nature from believers.[277] Luther found the reason why 'the Holy Spirit sometimes lets His Christians fall, err, stumble, and sin' from the divine purpose

---

[271] Choi, 'Historical Studies on Ratio in Luther', 114.
[272] LW 26:139-140.
[273] Gerrish, *Reason*, 69.
[274] Gerrish, *Reason*, 71.
[275] LW 27:65.
[276] LW 26:140.
[277] LW 27:65.

'to forestall any complacency, as though we were holy of ourselves, and to teach us to know ourselves and the source of our holiness', lest we 'become arrogant and overweening'.[278] For Luther, God continues to be 'feared, revered, and worshipped' when believers continue to realize their sinfulness before God.[279] Simply put, God leaves believers in the state *simul justus et peccator* to make them humble before God in dependence on His sheer grace for their salvation. In consistence with his own view of major sin as unbelief, pride, or self-centredness which make sinners independent from God, he contended even that to save them from such major sins, God allows believers to fall into sin.

Wesley agreed with Luther that in believers sin may remain, and still Christ may be present in their 'heart where sin is'. 'Christ indeed cannot *reign*, where sin *reigns*; neither will He *dwell* where any sin is *allowed*'; 'He *is* and *dwells* in the heart of every believer, who is *fighting against* all sin; although it be not yet purified'.[280] In his sermon, 'The First Fruits of the Spirit' (1746), Wesley wrote:

> Although they feel the flesh, the evil nature in them; although they are more sensible, day by day, that their 'heart is deceitful and desperately wicked'; yet, so long as they do not yield thereto; so long as they give no place to the devil; so long as they maintain a continual war with all sin, with pride anger, desire, so that the flesh hath not dominion over them, but they still 'walk after the Spirit'; 'there is no condemnation to them which are in Christ Jesus'. God is well pleased with their sincere though imperfect obedience: and they 'have confidence toward God', knowing they are His, 'by the Spirit which He hath given' them.[281]

Wesley's different nuance from Luther's should be discerned. Wesley maintained, 'A man may be in God's favour though he feels sin; but not if he *yields* to it. *Having sin* does not forfeit the favour of God; *giving way to sin* does. Though the flesh in you "lust against the Spirit", you may still be a child of God; but if you "walk after the flesh", you are a child of the devil'.[282]

Randall C. Zachman points out that Luther represented the conscience of believers rather than their will as the main 'anthropological locus toward which the grace of God is directed'. Whereas outside of Christ, the conscience is inevitably condemned, the gospel of Christ 'frees the conscience' from guilt and, thus, 'from its attempt to

---

[278] LW 24:172; LW 21:301.
[279] LW 6:85-86.
[280] S. Sin, III. 8; IV. 6-7.
[281] S. Fruits, II. 6.
[282] S. Sin, IV. 13.

justify itself before God' through works.²⁸³ In contrast with Luther, Wesley emphasized the works of God's grace on believers' wills as well as on their consciences. In his sermon, 'The Witness of Our Own Spirit' (1746), Wesley taught that to have 'a good conscience toward God', four things are required: (1) 'a right understanding' of God's 'holy, and acceptable, and perfect will concerning us' revealed in 'the word of God', 2) 'a true knowledge of ourselves', (3) 'an agreement' between God's will and believers' hearts and lives, and (4) a 'habitual perception' of this agreement.²⁸⁴ After God's grace freed believers' consciences from guilt and witnesses His love toward them, Wesley stressed, believers *can* and *should* live a holy life with their grace-enabled free will.²⁸⁵ In agreement with Luther, Wesley believed that God's creation of human beings in His image was motivated by His 'free grace'.²⁸⁶ However, in the restoration of the image of God, the same 'mere grace' has the element of the empowerment by the Holy Spirit that 'worketh in us both to will and to do of His good pleasure'.²⁸⁷

For Wesley, as God 'cannot deny Himself' or 'cannot counteract Himself',²⁸⁸ it cannot be possible that the holy God makes believers humble by making them commit sins. Wesley asserted that God cannot be the author of sin for any reason:

> Least of all can you with any colour of argument infer, that any man *must* commit sin at all. No: God forbid we should thus speak! No necessity of sinning was laid upon them. The grace of God was surely sufficient for them ... With the temptation which fell on them, there was a way to escape ... So that whosoever is tempted to any sin, need not yield; for no man is tempted above that he is able to bear.²⁸⁹

God's way of making believers humble is not leaving them in sins, that is, in the loss of the moral image. When Christ counteracts the works of the devil, 'the one medicine' for unbelief is faith.²⁹⁰ But, faith or the gospel does not always answer the end of the law,²⁹¹ and 'all that is written in the book of God' has its own use.²⁹² For the pur-

---

²⁸³ Zachman, *The Assurance of Faith*, 2.
²⁸⁴ S. Witness (3), 7.
²⁸⁵ S. Witness (1), I. 10-11; S. Working, III. 1-8.
²⁸⁶ S. Salvation, Intro. 1.
²⁸⁷ S. Working, I. 1; S. Witness (3), 15.
²⁸⁸ S. Providence, 15.
²⁸⁹ S. Perfection (1), II. 14.
²⁹⁰ S. Circumcision, I. 5-6; S. Coming, III. 1; S. Dissipation, 16.
²⁹¹ S. Established (1), I. 5.
²⁹² S. Established (2), I. 5.

pose of removing both outward and inward sin, sinners can benefit from warnings of the law or counsels of repentance as well as from the comfort of the gospel.[293] When Christ removes unholy tempers and affections, such as pride, self-will, and the love of the world,[294] Wesley emphasized that 'Our Lord has abundantly performed' His mission by teaching the inner law, mainly through His Sermon on the Mount.[295] Against Luther's teaching that God humbles believers by leaving them in sin, Wesley taught that God humbles believers by leaving them in the marring of the natural image in spite of the restoration of the moral image; in their 'bodily weakness, sickness, pain, and ... weakness of understanding':[296]

> 'Both ignorance and error belong to humanity'. He entrusts us with only an exceeding small share of knowledge in our present state; lest our knowledge should interfere with our humility, and we should again affect to be as gods. It is to remove from us all temptation to pride, and all thought of independency ... under the name of *liberty* that He leaves us encompassed with all these infirmities, particularly weakness of understanding; till the sentence takes place, 'Dust thou art, and unto dust thou shalt return!'[297]

From the belief that believers are restored to the moral image but not to the natural image, Wesley viewed orthopraxy rather than orthodoxy as a more reliable demonstration of true faith.[298] Whereas Luther confined believers within the state of *simul justus et peccator* to help them avoid the major sins of unbelief, pride, or independence from God, Wesley, denying that believers' dependence on God's grace is guaranteed by their sinfulness, emphasized a believers' obedience to God's law on the basis of the Spirit's empowerment as a crucial element of salvation. To make them humble and be dependent on Him, God does not remove human finitude on earth.[299] Distinguishing between voluntary transgression of the law and involuntary mistakes, Wesley related sin only to the former.[300] Without voluntary transgression, there may be ten thousand wandering thoughts and forgetful intervals.[301] Mistakes and infirmities are 'no way contrary

---

[293] S. Wilderness, III. 1-5; S. Established (1), I. 12.
[294] S. Coming, III. 2.
[295] S. Mount (5), I. 3-4; S. Mount (2), II. 1.
[296] S. Coming, III. 3.
[297] S. Coming, III. 3.
[298] S. Coming, III. 5.
[299] S. Coming, III. 3; S. Treasure, II. 4-5.
[300] S. Perfection (2), II. 9.
[301] Letters 5:322; WW 12:394.

to love, therefore, they are not, 'in the Scripture sense, sin'.[302] However, in that omissions, shortcomings, mistakes, and defects in the entirely sanctified believers are all deviations from God's perfect law, believers still need Christ's atonement.[303] For Wesley, God does not remove human finitude on earth to make them humble and dependent on Him.[304]

---

[302] *Plain Account*, 55.
[303] *Plain Account*, 55.
[304] S. Coming, III. 3; S. Treasure, II. 4-5.

Chapter 7

The Law in Practice

A. Martin Luther

I. The Law for the Church (Means of Grace)

Luther understood the Church as 'the assembly of ... true believers'[1] or 'a holy Christian people on earth, in whom Christ lives ... through grace and the remission of sin, and the Holy Spirit ... through daily purging of sin and renewal of life so that we do not remain in sin but ... lead a new life, abounding in all kinds of good works, as the Ten Commandments or the two tables of Moses' law command'.[2] The Church, according to Luther, is God's holy people who believe in the gospel and thereby obey God's law.

Practically, the church has external signs: preaching of the gospel and administration of the sacraments.[3] Like 'wherever God's word is, there the church must be', 'wherever baptism and the sacrament are, God's people must be, and vice versa'.[4] Against 'the charge of schism', Luther not only claimed that the Reformation Church had the true signs of the church, but also attacked 'traditions, rites, and ceremonies' of the Catholic Church as human inventions,[5] which Steven Ozment enumerates:

> ... mandatory fasting; auricular confession; the veneration of saints, relics, and images; the buying and selling of indulgences; pilgrimages and shrines; wakes and processions for the dead and dying; endowed masses in memory of the dead; the doctrine of purgatory; Latin Mass and liturgy; traditional ceremonies, festivals, and holidays; monasteries, nunneries, and mendicant

---

[1] *The Augsburg Confession*, 33.
[2] LW 41:143-144.
[3] *The Augsburg Confession*, 32; LW 41:152.
[4] LW 41:152.
[5] Forde, *Radical*, 159-160; Steven Ozment, *The Age of Reform 1250-1550* (New Haven: Yale University, 1981), 435.

orders; the sacramental status of marriage, extreme unction, confirmation, holy orders, and penance; clerical celibacy; clerical immunity from civil taxation and criminal jurisdiction; non-resident benefices; papal excommunication and interdict; canon law; papal and episcopal territorial government; and the traditional scholastic education of clergy.[6]

Against the Catholic view of holy things as meritorious causes, Luther represented his own view of the means of grace in his treatise *On the Councils and the Church* (1539).[7] Listing 'the seven holy possessions of the church' that help produce 'Christian sanctification',[8] Luther, firstly, described 'the holy word of God' which the Church proclaims 'orally' as 'the holiest of holy possessions' that 'sanctifies everything', exorcising 'pilgrimage-devils, indulgence-devils, bull-devils, brotherhood-devils, saint-devils, mass-devils, purgatory-devils, monastery-devils, priest-devils, mob-devils, insurrection-devils, heresy-devils, all pope-devils, also Antinomian-devils'.[9]

The second holy possession of the Church, Luther taught, is baptism. Luther called baptism 'the holy bath of regeneration through the Holy Spirit ... with which we are washed of sin and death ... in the innocent holy blood of the Lamb of God'.[10] 'Baptism is not merely water, but it is water ... connected with God's word'.[11]

The third is 'the holy sacrament of the altar', 'where Christ commanded His body to be eaten' in order that 'there is forgiveness of sins, consolation of souls, and strengthening of faith'. 'Wherever it is rightly administered, believed, and received', Luther taught, 'it transforms ... fleshly, sinful, mortal men' into 'spiritual, holy, living men... in faith'.[12]

The fourth holy possession is 'the office of the keys',[13] which 'was instituted by Christ' as 'a consolation and help against sin and a bad conscience'.[14] This office has a twofold use: 'public and private'. Publically, it can comfort and encourage believers who despair easily, having 'timid consciences', or 'who need to be ... instructed in Chris-

---

[6] Ozment, *The Age of Reform*, 435.
[7] LW 41:9-178; see Kleinig, 'Holiness', 76-91.
[8] LW 41:166.
[9] LW 41:148-150.
[10] LW 41:151.
[11] *BC*, 348.
[12] LW 41:152;.LW 37:101-102..
[13] LW 41:153.
[14] *BC*, 312.

tian doctrine'.[15] The keys can be applied to personal relationships with others as a way of loving neighbours.[16]

The fifth holy possession is the offices of ministries such as 'bishops, pastors, or preachers ... who ... use the aforementioned four things'.[17] There is no need for 'a hierarchical institution' for the purpose of mediating between God and human beings. This is the role of Christ.[18] All believers are equally priests in front of God. The only reason for ordaining church ministers is that 'the people as a whole cannot do these things, but must entrust or have them entrusted to one person ... to preach, to baptize, to absolve, and to administer the sacraments'.[19] What consecrates candidates in ordination is not chrism but the word of God, which Luther called the 'spiritual God-chrism'[20] What consecrates God's people through their ministry is God's word, not pastors' holiness.[21] God's words are free from 'the control of all elites' of the Church, but belong to all Christians; they are controlled by the words.[22]

The sixth holy possession is prayer.[23] David P. Scaer notes, for Luther, 'Prayer is motivated not only by the desperate need of the Christian, but also by the father-son relationship which God has with Christians'. God invites believers to prayer either in need of salvation and help, or in trust in God's promises to answer to their prayer.[24] In his *Personal Prayer Book* (1522), Luther explained prayer in the relationship between the Ten Commandments (the law), the Creed (the gospel), and the Lords' Prayer (prayer).[25] First being requested by the law and being promised by the gospel, believers come to God in prayer.[26] Prayer is dependent on God's words of the law and the gospel.[27]

The last one is 'the sacred cross' which makes believers 'steadfastly adhere to Christ and God's word'.[28] Kleinig explains that the

---

[15] *BC*, 312; LW 41:153.
[16] LW 21:148-155.
[17] LW 41:154.
[18] Lindberg, *Beyond*, 98-99.
[19] LW 41:154.
[20] LW 38:185-186.
[21] Kleinig, 'Holiness', 83; LW 41:155.
[22] Lindberg, *Beyond*, 98.
[23] LW 41:164.
[24] Scaer, 'Prayer', 305-306.
[25] LW 43:13-14.
[26] Nestingen, 'The Lord's Prayer in Luther's Catechism', 36-48.
[27] Scaer, 'Prayer', 305.
[28] LW 41:164-165.

cross is 'not a new holy thing', but the circumstances which 'lies behind the other six holy things' and 'in which the holy things of God take their full effect in human existence'.[29] Luther enumerated the cross as: 'every misfortune and persecution, all kinds of trials and evil from the devil, the world, and the flesh ... by inward sadness, timidity, fear, outward poverty, contempt, illness, and weakness'.[30]

Overall, in Luther's understanding of the means of grace for sanctification, which is no other than confirmation of justification, the preaching of the gospel becomes the most essential and fundamental element, which pervades all the other holy possessions and changes them into means of grace.[31]

II. The Law for the World (Christian Ethics)

i. Two Kingdoms of God

Luther's teaching of the two kingdoms of God deals with the relationship of believers to the world, especially what they should follow in the secular kingdom between the law of Christ given exclusively to believers and the positive laws of their society. There are explicit contradictions between the law of Christ which commands to forgive, not to resist evil, to endure violence, to love enemies, and the law of this world which commands punishing of sinners, resistance of evil, and revenge on enemies. To solve the paradoxes between contradictory laws, Luther said:

> We must sharply distinguish between these two, the office and the person ... He [God] makes you a child and me a father, one a master and another a servant, one a prince and another a citizen ... – not simply Hans or Nick, but the Prince of Saxony, father, or master ... here [in the Sermon on the Mount] ... He is talking merely about how each individual, natural person is to behave in relation to others.
>
> Therefore if we have an office or a governmental position, we must be sharp and strict, we must get angry and punish ... In other relations, in what is unofficial, let everyone learn for himself to be meek toward everyone else, that is, not to deal with his neighbour unreasonably, hatefully, or vengefully ...[32]

By the distinction between 'the office and the person', Luther did not mean that the law of Christ does not apply to the secular king-

---

[29] Kleinig, 'Holiness', 83; LW 41:164.
[30] LW 41:164.
[31] Kleinig, 'Holiness', 89-90.
[32] LW 21:23.

dom. On the contrary, love is the single principle of the laws of both kingdoms,[33] and believers are citizens of both kingdoms.[34] Therefore, 'the virtues of the Sermon on the Mount should prevail in the secular kingdom, too'.[35] However, there is a limitation in applying the law of Christ in the secular kingdom. The law of Christ is to rule believers' 'attitudes of the hearts' and their personal relationships with others, but it cannot be public rules of 'the secular society'.[36] In public office, believers' manners, methods, or ways of loving others should follow the civil law, even though their heart or their personal relationship is still motivated and ruled by the law of Christ.

In his treatise, *Temporal Authority: To What Extent It Should Be Obeyed* (1523), dividing human beings into two – 'true believers' who belong to both kingdom of God, and those who belong only to the earthly kingdom – Luther contended that true believers 'do of their own accord much more than all laws and teachings can demand', thus, for them 'there is no need for any suit, litigation, court, judge, penalty, law, or sword'.[37] But, Luther quickly added that 'there are few true believers ... Christians are few and far between ... the wicked always outnumber the good.[38] Besides, as long as believers are sinners, they also should be under the control of the sword of the secular kingdom. Arguing against dangerous attempts 'to rule the world by the gospel and to abolish all temporal law and sword' by radical reformers such as Anabaptists and leaders of the Peasants' War, Luther warned that such an attempt is like 'loosing the ropes and chains of the savage wild beasts and letting them bite and mangle everyone', since people will wickedly 'abuse evangelical freedom' and 'carry on their rascality' in the name of Christ.[39] Luther said,

> A man who would venture to govern an entire country or the world with the gospel would be like a shepherd who should put together in one fold wolves, lions, eagles, and sheep, and let them mingle freely with one another, saying, 'Help yourselves, and be good and peaceful toward one another. The fold is open, there is plenty of food. You need have no fear of dogs and clubs'. The sheep would doubtless keep the peace and allow themselves to be fed and

---

[33] Meistad, *Mount*, 18.
[34] Meistad, *Mount*, 14-15.
[35] Meistad, *Mount*, 18.
[36] Meistad, *Mount*, 15.
[37] LW 45:88-89.
[38] LW 45:90-91.
[39] LW 45:91.

governed peacefully, but they would not live long, nor would one beast survive another.⁴⁰

Since 'among thousands there is scarcely a single true Christian', the result will be that 'men would devour one another' and finally 'the world would be reduced to chaos.⁴¹ Therefore, as Meistad exemplifies in many examples, Luther taught that believers who inwardly and personally obey the law of Christ should act according to the secular law publicly, especially when the laws of two kingdoms seem to contradict each other.⁴² Believers should 'keep the relations between individuals and society in a proper perspective',⁴³ as Bornkamm explains:

> In speaking of two 'kingdoms' Luther is describing ... the two sets of relationships within which the Christian lives. On the one hand, there is his own existence, his personal attitude to his fellow men, his witness for the gospel – in this realm the unconditional commandment of forgiveness, endurance, and sacrifice prevails. On the other hand, there is the common 'life together' of mankind in general, in which law must of necessity set firm limits against evil; here the Christian must help to see that no one suffers injustice or becomes the victim of another.⁴⁴

On a proper distinction, the two kingdoms can be complementarily cooperative. While the spiritual kingdom of God produces inner righteousness before God, His secular kingdom prevents outer evils and preserves external peace. 'Neither one is sufficient in the world without the other'. The spiritual kingdom alone opens the door to 'all manner of rascality', and the secular kingdom cannot make people 'truly righteous'. Therefore, 'both [governments] must be permitted to remain'.⁴⁵ As Bornkamm points out, 'the Christian must therefore, in his own life, "satisfy" both realms'.⁴⁶

ii. Christian Vocation

In Luther's theology, a believer's realization that human works cannot add anything to God's salvific works causes a fundamental

---

⁴⁰ LW 45:91-92.
⁴¹ LW 45:90-91.
⁴² Meistad, *Mount*, 9-80.
⁴³ Meistad, *Mount*, 18; LW 45:96.
⁴⁴ Heinrich Bornkamm, *Luther's Doctrine of the Two Kingdoms* (Philadelphia: Fortress Press, 1966), 8; for more detailed discussion, see Joo-Han Kim, 'Personal Piety and the Common Good: Luther's Interpretation of the Sermon on the Mount and his Two Kingdoms Doctrine', (Ph.D. thesis, Boston University, 1999).
⁴⁵ LW 45:92.
⁴⁶ Bornkamm, *Luther's Doctrine of the Two Kingdoms*, 7.

change in the direction and the purpose of their ethical behaviour. The change is fourfold. Firstly, they give up the upward approach to God through pious activities and good works, with which they sought to obtain God's favour and salvation,[47] and 'the contemplative life' devised by the monastics and the scholastics for the purpose of 'elevating themselves above every other kind of life'. Believers, on the foundation of God's grace received in faith, obey His will in gratitude on earth.[48]

Secondly, what is intimately connected with the down-to-earth nature of Luther's ethics is altruism. Justification changes the direction of ethical behaviour from inward to outward. For Luther, the upward approach to heaven cannot be freed from an egocentricity that uses both relationships with God and with neighbours as a means of salvation.[49] Even the 'relationship of brotherhoods' in the late medieval Catholic Church was no more than 'group selfishness' that pursued their own salvation.[50] However, for Luther, Carter Lindberg states, since salvation is the foundation of Christian life, not the teleological goal, 'the energy and resources poured into acquiring other-worldly capital can be redirected to this-worldly activities'.[51] William H. Lazareth also states, 'With their salvation thus assured in the unmerited forgiveness of Christ, grateful Christians are free to redirect their reason and good works toward serving their neighbours' welfare'.[52] The consequence is that works done in faith have neighbours themselves as the object of service. To believers, 'no creature toward which you should practice love is nobler than your neighbour'.[53] Luther endeavoured to integrate social service for the poor such as gathering 'a common fund' regularly for distributing among those who are in need, into the worship service.[54] This is a practical example of how Luther connected justification by faith to a believers' altruistic service to others in the context of worship and sacraments.

Thirdly, justification denies human distinctions between great and trivial works. Human beings commit sins not only 'by neglecting what God has commanded' but also 'by doing more than God has

---

[47] LW 31:55-56 ('Heidelberg Disputation', Thesis no. 25).
[48] LW 5:345-346.
[49] LW 2:119.
[50] Lindberg, *Beyond*, 101.
[51] Lindberg, *Beyond*, 97.
[52] LW 44: xi-xvi.
[53] LW 27:58.
[54] LW 35:57, 68-69; Lindberg, *Beyond*, 100-110.

commanded'. The erroneous pursuit of *doing more* originates from 'the madness of human wisdom' that 'takes delight in what is magnificent', 'unusual things that are impressive', and 'something better or more difficult'.⁵⁵ For Luther, such 'a distinction of works' is made by those who do not trust in God's favour, but attempt to 'gather merits' in a more efficient way in order 'to do enough and to influence God' to 'win [His] favour'.⁵⁶ They disregard 'ordinary, unimportant, laughable' things which the God's law commands.⁵⁷ However, Luther stressed, 'when we are dealing with God's commands ... one must consider, not what is being said ... but Who is speaking ... He who considers the One who gives the commands will surely regard as most important even those things that seem most trivial'.⁵⁸ What 'glorifies all the works of believers and makes them grand' is God.⁵⁹ Comparing believers to 'a husband and a wife' who devote themselves to each other in both trivial and great things, since they 'really love one another ... and thoroughly believe in their love', Luther affirmed, in faith 'all works become equal ... distinctions between works fall away'.⁶⁰

Fourthly, the doctrine of justification by faith abolishes not only 'a distinction of works' but a distinction between priests and laity and between spiritual and secular works. Denying the Catholic distinction between 'the spiritual estate' of priests and 'the temporal estate' of the others, Luther asserted, 'all Christians are truly of the spiritual estate, and there is no difference among them except that of office'.⁶¹

By contending that human works cannot make a Christian, and also that Christian faith 'does not make me a prince ... a husband, or ... a priest',⁶² Luther implied that faith makes any vocation spiritual, but without faith even the station of the church is not in itself spiritual. Consistently, Gustaf Wingren points out that Luther used the term *Beruf* ('vocation') to indicate Christians' both earthly and spiritual works through their occupation.⁶³ Since 'every occupation has its own honour before God, as well as its own requirements and du-

---

⁵⁵ LW 2:77-79.
⁵⁶ LW 44:26-28.
⁵⁷ LW 2:77-79.
⁵⁸ LW 2:78-79.
⁵⁹ LW 4:103.
⁶⁰ LW 44:26-28.
⁶¹ LW 44:126.
⁶² LW 24:220-221.
⁶³ Gustaf Wingren, *Luther on Vocation*, tr. Carl C. Rasmussen (Eugene: Wipf & Stock Publishers, [1957], 2004), 1-2.

ties',[64] Luther contended that believers should have a confidence that their vocations 'are pleasing to God'. All good governors, diligent labourers, and 'pious spouses and mothers' will be rewarded 'on Judgment Day' for their faithful works of vocations done in faith.[65] Believers are all priests who serve God in different areas.[66]

The fourfold change in the direction and purpose of Christian ethics is related to Luther's understanding of the law. For Luther, believers see that God's creation remains good, though human beings are depraved:[67]

> It is foolish and wicked when many preachers inveigh against glory, power, social position, wealth, gold, fame, beauty, or women, thus openly condemning a creation of God ... God has made all things to be good and to be useful for some human purpose. What is being condemned ... is not the creatures but the depraved affection and desire of us men ... there is nothing better for any man than to find enjoyment and make life pleasant for himself, to eat and drink and enjoy his toil, etc.[68]

> God's creation in itself does not need to be redeemed through sacraments.[69] From this, once God's creation recovers its goodness, it recovers the status as the locus of Christian life:[70]

> When it is recognized that God is gracious ... then I go out and turn my face from God to human beings, that is, I tend to my calling. If I am a king, I govern the state. If I am the head of a household, I direct the domestics; if I am a schoolmaster, I teach pupils, mold their habits and views toward godliness. These works are rightly called a worship of God ... the real chief points of godliness and of true religion are these: faith toward God ... next, the works of our calling with reference to our neighbour, that you rule, prescribe, teach, comfort, exhort, make a living by working, etc.[71]

Believers realize that stations, offices, or vocations in the realm of God's creation are a special kind of God's law, in that they are imposed on every human being by God as an imperative to love others. Since every life station contains in it what believers can do for others, each station can be regarded as the law inherent in God's creation. The natural law, the Decalogue, or the law of the gospel teaches the principles of human duties 'valid everywhere and for all people'.

---

[64] LW 46: 246.
[65] LW 24:220-221.
[66] LW 44:130.
[67] LW 15:8; LW 46:304.
[68] LW 15:8.
[69] Forde, *Where*, 69-70; Scott Hendrix, 'Luther on Marriage', *LQ* 14 (2000), 336-338; LW 44: xi-xvi.
[70] Forde, *Where*, 46-47, 56-60; Forde, *Radical*, 145-150; Kleinig, 'Holiness', 86.
[71] LW 3:117-118.

However, each life station gives 'very definite or detailed instructions about what we as individuals ought to do here and now in living together with one another'.[72] In organic relationships with other stations, which have 'a useful and necessary function in the life of the world', every station is dependent on the others.[73]

Therefore, for Luther, life stations are God's law that is already and naturally 'built into the creation' by God the Creator.[74] Lazareth maintains, 'for Luther's social ethic, all offices and stations of life ... embody in institutional form a particular command of God's law. They are all integrated within the earthly kingdom of men'.[75] Since human beings are 'naturally suited for a civilized and social existence', those in stations, even when they do not know that they are serving others, are still serving others.[76] Luther asserted,

> If you are a manual labourer, you find that the Bible has been put into your workshop, into your hand, into your heart. It teaches and preaches how you should treat your neighbour. Just look at your tools – at your needle or thimble, your beer barrel, your goods, your scales or yardstick or measure – and you will read this statement inscribed on them. Everywhere you look ... All this is continually crying out to you: 'Friend, use me in your relations with your neighbour just as you would want your neighbour to use his property in his relations with you'.[77]

The implication of Luther's view of life stations is that Christians do not need the so-called third use of the law. As Lazareth underlines, for Luther, since there is no 'particularly Christian form' of orders of God's creation, but 'the natural orders', there is no 'particularly Christian form' of the law for the life on earth.[78] The civil law or the law of stations, being founded on the natural law that contains 'almost endless' laws in a brief principle of the golden rule, teaches Christian duties toward neighbour to the point that nothing needs to be added to it.[79] Commenting on John 16:20, Luther maintained that if believers faithfully perform the duties of their vocation, it will even mortify believers, just like they bear their own cross.[80] Forde contends,

---

[72] Althaus, *Ethics*, 36, 38; LW 5:72; LW 41:177; Grobien, 'Natural Law', 211-217.
[73] Althaus, *Ethics*, 37; LW 7:190; LW 51:348; LW 51:351-352.
[74] Forde, *Radical*, 154.
[75] LW 44: xi-xvi.
[76] LW 27:58.
[77] LW 21:237.
[78] LW 44: xi-xvi.
[79] LW 27:56.
[80] LW 24:377-379.

Luther spoke explicitly of only two uses of the law: the political use – perhaps we could call it the ethical use – and the theological use ... Politically speaking ... law preserves order and restrains evil ... theologically speaking, it judges us, convicts of sin ... so that we can be saved ... When one is looking for a positive use for law in life and ethics in Luther's thinking, one should look to his understanding of the first use of the law, the political or ethical use ... We have all we need there; we do not need a third use![81]

While both Christians and non-Christians participate in and contribute to those stations,[82] the superiority of Christian ethics to infidels is that Christians receive their stations as vocation,[83] and faithfully perform them 'in the certainty that God has called' them and it pleases God.[84] Having 'all necessary devotion, desire, and daring', and being 'willing to obey God',[85] Christians are superior to the others in their performance as well as in their recognition of God's will contained in their vocation.[86]

'Above ... institutions and orders' of creation, Luther added one more order which pertains only to Christians, that is, 'the common order of Christian love'. Christians serve 'every needy person in general with all kinds of benevolent deeds, such as feeding the hungry, giving drink to the thirsty, forgiving enemies, praying for all men on earth, suffering all kinds of evil on earth, etc.'[87] Christian love that 'goes far beyond the regular duties' can be applied to all the other stations.[88] Christians obey not only the law of the secular kingdom, but also the law of Christ, which is 'a higher law'.[89]

Consequently, as an example, believers make better rulers than nonbelievers. Recognizing 'a higher judge' over themselves,[90] Christian rulers will regard the obligation of affording 'protection to divine worship' as 'the state's most solemn duties'.[91] Labouring for neighbours, they 'preserve peace, punish sin, and restrain the wicked' and 'help the poor, the orphans, and the widows'.[92] Luther as-

---

[81] Forde, *Radical*, 152-154.
[82] Grobien, 'Natural Law', 220.
[83] LW 44: xi-xvi.
[84] Althaus, *Ethics*, 40-41.
[85] LW 49:207-208.
[86] LW 13:368.
[87] LW 37:365.
[88] Althaus, *Ethics*, 40-41.
[89] Steinmetz, *Luther in Context*, 123.
[90] Heinrich Bornkamm, *Luther's World of Thought*, tr. Martin H. Bertram (Saint Louis: Concordia Publishing House, 1958), 246-247.
[91] Ibid., 247-248; LW 13:52-53, 59-60.
[92] LW 45:94; LW 13:53-67.

serted, 'there is no greater jewel in the world than a God-fearing lord'.[93]

Luther's own life and ministry demonstrated how Christians can contribute to the improvement of the social system. Personally, in Lindberg's words, Luther was so 'notoriously' generous in sharing 'his own income' for the needy as to make his wife worried about it.[94] Publically, while Luther emphasized the necessity of solving the problem of poverty by developing 'rational, urban, social welfare legislation' according to his own vocation of teaching and preaching, Lindberg notes, civil authorities, according to their own offices and powers, accepted and incorporated Luther's teaching into legislation in many towns such as Wittenberg, Leisnig, Altenburg, Nuremberg, Strasbourg, Hamburg, and Ypres. This demonstrates that, as Luther taught, in a believers' faithful performance of vocation, there exists the possibility of the improvement of the whole society.[95]

B. John Wesley

I. The Law for the Church (Means of Grace)

Wesley defined the Church as 'a body of believers', contending that 'it *is* holy, because every member thereof is holy'.[96] To have a holy nature and to live a holy life are the essential elements with which people can 'be and continue living members' of the Church.[97]

Wesley's view of the church reflected his emphasis on the law as a means to sanctification.[98] Teaching that God ordains to use the means of grace as the 'very means... for the bringing it [love]' into human heart,[99] Wesley emphasized that benefitting from the means of grace is an important part of the law: 'the express direction'; 'peremptory' command; an 'explicit command'; and 'a plain duty'.[100] Since the means of grace are 'the ordinary channels whereby He [God] might convey to men, preventing, justifying, or sanctifying

---

[93] LW 13:60.
[94] Lindberg, *Beyond*, 119.
[95] Lindberg, *Beyond*, 128-160; LW 44: xi-xvi.
[96] S. Church, 28.
[97] S. Riches (2), Intro. 4; S. Church, 20-30.
[98] Baker, *John Wesley and the Church of England*, 137-159; Gwang Seok Oh, *John Wesley's Ecclesiology: A Study in Its Sources and Development* (Lanham: Scarecrow Press, 2008), 22; Howard A. Snyder, *The Radical Wesley and Patterns for Church Renewal* (Eugene: Wipf & Stock Publishers, 1996), 19, 154-157.
[99] S. Means, I. 2; II. 2.
[100] S. Means, III. 1-2; III. 7, 11; S. Sick, Intro. 4; S. Communion, I. 1.

grace', Wesley stressed, 'all who desire the grace of God are to wait for it in the means which He hath ordained; in using, not in laying them aside'.[101]

In his sermon, 'On God's Vineyard' (1779), Wesley reported that the systematized structure of the Methodist meetings was intended for providing them with suitable Christian disciplines according to their spiritual progress.[102] Lindström notes:

> The idea of gradual advance in sanctification ... was applied to the organization of the Methodist societies. They were organized in classes and bands... select bands or societies. The members belonged to one or the other of these according to their spiritual state and experience. The first category contained those who 'earnestly desired to avoid the wrath to come', the two latter the regenerate or fully sanctified. The categories corresponded to the stages in the progress of salvation: first repentance (repentance before justification), justification, and entire sanctification.[103]

Works of piety performed through 'instituted', 'general', or 'prudential' means of grace[104] become 'an excellent help to religion'.[105] As general means of grace Wesley taught 'universal obedience ... keeping all the commandments ... denying ourselves, and taking up our cross daily'; as 'instituted' means of grace, prayer, searching the scriptures, and attending the Lord's supper. Wesley also advised to employ 'prudential' means of grace, such as particular rules, meetings, habits according to believer's own discretion.[106] They make believers continually dependent on God, nurture 'all those tempers with which we are to approach to God',[107] give 'a clear knowledge of the divine will',[108] and strengthen believers' souls with spiritual food.[109] The works of piety help persuade nonbelievers to seek salvation, and help increase a believers' love for God.[110]

---

[101] S. Means, II. 1, III. 1; S. Enthusiasm, 27.
[102] S. Vineyard, II. 1 - III. 3.
[103] Lindström, *Sanctification*, 122; For a more detailed discussion, see Snyder, *The Radical Wesley and Patterns for Church Renewal*, 53-64.
[104] WW 8:322-324; Collins, 'Law', 227-228, 230-238.
[105] S. Sick, Intro. 1; see S. Means, III. 1-12; S. Question, III. 1, III. 5; S. Pleasing, Intro. 1.
[106] WW 8:322-324; for Wesley's eudemonistic view of holiness, and a detailed discussion on his distinction between 'instituted and prudential' means of grace, see Collins, *Law*, 227-228, 230-238.
[107] S. Mount (6), II. 5; III. 3.
[108] S. Eye, I. 3.
[109] S. Communion, I. 2.
[110] S. Question, III. 4.

Doing 'works of mercy' toward neighbours becomes the way of both receiving God's grace[111] and of deepening love for other people.[112] They deliver particular graces which cannot be received otherwise than by doing them.[113] Taking an example, Wesley contended, without visiting the sick, the chances of getting 'an excellent means of increasing your thankfulness to God, who saves you from this pain and sickness, and continues your health and strength; as well as of increasing your sympathy with the afflicted, your benevolence, and all social affections' will be lost.[114] Wesley said:

> One great reason why the rich, in general, have so little sympathy for the poor, is, because they so seldom visit them. Hence ... one part of the world does not know what the other suffers. Many of them do not know, because they do not care to know: they keep out of the way of knowing it; and then plead their voluntary ignorances an excuse for their hardness of heart.[115]

Wesley warned that 'voluntary ignorances' about the needy will result in decrease of grace and make believers self-indulgent.[116] Works of mercy become both a way and a consequence to love one's neighbour.[117]

Dividing works of mercy into temporal works to the bodies and spiritual works to the souls of people,[118] Wesley taught that, as Collins observes, though spiritual needs have 'valuational priority', 'the material needs of the neighbour have chronological priority (they are the very first things that must be done)'.[119] In that doers of works of temporal mercy can have exceptional chances to care for their neighbours' spiritual affairs, Wesley advised doers of temporal mercy to proceed to spiritual mercy.[120] However, Maddox notes, this does not mean that Wesley considered works of mercy as a mere instrumental 'enticement of uncommitted persons to embrace the Christian faith'. On the contrary, against the tendency that many Christians have been 'the grand stumbling-block' to others, failing to

---

[111] S. Question, III. 5; S. Pleasing, Intro. 1.
[112] S. Sick, I. 3.
[113] S. Sick, Intro. 1; see Maddox, 'Visits', 76-80.
[114] S. Sick, Intro. 1; I. 2; see Randy Maddox, '"Visit the Poor": John Wesley, The Poor, and the Sanctification of Believers', in Richard P. Heitzenrater ed., *The Poor and the People Called Methodists 1729-1999* (Nashville: Kingswood Books, 2002), 76-80.
[115] S. Sick, I. 3.
[116] S. Inefficacy, 16.
[117] S. Question, III. 5.
[118] S. Mount (3), II. 5-6, III. 10; S. Mount (7), IV. 7; S. Sick, I. 5, II. 4, III. 3-4; S. Way (2), III. 9-10; S. Reward, I. 5; S. Question, III. 5
[119] Collins, *Theology*, 283; S. Zeal, II. 9.
[120] S. Sick, II. 4.

show Christian love to the needy, the central rationale of Wesley's serious view of works of mercy was that only those who endeavour to do both works of spiritual and physical mercy for other people can 'overcome the widespread crisis of credibility of Christian witness'.[121]

Wesley taught that every single work of temporal mercy may have the possibility of incalculable virtues in itself, even though it does not serve directly for works of spiritual mercy. By illustrating an occasion of saving a nearly drowned person, Wesley explained how people can benefit both temporarily and spiritually from a work of mercy:

> How many miracles of mercy ... are contained in one! That poor man ... may again ... provide them [his family] with all the necessaries of life... you have prevented, that sickness which might naturally have arisen from their want of sufficient food ... You have hindered those orphans from wandering ... from being lodged in a dreary, comfortless prison ... The husband ... may now again strengthen her [wife's] hands ... He may again join with her in instructing their children, and training them up in the way wherein they should go; who may live to be a comfort to their aged parents, and useful members of the community ... It may be, you have snatched the poor man himself ... from ... the jaws of everlasting destruction.[122]

Wesley presented a principle of using the means of grace which can be applied to all situations: 'we are obliged to keep every command as far as we can'.[123] The reasons are: 'Considering this as a command of God, he that does not communicate as often as he can has no piety; considering it as a mercy [of God], he that does not communicate as often as he can has no wisdom'.[124] Wesley affirmed that to neglect the means of grace is to disobey God's law, 'setting at nought both His mercy and authority'.[125]

II. The Law for the World (Christian Ethics)

i. Christian Personal Ethics

Wesley's ethics can be called the ethics of Christian love. Christian love becomes a powerful motive for 'doing no harm' and 'doing

---

[121] Maddox, '"Visit the Poor": John Wesley, The Poor, and the Sanctification of Believers', 68-69.
[122] S. Reward, II. 4-6.
[123] S. Communion, II. 4.
[124] S. Communion, II. 5.
[125] S. Communion, II. 9.

good', which are the sum of the law.[126] Since love constrains us to do good works,[127] inward and outward religion is joined together.[128] However, in order that believers continue to love, they should act against human sin and self-love. As practical ways of overcoming those hindrances, and of sustaining and increasing love, Wesley emphasized both self-denial and good stewardship.[129]

In his sermon, 'Self-Denial' (1760), Wesley taught that self-denial or taking up one's own cross is 'the most universal ... absolutely, indispensably necessary' command of Christ for 'all times, and all persons ... and all things', without which Christians cannot follow Christ.[130] As an exceedingly broad command, it applies to a believer's everyday life against numberless hindrances to love.[131] Self-denial is necessary not only because God is wiser than us, but also because, as depraved creatures, we should resist our corruption in order to love.[132] 'In propagating religiously motivated inner-worldly asceticism, Wesley was influenced by biblical, and especially by Puritan tradition',[133] as well as by Thomas à Kempis and William Law.

Wesley also represented stewardship as an essential attitude of believers to whom God has committed what they have. Gary L. Ball-Kilbourne notes that the theme of good stewardship as 'the appropriate life-style for the Christian' is found 'widely throughout Wesley's writings'.[134] For Wesley, among various aspects of the relationship between God and human beings, there is no better concept that expresses the ethical responsibility of human beings than the one between the Lord and His stewards:[135]

> Although a debtor is obliged to return what he has received, yet until the time of payment comes, he is at liberty to use it as *he* pleases ... a steward ... is not at liberty to use what is lodged in his hands as he pleases, but as his master pleases ... this is exactly the case of every man, with relation to God ... With all these temporal things we are barely entrusted ... on this express

---

[126] WW 8:270-271; S. Established (2), III. 3.
[127] S. Mount (4), III. 2.
[128] S. Mount (4), III. 3.
[129] Collins, *A Faithful Witness*, 170-177.
[130] S. Denial, Intro. 1-2.
[131] S. Denial, Intro. 4; II. 1-7.
[132] S. Denial, I. 2-14; Mark Lewis Horst, 'Christian Understanding and the Life of Faith in John Wesley's Thought', (Ph.D. thesis, Yale University, 1985), 201-206.
[133] Marquardt, *Social*, 41.
[134] Gary L. Ball-Kilbourne, 'The Christian As Steward in John Wesley's Theological Ethics', *Quarterly Review* 4:1 (Spring 1984), 43, 48.
[135] S. Steward, Intro. 1-2; I. 1-8.

condition that we use them only as our Master's goods, and according to the particular directions which He has given us in His Word.[136]

Wesley applied both self-denial and good stewardship to various areas of common life: how to use money, what clothes to wear, what amusements to allow, and how to use time.[137] As examples, Wesley opposed distillation of liquors and excessive drinking, because such things are against both self-denial and good stewardship.[138] Excessive drinking not only leads people to 'earthly, sensual, devilish' tempers such as 'anger, or malice, or lust',[139] but also the breweries and distilled liquors cause starvation of the poor, consuming 'immense quantities' of food.[140] Both evil tempers and causing destitution are against love, self-denial, and stewardship.

In his sermon, 'The More Excellent Way' (1787), applying both motives of self-denial and good stewardship to uses of time and money, Wesley advised believers to redeem the time and money in order to 'promote health both of body and mind'; 'to provide things necessary for myself and my family'; 'to do the will of God on earth'; and to help the needy.[141] Wesley urged, 'Choose in all the ... particulars the "more excellent way" ... both with regard to sleep, prayer, work, food, conversation, and diversions; and particularly with regard to the employment of that important talent, money'.[142] He viewed money as one of the precious blessings of God.[143]

In his sermon, 'The Use of Money' (1760), Wesley taught three rules of economic ethics for Christians; 'Gain all you can ... Save all you can ... Then give all you can'.[144] Randy Maddox explains that the first rule focuses on 'the manner' of acquiring 'property, capital, or the means of production'; the second emphasizes 'self-denial in use of one's resources' against 'wasting them on idle expenses or luxuries'; and the third rule urges to 'meet the needs of our neighbours' against accumulating anything 'above what meets one's basic needs'.[145] In another sermon, 'Causes of the Inefficacy of Christianity'

---

[136] S. Steward, I. 1.
[137] Collins, 'Law', 238-246.
[138] Collins, 'Law', 242-244.
[139] WW 11:169-70.
[140] Letters 5:350; WW 11:53-55; see Marquardt, *Social*, 44.
[141] S. Excellent, I. 1 - VI. 6.
[142] S. Excellent, VI. 6.
[143] S. Steward, I. 7; S. Money, Intro. 2.
[144] S. Money.
[145] Randy Maddox, '"Visit the Poor": John Wesley, The Poor, and the Sanctification of Believers', 62.

(1789), Wesley warned, 'all who observe the two first rules without the third, will be twofold more the children of hell than ever they were before'.[146] Maddox summarizes Wesley's economic ethic into four points: '1) ultimately everything belongs to God; 2) resources are placed in our care to use as God sees fit; 3) God desires that we use these resources to meet our necessities (i.e., providing shelter and food for ourselves and dependents), and then to help others in need; thus, 4) spending resources on luxuries for ourselves while others remain in need is robbing God!'.[147]

Wesley warned that, in relation to God, we should not 'rob God' by using anything against His will.[148] 'The ground of mistake' is to regard any possession as our own. In relation to neighbours, we should not ascribe all misfortune of the poor and the miserable to God. Much of those miseries are due to lack of our self-denial and bad stewardship:

> The more you lay out on your own apparel, the less you have left to clothe the naked, to feed the hungry, to lodge the strangers, to relieve those that are sick and in prison, and to lessen the numberless afflictions to which we are exposed in this vale of tears ... every shilling which you needlessly spend on your apparel is, in effect, stolen from God and the poor![149]

Wesley synthesized both good stewardship and self-denial with the command of love or the golden rule as the definite attitude desired of the rich in helping the poor:

> You may consider yourself as one in whose hands the Proprietor of heaven and earth and all things therein has lodged a part of his goods, to be disposed of according to His direction. And His direction is, that you should look upon yourself as one of a certain number of indigent persons who are to be provided for out of that portion of His goods wherewith you are entrusted.[150]

Failing to act according to love, self-denial, and good stewardship is to make the poor remain destitute, as well as to 'poison both yourself and others as far as your example spreads, with pride, vanity, anger, lust, love of the world, and a thousand foolish and hurtful desires'.[151] Wesley asserted that if we use properly what is actually not

---

[146] Sermon, 'Causes of the Inefficacy of Christianity', 8.
[147] Maddox, '"Visit the Poor": John Wesley, The Poor, and the Sanctification of Believers', 62.
[148] S. Riches (3), I. 12-13.
[149] S. Dress, 14-16.
[150] S. Excellent, VI. 4.
[151] S. Dress, 18, 27.

'our own things' but the Lord's, He will reward us with 'eternal things' as 'our own'.[152]

ii. Christian Social Ethics

Thomas W. Madron notes that for Wesley love is 'a social concept rather than an individualistic one', and sanctification has the dimension of 'political and social reform'.[153] Against 'solitary religion' and Christian ethics viewed merely as personal, Wesley affirmed, 'Christianity is essentially a social religion':[154] firstly, because Christian holy dispositions or tempers can be cultivated through 'some intercourse even with ungodly and unholy men';[155] and also because Christians can spread, diffuse, and communicate 'to all those among whom you are ... whatever grace you have received of God'.[156] The Methodist social activities started by aiding for the poor, the marginalized, and the oppressed, but extended to the point of resisting financial and moral evils in society. Paired with the Methodist teaching of Christian love, Methodist social activities demonstrate how Wesley endeavoured to integrate Christian social service based on Christian love into Christian faith.

From when Wesley was an Oxford student, the involvement in social undertakings appeared: 'in the two city prisons in Oxford, among poor families, in the work house, and in a school for underprivileged children'.[157] When Methodism was expanded into a popular movement from 1738, Wesley synthesized various Methodist social services into the activities of the Methodism. Those activities were inclusive of 'the provision of foodstuffs and clothing'; 'free medical care'; providing 'interest-free loans'; 'initiation of work projects';[158] establishing schools and educating 'children from poor families'; promoting 'the Sunday school movement' as well as 'adult education' especially for the 'illiterate miners and simple people'; and educating through publications.[159] Madron says, 'the old Foundery in London ... became a veritable melting pot of projects – "a house of mercy for

---

[152] S. Steward, I. 1.
[153] Thomas W. Madron, 'John Wesley on Economics', in Theodore Runyon ed., *Sanctification and Liberation* (Nashville: Abingdon Press, 1981), 106.
[154] S. Mount (4), Intro. 5.
[155] S. Mount (4), I. 1-7.
[156] S. Mount (4), I. 7-8.
[157] Marquardt, *Social*, 24.
[158] Marquardt, *Social*, 27-30.
[159] Marquardt, *Social*, 51-60.

widows, a school for boys, a dispensary for the sick, a work shop and employment bureau, a loan office and savings bank, a book room ..."'.[160]

Being not content to simply give alms to the poor or organize self-help projects,[161] Wesley, analysing the causes as well as 'an oddly connected sequence of interrelated problems' in 'poverty and unemployment', attacked the moral evils hidden in financial injustice.[162] He criticized the enclosure laws that 'denied the peasants access to common grazing lands, and drove them off the land and into the cities to become the great disenfranchised urban proletariat'.[163] Against early capitalism and the claim of 'governmental non-intervention', Wesley advocated 'governmental planning and control' especially 'in times of economic crisis'.[164] Wesley was enthusiastic in attacking the slave trade, regarding it as 'the worst abomination found in the Christian world'.[165] He rebuked slaveholders,[166] and encouraged and sanctioned Wilberforce's antislavery cause.[167]

Further, in his sermon, 'The Reformation of Manners' (1763), reporting the good social services done by The Society for Reformation of Manners, Wesley urged true Christians 'to join together' for the purposes of opposing 'the works of darkness' and of promoting 'His [God's] kingdom upon earth', which includes not only support of the needy but also the repression of 'all the ungodliness and unrighteousness' such as Sabbath-breaking, gambling, prostitution, profane swearing, and public nuisance.[168] In Wesley's vision, the extent to which Christian ethics should function covers 'the whole realm' of business, labour, education, health care, and human rights.[169]

Irv A. Brendlinger observes that though 'Wesley believed the individual was the most effective means to achieve lasting social improvement', occasionally he urged 'individuals to band together and organize in order to have greater impact against social evils'. However, 'by the late 1780s', as illustrated in his attack against slave trade, Wesley, moving 'beyond an exclusively individualistic ap-

---

[160] Madon, 'Economics', 113.
[161] Runyon ed., *Sanctification and Liberation*, 11-12.
[162] Madon, 'Economics', 110-113.
[163] Runyon ed., *Sanctification and Liberation*, 11-12.
[164] Madon, 'Economics', 114-115.
[165] Runyon ed., *Sanctification and Liberation*, 12.
[166] WW 11:78.
[167] Letters 8:265; Runyon ed., *Sanctification and Liberation*, 12.
[168] S. Manners, Intro. 1 - II. 12.
[169] Madron, 'John Wesley on Economics', 113.

proach', requested his followers 'to petition Parliament' to change the law. This shows 'a clear modification' of his earlier individualistic approach toward social evils.[170] H. Richard Niebuhr's criticism that Wesley 'envisaged sin as individual vice and laxity, not as greed, oppression, or social maladjustment', thus, in Wesley's ethics 'the hope of a thorough-going social reconstruction was almost entirely absent',[171] cannot be accepted. Brendlinger properly contends, 'Wesley did envision a complete social reconstruction, albeit emanating from the smallest societal unit, the individual, rather than through a reformation of structures themselves'.[172] Was Wesley right, and was his plan successful? According to Brendlinger, the answer is quite positive:

> Although Wesley did not normally relate his social ethic to the structures of society, as time went on the persons he influenced did. The second and third generations of Methodist leaders were more effective in carrying his message to the nerve centres of policy formation ... through petitions and boycotts. In the late-eighteenth and early-nineteenth centuries, legislative reform was influenced by the evangelical revival and produced reforms such as the temperance movement, organizations to prevent cruelty to children and animals, and even the more fully developed antislavery movement ... The changed individual is inspired to address the social structure. Such individuals then inspire support to carry through social reform ... Near the end of his life, Wesley was approaching such a synthesis. He never lost sight of the importance of the individual's integral role in society, but he did come to grips with the real power of structures.[173]

C. Observations and Analysis

I. Means of Grace as the Gospel vs. Means of Grace as the Law

In defining the church, Gwang Seok Oh says, 'the most significant common element between Luther and Wesley ... is that the church is primarily a *congregation of holy people of God*'.[174] While Wesley in his definition of the church followed Article XIX, 'Of the Church', of the

---

[170] Brendlinger, *Justice*, 141-143.
[171] H. Richard Niebuhr, *The Social Sources of Denominationalism* (New York: Henry Holt & Co., 1929), 66-67. Quoted by Brendlinger, *Justice*, 144.
[172] Brendlinger, *Justice*, 144.
[173] Brendlinger, *Justice*, 145-146; see Meistad, *Mount*, 243-245.
[174] Oh, *John Wesley's Ecclesiology*, 52.

Thirty-Nine Articles of the Church of England,[175] the Article was influenced by Article VII of *The Augsburg Confession*,[176] and was thus 'partly Lutheran in tenor'.[177]

There are also fundamental differences between the two theologians' views of the Church. Luther's view of the church is, in Gwang Seok Oh's words, 'essentially ... evangelical and Christological': 'it is evangelical in the sense that ... the gospel constitutes the reality of the church and is the one thing needful to ensure its existence'; and it is Christological, 'because Christ is the gospel'.[178] Luther's ecclesiology is also theocentric. John W. Kleinig notes, for Luther, 'God alone is intrinsically holy', and if believers can ever be called holy, it is 'derived from' God.[179] This 'holiness is not a moral concept', but 'a liturgical reality' believers passively receive from God in faith.[180] A believers' active holiness is dependent on what gives them faith and the Holy Spirit, that is, the word of God.[181]

Luther found the necessity of the means of grace of the church from the fact that, as Gerrish points out, faith is 'not implanted in the soul once and for all', but 'its continued existence depends on the proclamation of the gospel'.[182] By representing the means of grace as the way of delivering and renewing God's words, Luther redefined 'the basic nature of' the means of grace not as 'something in which we are raised to His [God's] level', but as the way in which 'He comes to us on our level'. It means that in practice as well as in doctrine Luther reversed the direction in the relationship between God and humanity from upward to down-to-earth.[183] Luther said, 'God governs us in such a way that wherever He speaks with us here on earth, the approach to the kingdom of heaven is open ... There is no reason for you to run to St. James's or ... to hide yourself in a monastery ... look in faith at the place where the Word and the sacraments are ... and

---

[175] Gilbert Burnet, *An Exposition of the Thirty-Nine Articles of the Church of England by Gilbert, Bishop of Sarum*, ed. James R. Page (New York: D. Appleton and Company, 1866), 233. Quoted by Oh, *John Wesley's Ecclesiology*, 51.
[176] *BC*, 32.
[177] Oh, *John Wesley's Ecclesiology*, 51-52.
[178] Ibid., 48-49.
[179] Kleinig, 'Holiness', 76-77; LW 12:325; LW 30:6.
[180] Kleinig, 'Holiness', 78-79; LW 30:32; LW 26:25; LW 27:82.
[181] Kleinig, 'Holiness', 79.
[182] Brian. A. Gerrish, 'Priesthood and Ministry in the Theology of Luther', *Church History* 34:4 (Dec. 1965), 409-410.
[183] Forde, *Where*, 69-70.

there write the title THE GATE OF GOD.[184] Christ is 'certainly found' in God's words, and in sacraments.[185] As Luther's own conversion was the outcome of his study of Scripture,[186] his emphasis on the use of the means of grace was mainly focused on the gospel. Lazareth asserts, what is 'primary and central' for Luther's teaching of the means of grace is 'the gospel and faith'.[187]

Whereas for Luther believers' works are only the outcome of Christian faith, not vice versa, for Wesley, believers' works are not only grounded in Christian faith, but also have 'the *formative* role' that develops Christian spirituality.[188] Faith goes 'before works and together with them' and 'works do not give life to faith'. However, works also have their own 'energy and operation' distinguished from those of faith. Wesley emphasized, 'faith begets works, and then is perfected by them ... Faith hath not its being from works, (for it is before them,) but its perfection'.[189] Faith and works increase and perfect each other. Likewise, the gospel and the means of grace are mutually interdependent. As much as Luther emphasized that good works are the consequence of justifying faith, Wesley stressed that the same faith should be sustained, increased, and perfected through constant use of the means of grace.

The means of grace help the actualization of Christian doctrine both in the world and in Christian life.[190] Conversely, to disregard 'any of the means of grace' may eventually cause 'shipwreck of faith'.[191] In a sermon, 'Causes of the Inefficacy of Christianity' (1789), written near the end of his life, Wesley asked two questions: firstly, 'Why has Christianity done so little good in the world?'[192] Secondly, why do most Christians fail to change their tempers or lives in spite of their knowledge of the Christian doctrine? He found the answer from the lack of Christian discipline through the use of the means of

---

[184] LW 5:247; John Kleinig, 'Where is Your God? Luther on God's self Localization', in Dean O Wenthe and others eds., *All Theology Is Christology: Essays in Honor of David P. Scaer*, (Concordia Theological Press: Fort Wayne, 2000), 117-131.
[185] LW 3:108.
[186] McKim ed., *The Cambridge Companion to Martin Luther*, 89.
[187] LW 38: Introduction.
[188] Maddox, '"Visit the Poor": John Wesley, The Poor, and the Sanctification of Believers', 64; S. Way (2), III. 3-13; S. Working, II. 1; III. 1-8.
[189] ENNT Ja 2:22.
[190] S. Dress, 4.
[191] Letters 1:207.
[192] S. Inefficacy, 1.

grace: 'Whatever doctrine is preached, where there is not discipline, it cannot have its full effect upon the hearers'.[193]

As a practical example, Wesley reminded his reader of the elderly Luther's regret that though he 'reformed in opinions and modes of worship', he could not make his followers' 'hearts and lives ... a jot better than the Papists', implying that many Lutherans 'made shipwreck of faith and a good conscience' because of lack of Christian discipline.[194] In the same sense, Wesley mentioned that Whitefield had much sorrow because a majority who were influenced by his preaching had turned back from God's words later.[195] Comparing those examples with the Methodists' continuing effectiveness, Wesley argued that without proper discipline through Christian connection for mutual care of each others' souls, those who were once blessed by preaching may fall from God's grace again: 'if any fell into lukewarmness, or even into sin, he had none to lift him up: He might fall lower and lower, yea, into hell, if he would, for who regarded it?'[196] Quoting a saying from the early church, Wesley stressed the use of the means of grace; 'The soul and the body make a man; the spirit and discipline make a Christian'.[197]

Like Luther, Wesley opposed monastic solitary religion. But, he stressed that 'in the midst of a world in which God has been forgotten', it is quite necessary for believers to gather together 'from time to time as a distinctive Christian community', in order to be aware of the presence of God and strengthen each other's faith.[198]

To guard the doctrine of sanctification from abuse of antinomians Wesley placed 'a high degree of moral responsibility' upon believers. Though God gives sanctifying grace through faith in an instant, Coppedge contends, it should be maintained 'by spiritual accountability and the use of the means of grace'.[199] To teach of the need for accountability and of the formative role of the means of grace is 'not to expect salvation due to our own work', but, on the contrary, to put trust in 'Christ who has promised to meet us in the means of grace'.[200] What Wesley taught was not 'to trust in' those means, but

---

[193] S. Inefficacy, 7.
[194] S. Counsels, 10.
[195] S. America, I. 6.
[196] S. America, I. 7.
[197] S. Inefficacy, 7; S. America, I. 7.
[198] Henry H. Knight III, *The Presence of God in the Christian Life: John Wesley and the Means of Grace* (Lanham: The Scarecrow Press, 1992), 96-99.
[199] Coppedge, *John Wesley in Theological Debate*, 268.
[200] Knight, *The Presence of God in the Christian Life*, 43.

'to use them', though the Moravians did not distinguish them from each other.[201] The means do not have 'any intrinsic power', unless the Holy Spirit works 'in them and by them'.[202] Believers' attitude toward God in using the means of grace is 'to wait in them as a beggar waits at a man's door'.[203]

II. Ethics of Creation vs. Ethics of Heaven

Christian ethics are intimately connected with salvation. How to understand salvation characterizes what Christian life should be like. Teaching that Christian life is freed from all upward approach, selfish meritorious cause, distinction of works, and distinction between spiritual and temporal estates, Luther taught that the earth, 'among the neighbour', vocation, and the secular stations become the main locus of Christian life. Luther believed he emancipated not only God's words from the Catholic Church,[204] but also believers from the system of the ladder to heaven. Believers who realize that we can do nothing for God, understand paradoxically that to live a creaturely life, not to transcend our being or to transform our nature into the divine one, is to obey God's will. Christian ethics is not a heavenly ethics, but an ethics of creation.

Luther was both 'a kind of natural law ethicist' and a realist, not a nominalist. For him, the law does not need to be 'a mimetic copy or imitative reflection of eternal law', like Wesley's Platonic concept of the law.[205] Imitation piety disregards 'what every person owes to God according to his calling', but magnifies 'those works which among men are highly esteemed and which people admire'.[206] However, the law does not need to be a 'supernatural' one. The 'law is natural, in the sense that it was built into the creation' as requirements for daily life among neighbours.[207]

José Míguez Bonino's analysis of Wesley's ethics can be seen as a good representation of Luther's criticism of Wesley. From Luther's viewpoint, Wesley's theology contains 'radical dualism' between human beings as spiritual beings who have a 'reality' of their own

---

[201] Ibid., 41; Starkey, *Spirit*, 84; see S. Mount (4), III. 6-7.
[202] S. Means, II. 3.
[203] Starkey, *Spirit*, 84.
[204] Lindberg, *Beyond*, 98.
[205] Kenneth J. Collins, 'John Wesley's Platonic Conception of the Moral Law', *WTJ* 21 (1986), 116-128.
[206] LW 25:408.
[207] Forde, *Radical*, 154.

and their subsidiary or circumstantial 'earthly, social, bodily life'. Of the two, Wesley gave superiority to the former.[208] Accordingly, Wesley's teaching is not free from the dualism of the spiritual and the temporal estates, between which Wesley gave superiority to the former.

Also, though Wesley repeatedly emphasized 'the social character of the Christian life' against 'a solitary religion', in Wesley's view, society was 'simply a convenient arrangement for the growth of the individual'; 'it is the individual soul that finally is saved, sanctified, perfected. The fellowship is, in the last instance, an external support … The drama of justification and sanctification takes place in the subjectivity of the inner life – although it seeks objective expression in works of love'.[209]

In addition, by leaving justification behind 'as a moment' and teaching that there is another moment of final justification that is determined by sanctification, Wesley not only obscured both the nature of justification as a total gift by God's grace and 'the faithfulness and unity of God's grace', but also implied ethically that believers cannot be freed from self-centredness as well as from an upward approach toward heaven by way of the works of the law. Sanctification should still be pursued by way of 'the mediation of a divine moral code' even after justification. Similarly to the Catholic Church's ethics that weighs between great and trivial works with individualistic and upward concerns, Wesley's ethics remains under the bondage to the law and, consequently, cannot have the freedom and power of 'wrestling with actual historical conditions', which is given only by the gospel.[210]

The result is, Bonino insists, that Wesley 'was not able to develop a theology of sanctification in which the unity of creation and redemption could be the centre of articulation. Had he done so, his concern for human life in its entirety, and for social conditions, would have become integral and not subsidiary to his doctrine of sanctification'.[211] Though Rupert E. Davies speaks for liberation theology, not for Reformation theology, his argument that lest 'temporal realities lack autonomy', Christians should be able to 'come right

---

[208] José Míguez Bonino, 'Wesley's Doctrine of Sanctification From a Liberationist Perspective', in Runyon ed., *Sanctification and Liberation* (Nashville: Abingdon Press, 1981), 56-57.
[209] Ibid., 55.
[210] Ibid., 56-57.
[211] Ibid., 58.

down into the arena of political and social' reality, rather than relying on any 'form of pietism' or 'any kind of concentration on the unworldly',[212] can be Luther's criticism on Wesley's ethics. Luther's ethics does not align with a pietistic upward approach to heaven, but are firmly founded on and motivated by Christian freedom from any upward, self-centred, or meritorious concerns.

It is time to turn to Wesley's position. Firstly, compared with Luther's down-to-earth approach, Wesley's ethics has a teleological concern.[213] In the preface to his *Sermons on Several Occasions* Wesley wrote that what he aimed for by everything he did was to pursue 'one thing – the way to heaven'.[214] He described Christ's Sermon on the Mount as 'the royal way' to heaven.[215] Insisting that human beings 'were not created ... to seek happiness in any created good',[216] he lamented that believers do not pursue the heavenly life.[217] Wesley expected in the Methodist movement that believers 'would have lived like angels here below ... walking in eternity'.[218] For him, 'walk by faith' meant to devalue visible things in preference to 'things invisible and eternal';[219] 'religion is no less than living in eternity ... on earth'.[220]

Whereas Luther, regarding imitation piety as a sort of upward approach to God, which originates from human pride and self-idolatry, represented humanity only as God's creatures and emphasized an ontological difference between the two, Wesley accepted the medieval 'ethics of imitation'.[221] Wesley taught that human beings are not only created in God's image, but also can perfect their nature by adapting themselves to God's law.[222] What Wesley meant by the conceptions of 'to be like God' or 'to go heaven' is not that believers transcend their human nature, against which Luther warned, but that they are recovered from a depraved state to their original image of God.[223] Even in a depraved state after the fall, Wesley be-

---

[212] Rupert E. Davies, 'Justification, Sanctification, and the Liberation of the Person', in Runyon ed., *Sanctification and Liberation*, 72.
[213] Collins, 'Law', 228-230.
[214] WW 5:3.
[215] S. Mount (1), Intro. 3.
[216] S. Man (2), 13, 15.
[217] WW 8:302.
[218] S. Vineyard, V. 1.
[219] S. Walking, 14, 17-18.
[220] S. Walking, 17-18.
[221] Hynson, *To Reform the Nation*, 22.
[222] S. Law, I. 2-3.
[223] S. New (1), I. 1.

lieved, every human being has an absolute and incomparable value which originates from God's grace.[224] To trace human nature to its origin from God's nature is not to idolize human beings, but to accept the noble position which God has granted to us in gratitude and responsibility. Whereas Luther thought that imitation piety put people under the bondage of the ladder system, for Wesley it becomes the theological foundation for freeing human beings not only from personal sins but also from social injustice, oppression, or discrimination.[225] Imitation piety has the potential of healing personal and social evils.[226]

Secondly, concerning the altruistic aspect of Luther's ethics, Wesley would agree that Christian ethics has entirely altruistic motives. However, he did not deny that happiness is a goal as well as a consequence of Christian love.[227] What causes unhappiness is not only outward sins but inward sin itself, that is, unholy tempers, whereas love and holy tempers not only counteract the results of sins, but they themselves give happiness.[228] Differently from Luther's negative attitude toward eudemonism, for Wesley, happiness is not a mere individual or self-centred concept, but the peace with God, with others, and with oneself.[229]

Happiness is inevitably connected with our pursuit of heaven and eternity, since transient happiness cannot be true happiness. When believers deny themselves and serve their neighbours on earth, it is because faith makes them fix their eyes to heaven and eternity. The eschatological hope for eternal happiness and for reward from God becomes a great inducement to a believers' holy and altruistic life.[230] In Wesley's Christian ethics, all of the concern for heaven, altruism, and eudemonism are joined together:

> Had all men a deep sense of this [the final judgment], how effectually would it secure the interests of society! For what more forcible motive can be conceived to the practice of genuine morality? to a steady pursuit of solid virtue? an uniform walking in justice, mercy, and truth? What could strengthen our hands in all that is good, and deter us from all evil, like a

---

[224] S. Man (1), II. 5-7, 14.
[225] Hynson, *To Reform the Nation*, 45-51; Brendlinger, *Justice*, 74-83.
[226] For more detailed discussion, see Kim, 'Anthropology', 211-233.
[227] Collins, 'Law', 226-228.
[228] S. Riches (1), I. 18-19; S. Schism, I. 12; S. Question, III. 10; S. Fall, I. 2; S. Idolatry, II. 2.
[229] S. Speaking, III. 5; S. Fall, I. 2; S. Worship, III. 1-8; S. Idolatry, II. 3; S. Unity, 17.
[230] S. Eternity, 12-17; S. Dissipation, 19; S. Reward.

strong conviction of this, 'The Judge standeth at the door'; and we are shortly to stand before Him?[231]

From Wesley's viewpoint, Luther's ethics may look too idealistic or optimistic in arguing that justified believers can be totally altruistic, or that they would obey God even if there is no reward in heaven or no punishment of the hell.[232] At the same time, he may look too pessimistic regarding the state of believers as sinners. Althaus admits, 'Luther's ethics is determined in its entirety, in its starting point and all its main features, by the heart and centre of his theology, namely, by the justification'.[233] Putting this in another way, Brian Hebblethwaite contends, Luther's ethics are 'eschatological', since that though the final judgment will determine 'heaven or hell', believers already experience either of them in their conscience *now*.[234] Gordon Rupp calls Luther's eschatology 'an eschatology of faith',[235] implying that the eschatological moment comes 'when one accepts what God has done for us in Christ'.[236] From the viewpoint of Luther's 'ethics of justification', Hynson notes, Wesley's 'sanctification ethics' may seem 'to lack something of the freedom or spontaneity of the justification ethic, by its deliberate quest for holiness';[237] it may seem 'to be a nervous kind of Christianity which strips the Christian life of some of the joy and power it bears'.[238]

However, is the entirety that Luther ascribed to justification compatible with his anthropology? Luther's altruistic ethics is dependent on a total trust in God's grace. Can believers have such a faith? For Luther, faith in believers is not a perfect one, thus, it needs to be sustained by continuous confirmation of the gospel through the means of grace. Then, is it not to choose between all or nothing to base Christian ethics on the entirety of justification?

For Wesley, though justifying faith initiates and gives foundation to Christian ethics, it cannot exist in believers with such an entirety

---

[231] S. Assize, Intro. 3.
[232] LW 33:153; LW 44:26-28.
[233] Althaus, *Ethics*, 3; see Leon O. Hynson, 'Christian Love: The Key to Wesley's Ethics', *MH* 14 (October 1975), 49.
[234] Brian Hebblethwaite, *The Christian Hope* (New York: Oxford University Press, 2010), 71.
[235] Rupp, *The Righteousness of God*, 255.
[236] Hebblethwaite, *The Christian Hope*, 71; Winfried Vogel, 'The Eschatological Theology of Martin Luther, Part 1: Luther's Basic Concepts', in *Andrews University Seminary Studies* 24:3 (Autumn 1986), 252, 254.
[237] Hynson, 'Christian Love: The Key to Wesley's Ethics', 52.
[238] Ibid., 53.

as Luther taught without receiving further grace of sanctification, existing only as 'faith ... mixed with doubts and fear'.[239] With such faith, a believer can love others merely 'in a low degree, in proportion to the degree of his faith'. Only when faith grows, the altruism in a believer can grow in 'the same proportion as he grows in faith'.[240]

Even after believers are blessed with 'a full conviction of present pardon',[241] this assurance can be confirmed and continued by 'the witness of our own spirit' through continuous exercise of love.[242] This means that believers should not remain in justifying grace, but proceed to and grow in sanctifying grace.[243] Believers can be totally altruistic on the precondition that their faith and love are perfected in sanctifying grace and they continue and grow in the same grace.[244]

Thirdly, compared with Luther who removed distinction between works, Wesley taught that differences exist in 'degree[s] of goodness that is in its object' or 'comparative value of the several parts of religion'. According to these different values, Wesley ordered holy works and tempers from the lowest to the highest; the Church, works of piety, works of mercy, holy tempers, and love.[245] This ordering does not mean that the higher part has more merit than the lower one. Rather, it means that since faith cannot be perfected in an instance but needs to grow and be strengthened,[246] believers should discern what means of grace, what attitude of the heart, or what works are more substantial in supporting their faith. It also means that the higher works verify the depth and the authenticity of its holder's faith more credibly than the lower ones.

Fourthly, concerning the subject of priesthood of all believers, Wesley would have agreed entirely with Luther in principle in the sense that the secular world is the realm of God's government and believers' works in this world are regarded as ways of serving God. The principle of the priesthood of all believers was well accepted in Wesley's Methodist movement, in which lay persons and women

---

[239] Letters 3:305.
[240] S. Patience, 10.
[241] Letters 3:305.
[242] S. Witness (1), I. 1-6.
[243] Hynson, 'Christian Love: The Key to Wesley's Ethics', 49.
[244] Collins, 'Law', 230.
[245] S. Zeal, II. 5-11.
[246] S. Adoption, IV. 1; S. Perfection (1), II. 1.

played crucial roles as good examples of practising their priesthood.[247]

However, as much as sanctification remains the teleological end of Christian life, and as there exist differences of 'comparative value' of works, believers should have more concern for those works which will make them holier. Secular works have their own goodness, but their values depend on how they contribute to sanctification. Wesley did not remove the distinction in value between the spiritual estate and the temporal estate, evaluating the former more highly.

While Luther represented Christian life on earth as vocation, what is equivalent to vocation in Wesley's teaching would be stewardship. In both God is the ultimate governor over all. The difference is that whereas Luther's vocation is exercised in God's secular kingdom with gratitude for the entirety of the already received salvation, Wesley's stewardship is for those who are pursuing a sanctified life, living between initial justification and final justification. Whereas vocation as a fruit of God's grace demonstrates the theocentricity of Luther's theology, Wesley's stewardship has a bifocal emphasis on both God's sovereignty and human responsibility. Whereas in Luther's concept of vocation a believers' horizontal 'service to the neighbour' will prove their true faith on the last day,[248] in Wesley's idea of stewardship it seems that a vertical relationship with God is more important.[249]

For Luther, while the 'common standard' of Christian service to others is achieved through life stations or vocation, believers' works of love according to the law of Christ are regarded as 'extraordinary' ones.[250] For Wesley, when believers serve others in their life on earth, their standard of Christian ethics is the law of Christ.[251] Delivered by the original Law-Maker, their works are far superior to inferences by human reason.[252] Their works are not too abstract or too idealistic, but are applicable to all 'relations' as well as to all 'circumstances', containing 'the everlasting fitness of all things' in them.[253]

In solving the problem of social evils, whereas Luther stressed the role of the public law which is performed by civil authorities in their

---

[247] Snyder, *The Radical Wesley and Patterns for Church Renewal*, 19, 154-157; Collins, *John Wesley: A Theological Journey*, 21.
[248] LW 45:286; Lindberg, *Beyond*, 97-98.
[249] S. Steward, III. 3-6.
[250] Althaus, *Ethics*, 40-41; LW5:311.
[251] S. Established (1), III. 4.
[252] S. Mount (1), Intro. 2.
[253] S. Law, II. 5; III. 5; S. Mount (1), Intro. 7.

vocation, Wesley's ethic approaches the same problem in a more individualistic way. Wesley partly admitted the positive role of the civil law in checking human sins outwardly in society. However, without recovering individuals who are members of society from their depravity to the image of God, the improvement of society is limited.[254] As Brendlinger points out, since 'individual sin became social when experienced by the masses', each individual's interaction with others becomes 'the core of social structure'.[255] The solution should be what overcomes and removes sins first from the individuals, that is, God's sanctifying grace.[256] In this sense, although Wesley 'in the name of Christian love' actively criticized 'the many social evils that prevailed' in human life, Robert W. Burtner contends, for Wesley, Christian social ethics should be an application and an extension of the sanctification of individuals.[257]

---

[254] S. Manners, II. 8.
[255] Brendlinger, *Justice*, 144; S. National, Intro. 5; I.1 - II.7.
[256] S. National, II. 9-10.
[257] Robert W. Burtner and Robert E. Chiles eds., *A Compend of Wesley's Theology* (New York & Nashville: Abingdon Press, 1954), 223.

Conclusion

The theologies of the law in Martin Luther and John Wesley have been examined in relation to other subjects of systematic theology: the nature and works of God the Father, Christ's atonement and His teaching of the law, the Holy Spirit's illumination of the law and sanctification, the respective roles of faith and works in the order of salvation, the three states of human beings (original, depraved, and restored), and the uses of the law for the Church and for the world. In each chapter, the theologies of the law in Luther and Wesley have been investigated firstly in their theological systems, and, secondly, they have been compared and contrasted with each other.

In the first chapter, general agreements between both theologians' views of the law have been observed. Luther and Wesley agreed with each other that the law originates from God's nature of holy love, and that God's will is that the law is obeyed from the heart. For both, if God's love is accepted through faith, it produces our responsive love which voluntarily obeys His law. But, at the same time, the law, having a strictness that requires perfect obedience, judges whoever breaks even a small part of it as deserving death.

It has also been observed that, having different theological motives which were connected to their efforts to combat different errors, Luther and Wesley diverged in many points. Whereas Luther's discussion of the law focused on the accusing effect of the law when its holy nature is applied to sinners, Wesley, viewing the law from the point of its origin, which is God's nature, focused on its potential to show sinners the way of recovering their depraved nature according to God's nature.

Luther ascribed any positive relationship of believers with the law – proper understanding and fulfilment – to faith, the Holy Spirit, and God's works, leaving only an accusing role to the law. Even the power of accusing sin is not in the law itself. The law is just dead letters without words and actions of God, who condemns sinners with or without the law; through all things, events, and people. Ascribing the role of teaching Christian duties to a believers' reason, to faith working by love, or to requirements of life stations, Luther in reality did not attribute anything positive to the law, only the negative attribute of accusation.

In contrast, Wesley, focusing on the law in the Scripture, represented human ability to understand the prescription of the law and to respond to it through prevenient grace more positively. He consistently stressed that the justified can fulfil the law empowered by the Holy Spirit. His positive view of the law as a way of sanctification has been investigated with regard to his teachings of the covenant of grace, Christian dispensation, and covered promises.

In Luther's teaching of two uses of the law – the civil use and the theological uses – in relation to God's two kingdoms, the law cannot enable salvation in God's spiritual kingdom, but can be a way of knowledge of how to serve other people in God's earthly kingdom. What is equivalent to Luther's civil use of the law is Wesley's concept of prevenient grace in its restraining power. However, whereas he advocated the third use of the law for sanctification of believers, Luther taught that the civil use of the law is enough for Christian ethics, denying the third use.

In the second chapter, both theologians' different views of the law were investigated in relation to their thoughts of God. How they understand the law contains implications on who God is, what relationship He wants to establish between Himself and humans, and what the most central command of the law is.

The implications of Luther's teaching that God works all things according to His own will, were examined from different viewpoints. When the subject 'God' was emphasized, Luther made God's sovereignty the antithesis to human passivity. When he dealt with 'all things', his focus was on God's complete control. When 'God's own will' became an issue, Luther's voice took on a very radical tone that even eternal reprobation is by His intentional will. By teaching God's all-sufficiency, compete control, and absolute freedom, Luther taught that the law commands one to have a total faith in God in fear and love as a proper attitude toward God positively, and, negatively, to avoid any idolatry, arrogance, and self-complacency. The law cannot influence God; it just makes human beings humble before the sovereign God.

Wesley had a shared concern for God's glory with Luther. But, teaching that there is a unity between God's nature, His works, and the demands of the law, and correlating God's grace and His law,

Wesley endeavoured to establish the law as God's will and His instrument for sanctifying believers. For him, the law requires believers to imitate the God of holy love. To imitate God not only sanctifies believers, but also makes them co-workers with God for His providential works for other people.

In contrast to Luther who taught that the concept of the hidden God is a way of removing human arrogance and self-complacency, and of strengthening believers' dependence on God's grace, Wesley denied the doctrine of predestination from the viewpoints of the Scriptural teaching of God's love, and of human ability and responsibility to obey the law. Wesley related the fact of the incomprehensibility of God not merely to God's sovereignty but to His wisdom and goodness, which sanctifies believers by making them humble and dependent on God.

In the third chapter, Luther's teaching of Christ's atonement both for penal substitution and for the imputation of His righteousness to believers, and Wesley's acceptance of only penal substitution was contrasted. Whereas Luther's teaching aimed to ascribe all righteousness solely to Christ, Wesley wanted to make room for the necessity of a believers' own righteousness and for the role of the law in the process of gradual sanctification.

Luther, representing Christ as the gospel, attacked sinners who refuse accepting Christ, choosing the law as their way of achieving salvation with their own power, and glorifying human works against God's grace. However, Wesley's teaching on the three – prophetic, priestly, and kingly – offices of Christ in a threefold process of salvation – justification, sanctification, and final justification – is well organized to rectify an antinomian claim that Christ's priestly work is enough for salvation. Wesley confirmed the importance of the law as a way of sanctification with regard to all of Christ's offices.

Contrary to Wesley's criticism, Luther justified his grouping of the law among evil powers such as sin, death, the devil, and hell, arguing that without the law, all other enemies lose their power. From this, Luther taught, Christ firstly won His victory over the law through His perfect obedience to God's law, and, next, He imputes to believers His own victory in faith. Wesley agreed that Christ won victory through His perfect obedience to God's law. However, believers should win their victory through their own obedience to the law, on the foundation of Christ's victory and His reign in their heart.

In the fourth chapter, both theologians' pneumatologies were compared with particular focus on the law. Luther taught that the

Holy Spirit comforts believers in spiritual trials and various hardships by confirming the truth of God's justifying love. For him, sanctification is no other than believers' appreciation of the fact of their justification. Thus, in sanctification as well as in justification, there is no room for the role of the law. In contrast, Wesley related the witness of the Holy Spirit not only to the Spirit's revealing God's salvific love, but also to the Spirit's illumination of the essential nature of God's law, of the motive of God's giving the law, and of fruits which keeping God's law will produce, that is, holy love.

For Luther, the Spirit's role for sanctification is mainly to repeatedly confirm what God has done for believers. In sanctification, believers are passive receivers of comforts of the Spirit as well as spiritual trials imposed by God. However, in Wesley's teaching, the Spirit has a persuasive role which requires human response after receiving God's free grace, and an enabling role for those who accept the Spirit's persuasion to love God and obey His law.

In Luther's teaching, in spite of the Spirit's comfort and His repression of sin and the flesh in believers, believers themselves remain sinners, and their progress in their own holiness is hindered by sin and the flesh. But, for Wesley, the presence and empowerment of the Holy Spirit grants believers a new nature and a real righteousness, with which they obey the law and do not sin.

For Luther, the Spirit's confirmation of God's salvific love and of the justification of sinners, having trans-experiential character, counteracts believers' own experience of their sinfulness and of the accusation of the law. Justification cannot be an experiential event, though it is a real event. It is believed and accepted in faith. For Wesley, Christian assurance of God's love through the witness of the Spirit and through the witness of a believers' own conscience through conforming to God's law is experiential. Their happiness produced by sanctification is experiential as well. A believers' obedience to the law closely relates to the experiential character of Christian religion.

The fifth chapter compares the two theologians' views on the respective roles of faith and works and their relationship in salvation and the Christian life. For Luther, since love commanded by the law is weak and imperfect in believers, justification cannot be produced by love. The Scriptural teaching that love fulfils the law in reality does not apply to sinners' love. Accordingly, Luther opposed the third use of the law, stressing that only faith recognizes and fulfils God's will contained in the law, but love depends on faith. Attributing fulfilment of the law to faith is Luther's peculiar way of depreciating human works and, at the same time, of preserving the importance of love and good works in the Christian life as fruits of faith. In contrast, for Wesley, except the instants when we receive God's prevenient, convincing, justifying, and sanctifying grace, the law should be kept either as fruits of already received grace or as a preparation for receiving further grace. Love not only has its own power of preserving and strengthening faith, but also becomes the goal for which faith exists.

Whereas Luther opposed the medieval teachings of God's grace that changes human will (Augustine), of infused love that perfects infused faith (Aquinas), and of 'the human *in se*' which is considered necessary in order to complete Christ's merit (Biel), Wesley stressed the aspect of God's grace that changes the human will more than Augustine, advocated partly Aquinas' idea of infusion of love though he based this idea on Luther's teaching of saving faith, and also accepted Biel's teaching of 'the human *in se*' through the concepts of the covenant of grace and prevenient grace. Wesley, synthesizing the Protestant emphasis of God's grace as favour and the Catholic conception of grace that perfects human nature, made a believers' obedience to the law not only a verification but also the purpose of true faith.

In the sixth chapter, the three states of humanity in creation, after the fall, and in salvation have been investigated. Luther, emphasizing the great difference between God and humans, described humanity as God's creatures; understood the major sin as sinners' attempts to be like God through intellectualism and moralism; and taught that Christians remain always sinners. In contrast, Wesley, emphasizing humanity as the image of God, described human nature from the viewpoint of its resemblance with God's nature; understood the major sin as deviation from God's nature, as well as unbelief; and considered Christians as beings restored to the moral image of God in spite of the marring of the natural image of God.

Whereas Luther taught the main locus toward which God's grace works is the conscience of believers, Wesley taught that God's grace works on both the conscience and will of believers. Though Wesley criticized that Luther devalued human reason too much, Luther's distinction of the original, the depraved, and the restored states of human reason was not much different from Wesley's. If Wesley appraised Luther's view properly, he might have criticized Luther's too high evaluation of a believer's reason so as to deny the necessity of the prescriptive role of the law for believers.

In the last chapter, the uses of the law for the Church and for the world were investigated. Since Luther believed that Christian life is fruits of faith, he believed that the means of grace is no other than repeated proclamation of the gospel. Wesley regarded the means of grace as Christian discipline for strengthening faith and love.

For Luther, believers, being freed from the law as a way of placating God, serve their neighbours in life stations mainly by faithfully fulfilling their civil responsibilities, though Luther admitted that Christians can serve the needy in extraordinary ways with Christian love. However, Wesley regarded Christian love which Christ taught in His Sermon on the Mount as the standard of Christian life and their service for others. To teach Christian love, Wesley stressed that believers' self-denial and good stewardship on the foundation of God's sanctifying grace are necessary. Whereas Luther's ethics is the ethics of life stations, Wesley's ethics is ethics of Christian love which aims to fulfil the high standard of Christian perfection.

This book employed the analysis of two Luther scholars of the overall theology of Luther as a framework for interpreting Luther's theology: Philip Watson's theocentric motif and Brian Gerrish's doctrines of justification by faith and of two kingdoms. Both analyses have been verified as foundational thoughts of Luther, which give insights for understanding his theology of the law.

Arguing that both religious intellectualism and moralism form the theological system of the Catholic Church, Luther represented all aspects of God's all-sufficiency, His absolute freedom, imputation of Christ's righteousness, spiritual trials and comfort by the Holy Spirit, justification and sanctification by faith, human beings as earthly creatures, Christians as saints and sinners, two uses of the law in the two kingdoms of God, as countermeasures of the human-centred religion of the Catholicism. In all those subjects, Luther made the law a device that reveals sinners' inability to merit salvation by the law and, at the same time, preserve the necessity of good works which are led by Holy Spirit, produced by faith, and performed in life stations.

On Wesley's side, Kenneth Collins' analysis of the two-fold axial theme in Wesley's theology – holiness (holy love) and grace (free & co-operant) – together with various conjunctions, also have been confirmed as a reliable framework for understanding Wesley's theology of the law.

Against both antinomianism which Luther's over-reaction to the Catholic doctrine of merit caused, and legalism of the Roman Catholic Church, Wesley synthesized the Protestant emphasis on God's grace as favour received in faith instantaneously, and the Catholic emphasis on God's grace that requires a believers' response in the process of salvation. In all subjects of God's works of creation, salvation, and providence, the three offices of Christ, namely, Christ's penal substitution as Priest, His full exposition of the law as Prophet, and His ruling as King through the law, the witness and empowerment of the Holy Spirit, faith as handmaid of love, and the third use of the law, human beings as the image of God, and sanctification as renewal of person and cosmos, it has been demonstrated that Wesley's evangelical synergism makes room for the role of the law on the foundation of God's grace.

As a study that has investigated the theologies of the law in Luther and Wesley according to subjects of systematic theology, this book has tried to make clearer the historical and religious settings which had shaped their theologies, as well as the primary motives and the emphases in major subjects of their systematic theology. However, whereas Luther's view of the law has been investigated by scholars in a thorough way, Wesley's theology of the law has been underexplored. One of subject which deserves further investigation is Wesley's indebtedness to the Puritan theology of the law as an essential source of Wesley's theology of the law, which developed and deepened Calvin's positive representation of the use of the law for Christian holy life.

Selected Bibliography

I. Primary Sources

1. Martin Luther

Luther, Martin. *Luther's Works.* eds. Jaroslav Pelikan and Helmut T. Lehmann. 55 vols. Saint Louis: Concordia / Philadelphia: Fortress, 1955-86.
Plass, Ewald M., ed. *What Luther Says, an Anthology.* 3 vols. Saint Louis: Concordia Pub. House, 1959.
Tappert, Theodore G., tr. and ed. *The Augsburg Confession: Translated from Latin.* Philadelphia: Fortress Press, 1959.
_____., tr. and ed. *The Book of Concord: the Confessions of the Evangelical Lutheran Church.* Philadelphia: Fortress Press, 1959.

2. John Wesley

Burtner, Robert W. and Robert E. Chiles, eds. *A Compend of Wesley's Theology.* New York & Nashville: Abingdon Press, 1954.
Cragg, Gerald R., ed. *The Works of John Wesley.* Bicentennial ed. Vol. 11: *The Appeals to Men of Reason and Religion and Certain Related Open Letters.* Nashville: Abingdon Press, 1975.
Curnock, Nehemiah, ed. *The Journal of Rev. John Wesley.* 8 vols. London: Epworth Press, 1909-1916.
Hurley, Michael, ed. *John Wesley's Letter to a Roman Catholic.* London: G. Chapman, 1968.
Jackson, Thomas, ed. *The Works of Rev. John Wesley.* 14 vols. London: Wesleyan Methodist Book Room, 1829-1831. Reprinted Grand Rapids: Baker Book House, 1978.
Outler, Albert C., ed. *John Wesley.* New York: Oxford University Press, 1964.
_____., ed. *The Works of John Wesley.* Bicentennial ed. Vols. 1-4: Sermons. Nashville: Abingdon Press, 1984-1987.
Outler, Albert C., and Richard P. Heitzenrater, eds. *John Wesley's Sermons: An Anthology.* Nashville: Abingdon Press, 1991.
Sugden, Edward H., ed. *Wesley's Standard Sermons.* 2 vols. London: Epworth Press, 1951.
Telford, John, ed. *The Letters of the Rev. John Wesley.* 8 vols. London: Epworth Press, 1931.

Wesley, John. *Explanatory Notes upon the New Testament.* Grand Rapids: Baker Book House, 1987.

_____. *Explanatory Notes upon the Old Testament.* 3 vols. Salem, OH: Schmul Publishers, 1975.

_____. *A Plain Account of Christian Perfection.* London: Epworth Press. Philadelphia: Trinity Press International, 1990.

3. Others

Aquinas, Thomas. *Summa Theologica.* tr. Fathers of the English Dominical Province. 5 vols. New York: Benziger Brothers, 1948.

Augustine. *Confessions. NPNF.* vol. II. ed. Philip Schaff. Grand Rapids: Wm. B. Eerdmans, 1956.

_____. *De civitate Dei* (City of God). *NPNF.* vol. II. ed. Philip Schaff. Grand Rapids: Wm. B. Eerdmans, 1956.

_____. *De Trinitate* (On the Trinity). *NPNF.* vol. III. ed. Philip Schaff. Grand Rapids: Wm. B. Eerdmans, 1956.

_____. *On Grace and Free Will. NPNF.* vol. V. ed. Philip Schaff. Grand Rapids: Wm. B. Eerdmans, 1956.

Burnet, Gilbert. *An Exposition of the Thirty-Nine Articles of the Church of England by Gilbert, Bishop of Sarum*, ed. James R. Page. New York: D. Appleton and Company, 1866.

Mcneil, John. T., ed. *Calvin: Institutes of the Christian Religion.* Louisville: Westminster Press, 1960.

II. Secondary Sources

1. Martin Luther

Books and Articles

Althaus, Paul. *The Theology of Martin Luther.* Philadelphia: Fortress Press, 1966.

_____. *The Ethics of Martin Luther.* Philadelphia: Fortress Press, 1972.

Arand, Charles P. 'Luther on the God behind the First Commandment'. *LQ* 8 (1994), 397-423.

Aulén, Gustaf. *Christus Victor: An Historical Study of the Three Main Types of the Idea of the Atonement.* London: S.P.C.K., 1970.

Badcock, Gary D. *Light of Truth and Fire of Love: A Theology of the Holy Spirit.* Grand Rapids: Wm. B. Eerdmans, 1997.

Bainton, Roland H. *Here I Stand: A Life of Martin Luther.* Tring: Lion Publishing plc, 1987.
Bayer, Oswald. *Martin Luther's Theology: A Contemporary Interpretation.* Grand Rapids: Wm. B. Eerdmans, 2008.
_____. 'I Believe That God Has Created Me With All That Exists: An Example of Catechetical-Systematics'. *LQ* (Summer 1994), 129-161.
Beach, J. Mark. 'The Real Presence of Christ in the Preaching of the Gospel: Luther and Calvin on the Nature of Preaching'. *Mid-America Journal of Theology* 10 (1999), 77-134.
Becker, Siegbert W. *The Foolishness of God: The Place of Reason in the Theology of Martin Luther.* Milwaukee, WI: Northwestern Pub. House, 1982.
Beecroft, Mason and J. Scott Horrel. 'Review of Union with Christ: The New Finnish Interpretation of Luther'. *Bibliotheca Sacra* 157 (April-June 2000), 250-251.
Bell, Theo M.M.A.C. 'Man Is a Microcosmos: Adam and Even in Luther's *Lectures on Genesis* (1535-1545)'. *CTQ* 69:2 (April 2005), 159-184.
Boer, Theo A. 'Is Luther's Ethics Christian Ethics?'. *LQ* 21:4 (2007), 404-421.
Bornkamm, Heinrich. *Luther's World of Thought.* Saint Louis: Concordia Pub. House, 1958.
_____. *Luther's Doctrine of the Two Kingdoms in the Context of His Theology.* Philadelphia: Fortress Press, 1966.
_____. *Luther and the Old Testament.* Philadelphia: Fortress Press, 1969.
Braaten, Carl E., and Robert W. Jenson, eds. *Union with Christ: The New Finnish Interpretation of Luther.* Grand Rapids: Wm. B. Eerdmans, 1998.
Carlson, Arnold E. 'Luther and the Doctrine of the Holy Spirit'. *LQ* 11 (May 1959), 135-146.
Clark, R. Scott. '*Iustitia Imputata Christi*: Alien or Proper to Luther's Doctrine of Justification'. *CTQ* 70 (2006), 269-310.
Dorman, Ted. 'Review of Union with Christ: The New Finnish Interpretation of Luther'. *First Things* 98 (December 1999), 49-53.
Ebeling, Gerhard. *Luther: An Introduction to His Thought.* Philadelphia: Fortress Press, 1970.
_____. *Word and Faith.* Philadelphia: Fortress Press, 1963.
Elert, Werner. *Law and Gospel.* Philadelphia: Fortress Press, 1967.

Forde, Gerhard O. *A More Radical Gospel: Essays on Eschatology, Authority, Atonement, and Ecumenism*. eds. Mark C. Mattes and Steven D. Paulson. Grand Rapids: Wm. B. Eerdmans, 2004.

_____. *The Law-Gospel Debate: An Interpretation of Its Historical Development*. Minneapolis: Augsburg, 1968.

_____. *Where God Meets Man: Luther's Down-to-Earth Approach to the Gospel*. Minneapolis: Augsburg, 1972.

_____. *On Being a Theologian of the Cross: Reflections on Luther's Heidelberg Disputation, 1518*. Grand Rapids: Wm. B. Eerdmans, 1997.

_____. *The Preached God: Proclamation in Word and Sacrament*. Grand Rapids: Wm. B. Eerdmans, 2007.

_____. *The Captivation of the Will: Luther Vs. Erasmus on Freedom and Bondage*. Grand Rapids: Wm. B. Eerdmans, 2005.

Forell, George Wolfgang. *Faith Active in Love: An Investigation of the Principles Underlying Luther's Social Ethics*. New York: American Press, 1954.

_____. 'Justification and Eschatology in Luther's Thought'. *Church History* 38:2 (1969), 164-174.

Gerrish, B. A. *Grace and Reason: a Study in the Theology of Luther*. Oxford: Clarendon Press, 1962.

_____. *The Old Protestantism and the New: Essays on the Reformation Heritage*. Chicago: University of Chicago Press, 1982.

_____. 'Priesthood and Ministry in the Theology of Luther'. *Church History* 34:4 (December 1965), 404-422.

Gritsch, Eric W. 'The Worldly Luther: Wholistic Living'. *Word & World* 3/4 (1983), 355-363.

Grobien, Gifford. 'A Lutheran Understanding of Natural Law in the Three Estates'. *CTQ* 73 (2009), 211-229.

Headley, John M. *Luther's View of Church History*. New Haven: Yale University Press, 1963.

Hebblethwaite, Brian. *The Christian Hope*. New York: Oxford University Press, 2010.

Heckel, Johannes. *Lex Charitatis: A Juristic Disquisition on Law in the Theology of Martin Luther*. tr. and ed. Gottfried G. Krodel. Grand Rapids: Wm. B. Eerdmans, 2010.

Heinz, Johann. *Justification and Merit: Luther vs. Catholicism*. Eugene, OR: Wipf and Stock Publishers, 2002.

Hendrix, Scott H. 'Luther on Marriage'. *LQ* 14 (2000), 335-350.

Jastram, Nathan. 'Man as Male and Female: Created in the Image of God'. *CTQ* 68:1 (Jan. 2004), 5-96.

Ji, Won Young. 'The Work of the Holy Spirit and the Charismatic Movement, from Luther's Perspective'. *CJ* 11:6 (Nov. 1985), 204-213.
Johnson, Dale A. 'Luther's Understanding of God'. *LQ* 16:1 (Feb. 1964), 59-69.
Kirwan, Christopher. *Augustine*. London, New York: Routledge, 1989.
Kleinig, John W. Luther on the Reception in God's Holiness'. *Pro Ecclesia* 17:1 (Winter 2008), 76-91.
_____. 'Where is Your God? Luther on God's self Localization', Dean O Wenthe et. al. eds. *All Theology Is Christology. Essays in Honor of David P Scaer.* Concordia Theological Press: 2000, 117-131.
Kolb, Robert. 'Luther on the Theology of the Cross'. *LQ* 16:4 (Winter 2002), 443-466.
Laato, Timo. 'Justification: The Stumbling Block of the Finnish Luther School'. *CTQ* 72 (2008), 327-346.
Lee, Jeha. 'A New Interpretation of Faith Active in Love in Martin Luther'. *Mission and Theology* 21 (2011), 41-67.
Lienhard, Marc. *Luther, Witness to Jesus Christ: Stages and Themes of the Reformer's Christology*. Minneapolis: Augsburg Pub. House, 1982.
Lindberg, Carter H. *Beyond Charity: Reformation Initiatives for the Poor*. Minneapolis: Fortress Press, 1993.
Lohse, Bernhard. *Martin Luther's Theology: Its Historical and Systematic Development*. tr. Roy A. Harrisville. Edinburgh: T & T Clark, 1999.
Lowe, Mary E. 'Sin from a Queer, Lutheran Perspective'. ed. Mary J. Streufert, *Transformative Lutheran Theologies: Feminist, Womanist, and Mujerista Perspectives* (Minneapolis: Fortress Press, 2010), 71-86.
MacKenzie, Cameron. A. 'The Origins and Consequences of Original Sin in Luther's Bondage of the Will'. *CJ* 31:4 (Oct. 2005), 384-397.
Malcom, Lois. 'A Hidden God Revisited: Desecularization, the Depths, and God's Sort of Seeing'. *Dialog* 40 (Sept. 2001), 183-191.
Mann, Jeffrey K. 'Luther and the Holy Spirit: Why Pneumatology Still Matters'. *Currents in Theology and Mission* 34:2 (2007), 111-116.
Mannermaa, Tuomo. *Christ Present in Faith: Luther's View of Justification*. ed. Kirsi Irmeli Stjerna. Minneapolis: Fortress Press, 2005.
Martinus Luther: 450th Anniversary of the Reformation. Bad Godesberg: Inter Nationes, 1967.

McDonough, Thomas M. *The Law and the Gospel in Luther: A Study of Martin Luther's Confessional Writings*. London: Oxford University Press, 1963.

McGrath, Alister E. *Iustitia Dei*, vol. 1. Cambridge: Cambridge University Press, 1986.

_____. *Luther's Theology of the Cross: Martin Luther's Theological Breakthrough*. Oxford; New York: B. Blackwell, 1985.

_____. 'The Moral Theory of the Atonement: An Historical and Theological Critique', *Scottish Journal of Theology* 38 (1985), 205-220.

McKim, Donald K. *The Cambridge Companion to Martin Luther*. Cambridge; New York: Cambridge University Press, 2003.

Nestingen, James A. 'The Lord's Prayer in Luther's Catechism'. *Word & World* 22:1 (Winter 2002), 36-48.

Niebuhr, H. Richard. *The Social Sources of Denominationalism*. New York: Henry Holt & Co., 1929.

Noble, T. A. 'Doctrine of Original Sin in the Evangelical Reformers'. *European Explorations in Christian Holiness* 2 (2001), 70-87.

Nygren, Anders, *Agape and Eros*. tr. Philip S. Watson. London: SPCK, 1953.

Oberman, Heiko Augustinus. *Forerunners of the Reformation; the Shape of Late Medieval Thought*. New York: Holt, 1966.

_____. *The Harvest of Medieval Theology: Gabriel Biel and Late Medieval Nominalism*. Grand Rapids: Wm. B. Eerdmans, 1967.

_____. *Luther: Man Between God and the Devil*. tr. Eileen Walliser-Schwarzbart. New York: Image Books, 1992.

_____. '"IUSTITIA CHRISTI" and "IUSTITIA DEI": Luther and the Scholastic Doctrines of Justification'. *Harvard Theological Review* 59:1 (January 1966), 1-26.

Ozment, Steven E. *The Age of Reform (1250-1550): An Intellectual and Religious History of Late Medieval and Reformation Europe*. New Haven: Yale University Press, 1981.

Pelikan, Jaroslav. *Luther the Expositor*. St. Louis: Concordia, 1959.

Pinomaa, Lennart. *Faith Victorious: an Introduction to Luther's Theology*. Philadelphia: Fortress Press, 1963.

Prenter, Regin. *Spiritus Creator*. Philadelphia: Muhlenberg Press, 1953.

Rasmussen, Larry. 'Luther and a Gospel of Earth'. *Union Seminary Quarterly Review* 51:1-2 (1997), 1-28.

Root, Michael. 'Aquinas, Merit, and Reformation Theology after the Joint Declaration on the Doctrine of Justification'. *Modern Theology* 20:1 (January 2004), 5-21.

Rupp, E. Gordon. *The Righteousness of God: Luther Studies*. London: Hodder and Stoughton, 1953.

Shelton, R. Larry. *Cross and Covenant: Interpreting the Atonement for 21st Century Mission*. Tyrone, GA: Paternoster, 2006.

Siggins, Ian D. Kingston. *Martin Luther's Doctrine of Christ*. New Haven: Yale University Press, 1970.

Steinmetz, David C. *Luther in Context*. Grand Rapids: Baker Academic, 2002.

Stephenson, Bret and Susan Power Bratton. 'Martin Luther's Understanding of Sin's Impact on Nature and the Unlanding of the Jew'. *Ecotheology* 9 (2000), 84-102.

Streufert, Mary J. *Transformative Lutheran Theologies: Feminist, Womanist, and Mujerista Perspectives*. Minneapolis: Fortress Press, 2010.

Vogel, Lawrence M. 'A Third Use of the Law: Is the Phrase Necessary?'. *CTQ* 69:3-4 (2005), 191-220.

Vogel, Winfried. 'The Eschatological Theology of Martin Luther, Part 1: Luther's Basic Concepts', *Andrews University Seminary Studies* 24:3 (Autumn 1986), 249-264.

Watson, Philip S. *Let God Be God: An Interpretation of the Theology of Martin Luther*. Philadelphia: Fortress Press, 1947.

Wengert, Timothy J. *Harvesting Martin Luther's Reflections on Theology, Ethics, and the Church*. Grand Rapids: Wm. B. Eerdmans, 2004.

_____. 'Fear and Love in the Ten Commandments'. *CJ* 21.1 (1995), 14-27.

Wingren, Gustaf. *Luther on Vocation*. Philadelphia: Muhlenberg Press, 1957.

Wood, Arthur Skevington. *Captive to the Word: Martin Luther, Doctor of Sacred Scripture*. London: Paternoster, 1969.

Yeago, David S. 'Martin Luther on Grace, Law, and Moral Life'. *The Thomist* 62:2 (1998), 163-191.

Yule, George. *Luther: Theologian for Catholics and Protestants*. Edinburgh: T. & T. Clark, 1985.

Zachman, Randall C. *The Assurance of Faith: Conscience in the Theology of Martin Luther and John Calvin*. Minneapolis: Fortress Press, 1993.

Theses and Dissertations

Choi, Inho. 'Historical Studies on Ratio in Luther: Comparison and Analysis of Luther's Two Commentaries on Galatians of 1519 and 1535'. Ph.D. dissertation, Luther Seminary, 2004.

Kim, Joo-Han. 'Personal Piety and the Common Good: Luther's Interpretation of the Sermon on the Mount and his Two Kingdoms Doctrine'. Ph.D. dissertation, Boston University, 1999.

Kim, Sun-Young. 'Luther on Faith and Love: The overriding thematic pair in the dynamics of Christ and the law in the 1535 Galatians Commentary'. Ph.D. dissertation, Princeton Theological Seminary, 2008.

Kvam, Kristen E. 'Luther, Eve, and Theological Anthropology: Reassessing the Reformer's Response to the "Frauenfrage"'. Ph.D. dissertation, Emory University, 1992.

Lee, Jeha. 'Love or Theosis? A Critique of Tuomo Mannermaa's "New Paradigm" of Lurther's Concept of Love in his Commentary on The First Epistle of John (1527)'. Ph.D. dissertation, Boston University, 1991.

2. John Wesley

Books and Articles

Arnett, William M. 'The Role of the Holy Spirit in Entire Sanctification in the Writings of John Wesley'. *WTJ* 14:2 (Fall 1979), 15-30.

Baker, Frank. *John Wesley and the Church of England*. London: Epworth Press, 1970.

Ball-Kilbourne, Gary L. 'The Christian as Steward in John Wesley's Theological Ethics'. *Quarterly Review* 4:1 (Spring 1984), 43-54.

Brendlinger, Irv A. *Social Justice Through the Eyes of Wesley: John Wesley's Theological Challenge to Slavery*. Ontario: Joshua Press, 2006.

Brown, Dale W. 'The Wesleyan Revival from a Pietist Perspective'. *WTJ* 24 (1989), 7-17.

Bryant, Barry E. 'John Wesley on the Origins of Evil'. *WTJ* 30:1 (Spring 1995), 111-133.

Cannon, William Ragsdale. *The Theology of John Wesley: With Special Reference to the Doctrine of Justification*. New York, Nashville: Abingdon-Cokesbury Press, 1946.

Carter, Charles W., R. Duane Thompson, and Charles R. Wilson, eds. *A Contemporary Wesleyan Theology: Biblical, Systematic, and Practical*. 2 vols. Grand Rapids: Francis Asbury Press, 1983.

Clapper, Gregory Scott. *John Wesley on Religious Affections: His Views on Experience and Emotion and Their Role in the Christian Life and Theology*. Metuchen, NJ: Scarecrow Press, 1989.

Cobb, John B. *Grace and Responsibility: A Wesleyan Theology for Today*. Nashville: Abingdon Press, 1995.

Collins, Kenneth J. *A Faithful Witness: John Wesley's Homiletical Theology*. Wilmore, KY: Wesley Heritage Press, 1993.

_____. *John Wesley: A Theological Journey*. Nashville: Abingdon Press, 2003.

_____. *The Scripture Way of Salvation: The Heart of John Wesley's Theology*. Nashville: Abingdon Press, 1997.

_____. *The Theology of John Wesley: Holy Love and the Shape of Grace*. Nashville: Abingdon Press, 2007.

_____. 'John Wesley's Platonic Conception of the Moral Law'. *WTJ* 21 (1986), 116-128.

Colon-Emeric, Edgardo Antonio. *Wesley, Aquinas, and Christian Perfection: An Ecumenical Dialogue*. Waco, TX: Baylor University Press, 2009.

Coppedge, Allan. *John Wesley in Theological Debate*. Wilmore, KY: Wesley Heritage Press, 1987.

Cox, Leo G. *John Wesley's Concept of Perfection*. Kansas City: Beacon Hill Press, 1964.

_____. 'John Wesley's View of Martin Luther'. *Bulletin of the Evangelical Theological Society* 7:3 (Summer 1964), 83-90.

Deasley, Alex R. G. 'Entire Sanctification and the Baptism with the Holy Spirit: Perspectives on the Biblical View of the Relationship'. *WTJ* 14:1 (Spring 1979), 27-44.

Deschner, John. *Wesley's Christology: An Interpretation*. Grand Rapids: Francis Asbury Press, 1988.

Dreyer, Frederick. *The Genesis of Methodism*. Bethlehem, PA: Lehigh University Press, 1999.

_____. 'John Wesley: ein englischer Pietist'. *MH* 15 (2001-02), 71-84.

English, John C. 'References to St. Augustine in the Works of John Wesley'. *Asbury Theological Journal* 60:2 (Fall 2005), 5-24.

Hambrick, Matthew and Lodahl, Michael. 'Responsible Grace in Christology? John Wesley's Rendering of Jesus in the Epistle to the Hebrews'. *WTJ* 43 (Spring 2008), 86-101.

Hammond, Geordan. 'John Wesley and "Imitating" Christ'. *WTJ* 45:1 (2010), 197-212.
Han, Young-Tae. *The Trinity and Holiness* (in Korean). Seoul: SeungKwang Press, 1992.
Hildebrandt, Franz. *From Luther to Wesley*. London: Lutterworth Press, 1951.
Hynson, Leon O. *To Reform the Nation: Theological Foundations of Wesley's Ethics*. Grand Rapids: Francis Asbury Press, 1984.
_____. 'Christian Love: The Key to Wesley's Ethics'. *MH* 14 (October 1975), 44-55.
Jones, Scott J. *John Wesley's Conception and Use of Scripture*. Nashville: Kingswood Books, 1995.
Kevan, Ernest Frederick. *The Grace of Law: A Study in Puritan Theology*. London: Carey Kingsgate Press, 1964.
Knight, Henry H. *The Presence of God in the Christian Life: John Wesley and the Means of Grace*. Metuchen, NJ: Scarecrow Press, 1992.
Lindström, Harald. *Wesley and Sanctification: A Study in the Doctrine of Salvation*. Nashville: Abingdon Press, 1946.
Logan, James C. ed. *Theology and Evangelism in the Wesleyan Heritage*. Nashville: Kingswood Books, 1994.
Long, D. Stephen. *John Wesley's Moral Theology: The Quest for God and Goodness*. Nashville: Kingswood Books, 2005.
Lyon, Robert W. 'Baptism and Spirit Baptism in the New Testament'. *WTJ* 14:1 (Spring 1979), 14-26.
Maddox, Randy L., ed. *Rethinking Wesley's Theology for Contemporary Methodism*. Nashville: Kingswood Books, 1998.
_____. *Responsible Grace: John Wesley's Practical Theology*. Nashville: Kingswood Books, 1994.
Marquardt, Manfred. *John Wesley's Social Ethics: Praxis and Principles*. Nashville: Abingdon Press, 1992.
McGonigle, Herbert. B. *Sufficient Saving Grace: John Wesley's Evangelical Arminianism*. Carlisle: Paternoster, 2001.
_____. 'Pneumatological Nomenclature in Early Methodism'. *WTJ* 8 (Spring 1973), 61-72.
McPherson, Joseph. 'Historical Support for Early Methodist Views of Water and Spirit Baptism'. Paper Presented at the Wesleyan Studies Summer Seminar at Asbury Theological Seminary, June 2011, 1-10.
Meistad, Tore. *Martin Luther and John Wesley on the Sermon on the Mount*. Lanham, MD: Scarecrow Press, 1999.

Monk, Robert C. *John Wesley: His Puritan Heritage, A Study of the Christian Life*. London: Epworth Press, 1966.
Oden, Thomas C. *John Wesley's Scriptural Christianity: A Plain Exposition of His Teaching on Christian Doctrine*. Grand Rapids: Zondervan, 1994.
Oden, Thomas C. and Leicester R. Longden, eds. *The Wesleyan Theological Heritage: Essays of Albert C. Outler*. Grand Rapids: Zondervan, 1991.
Oh, Gwang Seok. *John Wesley's Ecclesiology: A Study in Its Sources and Development*. Lanham, MD: Scarecrow Press, 2008.
O'Malley, J. Steven. 'Pietistic Influence on John Wesley: Wesley and Gerhard Tersteegen'. *WTJ* 31:2 (Fall 1996), 127-139.
Riss, Richard M. 'John Wesley's Christology in Recent Literature'. *WTJ* 45:1 (Spring 2010), 108-129.
Runyon, Theodore. *The New Creation: John Wesley's Theology Today*. Nashville: Abingdon Press, 1998.
_____., ed. *Sanctification & Liberation: Liberation Theologies in Light of the Wesleyan Tradition*. Nashville: Abingdon Press, 1981.
Snyder, Howard A. *The Radical Wesley & Patterns for Church Renewal*. Downers Grove, IL: Inter-Varsity Press, 1980.
Starkey, Lycurgus Monroe. *The Work of the Holy Spirit: A Study in Wesleyan Theology*. Nashville: Abingdon Press, 1962.
Turner, George Allen. 'The Baptism of the Holy Spirit in the Wesleyan Tradition'. *WTJ* 14 (Spring 1979), 60-76.
Vogt, Peter. '"No Inherent Perfection in This Life": Count Zinzendorf's Theological Opposition to John Wesley's Concept of Sanctification'. *Bulletin of the John Rylands University Library of Manchester* 85:2-3 (Summer-Autumn 2003), 297-307.
Watson, Philip. 'Wesley and Luther on Christian Perfection'. *Ecumenical Review* 15 (1963), 291-302.
Williams, Colin. *John Wesley's Theology Today*. Nashville: Abingdon Press, 1960.
Wood, Laurence W. *The Meaning of Pentecost in Early Methodism: Rediscovering John Fletcher as Wesley's Vindicator and Designated Successor*. Lanham, MD: Scarecrow Press, 2002.
_____. 'Exegetical-Theological Reflections on the Baptism with the Holy Spirit'. *WTJ* 14:2 (Fall 1979), 51-63.
Wynkoop, Mildred B. *A Theology of Love: The Dynamic of Wesleyanism*. Kansas City: Beacon Hill Press, 1972.
_____. 'Theological Roots of Wesleyan Understanding of the Holy Spirit'. *WTJ* 14 (Spring 1979), 77-98.

Yates, Arthur S. *The Doctrine of Assurance: With Special Reference to John Wesley.* London: Epworth Press, 1952.
Zehrer, Karl. 'The Relationship between Pietism in Halle and Early Methodism'. tr. James A. Dwyer. *MH* 17:4 (July 1979), 211-224.

Theses and Dissertations

Bence, Clarence. 'John Wesley's Teleological Hermeneutic'. Ph.D. dissertation, Emory University, 1981.

Bryant, Barry E. 'John Wesley's Doctrine of Sin'. Ph.D. thesis, University of London (King's College), 1992.

Burns, Michael T. 'John Wesley's Doctrine of Perfect Love as a Theological Mandate for Inclusion and Diversity'. Ph.D. thesis, University of Manchester (Nazarene Theological College), 2009.

Collins, Kenneth J. 'John Wesley's Theology of Law'. Ph.D. dissertation, Drew University, 1984.

Cunningham, Joseph W. 'Perceptible Inspiration: A Model for John Wesley's Pneumatology'. Ph.D. thesis, University of Manchester (Nazarene Theological College), 2010.

Fujimoto, Mitsuru S. 'John Wesley's Doctrine of Good Works'. Ph.D. dissertation, Drew University, 1986.

Hammond, Geordan. 'Restoring Primitive Christianity: John Wesley and Georgia, 1735-1737'. Ph.D. thesis, University of Manchester, 2008.

Han, Young-Tae. 'The Trinity and Holiness in the Theology of John Wesley'. Ph.D. thesis (in Korean), Seoul Theological University, 1990.

Horst, Mark Lewis. 'Christian Understanding and the Life of Faith in John Wesley's Thought'. Ph.D. dissertation, Yale University, 1985.

Im, Seung-An. 'John Wesley's Theological Anthropology: A Dialectic Tension Between the Latin Western Patristic Tradition (Augustine) and the Greek Eastern Patristic Tradition (Gregory of Nyssa)'. Ph.D. dissertation, Drew University, 1994.

Kim, Young Taek. 'John Wesley's Anthropology: Restoration of the Imago Dei as a Framework for Wesley's Theology'. Ph.D. dissertation, Drew University, 2006.

Kwon, Tae Hyoung, 'John Wesley's Doctrine of Prevenient Grace: Its Impact on Contemporary Missiological Dialogue'. Ph.D. dissertation, Temple University, 1996.

Lee, Hoo-Jung. 'The Doctrine of New Creation in the Theology of John Wesley'. Ph.D. dissertation, Emory University, 1991.

Matthews, Rex D. 'Religion and Reason Joined: A Study in the Theology of John Wesley'. Th.D. dissertation, Harvard University, 1986.

Park, Chang Hoon. 'The Theology of John Wesley as "Checks to Antimonianism"'. Ph.D. dissertation, Drew University, 2002.

Rainey, David. 'John Wesley's Doctrine of Salvation in Relation to His Doctrine of God'. Ph.D. thesis, University of London (King's College), 2006.

Rakestraw, Robert Vincent. 'The Concept of Grace in the Ethics of John Wesley'. Ph.D. dissertation, Drew University, 1985.

Renshaw, John R. 'The Atonement in the Theology of John and Charles Wesley'. Ph.D. dissertation, Boston University, 1965.

Rogers, Charles A. 'The Concept of Prevenient Grace in the Theology of John Wesley'. Ph.D. dissertation, Duke University, 1967.

Tyson, John H. 'The Interdependence of Law and Grace in John Wesley's Teaching and Preaching'. Ph.D. thesis, University of Edinburgh, 1991.

Wilson, Charles Randall. 'The Correlation of Love and Law in the Theology of John Wesley'. Ph.D. dissertation, Vandervilt University, 1959.

Yang, Jung. 'The Doctrine of God in the Theology of John Wesley'. Ph.D. thesis, University of Aberdeen, 2003.

Index

active righteousness, 100, 101, 126, 138
Adam, 15, 191, 192, 194, 197, 203, 205, 208, 212; after the fall, 15, 24, 203, 204; before the fall, 14, 31, 32, 191, 192, 193, 200, 201, 210, 211, 214; cause of his fall, 212; his life in Paradise, 208, 209; his temptation, 194; old Adam in us, 86; process of his fall, 194
Adamic law, 32, 33, 34, 42; content of, 211
altruism, 231, 252, 253, 254
Anabaptists, 229
angelic perfection, 34
angels, 75, 251
Anglican (tradition), Anglicanism, 6, 96, 97, 139, 149, 166, 169, 181, 187, 205
antinomianism, 5, 7, 42, 101, 102, 105, 112, 113, 117, 144, 145, 148, 167, 170, 186, 187, 248, 259, 262
anxiety, 3, 73, 147, 210
Apostles' Creed, 119, 124
Aquinas, Thomas, 175, 176, 178, 183, 184, 261
assurance, 5, 110, 112, 148, 149, 151, 260; and evangelical synergism, 254; degrees of, 149
atonement, 51, 83, 89, 90, 95, 96, 97, 99, 100, 101, 102, 104, 110, 111, 161, 167, 223, 257, 259; as distinguishing point between Christianity and heathenism, 99
axial theme, 9, 130, 205, 262
baptism, 226
believers' own fulfilment of the law, 101, 102, 104, 105, 112, 113, 116, 133, 135, 222, 259; and Christ's priestly office, 114; and evangelical synergism, 130; and the third use of the law, 159
believers' victory, 30, 87, 95, 104, 142, 155, 208; as mere occasional victory, 141; impossibility of believers' constant victory, 140; through the law, 116, 259
believers as saints and sinners, 110, 112, 113, 139, 142, 198, 262
believers' own righteousness, 51, 91, 93, 102, 105, 110, 259
believers' reason, 207, 217, 218, 258, 261
Beruf, 232
Biel, Gabriel, 176, 177, 261
bondage of the will, 7; Luther's metaphor on, 197
Bondage of the Will, 61, 62, 64
Bußkampf controversy, 111
Calvary, 3
capitalism, 244
caritas, 174
Catholic Church, 3, 4, 53, 58, 79, 121, 175, 225, 231, 249,

279

250, 262, 263; doctrine of, 4, 6, 262
Catholics, 6, 9, 58, 120, 174, 180, 262
cause of afflictions, 86
centrality of preaching, 135
ceremonial law, 22, 23, 38, 42, 47, 102
chain of being, 68
Christ: all-sufficiency of, 96; and paradoxical way of revelation, 84; as best expositor of the law, 108; as example, 88, 89, 96; as gift, 88; as preacher of the gospel, 87, 88, 89; as preacher of the law, 88, 89; as readeemer from the law, 87; as the law, 109; as Victor, 94, 95; cause of His cross, 90; Christ's cross as the law, 85, 86, 87; His active obedience and the prophetic office, 109; His cross as victory, 94; sinners' involvement and liability in His death, 90
Christ's fulfilment of the law, 94, 97, 167, 259; Wesley's view of, 108
Christ's humanity, 84, 98, 156
Christ's kingship: as Judge, 105; as Lawgiver, 103; as Lord of believers, 104
Christ's substitutional death, 100
Christ's victory, 90, 93, 94, 95, 96; and His divinity, 94; over the law, 117, 259; through the law, 116, 259

Christ's active and passive obedience, 100
Christ's active and passive righteousness, 101
Christ's divinity, 84, 94, 156, 157
Christ's fulfilment of the law, 113; Luther's view of, 87
Christ's humanity, 84, 95, 97, 156
Christ's perfect obedience, 92, 100, 105, 112, 113
Christ's righteousness, 91, 92, 93, 99, 100, 101, 105, 112, 113, 140, 146, 262
Christ's victory, 83, 95, 259; as victory of God's love over the law, 95; over the law, 96; tension between 'already' and 'not yet' in, 105; three stages of, 104
Christian dispensation, 143, 258; and sanctifying grace, 116; superiority of, 36, 108, 109
Christian ethics, 1, 161, 233, 235, 243, 244, 249, 252, 253, 255, 258
Christian love, 50, 59, 60, 69, 89, 154, 157, 162, 163, 171, 178, 187, 188, 189, 235, 239, 243, 252, 256, 262
Christian perfection, 52, 110, 142, 184, 262; as *perfecting* perfection and *limited* perfection, 168; as teleological end, 50, 51, 52, 255; Augustine's denial of, 184; negative effect of the doctrine of, 50, 52; positive effect of the doctrine of, 50

church: external sings of, 225;
   Luther's definition of, 225;
   Luther's view of, 246;
   Wesley's definition of, 236
Church of England, 5, 129,
   167, 181, 186, 236, 246
civil authorities, 18, 25, 236,
   255
civil law, 21, 22, 23, 37, 38, 47,
   48, 229, 234, 256
comparative value, 76; of holy
   works, 254, 255
complacency, self-
   complacency), 3, 45, 65,
   220, 258, 259
conflict between Christ and
   the law, 94
congruous merit and condign
   merit, 175
conscience, 3, 4, 16, 25, 27, 28,
   30, 44, 64, 65, 66, 85, 94,
   119, 121, 127, 128, 130,
   140, 141, 146, 149, 190,
   220, 226, 248, 253, 260,
   261
continuous creation, 54, 55
convincing grace, 46, 132,
   165, 166, 167, 206; and
   faith of a servant, 131; and
   prevenient grace, 166
co-operant grace, 9, 184
covenant of grace, 32, 34, 47,
   100, 185, 261; demand of,
   33, 34
covenant of works, 31, 32, 33,
   42, 100; demand of, 32
covered promise, 40, 41, 70,
   114, 134, 258
cross-bearing: as touchstone
   of Christian love, 89
cupiditas, 174

curvatus in se, 194
Decalogue, 14, 17, 18, 19, 21,
   23, 31, 53, 106, 119, 125,
   158, 233; as best
   representation of the law,
   106
Deed-Word, 54
demonic powers, 90
despair, 4, 26, 27, 49, 50, 51,
   52, 61, 113, 116, 120, 172,
   226
devil, 16, 22, 66, 90, 93, 94, 95,
   115, 128, 135, 140, 148,
   157, 196, 216, 218, 220,
   221, 226, 228, 259
devilish passions or tempers,
   204, 241
dialectic: between *Anfechtung*
   and comfort by the Holy
   Spirit, 127, 128; between
   Christ as the law and Christ
   as the gospel, 87, 91, 107;
   between cross as the law
   and cross as the gospel, 87;
   between God's strange
   work and His proper work,
   96; between the hidden God
   and the revealed God, 64;
   between the Holy Spirit as
   the law and as the gospel,
   124; between the law and
   the gospel, 26, 49, 51, 65,
   123
dispensation, 207; difference
   between the Jewish and the
   Christian dispensations, 35,
   108
distinction: between
   awakened sinners and
   hypocrites, 116; between
   Christ's eternal and actual

kingship, 104; between Christ and the law, 66; between Christ as gift and as example, 91; between Christ as grace and faith as gift, 91; between Christ as grace and the Holy Spirit as gift, 91; between Deed-Word and Call-Word, 54; between doctrine and life, 4; between faith as a divine work and love as a human work, 188; between faith of a servant and of a child of God, 131; between general universal history and special redemptive history, 48; between God's sovereignty in creation and God's accommodations to human freedom after creation, 182; between great and trivial works, 231, 254; between imputed and inherent righteousness, 91; between places and times for the law and for the gospel, 28; between prescriptive role of the law and the third use of the law, 159; between present and final justification, 105; between priests and laity, 232; between process through faith terminology and achievement through law terminology, 159; between regeneration and entire sanctification, 206; between roles of each person in the Trinity, 131; between roles of the civil law and the moral law, 37; between spiritual and temporal estates, 249; between the effects of original sin on human reason and on the will, 196; between the law and the gospel, 4, 11, 121; between the law as letter and the gospel as the spirit, 121; between the law before the fall and the law after the fall, 14, 15; between the natural law and the law of the Spirit, 122; between the nature and effect of the law, 44; between the office and the person, 228; between the spiritual use of the law and the spiritual law, 159; between the temporary and the everlasting aspects of the law, 42; between universal law for entire humanity and the law exclusively for Christians, 19; between voluntary transgression of the law and involuntary mistakes, 34, 222; between ways of God's working as Creator and as Governor, 67

divine determinism, 79, 80

down-to-earth approach, 231, 246, 251

dualism of the spiritual and the temporal estates, 250

Eastern Orthodox, 129

economic ethics, 241, 242

empowerment, 36, 47, 52, 129, 133, 134, 173, 221, 222, 260, 263
enmity between the law and sinners, 133
enthusiasm, enthusiasts, 120, 121, 144, 148
entire sanctification, 42, 105, 112, 143, 144, 169, 206, 237; as pure love, 206
eschatological hope, 51, 114, 141, 198, 252
ethics of life stations, 262
evangelical law, 34
evangelical synergism, 46, 78, 129, 138, 165, 166, 168, 181, 182, 186, 263; and convincing grace, 166
evil angels, 213
evil tempers, 72, 142, 150, 203, 213, 214, 241; as practical atheism, 214
facientis quod in se est, Deus non denegat gratiam, 181
faith: as (sum of) proper attitudes toward God, 56, 190; as all in all in justification and in Christian life, 155; as demand of the law, 71; as disposition of the heart, 190; as foundation of Christian life, 188; as fulfilment of the law, 93, 154, 155, 159, 160, 260; as handmaid of love, 164; as instument of love, 188; as lord of love, 157; as means of restoring love, 164; as new law, 155; as perfect quality for salvation, 157; as replacement of the law, 26, 155, 159, 160, 161, 178, 188; as sole condition of justification and sanctification, 179; as spiritual sight, 207; as understanding of the law, 14, 155, 159, 160; as union with Christ, 92, 93; as unique validity before God, 56; as worship of God, 71; content of, 33; definition of, 131; degrees of, 110, 111, 149, 254; highest degree of, 63; self-sufficiency of, 156, 160
faith and good works, 24, 156, 157, 160, 161, 163, 171, 181, 189, 231, 247, 262
faith and love, 59, 60, 89, 156, 159, 161, 163; Aquinas' view of, 175; as a means and the end, 188; as cause and result, 187; Luther's metaphors on, 156; Wesley's correlation between, 33; Wesley's metaphor on, 164
faith and reason, 217
faith and works, 247
faith formed by God's love, 183
faith formed by love, 183
faith working through love, 34, 187, 190
faithlessness, 71
fall: effects of, 213; essence of, 213
fall of humanity, 203
fear, 3, 4, 6, 18, 30, 38, 53, 56, 58, 64, 71, 73, 93, 106, 112,

114, 120, 131, 147, 149, 169, 178, 192, 194, 204, 210, 220, 228, 229, 236, 254, 258
fellowship with God: face-to-face fellowship in love, 211; mediated fellowship through faith, 211
Filioque, 119, 129
final justification, 104, 105, 250, 255, 259
Finnish Luther School, 91
First Commandment, 55, 56, 57, 58, 59, 63, 74, 88, 90, 106, 109; and the other commandments, 56, 57
flesh, 2, 19, 20, 25, 67, 86, 92, 93, 95, 97, 125, 126, 139, 140, 141, 142, 154, 155, 157, 159, 188, 189, 197, 198, 199, 212, 219, 220, 226, 228, 260
formative role of believers' works, 247
free choice, 74, 196, 214
free grace, 62, 137, 138, 184; and convincing grace, 166; and direct witness of the Spirit, 149; and fruits of the Holy Spirit, 134; and God's creation, 221; and justification, 137; and prevenient grace, 166; and regeneration, 168; and sanctification, 137, 221
free will, 45, 74, 82, 123, 139, 175, 176, 185, 195, 196, 214, 221
freedom, 192, 250; abuse of, 189, 229; and responsibility, 52; and the law, 67; from fear, 4; from sin, 70, 167; from the law, 113; not real, 74; of Adam, 201; of Christian, 4, 70, 157, 251, 253; of God, 45, 258, 262; of humanity, 129, 133, 182, 214, 215; of the hidden God, 63, 64, 78, 120; of the Holy Spirit, 120, 131; of the will, 184, 185, 200, 201, 214; to obey the law, 70, 167
fruits of faith, 124, 147, 164, 261, 262
fruits of the Holy Spirit, 31, 40, 105, 124, 134, 135, 141, 144, 149; and fulfilment of the law, 134
fulfilment of the law, 100, 159; by proxy, 102; in believers' heart, 134
fundamental sin, 109, 213
glorifying grace, 51, 165
God: all-sufficiency of, 73, 74; as 'fire and passion ... of love', 58; as Creator, 53, 54, 55, 67; as Governor, 67; as Ruler of everything, 77; as Saviour, 58; foreknowledge of, 74; God's grace and human responsibility, 75; God's providence and human responsibility, 77; God's works and human participation, 77; God's words as Deed-Word, 54; harmony between the works of God as Creator and as Governor, 67; hidden God as the law, 63, 64, 65; His reward as grace,

58, 60, 74, 172, 175; incomprehensibility of, 59, 61, 79, 80, 81, 259; majesty of, 55, 57, 61, 64, 72, 79, 95, 196; masks of, 55, 73, 74, 77; omnipotence of, 55, 71, 74; omnipresence of, 55; providence of, 75; sovereignty of, 63, 67, 71, 77, 80, 81, 129, 182, 213, 255, 258, 259; the hidden and the revealed, 61, 62, 63, 64, 65, 77, 78, 79, 120, 145, 259; three aspects of His grace, 173; wrath of, 3, 4, 12, 20, 25, 26, 38, 43, 44, 45, 46, 49, 57, 64, 79, 84, 85, 90, 93, 94, 96, 99, 106, 112, 120, 125, 127, 132, 139, 197, 205, 237

golden chain (of God's graces), 51

golden rule, 16, 162, 234, 242

good conscience, 221

good works, 6, 8, 12, 31, 42, 60, 115, 139, 156, 157, 164, 169, 170, 177, 179, 197, 209, 225, 231, 240, 261; and God's reward, 172; antinomian view of, 6; as antithesis to faith, 157, 188, 213, 214; as highest of all Christian graces, 6

gospel dispensation, 32, 142

happiness, 68, 74, 150, 151, 179, 183, 192, 211, 251, 252, 260

happy exchange, 92

holy love: as believers' new nature, 138, 149, 164, 206; as demand of the law, 9, 31, 37, 43, 44, 66, 72, 73, 76, 132, 149, 259; as God's nature, 9, 43, 44, 66, 76, 81, 96, 132, 149, 257; as image of God in believers, 71, 188; as instrument of God's providence, 72, 77; root and fruit of salvation, 72, 150, 260

Holy Spirit: and God's word, 121; and preaching, 136; and santification, 125; and theology of cross, 124; as Comforter, 128; as gift of salvation, 119; as Mediator of God and Christ, 119; as presence of God and Christ, 129, 133; as replacement of the law, 26, 159, 178; as Revealer of the law and the gospel, 122, 132; as Sovereign Saviour, 119; as the law, 127; as worker of mortification and vivification, 122; main office of, 121

human finitude, 18, 59, 79, 222, 223

human reason, 19, 48, 61, 79, 80, 85, 130, 139, 154, 195, 196, 206, 215, 216, 217, 218, 255, 261; and natural law, 121

human responsibility, 7, 75, 98, 113, 255

human-centred religion, 85, 262

humanity: as already graced beings, 185; as both divine and creaturely beings, 211; as earthly creature, 209; as

partakers of the divine nature, 211; as strictly creaturely beings, 192; in similitude to God's nature, 210
hypocrisy, 50, 52, 113
idolatry, 29, 57, 58, 85, 180, 199, 251, 258
image of brutes (or beasts), 204, 213
image of God, 1, 14, 31, 32, 49, 53, 65, 66, 67, 68, 71, 72, 98, 110, 114, 129, 133, 137, 144, 172, 191, 192, 193, 194, 195, 197, 200, 201, 203, 205, 206, 208, 210, 211, 219, 221, 251, 256, 261, 263; loss of the moral image, 32, 221; loss of the spiritual dimension of, 194; Luther's definition of, 192; mar of natural and physical dimensions of, 194; mar of natural image, 222; mar of the natural and the political images, 32; moral image, 32, 71, 200, 201, 202, 203, 206, 210, 211, 221, 222, 261; moral image as principal image of God, 201; natural image, 200, 202, 204, 206, 207, 222, 261; political image, 32, 68, 200, 201, 202, 204, 211
image of the devil, 72, 204, 206, 213
imago dei, 188
imitation piety, 124, 139, 249, 251, 252
imputed righteousness, 7, 47, 83, 91, 92, 93, 95, 99, 100, 101, 102, 110, 112, 113, 117, 140, 146, 147, 182, 198, 211, 259, 262; as basis of believers' own fulfilment of the law, 113
inbred sin, 51, 142
incarnation, 83, 85, 97, 103, 107, 157, 216; and atonement, 97; and the law, 97
infirmities, 32, 34, 41, 130, 204, 207, 222
infused faith, 154, 175, 178, 183, 261
infused love, 123, 154, 178, 183, 261; as dialectic between the law and the gospel, 123
ingratitude, 28, 45, 64, 112, 194
inherent righteousness, 47, 48, 50, 72, 83, 91, 93, 101, 102, 110, 111, 113, 117, 125, 134, 137, 138, 140, 141, 151, 176; degrees of, 111
initial justification, 255
inner relationship in the Godhead, 120
inner religion, 108
inspiration of the Spirit: Wesley's definition of, 130
inward impression on the soul, 132
Jewish dispensation, 109
justification: as part of salvation, 172; as whole of salvation, 171; two different understanding of, 170

justification and santification, 171
justification by faith, 5, 6, 9, 19, 48, 83, 99, 105, 110, 139, 141, 149, 169, 170, 180, 182, 231, 232, 262
justification by imputation, 112
justification by *theosis*, 91
justifying grace, 51, 137, 167, 186, 254
law: abolition of, 27, 28, 42, 126; abuse of, 3, 39, 50, 107, 248; accusatory role of, 3, 7, 11, 12, 13, 16, 22, 23, 25, 26, 27, 28, 43, 44, 45, 46, 47, 48, 51, 64, 66, 85, 86, 91, 107, 113, 115, 116, 128, 131, 132, 140, 141, 153, 158, 161, 171, 187, 213, 257, 258, 260, 262; after the fall, 15; among demonic powers, 90, 93, 94, 115; and Christ's kingship, 103; and evangelical synergism, 77, 78, 168; and human freedom, 67, 81, 129, 165; and human responsibility, 82, 113; and reward, 43, 57, 150, 151, 172, 176, 177; and structure of the world, 67, 68, 69; and the hidden God, 64; and the nature of God, 65; as anthesis to faith, Christ, grace, and the gospel, 158; as chief of all enemies, 94; as enemy to sin, 115; as God's judgmental activities, 16, 44; as instrument of God's providence, 78; as norm, 32; as objective information of God's will, 45; as way of recovering the image of God, 67; as worship of God, 15, 39; before the fall, 14, 15, 25, 32, 39; civil use of, 25, 47, 235, 258; definition of, 11, 12, 29, 30; demand of, 31, 100, 210, 212; effect of, 24, 25, 39, 44; existential character of, 45, 64; impossibility of fulfilment of, 8; inner observance of, 109; Luther's two uses of, 25, 47, 161, 235, 258; nature of, 23, 24, 38, 44; prescriptive role of, 7, 15, 25, 44, 46, 114, 115, 131, 153, 158, 159, 161, 258, 259, 261; Puritan view of, 7; semi-independence of, 45; sources of, 13, 14, 31; spiritual use of, 159; the third use of, 8, 13, 40, 47, 103, 107, 126, 158, 159, 160, 161, 234, 235, 258, 260, 263; theological use of, 25, 47, 48, 159, 235; unity between Christ and the law, 98; unity between God and His law, 66, 69; unity of, 24, 108; various forms of, 43, 44; Wesley's three uses of, 39, 47, 48
law and gospel, 11; correlation between, 40, 52, 69, 70; dialectic between, 26, 49, 51, 65, 123, 128; distinction between, 4, 11, 121

law of Christ, 14, 18, 19, 20, 32, 34, 35, 48, 60, 122, 126, 158, 228, 230, 235, 255; and law of this world, 228
law of faith, 20, 33, 34, 71
law of life stations, 234
law of love, 18, 20, 34, 164
law of Moses, 3, 14, 16, 18, 19, 20, 21, 22, 23, 32, 34, 35, 87, 88, 106, 108, 122, 225; perfectness of, 88
law of mutual love, 18, 126
law of stations, 234
law of the gospel, 15, 17, 233
law pauses, 165, 167
law remains, 165, 168
legalism, 6, 7, 8, 60, 96, 262
letter and spirit, 121
Levitical law, 27
Lex semper accusat, 44
liberty, 67, 82, 189, 200, 204, 207, 215, 222, 240; abuse of, 3, 42, 202, 203; Wesley's definition of, 201
life stations, 48, 233, 234, 235, 249, 255, 258, 262; as the law, 234; as vocation, 235
loss of faith, 61, 171, 189, 213
love: and good works, 34, 157, 240; as a divine work, 189; as antithesis to faith, 157; as cross-bearing, 88; as essence of the law, 18; as evangelical law, 34; as fulfilment of the law, 33, 157, 163, 164, 187; as goal of Christianity, 162; as goal of faith, 164; as God's nature, 59; as lord of faith, 164; as proof of faith, 157; as servant of faith, 157; as single principle of the laws, 229; as sum of the law, 240; as supernatural gift, 189; as the image of God, 211; Christian love, 60; difference between God's love and human love, 58, 60; God's love and Christian love, 60; Hellenistic acquisitive love, 60; Judaic meritorious love, 60; superiority of love to faith, 164

Luther's metaphor of three virgins, 145
Luther's negative description of the law, 8, 116; Wesley's criticism on, 115
Luther's positive appreciation of God's creation, 209
Luther's chronological transition, 91
Luther's negative description of the law, 6, 8
Luther's regret, 248
means of grace, 10, 30, 226, 236, 237, 239, 246, 247, 248, 253, 254, 262; and Methodist meetings, 237; Luther's view of, 228; Wesley's view of, 236; works of mercy, 31, 168, 238, 239, 254; works of piety, 31, 168, 237, 254
mediated immediacy, 74
medieval church. *See also* Catholic Church; doctrine of, 3, 58, 59, 136, 137, 174, 182, 186, 251, 261

meritorious, 6, 58, 59, 60, 75, 175, 176, 209, 226, 249, 251
metaphor of small lead coins, 176
Methodism, 2, 5, 6, 81, 110, 111, 134, 143, 144, 243
monergism, 46
moral law, 21, 23, 31, 32, 37, 38, 42, 46, 47, 102; as norm of the God-human relationship, 201
Moravian errors, 110, 112
Moravians, 6, 110, 111, 115, 148, 149, 150, 166, 169, 170, 249
mortification, 56, 86, 87, 107, 122, 127, 135, 155, 160, 171, 188
Mosaic dispensation, 32, 36, 142
Mosaic law, 17, 21, 22, 42
Moses: as best expositor of the law, 13, 18, 88
natural affection, 88, 189
natural law, 14, 15, 16, 17, 18, 19, 20, 21, 22, 32, 45, 46, 48, 66, 121, 122, 136, 158, 216, 233, 234, 249; and reason, 48
natural reason, 196
nominalism, 177, 181
office of Moses, 27
office of the keys, 226
Old Testament, 13, 21, 88, 106; as mirror of believers, 106
order of salvation, 1, 50, 165, 185, 206, 257
original righteousness, 14, 25, 47, 193, 194, 195

original sin, 179, 183, 185, 186, 195, 196, 197, 199, 206; as distinguishing point between Christianity and heathenism, 205
orthodoxy, orthopathy, orthopraxy, 190, 222
otherness: of God, 213; of God's word, 136; of works of the Holy Spirit, 137
Paradise, 15, 32, 195, 208, 209
passive holiness, 125, 126
passive righteousness, 100, 125, 137
Peasants' War, 229
penal substitution, 100, 167, 259, 263
Pharisees, 109
positive law, 17, 18, 22, 48, 164, 228
potentia absoluta, 182
potentia ordinata, 182
poverty, 41, 109, 116, 228, 236, 244
practical antinomianism, 189
practical atheism, 214
predestination, 7, 61, 63, 67, 78, 79, 80, 81, 82, 174, 184, 186, 259
prevenient grace, 34, 46, 47, 48, 49, 78, 129, 130, 165, 166, 185, 186, 206, 215, 258, 261; as irresistible grace, 166
pride, 4, 12, 26, 45, 64, 80, 85, 107, 109, 122, 138, 172, 194, 203, 204, 211, 213, 214, 220, 222, 242, 251; as essence of sin, 212; as fundamental sin, 212; as prime sin, 212

priesthood of all believers, 254; and Methodist movement, 254
Protestantism, 5, 6, 7, 9, 139, 166, 181, 182, 184, 261, 263
purgatory, 3, 225, 226
radical reformers, 229
recapitulation, 97
reformation, 2, 5, 6, 38, 85, 245
Reformation, 3, 37, 53, 58, 84, 107, 117, 119, 121, 123, 135, 139, 156, 166, 170, 174, 176, 178, 181, 184, 225, 244
Reformation theology, 179
regeneration: and evangelical synergism, 167
resemblance between God's nature and human nature, 71
resignation (to God), 80
resignation to hell, 127, 128
resurrection, 29, 55, 62, 95, 96, 103, 120, 124, 128, 135, 136
sacrament, 3, 62, 74, 78, 86, 121, 209, 225, 226, 227, 231, 233, 246
salvation: as restoration of the image of God, 205; order of, 51; Wesley's definition of, 76
salvation by grace, 186
sanctification: as alien purity, 93; as assimilation of justification into believers' perception, 125; as renewal in the image of God, 206; degrees of, 110, 111

sanctification by faith, 127
sanctification by imputation, 91, 110, 112
sanctification by the Holy Spirit, 127
sanctifying grace, 36, 49, 50, 51, 52, 115, 143, 150, 165, 168, 186, 189, 190, 207, 237, 248, 254, 256, 261, 262; as love expelling sin, 189
Satan, 2, 50, 51, 73, 79, 96, 104, 109, 183, 194, 196, 197, 202, 203, 212, 213
scholasticism, 58, 124
secular kingdom, 73, 228, 229, 230, 235; and vocation, 48, 255; Christian relationship with, 48
self-centredness, 56, 145, 194, 213, 219, 220, 250, 251, 252
self-defense (of sinners), 90
self-denial, 107, 240, 241, 242, 262
self-glorification, 209, 211, 213
self-justification, 107, 122
self-will, 109, 138, 203, 204, 213, 214, 222
Sermon on the Mount, 13, 19, 31, 103, 222, 228, 229, 230, 251, 262
seven holy possessions of the church, 226
simul justus et peccator, 220, 222
sin: definition of, 34; essence of, 212; two focuses in Wesley's view of, 213
Sinai, 3, 16, 26, 43

social evils, 244, 252, 255
social improvement, 244
social reform, 243, 245
social service, 231, 243, 244
sola fide, 58, 169, 187
sola gratia, 9, 46, 179, 186
solafidianism, 6
soli Deo gloria, 9
solitary religion, 243, 248, 250
spiritual law, 45
spiritual trials, 78, 86, 106, 127, 128, 147, 260, 262
splendid sins, 6
St. Augustine, 174, 175, 178, 183, 184, 261
stewardship, 240, 241, 242, 255, 262
Ten Commandments, 1, 12, 17, 22, 27, 56, 106, 225, 227
tension: between already and not yet, 104; between believers as sinners and believers as saints, 140; between God's grace and human co-operation, 182; between present righteousness and Christian perfection, 50, 51, 185
theocentricity, 74, 124, 135, 137, 148, 246, 255, 262; as prime motif of Luther's theology, 9
theodicy, 202
theology of cross, 83, 85, 107, 124, 146, 182
theology of glory, 85, 87, 107, 148, 182
Thirty-Nine Articles, 97, 186, 246

three basic phrases of Wesley's Pneumatology, 143
three offices of Christ, 87; and sanctification, 115; Christ's priestly office as basis of the other offices, 114; Christ as King, 102, 103, 104, 105, 114, 115, 116, 117; Christ as Priest, 99, 102, 103, 114, 117; Christ as Prophet, 98, 99, 103, 109, 114, 117; interactions among, 115
total depravity, 179, 183, 186
touchstone of the true Christian faith, 164
Tower Experience, 3, 127
Trinitarian unity, 84, 97, 98
true sign of the presence of the Holy Spirit, 121
two kingdoms, 9, 48, 49, 74, 228, 230, 258, 262
ultimate crescendo of the law, 87
unbelief, 22, 73, 79, 194, 213, 218, 221; as atheism, 213; as fundamental sin, 109; as major sin, 220, 222, 261; as parent sin, 203, 204, 214; as supreme sin, 194
unbelievers' reason, 216, 217, 218; Luther's negative view of, 217
unholy tempers, 125, 213, 222, 252
unity: of the nature of God and the nature of humanity, 211
universal depravity, 197
upward approach to God, 59, 231

usus politicus, 47
usus theologicus, 47
via media, 181
views of atonement: classical victory type, Latin legalistic type, and ethical type, 95
vivification, 122, 135, 188
vocation, 28, 48, 232, 233, 234, 235, 236, 249, 255, 256

witness of our own spirit, 148, 149, 151, 254
witness of the Holy Spirit, 131, 132, 147, 148, 149, 151, 260; and faith of a child of God, 132; persuasive nature of, 133
written law, 15, 17, 35, 45, 46, 154, 218

www.ingramcontent.com/pod-product-compliance
Lightning Source LLC
Chambersburg PA
CBHW030335240426
43661CB00052B/1638